Psy

Social Science Content for Preparing Educational Leaders

JACK CULBERTSON

*University Council for
Educational Administration*

ROBIN FARQUHAR

*Ontario Institute for
Studies in Education*

BRYCE FOGARTY

New York University

MARK SHIBLES

University of Connecticut

CHARLES E. MERRILL PUBLISHING COMPANY

A Bell & Howell Company
Columbus, Ohio

MERRILL'S SERIES FOR EDUCATIONAL ADMINISTRATION

Under the Editorship of

DR. LUVERN L. CUNNINGHAM, Dean

College of Education
The Ohio State University

and

DR. H. THOMAS JAMES, President

The Spencer Foundation
Chicago, Illinois

Published by
Charles E. Merrill Publishing Company
A Bell & Howell Company
Columbus, Ohio 43216

Library of Congress Catalog Card Number: 72-87505

International Standard Book Number: 0-675-09121-7

1   2   3   4   5   6   7   8   9   10   —   77   76   75   74   73

PRINTED IN THE UNITED STATES OF AMERICA

Preface

During the last two decades the use of the social sciences in programs to prepare school leaders has become a visible and clearly recognized movement. However, the movement has presented new problems to professors, students, and practitioners of educational administration, a central and basic one being the question: of all the social science content available, what is more and what is less relevant to the study and practice of educational administration? A related question is: what criteria can be used to determine the content which is most and least relevant to the preparation of students and practitioners of educational administration? These two questions pinpoint the central concerns of this book. The questions and the book itself originated in discussions of a UCEA Task Force on "The Social Sciences and the Preparation of Educational Administrators."

Four basic and somewhat discrete perspectives of relevance shape and help to define the book. These perspectives are 1) discipline-based relevance, 2) theory-based relevance, 3) problems-based relevance, and 4) career-based relevance. The beginning points for establishing relevance and the criteria used to judge what social science content is more or less relevant to the study and practice of administration vary depending upon the perspective used. Thus, the beginning points for determining relevance from a discipline-based perspective are the concepts and modes of inquiry in a given social science discipline; the criteria for selecting relevant concepts and modes of inquiry are inherent in the nature of a discipline. For the problems-based perspective the beginning point is administrative practice, and the standards for selecting pertinent social science content are defined dimensions of problems faced by administrators. Selected sets of concepts or modes of inquiry from administrative science constitute the beginning point for those using a theory-based perspective, and criteria derive from assumptions about uses of theory. Those selecting content from a career-based perspective begin with the goals pursued by those in the differing careers of research, synthesis, development, and administration, and the distinctive functions performed in these careers become standards for judging the relevance of social science content.

Five social science disciplines receive major emphases in the book: social psychology, sociology, anthropology, political science, and economics. They have been most frequently associated with educational administration during the last two decades. However, these disciplines are not the only ones available for use in preparatory programs, and there is no intent in the book to suggest that they are.

The first section of the book provides a framework for examining issues of relevance. Chapter 1 analyzes the relevance problem and describes major features of the career-based, problems-based, discipline-based, and theory-based perspectives for viewing relevance. Chapter 2 describes actual and reported uses of social science content in preparatory programs and relates the various uses to the different perspectives for viewing relevance.

The five chapters in the second section are written by social scientists. Each selects and presents the core concepts and essential modes of inquiry in his discipline. Each also discusses the boundaries of his discipline and shows how it is related to other social science disciplines. Thus, the authors present a picture of much of the content from which basic concepts and modes of inquiry can be selected for use in preparatory programs.

Authors in Part Three describe how and why content is selected for use in preparatory programs. In other words, their chapters are case studies based upon the experiences of professors who are actually engaged in preparing educational administrators. Data are selected and presented to illustrate differences in the four perspectives of relevance. Although the cases presented are not pure in the sense that they involve one perspective only, they do illuminate the different points from which content selection problems are approached.

In the fourth section authors set forth desirable criteria for selecting social science content. Criteria are presented for each of the perspectives of relevance. In contrast to the authors in the third section, authors in Part Four were not constrained by actual experience in preparatory programs. Rather, it was their task to project ideal guidelines for students and professors interested in the systematic selection of content.

Part Five presents a summary and a projection. The summary brings together the major findings and conclusions with regard to the relevance problem during the last two decades. Findings and generalizations are based upon data presented in this book and on other related studies. The final chapter in the section projects directions judged desirable for the future and elaborates basic assumptions underlying the projections.

The book is written principally for graduate students and professors of educational administration. It is judged to be especially pertinent to the needs of beginning students interested in exploring differing career options in educational administration and in examining differing criteria for selecting social science content to be studied. In addition to providing potential textual materials, the book offers professors insights into program design questions and issues. This is particularly true for professors of educational administration, but it can also apply to other professors who have special responsibilities for preparing public and private administrators.

Many persons have contributed to the conceptualization and development of this volume. Special appreciation is expressed to the more than a score of professors who participated at various times during the 1960s in the UCEA Task Force mentioned earlier. We are also especially indebted to the authors of the various chapters who have generously contributed their ideas and talents. We hope that their contributions will be of substantial value to students and professors interested in the effective use of the social sciences in the study and practice of educational administration.

Contents

Part One

An Overview

In this section two tasks are performed. First, the analytical scheme which gives shape to the book is elaborated. Second, actual and reported uses of social science content in preparatory programs for educational administrators are described in relation to the analytical scheme presented.

The analytical scheme is derived from a study of the concepts and events judged central to the social science movement of the last two decades. The following four perspectives of relevance are central to the scheme: career-based relevance, discipline-based relevance, theory-based relevance, and problems-based relevance. Significant ideas and events which have helped to define each perspective are delineated, and the criteria for selecting social science content implicit in each are set forth. Illustrations of practice from each perspective are also provided.

Available evidence is presented on actual uses of social science content in preparatory programs. Positions taken by departments of educational administration in official documents concerning the social science content required in preparatory programs are delineated. Then, data about courses actually taken are organized and presented. Finally, various strategies that institutions of higher education use to incorporate content into preparatory programs are discussed, and the relationships of these strategies to the four perspectives of relevance are illuminated.

1

The Social Sciences and the Issue of Relevance

Jack Culbertson and Mark Shibles

In 1946 the National Society for the Study of Education issued a yearbook entitled *Changing Conceptions in Educational Administration*. From the perspective of the present book, it is significant that the 1946 yearbook did not contain a single reference to studies conducted by political scientists, sociologists, economists, social psychologists, or anthropologists. Six out of the eight authors who prepared chapters for the yearbook were practicing educational administrators and the remaining two were professors of educational administration. One of the practitioners did call for "greater utilization of the resources of the university" in the preparation of school administrators.[1] However, his references were not to social science departments but to professional schools of architecture, engineering, and public affairs.

The year following the publication of *Changing Conceptions in Educational Administration*, a special subcommittee of the American Association of School Administrators requested funds from the W. K. Kellogg Foundation to support a national commission to study the school superintendency. While this initial proposal was not approved, it set in motion deliberations which eventually led to the W. K. Kellogg Foundation supported Cooperative Program in Educational Administration (CPEA). In the 1950-51 academic year, this program began at the University of Chicago; Teachers College, Columbia University; George Peabody College; Harvard University; and the University of Texas. It was expanded to include the Ohio State University; the University of Oregon; and Stanford University in 1951-52.

Very soon after the CPEA was initiated, the view that the social sciences had important uses in the study of educational administration and in the preparation of educational administrators began to have impact. At Harvard University on the East Coast, for example, a special concept of university staffing for educational administration was implemented when social scientists became members of the Graduate School of Education and were assigned major responsibilities for studying administration and for preparing educational administrators. These scholars and their students jointly began to conduct applied community studies as a part of preparation. Interdisciplinary teams undertook investigations of complex problems associated with school-community relations.[2]

On the West Coast, to take another example, those responsible for preparing educational administrators at the University of Oregon in 1951 offered for the first time an exploratory interdisciplinary seminar called "The Scope and Sequence of the Social Sciences." Included on the seminar staff was an anthropologist, a political scientist, a sociologist, an economist, and an educator. Early in the following year, faculty from the School of Education and professors from social science departments at the University of Oregon and leading school administrators held a three-day conference to examine the contributions which social scientists could make to the education of administrators. The results of the discussion reinforced the need for continuing the seminar initiated the previous year. In addition, a new seminar called "The Nature and Problems of Administrative Behavior" was projected and later implemented in the summer of 1952. It was staffed by professors of economics, psychology, sociology, political science, anthropology, and education.

The developments at Harvard University and at the University of Oregon in the early 1950s were matched by related developments at other CPEA Centers. However, perhaps enough has already been said to make clear that social science concepts and modes of inquiry affected selected preparatory programs in substantial ways in the early 1950s.[3] This particular turn in administrator preparation was a very significant one — so significant that future observers may conclude that it represented one of the most radical shifts in the history of educational administration. Although pervasive program change was not produced immediately, the concepts and assumptions associated with the use of social sciences represented a basic reorientation in the field. This reorientation helped establish directions and set in motion events which have already had, and unquestionably will continue to have, significant impacts upon administrative study and preparation.

One of the major immediate results of the movement was to raise a variety of questions about problems of administrator preparation. Even though many of the questions were not novel, they took on new meaning because of the social science perspective from which they were viewed. The questions raised dealt with such problems as rationales for using social sciences in preparation; objectives which should guide the inclusion of social science content in preparatory programs; staffing of departments or areas of educational administration to ensure effective social science use in programs; instructional methods for teaching social science and related content; needed changes in student qualifications; and kinds of research which should be pursued in educational administration.

This book is focused principally upon one of the basic problems related to the use of the social sciences in educational administration. Stated in general terms, the problem is that of relevance. Why and how, in other words, are the social sciences relevant to administrator preparation and, in turn, to the practice of educational administration? This question is judged to be basic since all other issues bearing upon the social science movement seem to be in one way or another related to it.

Emergence of the Issue of Relevance

"Relevance," according to Webster's dictionary, "implies a traceable, significant, logical connection."[4] Within the current context this means that social science concepts and modes of inquiry are relevant to administrator training when they have a "traceable, significant, and logical connection" with educational administration. Objectives of instruction in preparatory programs are key considerations since they should be logically related to the practice of educational administration and, at the same time, should provide a basic criterion for determining the relevance of given social content to administrator preparation. As will be demonstrated later in the chapter, there are different definitions of relevance depending upon the kinds of objectives established in preparatory programs.

A study of the professional literature on educational administration suggests that the issue of relevance remained largely implicit during the 1950s. Thus, *Administrative Behavior in Education*, which was the first major book to be influenced in a significant way by the social science movement, described various university arrangements for incorporating social content into preparatory programs, but it did not speak directly to the issue of program objectives or program relevance.[5] Some of the progress reports emanating from the various CPEA Centers did contain implied program objectives related to the use of social science content. One stated objective, for example, was that of providing future and practicing administrators a different outlook or perspective. In the words of Sargent and Flower: "Undoubtedly we educators can find much of value in looking at our own work for a change through the eyes of a sociologist or political scientist."[6]

The observation by Sargent and Flower was repeated in a variety of ways by different writers and was expanded to include such disciplines as economics, psychology, and anthropology. However, implied or stated program objectives oriented toward the changing of administrators' perspectives through social science content frequently encompassed such general targets as reasoning ability and analytical perspective — goals typically associated with a liberal education. Thus, the line between using social science content in preparation for liberal education purposes and for purposes specifically related to the context and practice of educational administration was not always clear.

In the early 1960s, the issue of the relevance of social science content to administration and administrator preparation became more explicit and received more specific attention than it did in the 1950s. In 1960, for example, at the first meeting of the UCEA Task Force on "The Social Sciences and the Preparation of Administrators," one of four major questions discussed was "what criteria can be used for determining what social science content is pertinent in training programs?" A monograph which grew out of a seminar co-sponsored by the University of Alberta and the University Council for Educational Administration and held in the Spring of 1962 at the Banff School of Fine Arts, Canada, focused directly upon the relevance issue.[7] Daniel Griffiths highlighted the necessity for dealing more effectively with the issue in the following terms:

> We in administration have taken, cafeteria style, anything we could get our hands on from the social scientists. True, it is time to exploit the social sciences to the utmost, but the look-and-grab technique of the cafeteria will no longer suffice.

Shortly after the Banff seminar, two events occurred which had further significance for the relevance issue. One was the commissioning of Keith Goldhammer by the UCEA Task Force on "The Social Sciences and the Preparation of Educational Administrators" to develop a position paper which would treat the role of the social sciences in administrator preparation comprehensively and would address further the issue of relevance.[9] At about the time Gold-hammer accepted the task of preparing the UCEA position paper, the National Society for the Study of Education (NSSE) established a commission to plan a yearbook on educational administration. The book planned by the commission and later published by NSSE drew together in summary form a substantial amount of social science content judged to be relevant to educational administration.[10] Four social scientists from outside schools of education contributed to the book. The 1964 NSSE publication contrasted sharply in a variety of ways with its 1946 predecessor.

In the second half of the 1960s the issue of relevance became even more prominent and visible. It was ever present, for example, in the continuing efforts of members of the UCEA Task Force on "The Social Sciences and the Preparation of Educational Administrators," as they sought to define criteria which would enable them to incorporate social science content systematically into courses, seminars, and other components of preparatory programs. The issue was especially visible when members undertook design work involving the actual incorporation and use of content from economics, political science, and sociology into preparatory programs. It also became clear that a number of different analytical perspectives were being used by different members of the Task Force as they dealt with the issue of relevance.

At the 1967 Spring meeting of the Task Force on "The Social Sciences and the Preparation of Educational Administrators," a decision was made to prepare a book which would draw upon past experience and which would seek to explicate and illustrate various perspectives for selecting and organizing relevant social science content. An examination of a number of unpublished papers and reports prepared by Task Force members and a study of practice in universities resulted in an identification of four interrelated but somewhat discrete perspectives for viewing relevance. These perspectives came to be labeled for purposes of this publication as follows: discipline-based relevance, theory-based relevance, problems-based relevance, and career-based relevance. Since these perspectives provide the basic framework for most of the chapters which follow, they require more detailed and illustrative treatments.

PERSPECTIVES FOR VIEWING RELEVANCE

There are two different approaches to establishing a "logical connection" between social science content and administrator preparation and practice. One is to start with social science concepts and modes of inquiry and, then, to establish their connections with administrator practice and preparation. The other approach is to start with dimensions of practice in educational administration and, then, identify or develop social science content which can illuminate these dimensions. Admittedly, the distinction between the two approaches is somewhat oversimplified in that the movement from content to practice and vice versa is not strictly a one-way process. There is inevitably a moving back and forth between practice and content in the reaching of decisions about relevance. However, the two approaches do represent important and different points to begin to establish relevance. The distinction is also pertinent to the four perspectives used in this book. The discipline-based and theory-based perspectives of relevance, which begin with content, represent one approach. The problems-based and the career-based perspectives of relevance, which start with practice, represent the other approach.

Table 1 (see pages 10 and 11) provides summary information highlighting some of the differences in the four prespectives for viewing relevance. However, it should be clear that while each of the four perspectives has unique characteristics, there is some overlap between and among them. It is also clear that universities in making program and instructional decisions about social science content typically use more than one perspecive during the process. At given points in the process, one perspective may predominate, while at some other point a different one will be used. Thus, the perspective used in curriculum design by staff may differ from the one used in planning a program for a given student, or the perspective used in one professor's seminar may differ from that used by another professor. In spite of such limitations, however, the four perspectives offer useful bases for analyzing relevance and a heuristic means for assessing program decisions and values.

Discipline-Based Relevance

The inter-disciplinary seminars which emerged in a number of CPEA Centers in the 1950s placed value, at least implicitly, upon discipline-based relevance. While content from a variety of disciplines was sampled in these and later seminars, sociology, political science, economics, social psychology, and anthropology have come to be the social science disciplines most frequently associated with educational administration during the last two decades. According to a recent study,[11] content from these disciplines is most frequently incorporated into preparatory programs by having students take courses "across campus" in social science departments. Since the study also demonstrated that almost all prospective superintendents in UCEA universities now study social science content during their preparation, it can be concluded that the perspective of discipline-based relevance is having an important impact on the planning of programs for prospective administrators.

The written record suggests, as Table 1 indicates, that those using the discipline-based approach have conceived of relevance in at least three ways. One is in terms of general relevance and the purposes associated with a "liberalizing" education. Thus, one of the purposes of the University of Oregon seminar entitled "Scope and Methods of the Social Sciences," for example, has been that of providing students "a general liberal education" at the graduate level and "a background of reading which would whet the appetite for further reading and give the basis for critical judgment of the major problems confronting American society."[12] A range of disciplines has been used in the seminar to develop liberally educated persons, which includes psychology, sociology, social psychology, economics, political science, and anthropology. Again, it should be emphasized that content from these disciplines has been explored in relation to *major societal* problems.

Others within the liberal education tradition hold a somewhat different concept of relevance. They argue that intensive study of one of the social sciences develops a "disciplined way of thinking" which can be applied generally by educational administrators in posts of leadership. In this argument, such objectives as enhanced reasoning ability, sharpened analytical skills, and a broadened perspective are emphasized on the assumption that such learnings provide prospective administrators tools for effective decision making. The specific discipline chosen is not so significant since it is assumed that such learnings can be acquired through depth study of any one of a number of disciplines.

Whether relevance is sought through depth study of one or breadth study of several disciplines, those adhering to the liberalizing view generally assume that students have a major responsibility for establishing "traceable, significant, and logical connections" between social science content and educational administration. This view perhaps helps to explain why conflict sometimes arises between professors in social science departments oriented toward the attainment of liberal education objectives and prospective educational administrators in their classes who are concerned with learnings relevant to more specific career-based objectives.

A second approach used by those adhering to discipline-based relevance involves the establishment of logical connections between

Table 1

Perspectives for Viewing Relevance: Some General Characteristics

General Perspectives for Viewing Relevance	Distinguishing Historical Events	Beginning Points for Establishing Relevance	Some General Instructional Goals Used in Selecting Social Science Content
Discipline-Based Relevance	1. Emergence of a number of inter-disciplinary social science seminars in CPEA Centers in the early 1950s. 2. Participation of leading social scientists in the 1954 meeting of The National Conference of Professors of Educational Administration. 3. Emergence in the early 1960s of the concept of substructures in disciplines (e.g., economics of education).	Concepts, research findings, generalizations, and modes of inquiry in social science disciplines	I. To develop liberally educated persons through the study of social science disciplines. II. To develop individuals who are sensitized to selected social science content in ways that enable them to understand significant dimensions of administration. III. To develop individuals who understand social science research in educational settings which illuminates relationships among important variables affecting *educational* administration.
Theory-Based Relevance	1. Establishment of the *Administrative Science Quarterly* in 1956. 2. The first UCEA Career Seminar in 1958 on *Administrative Theory in Education*. 3. Publication of *Behavioral Science and Educational Administration* (1964 Yearbook of The National Society for the Study of Education).	Theories of administration and organization associated with the science of administration	I. To develop individuals who understand theories which apply to organizations and administration generally. II. To develop individuals who understand theories which apply to educational organization and administration specifically.
Problems-Based Relevance	1. Development in the early 1950s of the first written case problems in educational administration. 2. Development in the late 1950s of in-	Problems confronting or likely to confront	I. To develop individuals who understand specific administrative problems and who can make effective decisions regarding these problems.

	basket and other simulated problems in educational administration. 3. Growing visibility in the mid-1960s of major administrative and leadership problems confronting educational institutions. 4. Growing emphasis on educational planning in the late 1960s and the establishment of educational policy centers.	educational administrators and leaders	II. To develop individuals with general understandings of pervasive leadership problems in education and with better bases for resolving these problems. III. To develop individuals with a capacity to anticipate future problems and with the skills to understand policy and program issues related to these problems.
Career-Based Relevance	1. Growing number of federal programs in the mid-1960s designed to advance research, development, and training and the emergence of NDEA programs to prepare professors of educational administration. 2. Generation of concepts in the 1960s related to the differentiation of preparatory programs for researchers and administrators. 3. Establishment at the University of Oregon in the mid-1960s of a program, which was distinctly different from the one for preparing administrators, and which was designed specifically to prepare researchers.	Career objectives and functions of personnel preparing to use knowledge in educational administration in different settings and for different purposes	I. To develop individuals in specialized and differentiated preparatory programs who can pursue effectively different career routes in educational administration (e.g., research, development, or leadership).

social science content and specific dimensions of educational administration. During the 1950s, for example, different writers argued that programs could develop educational administrators who grasped social science content in ways that made them sensitive to such environmental factors as community and human relations. More specifically, concepts and modes of inquiry from political science, economics, and sociology, it was argued, could help develop administrators who were sensitized in new ways to "community," "community analysis," and "community decision making." Or, to take another example, various CPEA reports maintained that content from social psychology and other disciplines could generate greater human understanding among practicing and prospective educational administrators. Specifically, the first textbook of the 1950s to be strongly affected by the social science movement dealt principally with human relations.[13]

Goldhammer, in the early 1960s, spoke in some detail about how a number of social science disciplines were generally related to different dimensions of educational administration.[14] Such logical connections as the following can be established from generalizations developed by Goldhammer: sociology can shed light on formal organization; psychology, social psychology, and group dynamics contain concepts which can clarify individual and group relationships; political science can illuminate power, political action, and government; anthropology can help explain socialization and acculturation; and content from economics can shed light on the allocation of economic resources.

More encompassing and general statements about relevance, such as the ones just noted by Goldhammer, were supplemented by statements of social scientists demonstrating specific ways concepts in given disciplines had relevance for selected dimensions of educational administration. Meno Lovenstein, for example, in the late fifties selected a number of concepts from economics including "efficiency," "capitalism," "resources," "planning," "economic analysis," and "labor markets." He established logical connection between these and such differing administrative functions as "community relations," "personnel," "business administration," "curriculum," and the development of an "educational philosophy."[15]

Developing individuals who understand social science concepts in ways which enable them to view significant aspects of administration sensitively becomes an instructional objective associated with the second approach to discipline-based relevance. In the words of a social scientist speaking from the perspective of sociology:

> The essential contribution of the sociologist, in my view, con-
> sists in making available to educational administrators a set of
> *sensitizing ideas and concepts* that emerge from his theoretical
> and empirical efforts that will allow the educational adminis-
> trators to examine in a more realistic and incisive manner the
> complex set of forces at work in his social environment.[16]

In the third approach to discipline-based relevance, which currently represents more of a hope than a firm accomplishment, the
objective is to achieve a more specific kind of relevance than in
either of the two approaches noted above. Specific relevance would
be achieved over a period of time by using the concepts and modes
of inquiry from given social science disciplines to study actual
problems, conditions, and variables in school systems and their
environment. Through such a process of study, substructures of
knowledge within social science disciplines would be developed.
These substructures would have immediate relevance since they
would be based upon actual research in educational systems or their
environments. Such substructures of knowledge are beginning to
emerge under such titles as the "politics of education," and the
"economics of education."

With well-developed substructures in social science disciplines,
professors could do more, it is argued, than to use concepts typically
developed from studies in noneducational settings to sensitize
administrators to conditions, problems, and factors affecting decision making. With more integrated sets of concepts or theories,
developed and tested through studies of phenomena in educational
settings, instructors could help administrators understand causal
relationships between and among variables which face them in
actual decision situations. A firm grasp of sets of integrated concepts would make it possible for administrators not only to understand interrelationships between decision variables but also to
achieve better control over administrative and educational events.
A clear understanding by educational policy makers of how investment in education is positively related to economic growth, for
example, could provide an important base for guiding policy decisions and for predicting their results.

In summary, then, those using the discipline-based perspective
for selecting social science content have developed different assumptions about relevance. Some argue that social science concepts and
modes of inquiry should be selected and used to develop liberally
educated persons. Others maintain that already existing social sci-

ence concepts should be selected and used to enable administrators to be more sensitive to significant dimensions of administration. A third viewpoint is that relevant content evolves when social science concepts and modes of inquiry are used in the actual study of educational administration within schools, school systems, and school settings.

Theory-Based Relevance

Theory-based relevance is related to discipline-based relevance. Theory development, for example, has proceeded largely through the borrowing and use of concepts and modes of inquiry already available in existing social science disciplines. However, there are important differences between the two perspectives. Those adhering to theory-based relevance are oriented not so much toward advancing knowledge in existing disciplines as they are in creating a new discipline — a science of administration. In developing a science of administration, proponents of the theory-based view want to achieve more focused and limited objectives. While a sociologist, for example, might study and theorize about subjects ranging from divorce and juvenile delinquency to social class structure and role behavior, those committed to developing the new science would tend to concentrate specifically upon administration. The process of developing a science of administration has proceeded to this point, however, largely through the synthesis of already existing social science concepts. The purpose of such synthesis has been to illuminate specific dimensions of administration. Synthesis has been advanced by scholars in social science departments and in professional schools committed to the preparation of administrators.

Another important difference between discipline-based and theory-based relevance has to do with the fact that social science disciplines, while placing a strong emphasis upon objectivity, reliability, validity, and replication, also encompass normative considerations. Some social scientists, in other words, deliberately generalize about what ought to be and develop specific recommendations for improving conditions associated with poverty, race relations, education, unemployment, and related matters. However, many of those concerned with formulating a science of administration, particularly in the 1950s, maintained that scholars committed to theory development should concentrate on descriptions, explanations, and predictions and avoid prescriptive generalizations about what organizations or administrators should do.[17]

Although the historical antecedents of the theory movement in education can be traced to the works of Taylor, Follett, Mayo,

Roethlisberger, Barnard, and Simon during the first half of the twentieth century, it was not until the 1950s that the movement began to have an impact on the study and teaching of educational administration. The late Walter Cocking in 1954 foreshadowed the theory-based orientation in education when he spoke of placing together in "one gigantic test tube all of the knowledges and processes of the various disciplines" and of heating "them with the need of school administration until at long last we have a residue which is no longer bits from various disciplines but a new substance which there is reason to believe is that needed by school administrators."[18] In the year following the remark by Cocking, the first systematic treatment of the concept of the theory appeared in educational administration in the form of a monograph by Coladarci and Getzels entitled *The Use of Theory in Educational Administration*.[19] Two years later, the very influential publication *Administrative Behavior in Education* emerged. This book provided discussions of the nature of theory, examples of theories, and ways of using theory in educational administration.[20]

In 1956 the *Administrative Science Quarterly* was established at Cornell University under the editorship of James Thompson, an exponent of the science of administration. In the first four issues of this publication, articles were included concerning administration in such diverse organizations as manufacturer-dealer systems, Soviet business operation, hospitals, British and American ships, and research corporations. Those founding this new *Quarterly* accepted the concept of administration *qua* administration and sought to develop and disseminate studies and theories which would apply generally to administrative organizations.

The *Quarterly* rapidly became one of the leading journals in the field of administration and the chief forum for expression of the administrative science point of view. The articles contained in the *Quarterly* over the past thirteen years have consistently reflected the view that administration in all organizations has common characteristics. Although controversial in concept, the success and prestige of the *Administrative Science Quarterly* attests to the fact that the concept of administration *qua* administration has been widely accepted.

The first UCEA career seminar on "Administrative Theory in Education," sponsored by the University of Chicago in 1958, was one of the high points in the theory movement.[21] At this seminar, such social scientists as Talcott Parsons, Jacob Getzels, John Hemphill, James Thompson, and Andrew Halpin presented papers examining or elaborating theories of administration as did such scholars from professional schools as Daniel Griffiths and Carroll Shartle. It is perhaps significant that the final paper entitled "What Peculiarities in Educational Administration Make It a Special Case" and presented by Roald Campbell raised questions which went beyond the concept of administration *qua* administration. However, papers with such titles as "Administration as a Social Process," "Administration as Problem Solving," and "Administration as Decision-Making" denoted the main thrust of the seminar.

In the mid and late 1960s, theorizing in educational administration began to focus more upon environmental factors in administration. With the emergence of social systems theory, for example, the tendency to focus narrowly and sharply upon theories of administrative behavior became less pronounced. A statement by Erickson in the foreword of the 1967 issue of the *Review of Educational Research* delineated the more recent trend in theory development.

> The erstwhile search for "administrative theory," for example, seems virtually abandoned today, though a few scholars still attempt to explain important events in terms of what The Leader is or does. There seems to be a growing tendency to assume that administrative procedures, instructional approaches, schools, and physical structures must be analyzed as systems or system components (in the broad sense) and that these systems may be extraordinarily open. Investigation has been widened to include not only the administrator himself . . . , but teachers as his prime interactors . . . , the organization as his context . . . , or even the major determinant of what occurs . . . , the allocative strategies that must be considered . . . , and a wide ranging politico-economic framework. . . .[22]

Thus, theories of administration, which were initially somewhat narrowly focused on the administrator himself, have more recently concentrated upon the larger organizational and societal context of educational administration.

In contrast to the perspective of discipline-based relevance, which has generally resulted in prospective administrators' studying in social science departments, those teaching from a perspective of theory-based relevance have tended to be located in professional schools. A study by Judson Shaplin in 1964, for example, showed that the second most popular group of specialists sought by major universities recruiting professors of educational administration were those prepared to teach theory.[23] "Administrative theory," "organizational behavior," and "decision-theory" were courses which denoted this specialization.

Those making decisions about relevant social science content from the theory-based perspective have generally assumed that theories of administration and organizations exist at different levels of abstraction. At the most general level, there is theoretical knowledge that is relevant to administration in all types of organizations. Those holding this view accept the concept of administration *qua* administration. Their instructional objective is to teach prospective administrators theories that can illuminate the characteristics of administration and organization generally, and this objective guides content selection. Thus, such chapter titles as "Administration as Decision Making," and "The Decision Making Process" suggest theoretical content related to this objective.[24]

A second level of theorizing might apply specifically to administration in such differing organizations as industries, hospitals, and schools. At this level of theorizing, professors might select or develop content that would illuminate educational administration specifically. However, it is evident that much of what is currently taught as theoretical content in educational administration is at the most general level of abstraction. Middle and lower level abstractions of theory, applied strictly to educational organizations, simply have not been widely developed as yet, even though some research has been generated within the context of educational administration. Role theories, for example, have generated considerable research within the specific context of educational administration. Other research based upon theories of administration and conducted in educational settings is beginning to be published in such journals as *Educational Administration Quarterly*.

The task of selecting content from a theory-based perspective is complicated by the fact that there are presently numerous "islands of theories" from which to select, and most of these have their origins in specific disciplines. Thus, there is a problem of determining the quality of available theories and their potential for helping individuals develop new understandings of organization and administration.

Few attempts have been made to explicate in rigorous fashion criteria for selecting concepts and/or theories which are both relevant and cogent. Sweitzer has identified several major sets of questions which can be posed to evaluate theories.[25] In a more extensive treatment of the qualitative aspects of theory, Charters has elaborated seven criteria against which a given theory, orientational view, or concept set may be judged for its potential contribution to administrative training.

1. Articulation of the theory or concept set. The greater the number and range of definite relationships incorporated in the theory, the higher its priority for inclusion in the training program. At the one extreme are highly abstract theories in which explicitly stated relationships among concepts have a substantial degree of empirical support. It goes without saying that this is a null class in the social sciences. At the other extreme, at a low level of priority, are simple taxonomies or classification schemes which suggest no relationships among the categories. It should be noted, however, that most taxonomies, unless they are entirely concretistic, do carry implicit suggestions of relationship with other conditions and concepts and may prove to be exceedingly fruitful for the practitioner. . . .

2. Dynamic referents in the theory or concept set. Candidates for inclusion in the training program should incorporate conceptions of process and change among its elemental concepts. Concept sets which imply circumstances or which propose movement toward an equilibrium without specifying the conditions creating disequilibrium should have a low priority. . . .

3. Person-environment interaction referents. The concept set should include both situational and personal concepts and suggest the interactive conditions of the two. That is, the orientation must not be exclusively environmental, accounting for no inter-individual variation, nor exclusively individual, accounting for no intra-individual variations from situation to situation. . . .

4. Operationality of the concepts. In keeping with criteria for good social science theories, the concepts presented to trainees should be those whose denominations are reasonably unambiguous and precise. But beyond this, the operations for the denotation of concepts must not demand information which is inaccessible to the practitioner. . . .

5. Relevance of scope. Social science theories and concept sets are designed to account for delimited classes of phenomena. Preference should be given to those which account for reasonably substantial amounts of variance in phenomena with which the practitioner must deal. . . .

6. Intervention capacity in the theory or concept set. Preference should be given to orientations and concept sets which propose causal conditions within the capacity of human agents to manipulate. The theory should be optimistic. This criterion should not preclude, however, acquaintance with theories failing to meet this criterion. . . .

7. Gain in power from a theory or concept set. This refers to the extent to which the social science contribution constitutes an improvement upon the schema available to the practitioner in any one of the above respects. This criterion cannot be applied, however, without some knowledge of the schema of the particular individuals — practitioners or trainees — in question.[26]

In summary, then, those using the theory-based perspective for selecting social science content have developed differing criteria for selecting content judged to be relevant to dimensions of administration. One approach involves the selection and use of theories which illuminate administration in organizations generally. Another involves the selection and use of theories which are based upon studies of administration within the specific context of education. Some scholars have developed criteria which help to denote the power and quality of given theories as they apply either to administration generally or educational administration specifically.

Problems-Based Relevance

In the very early stages of efforts to incorporate social science content into preparatory programs, observers noted that content and learning experiences had to be "built realistically about the actual problems and issues besetting the school administrator on the job."[27] In other words, the view offered was that efforts to achieve relevance should not begin in the library but rather with the problems facing educational administrators. Having identified field problems, it was then assumed, that social science content designed to help administrators understand or resolve defined problems could be identified and selected.

Those adhering to the problems-based perspective have evolved differing approaches to establishing the relevance of social science content. One approach, which emerged in the field of educational administration during the 1950s, was that of using case descriptions of problems as a base for establishing logical connections between social science concepts and administrative practice. Sargent and Belisle, for example, used case problems as a springboard to encourage students to select, study, and use concepts as "basic building blocks in organizing and relating knowledge or experience."[28] During the case study seminar, prospective administrators selected and studied a range of concepts to organize thinking and analysis. Illustrative concepts were "group dynamics," "culture," and "personality."

At the University of Oregon, a related method was used for establishing relationships between administrative problems and social science concepts.[29] The method, which also involved the use of decision problems depicted in written cases, required students initially to discuss a number of cases intensively without immediate and directed concern for linking problems to social science concepts or modes of inquiry. Out of the discussions of problems in cases, definitional and theoretical questions inevitably arose, and these were identified periodically. For example, the meaning of "leadership" was a concern which typically arose during discussions of decision problems in cases. At certain points in the seminar discussion, periods would be established to explore in depth a selected social science concept, concept set, or theory and to analyze its meaning in relation to problems identified in cases. Social scientists, on occasion, prepared written statements in which they used selected concepts from different social science disciplines to analyze case problems. The sociological concept of "profession" was used, for example, to analyze the school superintendent's behavior in a case entitled "The Valley City Consolidation Issue."[30]

Another related approach to problems-based relevance is found in the Jefferson, Madison, and Monroe City school district simulations. The simulation of these school districts represented, in one sense, a large case study, but the decision problems depicted were presented through the "in-basket" technique, films, kinescopes, and audio recordings, Much effort was expended by professors and students during the 1960s in establishing "logical connections" between "in-basket" problems and social science content. In 1967, a substantial inventory of concepts judged by professors to be relevant to problems represented in simulated situations were collected.[31] More specific illustrations of concept sets actually used by professors are found in the published inventory of resource materials. Among these are "causal chain and decision making," "types of power structure," "determinants of bureaucratic type," "model of small group properties," "a dynamic response model of the political system," and "model of adaptive motivated behavior." Thus, it is clear that professors and students have selected simulated problems and, then, have established relationships between these and social science concepts and theories in various ways. Concepts and theories selected are indigenous to given disciplines in some cases and are inherent in the science of administration in others.

What instructional objectives guide those using case problems and simulated decision situations to identify and select social science content? Two objectives seem to be paramount. One is to develop individuals who can effectively analyze and understand specific administrative problems. The second is to develop individuals with effective problem-solving and decision-making skills. Hunt has summarized this second objective as "the ability to use ideas, to test them against the facts of the problem, and to throw ideas and facts into fresh combinations, thus discovering ways to make them appropriate for the solution of the problem at hand."[32] In sum, then, social science concepts and modes of inquiry when used with cases and simulations are considered relevant if they can improve problem analysis, problem-solving, and decision-making abilities in prospective administrators.

A second approach used to establish logical connections between problems and social science concepts is represented in the so-called "problems" seminar. Problems within this context differ in several ways from those represented in cases and in-baskets. While problems represented in cases and in-baskets are specific to given positions and school districts, those in problems seminars are more generally defined. Typically, they are presumed to exist in different forms in a substantial number of school districts. They also tend to be viewed within the larger school system context, rather than within the context of sub-systems as is usually true with cases and simulation. Problem seminars, for example, might concentrate upon such areas as "Teacher Militancy," "Educational Innovation," "Education and Race Relations," "Student Unrest," and "Inter-Governmental Relations." The problems seminar involves identifying and describing a problem, selecting and organizing content in such a way as to facilitate analysis and understanding of the problem, and projecting possible developmental solutions.

In the problems seminar approach, instruction typically begins with the perceptions which practicing and/or prospective administrators have of the nature of given problems. After initial delineation of a problem area, a major thrust of the seminar effort is to seek more precise definitions and understandings of the problem and, in turn, more effective ways of resolving it. In these activities logical connections between defined dimensions of problems and selected social science concepts, findings, and generalizations are established. Specific illustrations of such connections can be provided in relation to the problem area of "Education and Race Relations."

A problems seminar on "Education and Race" could focus on any one of a number of issues. A general statement of the problem, such as "Providing Equality of Opportunity," leads directly to the need to define what "equality of opportunity" means. Familiar demographic data reflecting the racial balance or imbalance in public schools, economic data showing relative employment and income levels, information pertaining to political disenfranchisement, and psychological tests of school achievement all provide basic insights into the definitional problem. From data of the type just noted, definitions of equality of opportunity can be developed and tested against other studies or against practice in one or more selected school districts.

Further understanding of the problem can be gained by studying the social and psychological conditions which help to define it. Thus, Pettigrew in *A Profile of the Negro American* has made use of role theory to define relationships of whites and blacks and the attendant behaviors associated with these relationships.[33] The unique problem of "identification," involving such factors as physical appearance, ascribed status, and omission from decision making, has been analyzed by several social scientists. Drake, for example, has commented on one aspect of identity.

> The Black Ghetto forces him to identify as a Negro first, an American second, and it gives him geographical "roots." The job ceiling is an ever present reminder that there are forces at work which make him a second class American.[34]

Sociologists have used such concepts as that of "inclusion" to outline the major problems of the black in moving toward full citizenship.[35] Concepts illuminating political aspects are found in the work of Banfield and Wilson, who have characterized existing styles of black politics in cities whose political systems are: (1) ward-based, machine; (2) ward-based, weak organization or factions and followings; (3) proportional representation; and (4) non-partisan, at-large.[36]

Social science literature can also provide prospective leaders insights pertinent to the attainment of solutions to problems. Thus, Rainwater has identified three deprivation effects of caste victimization and has projected general remedies for each condition.[37] Pettigrew, to take one other example, has listed seven ways of achieving racially balanced education.[38]

Those using the problems seminar, then, as a basis for identifying, selecting, and using social science content in preparatory programs, seek two general objectives: first, to advance understanding of educational problems, their relation to larger societal problems, and their implications for leadership and, second, to achieve better bases for solving these problems. While these objectives are clearly related to those pursued by professors using case and simulation problems as bases for selecting social science content, there are two significant differences which deserve to be noted. First, the problems represented in cases and simulation tend to be more administrative in character. Those dealt with in problems seminars, as described here, are more developmental, and the problem-solving involved is more oriented toward change and leadership. Second, in understanding and making decisions about in-basket and case problems, descriptive and explanatory social science content has been chiefly used. On the other hand, problems dealt with in problems seminars have typically entailed the selection of normative content from social science disciplines, as well as descriptive and explanatory concepts and theories.

Another approach to selecting social science content from the perspective of problems-based relevance — an approach which is more emergent than established — focuses upon societal and educational issues of the future. Rather than dealing with existing problems in schools or school systems as those using cases and simulations do or concentrating on perceived general problems as those using the problems seminar approach tend to do, those committed to a "futures" orientation themselves are concerned with prospective educational conditions. The futures seminar, used in a few universities, provides opportunities for exploring prospective problems and issues. Processes of exploration include the use of social science content to describe and assess future problems and to project and examine alternative policies and programs related to these problems.

Harman describes the orientation of educational policy research as follows: "Educational policy research tends to emphasize strategic rather than tactical questions. It tends to be problem-centered rather than disciplined-centered."[39] Recently established educational policy centers supported by the federal government are concentrating on policy research, as are some university departments and non-profit organizations. Policy researchers come from a variety of social science and other disciplinary backgrounds. They approach problems on an inter-disciplinary basis, and their contributions interact with those of other specialists throughout the process.

Data relating to the problem of the future financing of education, for example, can be drawn from a number of social science disciplines, including economics, sociology, and political science. Thus, the sociologists Hauser and Taitel have presented statistical information on population growth by region, urban and rural areas, ethnic characteristics, and age groups for the 1970s.[40] The economist Colm has projected percentage increases in the enrollment of public schools and institutions of higher education in 1980.[41] Lecht has projected a GNP by 1975 of one trillion dollars, after correcting for inflationary influences.[42] Elazar has identified political conditions which will affect the financing of education during the seventies, including growth in the size of governments, increased intergovernmental cooperation, and expanded federal influence in policy making for other levels of government.[43] He has also identified some of the implications for education of expanding federal support.

Social scientists have not only provided data pertinent to the future financing of education; they have also helped generate policy alternatives. Colm, for example, has described five alternatives for future financing which are based upon expenditure projections for education and the possible development of federal, state, and local financial resources.[44] Such projections provide prospective leaders opportunities for studying and assessing alternatives.

The major purpose of using future-defined problems as bases for identifying and selecting social science content is to provide prospective leaders a clearer vision of alternative futures affecting education and better capacities for anticipating and coping with important policy problems. This purpose constitutes the criterion for selecting social science content. The "futures" approach differs from other approaches to problems-based relevance in several ways. It is more recent in its development than are other approaches. It gives major attention to future, in contrast to on-going situations. Finally, it tends to view problems more from a national than from a local perspective.

By way of summary, then, three somewhat distinct approaches have guided those selecting social science content from the problems-based perspective. First, case and simulated problems specific to given positions and school districts have been used as beginning points for identifying and selecting social science content. The content selected has typically been used to help prospective leaders understand administrative problems and to gain analytic and decision-making skills. Second, the problems seminar has provided prospective leaders opportunities to understand and define more general leadership problems found in many school districts and to obtain bases for generating solutions pertinent to these problems.

Social science content is selected to develop individuals who understand general leadership problems and who have concepts basic to resolving these problems. Finally, future-oriented problems, not yet widely recognized by school personnel, constitute another basis for identifying and selecting relevant social science content. The purpose of such content is to provide prospective leaders a better vision of alternative futures, both societal and educational, and clearer perceptions about policy problems and issues likely to be encountered by those giving leadership to educational institutions.

Career-Based Relevance

The fourth approach to relevance starts with career objectives in educational administration and the functions which personnel in different positions will likely perform. Universities, of course, long before the social science movement was initiated, were giving attention to student interests, backgrounds, and career motivations in program planning. However, during the last decade, especially, the concept of career-based relevance has taken on new meanings which have significant implications for those incorporating and using social science content in preparatory programs. These meanings stem largely from specialization tendencies inherent in educational administration — tendencies which have been stimulated, in part, through the social science movement. These tendencies are reflected in emergent new bodies of knowledge (e.g., "economics of education"), as well as in more specialized and intensive uses of knowledge in educational administration (e.g., research, development, and decision making).

Personnel at Harvard University made a clear distinction in the early fifties between preparing researchers and preparing administrators, as is indicated in Chapter Eight. However, throughout most of the 1950s, those engaged in incorporating social science concepts and modes of inquiry into preparatory programs were thinking largely about personnel preparing for administrative posts in school districts. It was not until the end of the decade that scholars more generally began to question the implicit assumption held by planners that programs for preparing school administrators and researchers should be the same. Thus, the Committee for the Advancement of School Administration in 1958 made the following statement: "The school administrator is a practitioner, not a researcher, and the research required of him in professional training will recognize this distinction."[45] Even though questions were raised about needed differences in preparation for researchers and administrators, these did not materialize in the 1950s. Program change was oriented almost entirely toward administrator preparation, and, as a result, the development of explicit and unique programs for researchers was not achieved. Thus, Daniel Griffiths, near the end of the 1950s, was able to observe that

> The past few years have seen some revisions in the programs of preparation of educational administrators at a few of the major institutions in the country. . . . There is, however, no source which describes changes in the graduate programs which would lead to more competent researchers — for the very apparent reason that little has been done. It would certainly be reasonable to say that a researcher needs preparation different from that of an administrator, yet nowhere is this difference taken into account.[46]

In the mid 1960s, Jean Hills analyzed some of the consequences of programs which recruit prospective professors and administrators from similar talent pools and provide them the same kind of curriculum during their preparation.[47] Most professors of educational administration, under such a practice, were "general-practitioner professors," to use Hill's term, rather than scholars with specialized research skills and critical attitudes toward the *status quo*. While agreeing that the "general-practitioner professor" has made substantial contributions in field service activities and in a role supportive of the practicing educational administrator, Hills argued that this type of professor is so immersed in the ideology of practice that he is not able to exercise a critical intellectual and leadership role in changing the goals and structures of existing educational organizations. Hills summarized some of his ideas as follows:

> The relative absence of a problem-solving emphasis can be observed in the fact that there are few specialties within the field of educational administration. Most professors operate as general practitioners. That is, they play a diffuse role both in relation to their public school clients and in relation to their students. Any given professor is likely to be called upon to perform services ranging from population projections to the solution of personnel problems. And he may be called upon to teach courses ranging from school finance, to the elementary school principalship. This in itself is a strong deterrent to scholarship. When it is coupled with the supportive-service orientation, an expectation for scholarly production is totally unrealistic. It seems clear, then, that the combined general practitioner-supportive service role of the typical professor

of educational administration effectively rules out scholarly production.[48]

Implicitly, then, Hills was making the case for recruiting and preparing a greater number of professors who could play a more specialized role toward changing existing educational systems, rather than toward supporting current ideology and practice. Although he did not spell out specific suggestions for training, he observed that some differentiation in professor roles and in their training was beginning to take place within the field of educational administration. This, he predicted, would lead to a more scholarly specialization on the part of professors and, in turn, would enable them to play a more important leadership role in educational administration.

Only a few writers have examined the issue of social science relevance specifically, in relation to differing career roles and functions. One of the first authors to discuss the issue in relation to differentiated training for personnel pursuing different career functions was John Andrews.[49] He postulated the need for the following four different types of personnel in the field of educational administration: social scientists, applied scientists, consultants, and practitioners. He defined the major functions of these various types of personnel as they relate to educational administration as follows: the social scientist is centrally concerned with producing general knowledge; the applied scientist with producing generalized applied knowledge; the consultant with applying knowledge to practice in some usable form; and the practitioner with implementing knowledge in actual administrative settings. In projecting guides for incorporating social science content into preparatory programs, Andrews offered the following general suggestions: the social scientist should have advanced specialization in one of the social sciences; the applied scientist should have partial specialization in one or more of the social sciences; the consultant should have a general background knowledge in several social sciences; and the practitioner should have useful knowledge selected from the social sciences.

Another analysis appearing in the late 1960s, which dealt with career-based relevance, concentrated specifically upon professors who plan to specialize in studying the politics of education and administrators who plan to head school districts.[50] A number of differences in preparation were postulated for these two classes of personnel on the assumption that their motivations, functions, and work places differ substantially. One of the recommendations bearing upon the issue of relevance, for example, was that school superintendents should take work in a number of social science disciplines and that professors planning to specialize in basic research in an area, such as the politics of education, should have depth study in political science.

As concepts were developed highlighting differing career functions in educational administration, and as arguments for differentiated programs to prepare researchers and administrators become more explicit in the mid-1960s, federally supported research and development programs grew in scope and number. In addition, funds became available to prepare professors through the National Defense Education Act and researchers through the Cooperative Research Program. Federal funds were made available to a number of universities to prepare professors of educational administration and the University of Oregon undertook a program designed specifically to prepare research professors in educational administration. These developments helped to raise further questions about "differentiated" preparation for researchers and administrators and served to make more explicit the concept of career-based relevance.

Clearly, the career-based perspective for viewing relevance is more general in orientation than are the three other perspectives discussed in this chapter. The perspective requires a comparative analysis of different knowledge-related functions and of the competencies needed to perform different functions. Functions to be performed by personnel pursuing different objectives become criteria for selecting social science content.

So far in educational administration, the career-based perspective has been used more for program analysis than for program design. It is assumed by those adhering to the career-based concept of relevance that the function of basic researchers who use knowledge to create new knowledge, for example, are quite distinct from those of administrators who use knowledge in decision-making and in influencing policy development. So far, analysis and design have been limited largely to the preparation of personnel to perform the differing functions of research and administration. These basic differences become beginning points for content selection.

SUMMARY

The last two decades have produced considerable ferment in thinking concerning the preparation of educational administrators.

Basic to this ferment have been questions and issues associated with the selection, organization, and use of social science content in preparatory programs. A fundamental issue which has received increasing attention and which relates to most other issues dealt with is that of *relevance*.

Given the large amount of social science content available, the important questions to be answered are what is more and what is less relevant to the preparation of educational administrators, and on what bases can this question be most wisely answered?

A number of analytical perspectives have evolved for identifying and responding to issues of relevance and for developing positions on these issues. Four analytical perspectives have been described in this chapter. They have been labeled as (1) discipline-based relevance, (2) theory-based relevance, (3) problems-based relevance, and (4) career-based relevance.

These perspectives, while not entirely discrete, do have unique characteristics, including different intellectual origins and histories. Those who employ them for selecting and using social science content start from quite different bases. Those adhering to discipline-based relevance start with the concepts, research findings, and generalizations of the social sciences; those committed to theory-based relevance begin with the theories associated with the science of administration; those holding to problems-based relevance start with the problems confronting or likely to confront educational administrators; and those accepting career-based relevance begin with the functions and objectives of personnel pursuing such differing careers as administration and research.

Personnel beginning at different points and from different perspectives tend to pursue differing instructional objectives. These instructional objectives become criteria for identifying, selecting, and organizing social science content in preparatory programs. The objectives, in other words, constitute the major bases for establishing "logical and significant connections" between social science content and educational administration.

FOOTNOTES

1. Alonzo Grace, "The Professional Preparation of School Personnel," in *Changing Conceptions in Educational Administration*, ed. Nelson B. Henry

(Chicago, Illinois: The University of Chicago Press, National Society for the Study of Education, 45th Yearbook, Part II, 1946), p. 181.

2. Cyril G. Sargent and George E. Flower, "C.P.E.A. in New England Deals With Community Situations: Seeks Help from Allied Disciplines," *Nation's Schools* 48, 6 (December 1951): 44.

3. For more details on the development of social science uses during the Cooperative Program in Educational Administration see Hollis A. Moore, Jr., *Studies in School Administration* (Washington, D. C.: American Association of School Administrators, 1957).

4. *Webster's Seventh New Collegiate Dictionary.*

5. Roald Campbell and Russell Gregg, eds., *Administrative Behavior in Education* (New York: Harper and Row, 1957).

6. Sargent and Flower, "C.P.E.A. in New England Deals With Community Situations," p. 44.

7. Lawrence W. Downey and Frederick Enns, eds., *The Social Sciences in Educational Administration* (Edmonton, Canada: Division of Educational Administration, The University of Alberta and the University Council for Educational Administration, 1962).

8. Daniel Griffiths, "The Social Sciences and Administration: A Rationale Response," *The Social Sciences in Educational Administration*, p. 14.

9. Keith Goldhamer, *The Social Sciences and the Preparation of Educational Administrators* (Columbus, Ohio: The University Council for Educational Administration, 1963).

10. Daniel Griffiths, ed., *Behavioral Science and Educational Administration* (Chicago: University of Chicago Press, National Society for the Study of Education, 63rd Yearbook, Part II, 1964).

11. Robin Farquhar, "Results of a Questionnaire Study," in Jack Culbertson, Robin Farquhar, Al Gaynor, and Mark Shibles, *Preparing Educational Leaders for the Seventies* (Prepared with the aid of a grant provided by the Cooperative Research Program of the USOE — Contract No. OEG-0-8-080230-2695[010], 1969).

12. Donald E. Tope, et al., *The Social Sciences View School Administration* (Englewood Cliffs, New Jersey: Prentice-Hall, Inc., 1965), p. 32.

13. Daniel Griffiths, *Human Relations in School Administration* (New York: Appleton-Century-Crofts 1956).

14. Keith Goldhammer, *Social Sciences and Preparation of Educational Administrators*, pp. 13–14.

15. Meno Lovenstein, *Economics and the Educational Administrator* (Columbus, Ohio: College of Education, The Ohio State University, in cooperation with the Joint Council on Economic Education, 1958). Also see Tope, et al., *The Social Sciences View School Administration*.

16. Neal Gross, "Sociology and the Study of Administration," *The Social Sciences in Educational Administration*, p. 31.

17. James Thompson, "Modern Approaches to Theory" in *Administrative Theory in Education*, ed. Andrew Halpin (Chicago: Midwest Administration Center, The University of Chicago, 1958), p. 31.

18. Walter Cocking, "Other Disciplines and School Administration," *School Executive* 73 (March 1954): 7.

19. Arthur P. Coladarci and Jacob W. Getzels, *The Use of Theory in Educational Administration* (Stanford, California: Stanford University Press, 1955).

20. Campbell and Gregg, eds., *Administrative Behavior in Education.*

21. Andrew Halpin, ed., *Administrative Theory in Education.*

22. Donald A. Erickson, "Foreword," *Review of Educational Research* 37. 4 (October 1967): 376.

23. Judson Shaplin, "The Professorship in Educational Administration: Attracting Talented Personnel," in *The Professorship in Educational Administration*, eds. Donald Willower and Jack Culbertson (Columbus, Ohio: The University Council for Educational Administration and The College of Education, Pennsylvania State University, 1964).

24. See Daniel Griffiths, *Administrative Theory* (New York: Appleton-Century-Crofts, 1959).

25. Robert E. Sweitzer, "An Assessment of Two Theoretical Frameworks," in *Educational Research: New Perspectives*, eds. Jack Culbertson and Stephen Hencley (Danville, Illinois: Interstate Printers and Publishers, Inc., 1963), pp. 199–232.

26. W. W. Charters, Jr., "Anthropology and the Study of Administration Response," *The Social Sciences in Educational Administration*, pp. 91–93.

27. Sargent and Flower, "C.P.E.A. in New England Deals With Community Situations," p. 46.

28. Cyril Sargent and Eugene Belisle, *Educational Administration: Cases and Concepts* (New York: Houghton Mifflin Co., 1955), p. 453.

29. Jack Culbertson, Paul Jacobson, and Theodore Reller, *Administrative Relationships: A Case Book* (Englewood Cliffs, New Jersey: Prentice-Hall, 1960), p. 97.

30. See "Case Analysis," *Administrative Relationships: A Case Book*, pp. 26–50.

31. The University Council for Educational Administration, *Resource Materials for Use in Simulation Workshops* (Columbus, Ohio: UCEA, 1967).

32. Pearson Hunt, "The Case Method of Instruction," *Harvard Educational Review* 21, 3 (Summer 1951): 178.

33. Thomas F. Pettigrew, *A Profile of the Negro American* (Princeton, New Jersey: Van Nostrand, 1964).

34. St. Clair Drake, "The Social and Economic Status of the Negro in the United States," *Daedalus*, 94, 4 (Fall 1965): 800.

35. Talcott Parsons, "Full Citizenship for the Negro American: A Sociological Problem." *Daedalus*, 94, 4 (Fall 1965).

36. Edward C. Banfield and James Q. Wilson, *City Politics* (New York: Random House, 1963).

37. Lee Rainwater, "Crucible of Identity: The Negro Lower-Class Family," *Daedalus*, 94, 1 (Winter 1966): 208.

38. Thomas F. Pettigrew, "Extending Educational Opportunities: School Desegregation," in *Educating an Urban Population*, ed. Marilyn Gittell (Beverly Hills, California: Sage Publications, 1967).

39. Willis W. Harman, "Technology and Educational Policy Research," in *Planning For the Effective Use of Technology in Education*, eds. Edgar L. Morphet and David L. Jesser (Denver: Designing Education for the Future, 1968), p. 254.

40. Philip M. Hauser and Martin Taitel, "The Changing Character of General Population: Implications for Education," in *The Emerging Role of State Education Departments with Specific Implications for Divisions of Vocational-Technical Education*, eds. Dick Rice and Powell Toth (Columbus, Ohio: The Center for Vocational and Technical Education, 1967).

41. Gerhard Colm, "Prospective Economic Developments," in *Prospective Changes in Society by 1980*, eds. Edgar L. Morphet and Charles O. Ryan (New York: Citation Press, 1968).

42. Leonard A. Lecht, "The Changing Occupational Structure with Implications for Education," in *The Emerging Role of State Education Departments.*

43. Daniel Elazar, "The American Partnership: The Next Half Generation," *Prospective Changes in Society by 1980.*

44. Gerhard Colm, "Prospective Economic Developments."

45. Committee for the Advancement of School Administration, *Something to Steer By* (Washington: The Committee, 1958), p. 9.

46. Daniel Griffiths, *Research in Educational Administration* (New York: Bureau of Publications, Teachers College, Columbia University, 1959), p. 50.

47. Jean Hills, "Social Science, Ideology, and the Professor of Educational Administration," *Educational Administration Quarterly*, 1, 3 (Autumn 1965): 23–39.

48. Ibid., p. 32.

49. John H. M. Andrews, "Differentiated Research Training for Students of Administration," *Educational Research: New Perspectives*, pp. 355–365.

50. Jack Culbertson, "Differentiated Preparation for Professors and Educational Administrators" (Vice-Presidential Address – Division A, American Educational Research Association, 1968).

2

Incorporating the Social Sciences in Administrator Preparation Programs: Some Empirical Evidence

Emil J. Haller and Edward S. Hickcox

In the previous chapter, Culbertson and Shibles suggest an analytic scheme for considering the relevance of the social sciences to administrator preparation programs. They propose that the "logical connection" between social science and administrative training can be examined from four perspectives: the social science discipline involved, administrative theory, problems and issues in education, and the careers of specialists in educational administration. Thus, they trace the development of training programs in educational administration from each of the four perspectives and are concerned with delineating criteria by which concepts, theories, and methodologies of the social sciences might contribute more effectively to training experiences.

In this chapter, we consider the question of *how* social science content has been incorporated in training programs. We do this in two ways. First, we examine the position taken by departments of educational administration regarding the use of social science disciplines in their graduate programs. That is, what are departmental expectations of graduate students? While it is clear that nearly all departments stress the interdisciplinary aspects of their training, considerable variation in emphasis and method is likely. Second, we examine the social science courses actually taken by a selected group of doctoral students in educational administration. By examining data on courses taken by students, their major and minor fields of study and their backgrounds, we obtain a second perspective on the interdisciplinary emphasis in training programs. This second approach seems appropriate since what departments say students do is not necessarily what they in fact do.

"OFFICIAL POSITIONS": DEPARTMENTAL PRONOUNCEMENTS

One index of a commitment to an interdisciplinary perspective is provided by the degree to which departments of educational administration encourage doctoral students to take courses offered by social science departments. Determining the extent of such encouragement was one of the problems addressed by Stolworthy.[1]

Stolworthy surveyed 61 NCATE accredited universities offering Ed.D.s in educational administration in 1964–65. He collected three varieties of data. The first consisted of announcements and program descriptions published by graduate schools, schools of education, and departments of administration. When these sources were in need of clarification, he supplemented them through personal correspondence with department chairmen. As a third source of data, he sent a questionnaire to all chairmen. Fifty-three (87%) of these men replied to the questionnaire. Thus, Stolworthy's study provides a snapshot of the official position which departments were taking in 1964–65 on the question of the use of social science and other non-education courses in preparing school administrators.

As part of his research, Stolworthy attempted to determine the stance of responding departments concerning course requirements in other disciplines as a condition for earning degrees. That is, departments may mandate such course work, or they may leave it to the discretion of students and their advisors. Using four categories, Stolworthy sought to categorize departmental positions on this question of discretion; he termed these categories "required," "expected," "encouraged and/or recommended," and "optional." Since the distinction between the first two of these is unclear (and since, in any case, the second category contained only two cases), we have collapsed his four categories into three — "required," "encouraged," and "optional." He found that of the 51 departments which he could classify, 37 (72%) required some course work in departments other than education, 5 (10%) encouraged or recommended such work, and 9 (18%) considered such work to be at the student's option.[2] By this index, there appears to be a strong interdisciplinary emphasis in the majority of training programs.

A somewhat different picture emerges, however, when one asks how intensive are these requirements for non-education courses. For example, how many semester hours in other departments are required of a student? Stolworthy was able to obtain data in this regard from 40 schools. Requirements for work in other departments ranged from 4 to 30 semester hours. The modal number of hours required was 12, or approximately four courses at the usual three hours per course. Remembering that these specifications represent requirements *beyond* the bachelor's degree, it can be seen that required non-education courses represent a relatively modest portion of a student's graduate course load at most schools. This is seen more clearly when non-education requirements are computed as a percentage of the total number of post-bachelor hours needed for an Ed.D.

Table 1

Minimum Proportion of Students' Total Programs Required in Other University Departments[a]

Proportion of Program Required in Other Departments	Number and Percent of Educational Administration Departments Requiring Outside Work	
0 — 10%	6	(15.0%)
11 — 20%	16	(40.0%)
21 — 30%	12	(30.0%)
31 — 40%	4	(10.0%)
41 — 50%	2	(5.0%)
Total	40	(100%)

[a]Adapted from Stolworthy, "Study of Use of Disciplines Outside Education," pp. 155-156.

Table 1 shows the distribution of the percentages of the total number of graduate hours required for an Ed.D. which students must take outside education. It can be seen that a majority of the educational administration departments required that less than one-fifth of a student's program be in other university departments. Thus, while most departments require students to take courses in other disciplines, these requirements are reasonably modest.

It is possible that many departments of educational administration incorporate social science content in their own courses and, therefore, feel that it is unnecessary to require students to take much outside work. One technique for incorporating social science is to utilize faculty of these disciplines in administration courses. Accordingly, Stolworthy asked department chairmen to indicate the extent to which non-education professors were used in seminars to discuss problems and subjects related to education. Table 2 presents his findings.

Table 2

*Extent to Which Non-Education Professors Are Used
in Educational Administration Seminars*[a]

Responses of Department Chairman	N	%
Often	17	(35.0)
Seldom	28	(60.0)
Never	2	(5.0)
Total	47	(100)

[a]Adapted from Stolworthy, "Study of Use of Disciplines Outside Education," p. 126.

It can be seen that the majority of departments "seldom" or "never" make use of professors from other disciplines to teach in administration courses. Unfortunately, it is difficult to interpret these data, since we have no idea what "often," "seldom," or "never" mean in this context. The reader is free to "plug in" whatever values for these terms he deems appropriate. As a personal guess, we suspect that only a very few students ever meet a social science professor in courses in educational administration. A small number of departments employ such men full-time (e.g. Chicago) and a few more make joint appointments (e.g. Syracuse). Using professors of other disciplines to assist in the teaching of educational administration does not appear to be a common device for achieving an interdisciplinary focus in training programs.

Another method for incorporating the social sciences into graduate programs is to utilize professors of those disciplines as minor members on students' advisory committees. When these committees are concerned with guiding students' course work and dissertations, *and* when they play an active role in those processes (the last condition, we suspect is by no means universally met), this procedure may be an effective one. For example, minor members from other disciplines may best insure that students treat their thesis problems within theoretically appropriate frameworks drawn from those disciplines. Presumably, these men are best equipped to guide the students' reading and course work within their area of expertise.

Similarly, they are presumably most familiar with their discipline's methodologies. Stolworthy asked departmental chairmen about the frequency of using "outside members" on student committees. Their replies are shown in Table 3.

Table 3

*Extent of Use of Non-Education Professors
on Student Advisory Committees*[a]

Response of Department Chairmen	N	%
Often	23	(46)
Usually	12	(24)
Seldom	13	(26)
Never	2	(4)
Total	50	(100)

[a]Adapted from Stolworthy, "Study of Use of Disciplines Outside Education," p. 129.

It appears that requiring students of educational administration to work with non-educationists on their doctoral committees is a commonly used procedure for incorporating an interdisciplinary perspective in training programs. Fully 70% of the responding departments "often" or "usually" make use of this device.

Undoubtedly, the most common strategy for securing a social science perspective in administrator preparation is to build it into a department's own courses. This might be done by preparing course curricula which deliberately include concepts, theories, and methods from those disciplines. This technique is aided considerably by the increasing number of textbooks in this field which explicitly treat school administration within one or more disciplinary perspectives.[3] During the last decade, we have witnessed a steady decline of texts written from an entirely prescriptive viewpoint. Further, authors who have revised their outdated prescriptive texts during this period have usually done so by attempting to include concepts and research findings from the social sciences.

Another common technique for including the social sciences directly into administration courses is to hire professors of educational administration who have been extensively trained in one or more of these disciplines, as well as in education. Stolworthy collected no data on this possibility. We will, however, present some evidence bearing on this strategy in the next section. Meanwhile, Shaplin can help us out. His research suggests that approximately 70% of the UCEA institutions place a "high" or "medium" emphasis on depth and/or breadth of social science training when recruiting assistant professors.[4] Shaplin's work was reported in 1964. Since then, it is probable that departments have increased their emphasis on this selection criterion. We may safely conclude that another commonly used technique for incorporating an interdisciplinary approach into training programs is to stress relevant social science content within educational administration courses themselves.

Finally, Stolworthy asked department chairmen to respond to an item regarding the frequency of use of courses in several non-education disciplines. Their responses relative to the social science disciplines are tabulated in Table 4.

Table 4

*Perceived Frequency of Use of Social Sciences
in Ed.D. Programs*[a]

Discipline[b]	Always N %	Usually N %	Seldom N %	Never N %	Totals
		Frequency of Use			
Anthropology	2(4.8)	14(34.1)	22(53.7)	3(7.3)	41
Economics	3(7.1)	23(54.8)	15(35.7)	1(2.3)	42
Political Science	6(13.6)	31(70.5)	7(15.9)	0	44
Sociology	7(16.3)	30(69.8)	5(11.6)	1(2.3)	43

[a]Adapted from Stolworthy, "Study of Use of Disciplines Outside Education," pp. 135-136.
[b]Social psychology was not included in the questionnaire.

We can see that chairmen of departments claim to make heaviest use of courses offered in sociology and political science, with substantially less utilization of economics, although over half of the respondents say they "usually" make use of the latter discipline. Anthropology falls far behind those three in perceived use.

From this survey, it seems clear that the "official position" of most departments is that their programs should incorporate content from the social sciences. Most are willing to mandate this inclusion by requiring some proportion of students' work to be outside education. However, most departments also seem inclined to keep 80% of their students' programs within education, typically requiring four post–B.A. courses in other disciplines. The majority of the departments surveyed made infrequent use of professors of other disciplines to actually teach courses and seminars in educational administration. A very common technique for securing an inter-disciplinary emphasis in doctoral programs seems to be to include non-educationists on students' doctoral committees. Finally, incor-porating social science content is frequently accomplished by in-cluding it in administration courses, through textbook adoptions, and hiring professors who were themselves trained in interdisplinary programs.

The Course Content of Student Programs

While the previous section indicated what departments say they would like students to take, this section will examine actual pro-grams for evidence of a social science emphasis. Data for this sec-tion comes from forms circulated by UCEA in 1968–69 to students in all member institutions who were interested in professorial posi-tions. The purpose of these forms is to provide member institutions with data on each year's crop of new doctorates. In 1968–69, these forms were completed by 74 doctoral candidates representing 35 universities. Among the items on this form is one which asks stu-dents to list all graduate courses which they have taken. By com-paring these responses with current catalogues, it was possible to identify the courses which students took in social science depart-ments.

It is recognized that these forms provide a non-representative sample of students. That is, these forms are completed only by that minority of students who are considering a professorship of educa-tional administration as post-doctoral employment. (In the 1968–69 academic year, universities graduated approximately 1,000 Ed.D.s and Ph.D.s in educational administration.[5] While we cannot be sure of the effect that examining this minority has on the following tab-ulations, we assume that it tends to inflate the number of social science courses shown. Students considering a professorial career are more likely to have taken a greater number of non-education courses than students planning on careers as practitioners. Shaplin's study supports this assumption.[6] Thus, this index of an interdis-ciplinary emphasis in preparation programs is likely to be *higher* than would a similar measure based on all doctoral candidates.

How much course work do students actually take outside their own departments? Table 5 presents the percentage of post–B.A. courses taken in other departments for each 1969 graduate.

Table 5

Percentage Distribution of Non-Education
Courses for 1969 Graduates

Percent of Program in Non-Education Departments	Number of Students	%
0 — 5%	11	(14.9)
5.1 — 10	9	(12.2)
10.1 — 15	11	(14.9)
15.1 — 20	14	(18.9)
20.1 — 25	8	(10.2)
25.1 — 30	3	(4.1)
31.1 — 35	6	(8.1)
35.1 — 40	3	(4.1)
40.1 — 45	3	(4.1)
45.1 — 50	1	(1.4)
Over 50	5	(6.8)
Total	74	(100)

A wide variation in the percentage of non-education course work taken by these students is apparent. A large majority (53) had less than 25% of their work outside education. The modal group falls into the 15-20% category. This figure closely approximates Stolworthy's finding regarding departmental requirements — the typical requirement for non-education courses is that they represent about 20% of a student's total program.

A more relevant question is the extent to which these students have actually included social science courses in their graduate programs. That is, the previous tabulation included all non-education courses regardless of the department in which they were offered. In Table 6, we have utilized the distinction made by the editors of this book. The social sciences are divided into sociology, social psychology, political science, economics, and anthropology. The following table indicates the percentage of all courses taken by students in any of the five listed disciplines.

Table 6

Percentage Distribution of Social Science Courses

Percent of All Courses Taken in Social Science Departments	Number of Students	%
0%	19	(21.8)
1 — 5	17	(19.6)
6 — 10	11	(12.7)
11 — 15	15	(17.3)
16 — 20	8	(9.2)
21 — 25	6	(6.9)
26 — 30	3	(3.4)
31 — 35	1	(1.1)
36 — 40	2	(2.3)
41 — 45	0	(0)
46 — 50	2	(2.3)
51 — 55	2	(2.3)
56 — 60	1	(1.1)
Total	87	(100)

Under this definition of social science, fully one-fifth of these students have taken no courses in these fields in their graduate programs. Over one-half have taken less than 10% of their course work in one of those disciplines. The proportion of students taking more than 15% of their work in social science departments drops rapidly, terminating with the case of three who took more than one-half of their work outside the department of education.

It should be emphasized that nearly all of the students falling in the low end of this continuum have a larger proportion of non-education courses in their programs than Table 6 indicates. Many of these students have taken some work in psychology, particularly educational psychology, which does not show in these tabulations. In addition, many have taken a significant proportion of their work in departments of business administration, history, and so on. This distribution does indicate that many students take no formal social science courses in their graduate careers.

From the UCEA form, one can determine the social science disciplines which these students tend to elect. This is shown in Table 7.

Table 7

Social Science Courses Taken by Prospective Professors[a]

	Number of Courses	%
Political Science	120	(45.4)
Sociology	96	(36.2)
Economics	20	(7.5)
Anthropology	17	(6.4)
Social Psychology	12	(4.4)
Totals	265	(99.9)

[a]Including work taken in MA programs.

Among 1969 doctorates, political science courses were the most popular, with sociology following closely behind. Economics, anthropology, and social psychology were taken much less frequently. This ordering agrees with Stolworthy's findings regarding departmental emphases and with Haller's analysis of professorial research.[7] Thus, we conclude that students actually take something less than 25% of their post–B.A. work outside education; and that when this work is in the social sciences, it is typically in sociology or political science. Finally, it appears that course work in social science accounts for no more than 15% of most students' programs.

One possible technique for incorporating social science content in preparation programs would be to recruit doctoral students who already have strong backgrounds in one of these disciplines. This technique would substantially free departments from having to send their students "across campus" for social science courses or from having to duplicate the relevant content within their own course structures. To check the possibility that departments are doing this, we have tabulated the bachelor's and master's degree majors of each Ed.D. in Table 8.

It appears that departments can not place a great deal of emphasis on deliberately recruiting students with backgrounds in the

Table 8

*Major Fields of Study at the Bachelor's and
Master's Degree Levels of Ed.D.s in Administration*

Major Field	Bachelor's Degree		Master's Degree	
Education	21	(28.4)	57	(77.0)
Social Science	16	(21.6)	5	(6.8)
Humanities	14	(18.9)	3	(4.1)
Science-Mathematics	13	(17.6)	4	(5.4)
Business	8	(10.8)	1	(1.4)
Other	2	(2.7)	4*	(5.4)
Totals	74	(100)	74	(100.1)

*3 earned no M.A.

social sciences. Students with such undergraduate majors constitute a little over one-fifth of the total group, and this figure is probably inflated over the corresponding figure for all doctoral candidates. This inflation would result from the practice of a few departments of specifically recruiting social science majors for training as professors.[8] The modal undergraduate major is education. In the case of the M.A., the vast majority have done their work in this field. Thus, this recruiting strategy for incorporating a social science perspective may not be a common one.

DISCUSSION

The data presented indicate that the social sciences are currently being incorporated into preparation programs for educational administrators. By this we mean that the intent of training programs is to expose students to social science content. Further, we can expect this interdisciplinary emphasis to continue in various forms for some time, although Button suggests otherwise.[9] The three most common strategies used by departments of educational administration for incorporating social science into their training programs are the "requirement strategy," which requires doctoral students to take some proportion of their course work outside the department of education; the "minor member," strategy which requires that doctoral candidates include non-educationists on their committees; and the "in-house strategy" in which professors of educational administration introduce relevant social science concepts and theories into their own courses. Undoubtedly, most universities utilize all three of these methods to varying degrees. In the remainder of this chapter, we shall examine these strategies and attempt to relate them to the relevance perspectives outlined in the first chapter.

As a preliminary comment, it is important to note that only a minority of all graduate students of educational administration are affected by the requirement and minor member strategies. This is because *most* students of educational administration are part-time, non-degree candidates who enroll in after-hours courses, usually only long enough to satisfy state certification requirements. Requirements for non-education courses and the composition of doctoral committees are of little concern to these people. Thus, their exposure to social science concepts and theories depends entirely on their professors of educational administration. It appears that these extramural students have almost no exposure to professors in other fields, to interaction with students in other disciplines, or extensive opportunities to utilize libraries of social science materials.

This situation points up a certain anomaly in the position of many departments of educational administration. On grounds that extensive exposure to relevant social science content is necessary to the successful practice of administration, most departments adopt requirement, minor member, and in-house strategies to ensure that students confront these disciplines. However, the necessity of social science exposure apparently is seen as less crucial for part-time students. Yet, it is from the ranks of these students that the majority of practicing administrators come. On what basis are part-time students, preparing for the same roles as their full-time counterparts, exempted from these techniques for relating the social sciences to administration? It seems that departments' commitments to the social science perspective has often been compromised by the limitations of resources, the financial attractiveness of having large numbers of part-time students, and the narrow focus of state certification requirements.

The Requirement Strategy

Turning first to a discussion of the requirement strategy as it has been applied to training programs, we note that the data presented earlier suggests this to be an effective technique for insuring that doctoral students get some exposure to other disciplines besides education. Indeed, taking in conjunction Stolworthy's data and that derived from the pre-professor forms, one finds the correspondence of departmental requirements and student behavior striking. (Stolworthy's data, indicating that doctoral candidates take about 20% of their work in non-education courses, corresponds quite closely to our finding that, for students submitting pre-professor forms to UCEA, the modal percent of non-education courses actually taken also approximates 20%. In this limited sense, "distribution" requirements seem to work.)

The similarity in these two analyses, however, also suggests the workings of one of the classic dysfunctions of rules.[10] That is, rules which define minimally acceptable behavior tend to produce exactly that — minimally acceptable behavior. If a goal of these departments is for students to take an integrated interdisciplinary program, it may be dysfunctional to define operationally this goal as some required number of hours outside the department even aside from the obvious inadequacy of that operationalization. Such a procedure may well define the *maximum* number of hours students will take.

There are several reasons to believe that graduate students of educational administration will tend to take a few courses as they must in other departments. Our students are practical men, usually working administrators on a sabbatical, intent on earning a degree and returning to their jobs as quickly as possible. For most of them, graduate education is seen from an entirely instrumental perspective. That is, the doctorate is viewed as a necessary prerequisite to successful competition in the job market. For such men, the relevance of courses offered by other departments may not be immediately apparent. A course in community politics, for example, taught in the Department of Political Science, is by no means necessarily useful to a man concerned with passing referendums and even less to a man primarily concerned with getting a larger superintendency.[11]

For another very practical reason, doctoral students tend to avoid going across campus. The competition is often tough. Typically, the social science courses most obviously relevant to their needs (e.g., a course in community politics) are taught at the graduate level, where their classmates, in addition to being somewhat brighter,[12] are also better prepared for the courses by virtue of possessing undergraduate and/or graduate majors in the discipline. Thus, students are often ill-prepared for just those social science courses which might be of greatest use to them. Students are not oblivious to this disadvantage.

The converse of this problem of lack of preparation is the issue of prerequisites. Whether because of a belief in the cumulative knowledge structure of their own disciplines or, more cynically, from a simple desire to reduce class sizes, professors of social science often attach prerequisites to their graduate courses. These effectively bar many students of educational administration. With only a year of sabbatical leave to spend in full-time study (education majors probably spend less time on campus earning a doctorate than students in any other discipline),[13] they are understandably loathe to fill their programs with courses to satisfy prerequisites. The prerequisite problem is further exacerbated by the fact that the majority of the graduate courses taken by students who eventually earn a Ph.D. or Ed.D. are taken in the evenings or summers, when few graduate courses are offered by other departments. These problems of prerequisites and scheduling are reflected in the replies to Stolworthy's questionnaire.

One of the open-ended items in Stolworthy's survey asked department chairmen to list any problems they have had in utilizing non-education courses in their programs. Table 9 classifies their responses into eight categories. The first of these provides evidence

Table 9

Problems Mentioned by Department Chairmen in Utilizing Non-Education Courses in Educational Administration Programs

Problem	Number of Times Mentioned
1. Difficulties of scheduling	8
2. Students unable to meet specified prerequisites	9
3. Lack of interest and commitment among non-education professors to students and programs in educational administration	14
4. Lack of suitable or relevant courses in other departments	7
5. Inter-departmental antagonisms, problems of prestige and communication	5
6. Other problems, not classified	2
7. No problems mentioned	7
8. No answer	6

that scheduling non-education courses into students' programs presents difficulties which result from having a relatively limited amount of on-campus time with which to work. Most students are required to take courses in their major field. Since most have only their sabbatical year to spend in full-time study and since social science departments seldom offer anything but survey-type undergraduate courses in summer sessions and after hours, it is difficult to schedule extensive work in other departments into students' programs. Eight department chairmen made reference to this problem. Similarly, nine chairmen noted the problem of meeting prerequisites specified in non-education courses. The fourth response, "lack of suitable or relevant courses in other departments," may also reflect these problems.

A final structural feature of graduate courses in other disciplines, which may deter some administration students from taking them, is student visibility. Often these courses have small enrollments and are operated as seminars. These features deny to the disciplinary novice a very desirable quality — invisibility. Seminars in unfamiliar fields, calling for active student participation, may be threatening to many students who might much prefer to sit in the back of a large lecture hall and take notes.

Caught between departmental rules mandating some specified number of hours in unfamiliar and, perhaps, threatening fields in order to graduate and their own strong motivation to finish as quickly as possible in order to return to their jobs, it is not surprising that students develop adaptive mechanisms to cope with the situations in which they find themselves. Nor is it surprising that these adaptations have some unanticipated consequences for interdisciplinary programs in educational administration. One such adaptation among students is the development of a kind of folklore regarding courses and professors in other departments. Such lore includes judgments about the relevance of particular courses to educational practice and administrators' careers, as well as the usual valuing of teaching competence, grading, and course requirements which are endemic aspects of graduate student culture. One of the important functions of advanced students is to "clue in" their novice peers to the courses offered in other departments which will simultaneously meet departmental distribution requirements, satisfy major advisors, have issue and career relevance, and provide unprepared students with a reasonable chance of success.

A consequence of courses having to meet all of these criteria is that students may tend to pick up a course or two in several departments which meet these criteria and which may have little relation to each other, rather than pursuing a program designed to provide an integrated interdisciplinary experience. While this "cafeteria approach" may indeed yield a sequence of courses of use to both practitioners and potential professors, it probably does not provide a coherent grasp on any particular social science discipline or help to integrate several disciplines. Such a grasp may be less important for the practitioner than it is for the prospective professor. In the latter instance, a student's future capability to conduct theoretically-grounded research and interdisciplinary classes may be impaired by a cafeteria approach to non-education courses.

There are other problems involved in the requirement strategy evident from the data presented earlier. Professors of the social sciences will probably spend little, if any, of their course time relating their discipline to school administration. As a result, administration students must perform the often difficult process of correctly applying the social science to administration, a process which may well be beyond the capabilities of many of them. The assumptions which departments utilizing this strategy seem to make is that even if the student fails to integrate his social science work with educational administration, he will at least learn a few useful concepts, and in any case, no positive harm will be done. The latter assumption, especially, may be unwarranted. First, the on-campus time of graduate students is a precious commodity, departments have little more than a year of it at their disposal. To require that 20% of this scarce resource be expended to "learn a few concepts" may well be irresponsible.

In a second sense, a great deal of harm may be done by requiring students to take a minimum of non-education courses. The student who fails to see the relevance of sociology, for example, to his chosen field of work may come away from his experiences in that field with more than a few concepts. He may well come away with the conviction that administering schools is one thing and that sociology is quite another, and he may contend that the study of the latter has little to recommend it to men concerned with the former. In fact, if he is reasonably bright, he will recognize the inchoate structure of the social sciences, the ill-defined nature of most of their concepts, and the weak explanatory power of their "theories." Students bright enough to recognize these weaknesses may come away angry, perceiving their time to have been wasted. It may well be the dull student who immediately perceives the "relevance" of social science to school administration. It is these students who begin to call teacher car-pools "informal organizations," believing that the new label explains something. More importantly perhaps, since they do not recognize the "vicious abstractions" which many concepts and theories represent, their attempts to apply these poorly understood formulations to the practice of administration may be positively harmful to the operation of their schools. Few students seem to develop the "cynical grasp" of social science theories which Schwab has advocated.[14]

That many students are baffled and occasionally angry with their experiences in interdisciplinary programs is clear from their comments on the back of the UCEA pre-professor form. On that page they are asked to "discuss the major concerns you have about the preparation of leaders for our nation's schools and the practice of educational administration." Without doubt, the most frequently voiced concerns dealt with integrating theory and practice and relating the social sciences to educational administration. One wonders about the efficacy of training programs which lead a majority of their graduates to see these issues as major concerns. In an era of racial strife surrounding schools, declining revenues coupled with rising expectations, teacher and pupil strikes, and ill-starred attempts at decentralization, "relating theory to practice" hardly seems to be crucial. It certainly would be *if* course work did, in fact, concern *theories* of racial strife in schools, decentralization, and so on. Usually they do not. At best, most courses present a host of poorly defined concepts, weakly or totally unrelated to each other, applied to these administrative problems.

In order for theory in social sciences to contribute to an individual's understanding of administration and his potential for the performance of administrative tasks, it would appear that students need to know something about theory building and something about the kinds of theoretical concepts which might be appropriate for administrative models. Courses in sociology and political science, for example, taken across campus, might provide enough background for students to grasp the beginnings of the principles of theory building, but we doubt that this is the case. The exposure of most students to such principles must be somewhat superficial, given the limited number of courses they can be expected to take.

On the one hand, and in terms of the "types" of relevance discussed by Culbertson and Shibles in the previous chapter, the requirements strategy certainly has at least the potential of providing what they have called disciplinary relevance. On the other hand, it would seem to have less potential for providing career and problem-based relevance. Formal courses in sociology and political science, for example, probably offer little direct guidance concerning the superintendency or the real problems faced by the incumbents of that role. A solid understanding of the career and problems of the superintendent will continue to come from work in departments of education.

While noting the limitations of the requirements strategy in terms of career relevance for those students intent on becoming practicing administrators, we suggest that this strategy may be successful in providing career relevance for students preparing for professorships. For example, students can be required to obtain training in research methodology through courses in the sociology department, the political science department, and the anthropology department. In fact, research skills obtained in this way may be more effective than those obtained by requiring students to take methodology courses in the education schools.[15] Research methodology in education has traditionally emphasized experimental methods, the use of control groups, and the ability to manipulate variables. Yet, in research in educational administration, there is seldom a chance to use genuine experimental designs. What is needed, rather, are skills in survey research and observation techniques which can be applied to gaining knowledge about organizations.

The Minor-Member Strategy

The second major departmental strategy for fusing social science content with administrator preparation programs is to require that students add one or more non-educationists to their doctoral committees. Presumably, the intent of this strategy is to insure that students' course work and dissertations incorporate relevant disciplinary concepts and methodologies. Typically, committees are initiated at one of two points in a student's career. At some universities, they are formed immediately upon his entry into graduate school. This committee then formulates a program of courses which the student follows. The second point at which committees are often formed is at the dissertation proposal stage. In this case, their function is to oversee and evaluate the conduct of that research. In both instances, the usual practice is for a member of the educational administration department to act as chairman, with the non-educationist in the role of minor member.

When a committee is formed on a student's entry, one of its major functions is to set out a program of studies. Recommending the non-education components of this sequence is an important role of the outside member. This procedure has the advantage of immediately getting expert advice into the decision-making process regarding appropriate course work in other fields. For example, when the minor member is a sociologist, he is presumably most knowledgeable about the content of the courses taught in his department and the people teaching them. However, the effectiveness of this procedure depends heavily on his understanding of the field of educational administration. There is no reason to believe that a practicing sociologist will necessarily appreciate the importance of the theory, issue, or career relevance of his department's courses to students of educational administration. Thus, his decisions about non-education courses will tend to be made primarily in terms of disciplinary relevance. The minor member may scan the current catalogue of his department's offerings and ask himself which combination of courses will best acquaint the student with his discipline. The resulting list may or may not meet the relevance criteria of administration theory, educational issues, or the projected career of the student.

When courses are selected in this manner, their appropriateness may go unchallenged. Although the universities which utilize this procedure, and with which we are familiar, urge students to actively participate in the formulation of their programs by questioning professorial recommendations and offering alternatives, it has been our experience that they seldom do so. Their unfamiliarity with the university and with the discipline represented, together with the lopsided authority structure of any faculty-student committee, effectively prevent many students from playing anything more than a relatively passive role in the formulation of their own programs. The major advisor from educational administration, on the other hand, may be loathe to question his colleague's judgment, and this will be especially so should he be unfamiliar with the specifics of the noneducation courses proposed by the minor member. This problem is intensified by the very nature of school administration. There are virtually no social science courses which are entirely irrelevant as the relevance question is always one of degree. Unless the major advisor (i.e., the professor of educational administration) is thoroughly familiar with social science courses *as they are taught in his particular university*, the tendency may be to allow the minor member to make such judgments.

The alternative procedure, that of forming an interdisciplinary committee at the time a student prepares his dissertation proposal, has certain advantages. Inputs of the social science member are directly related to the thesis topic. Rather than requiring the minor member to make judgments about his department's courses and their relevance to educational administration, he may focus his attention on the much narrower problem of directing the student's study of substantive and methodological issues bearing on the research topic. This usage of non-educationists may be one of the reasons for the steady increase in the proportion of explanatory, social science oriented dissertations completed in educational administration in the past ten years.[16] However, reliance on this procedure has the disadvantage of incorporating social science content relatively late in a student's career. More importantly perhaps, this "research relevance" may be entirely unrelated to any of the other types of relevance discussed by Culbertson and Shibles. The vast majority of doctoral students in this field probably never conduct another research study in their professional lives. To put that much stress on the value of other disciplines for the conduct of research in educational administration, at least for those students intent on becoming practitioners, may serve no useful purpose.

Finally, the success of the minor-member strategy depends almost entirely on the willingness of these non-educationists to devote considerable time to the training of someone else's students. The reward structure of universities does not encourage such behavior. Serving as a minor member on student doctoral committees, particularly for students of another field, is probably well down on most professors' list of priority activities. Their primary obligation, after all, is to the students in their own departments. Consequently, there is probably a tendency to spend little time in the advisor's role. An example of this is the common practice among minor committee members of spending a short while helping a student formulate his thesis problem and, then, telling him to go away until the thesis is completed to his major advisor's satisfaction.

As was the case with the requirement strategy, the minor member strategy appears to have the most potential for achieving discipline and theory-based relevance in terms of effectively incorporating social science content in administrator training programs. Especially for discipline-based relevance, as we have noted previously, the minor-member strategy has strong potential. This is because the minor professor is a card-carrying member of his discipline, probably does all his teaching and research in that discipline, and attends its conventions and meetings. As a committee member for a student in administration, he has an obligation to the individual of a more particularistic nature than he has as an instructor of a course. He can insist on a reasonable grounding in the discipline before approving the candidate's degree.

In regard to career and problems-based relevance, the minor member may at best make only a small contribution. In a general sense, the minor member can offer guidance to the student in terms of readings which the student can then transfer to the roles he sees in educational administration, but it would be up to the major committee member from education to offer the cogent comments and criticism. The minor member is at a particular disadvantage in applying his knowledge to problems and issues in education. Perhaps the most that many can do, with any confidence, is express interest in the peculiar problems of schools and search for commonality in other kinds of social settings. Yet, even these commonalities may be deceptive.

Consider, for example, a student in administration who is interested in board-administrator relationships. This common problem area in administration has some unique aspects in education in that the relationship between the board, which legally controls the system, and its administrators is that of layman to professional. By contrast, the board of directors of a typical corporation is made up of business experts who will be quite familiar with business techniques and problems. Thus, the professional manager of the business is communicating with other professionals in the same business, while the educational manager is communicating with laymen.[17] The minor member in sociology or business administration, working with a student concerned with board-administrator relationships, might fail to discriminate between the case in business and the case in education when helping the student formulate his problem. Once the situation is described, of course, the minor member is in a position to comment on the difference.

The In-House Strategy

The last strategy to be considered is to incorporate social science directly into administration courses through the teaching of professors of educational administration who themselves possess the requisite knowledge and training. Undoubtedly, this strategy is the most common of the three mentioned.

Unfortunately, we have very little data on professors or the professorship of educational administration. It is possible to infer, however, from the data that is available that many have had little training in the social sciences and their attendant research methodologies. Griffiths reported that, in the period 1957-64, few professors of educational administration were conducting funded research. Of 916 studies supported by the Cooperative Research Programs of USOE, 47 or 5.1% concerned administration, and many of these were conducted by professors of other disciplines. Griffiths concludes that "the veritable flood (of presumed research in educational administration) is a dubious dribble."[18] In regard to the level of interdisciplinary training among professors of educational administration, Hills' 1965 study of a sample of members of NCPEA provides some additional evidence. For example, if reading interdisciplinary journals is any indication of a commitment to study education from other perspectives, such commitment does not seem to be pervasive in this field. Only 37% of his sample regularly read *Harvard Educational Review*. Similarly, only 10% read *Administrative Science Quarterly*, and only 20% read any kind of social science journal at all. Hills concludes that "not only is the interdisciplinary emphasis more imagined than real, but also that most professors of administration do not even read the more sophisticated journals in the field of education."[19] If this conclusion is correct, the in-house strategy for achieving a social science orientation in training programs may be less effective than presumed.

Further supporting evidence for such a conclusion comes from the UCEA pre-professor forms. It will be recalled from Table 6 that the large majority of students take less than 15% of their course work in social science departments. In contrast, the mean number of *administration* courses taken by these students was 11; the mean number of education courses was 22. Two students had more than 20 courses in educational administration. The majority listed minor concentrations in other aspects of education (e.g., curriculum). Nor was there a significant social science input to their training at earlier points in time. As we have seen, only 16 (22%) had undergraduate majors in one of the social sciences, and this figure is even lower at the master's level (4%).

These data suggest that there is little immediate prospect of substantially incorporating sophisticated social science perspectives into training programs by using the in-house strategy. Many professors of educational administration appear to lack adequate preparation to do so. Further, most students aspiring to the professorship are not getting that kind of preparation. There are few programs which are specifically devoted to the preparation of professors, and most of these make no major differentiation between students who will practice and those who will profess.[20] This undifferentiated approach characterizes recruiting, as well as preparation programs. Students aspiring to the professorship seem to be very like those aiming for a superintendency. Both groups have typically been teachers and administrators. Although Shaplin suggests that prospective professors are typically younger, they would seem to be, on the average, somewhat older than doctorates in other disciplines. For example, the median age of those filling out the UCEA forms in 1969 was 36. At that age, most men are already well into their productive lives.

Despite the rather discouraging evidence to the effect that professors of educational administration have only a sketchy background in the social sciences, this strategy has potential for achieving certain kinds of relevance, assuming that the long and painful process of training a cadre of professors with substantial social scientific knowledge and research skills can be carried out.

In contrast to the other two strategies, the in-house strategy is likely to have great impact in achieving problems-based relevance and career-based relevance. The likelihood of achieving theory and discipline-based relevance, however, may be less than with the requirements and minor-member strategies.

The educational administration professor with a thorough grounding in social science has a commitment to two fields. Presumably, he has the basic skills to keep up in his particular discipline, and, at the same time, he interacts with educators and is familiar with the real problems facing school systems. This enables him, ideally at least, to help his students define administrative roles, to identify appropriate readings from the disciplines, to contribute to the understanding of these roles, and to ensure that his students can apply the appropriate research techniques to administrative problems.

The in-house strategy, however, may preclude the professor from maintaining much more than a token commitment to a social science discipline. "Keeping up" in one field is difficult; in two fields it may be impossible. His day-to-day activities, his field contacts with practitioners, and the reward structure of his department all help to ensure that, over the course of time, the novice professor's commitment toward a particular social science will weaken. This increasingly tangential relationship to a social science suggests that professors, even when thoroughly prepared in an interdisciplinary graduate program, may be less and less effective in achieving discipline-based relevance.

CONCLUSION

In this chapter, we have analyzed the strategies used in universities to incorporate social science content into training programs for educational administrators. We have suggested that the various strategies have potentially different impacts in achieving the kinds of relevance outlined by Culbertson and Shibles.

Through an analysis of official departmental regulations and evidence regarding the actual exposure of students to social science courses, we have identified three strategies commonly used in university departments of educational administration to integrate social science content into training programs. These are the requirements strategy, in which students are required to take courses in other disciplines; the minor-member strategy, in which at least one member of the student's program and/or dissertation committee is a professor from outside of education; and the in-house strategy, in which social science content is incorporated into courses in educational administration taught by professors of educational administration.

Despite the widespread use of one or more of these strategies in training programs for administrators, we have suggested that, for a variety of reasons, students in administration tend to receive only minimal exposure to the social sciences during their academic careers.

Recognizing problems in the effective use of these strategies in current practice, we suggest that each of the strategies has potential for achieving particular kinds of relevance to the practice of administration. On one hand, the requirement and minor-member strategies have higher potential for achieving theory-based relevance and discipline-based relevance than for achieving issue and career-based relevance. On the other hand, the in-house strategy, if employed effectively, would seem to be more useful for achieving career and issue-based relevance.

We have predicted that the social science emphasis will continue for some time. While suggesting that we need to question the appropriateness of continuing this emphasis in terms of its actual effect on administration, we note also that the mix of strategies will determine to an extent the kinds of relevance potentially possible. Thus, if a department considers that problems-based relevance might have the best chance of really making a difference in the practice of administration, then it would do well to develop its in-house strategy, sublimating the requirements and minor-member strategies. We suspect that social science content of some kind will always be appropriate to administrative training, but we advocate a critical, on-going examination of its relationship to practice, and the adoption of a combination of strategies which will provide the kind of relevance most likely to have a beneficial effect on the way schools are administered.

FOOTNOTES

1. Reed L. Stolworthy, "A Study of the Use of Academic Disciplines Outside the Department of Education in Doctoral Programs of Educational Administration" (Ed.D. dissertation, Brigham Young University, 1965). We are indebted to Professor Stolworthy for allowing us to use his data in the preparation of this chapter.

2. Ibid., pp. 93–94.

3. See, for example, J. W. Getzels, et al., *Educational Administration as a Social Process* (New York: Harper and Row, 1968); Lane, et al., *Educational Administration: A Behavioral Analysis* (New York: Macmillan, 1967).

4. Judson T. Shaplin, "The Professorship in Educational Administration: Attracting Talented Personnel," in *The Professorship in Educational Administration*, eds. Donald J. Willower and Jack Culbertson (Columbus, Ohio: University Council for Educational Administration, 1964), p. 6.

5. Personal communication based on a current research project being conducted by Professor M.P. Robbins, Ontario Institute for Studies in Education.

6. Shaplin, "Professorship in Educational Administration: Attracting Personnel."

7. Emil J. Haller, "The Interdisciplinary Ideology in Educational Administration: Some Preliminary Hypotheses on the Sociology of Knowledge," *Educational Administration Quarterly* 4 (Spring 1968), p. 67.

8. Shaplin, "Professorship in Educational Administration: Attracting Talented Personnel."

9. H. Warren Button, "Doctrines of Administration," *Educational Administration Quarterly* 2 (Autumn 1966): 216.

10. Alvin W. Gouldner, *Patterns of Industrial Bureaucracy* (Glencoe, Illinois: Free Press, 1954), pp. 174–180. See also, Robert K. Merton, *Social Theory and Social Structure* (New York: Free Press, 1957), p. 199.

11. Ward S. Mason and Neal Gross, "Intra-Occupational Prestige Differentiation: The School Superintendency," *American Sociological Review* 20 (June 1955): 326–331.

12. Emil J. Haller, "The Questionnaire Perspective in Educational Administration: Notes on the Social Context of Method" (paper read at the annual convention of the American Educational Research Association, Minneapolis, 1970).

13. The UCEA forms indicate that the majority spend little more than one year in residence for their degrees. See also, B. Berelson, *Graduate Education in the United States* (New York: McGraw-Hill, 1960).

14. Joseph J. Schwab, "The Professorship in Educational Administration: Theory-Art-Practice," in *Professorship in Administration*, eds. Willower and Culbertson, p. 61.

15. Haller, "The Questionnaire Perspective."

16. Data from a study of student research in educational administration, which Haller is currently conducting, indicates that the proportion of dissertations utilizing perspectives from one of the social sciences increased from 15% to nearly 45% in the period from 1956 to 1966.

17. R. E. Campbell, "Peculiarities in Educational Administration," in *Administrative Theory in Education*, ed. Andrew W. Halpin (New York: The Macmillan Co., 1967), p. 177.

18. D. E. Griffiths, "Research and Theory in Educational Administration," in *Perspectives on Educational Administration and the Behavioral Sciences*, eds. Jack Culbertson, et al., (Eugene, Oregon: Center for Advanced Study of Educational Administration, 1965), p. 42.

19. Jean Hills, "Educational Administration: A Field in Transition?" *Educational Administration Quarterly* 1 (Winter 1965): 54.

20. Shaplin, "Professorship in Educational Administration: Attracting Personnel."

Part Two

Core Content
from the Social Sciences

Content from social science disciplines can be classified in various ways. In economics, for example, there are facts as illustrated in the question of what the Gross National Product was in 1971. Principles are also a part of knowledge as, for example, the well-known law of "supply and demand." There are also basic building block concepts in disciplines as represented in the term "scarcity." Finally, there are the modes of inquiry by which a discipline establishes, extends, and re-creates itself.

The five social scientists who prepared the chapters in this part were asked to elaborate the core concepts and the essential modes of inquiry in their disciplines. They were also asked to delineate the boundaries of their respective disciplines and the relationships of the boundaries to other disciplines. Since it was recognized that different social scientists in a given discipline might arrive at different judgments about core concepts and essential modes of inquiry, each author was also invited to make explicit assumptions concerning his own approach to the task.

The five chapters on social psychology, sociology, anthropology, political science, and economics offer a unique summary of core concepts and modes of inquiry in the social sciences. For this reason, the summary should be pertinent to the interests of students and professors regardless of the perspective of relevance which they value most.

3

An Overview
of Social Psychology

Herbert J. Walberg

Psychology is the science of behavior. If behavior is the response of the organism to the environment, and if other organisms constitute an important part of the environment, then by definition, psychology always includes social psychology. Indeed, because psychology holds the unifying element in the social sciences — the individual organism in the behavioral system — all the social sciences might be included as or reduced to aspects of psychology. For a half-century, there has been a growing psychological emphasis in social anthropology, economics, political science, and sociology, as well as in applied fields, such as education, social work, and public administration. Thus, this chapter is an overview of social psychology as psychology, rather than, say, psychological sociology.[1]

Yet, it should be noted at the outset that, unlike physics in relation to chemistry and biology, psychology has yet to fulfill its objective of reduction; nor have psychological concepts been significantly reduced to biology. Except for high level (and perhaps unscientific) abstractions that are not explicitly linked to empirical referents, psychology holds no core of integrated, universally accepted concepts and paradigms in Kuhn's sense.[2] In the last two decades, cooperative efforts to develop a unified treatment of psychology have only illustrated its pluralism and far-reaching clashes of ideas and methods.[3] And, in the last five years, some psychologists have even questioned the capacity of psychology to contribute constructively to the solution of individual and social problems. Perhaps these are not the signs for despair but for hope in an immature but growing and healthy discipline; for, in a Hegelian sense, there can be no synthesis before antithesis, and to contribute effectively to social problem solving, a discipline must set forth its current limitations, as well as its ultimate aspirations. The important point here is that any overview of social psychology (including this one) is likely to be subjective in terms of the selection and emphasis of content. To afford the reader a broader, more objective view, the next section briefly outlines the scope of social psychology, first, by tracing historically some of its persisting substantive concepts and issues and, second, by presenting content analyses of the field as viewed both by social psychologists and by other social scientists. Hopefully, these analyses will give the reader an idea of the boundaries of knowledge from which the present chapter samples, as well as references to important concepts and writings that cannot be summarized here. The remainder, and major part, of this chapter is avowedly subjective and treats in three sections the key thought processes and modes of inquiry in social psychology, some basic concepts and systematic positions, and, finally, some speculations about the future of the discipline.

THE SCOPE OF SOCIAL PSYCHOLOGY

Historical Perspectives

Though the intellectual ancestors of modern social psychology did not have the precise instruments and scientific methods of this century, they structured the substance of the field in ways that survive to the present day. Along with such creative artists as Sophocles, Shakespeare, and Dostoyevski, they made shrewd insights into the socio-psychological nature of man that have a continuing relevance. However, social psychologists, perhaps because of specialized training and research,[4] are sometimes unaware of this heritage, and a definitive history of the field is yet to be written.[5]

Yet, the central triumvirate of theories in social psychology can be traced to Plato's *Republic* and his other writings.[6] Plato, like Freud, conceived three faculties or institutions that constitute human nature and society (see table 1). For Plato, the head was the center of thought; the breast, of striving; and the abdomen, of feeling. Society's three analogous classes were philosopher-kings (or guardians), warriors, and slaves. Placing the three faculties in both the individual and society parallels the moot placement of psychology in the biological or social sciences and the divisiveness of "biotropes" and "sociotropes"[7] within psychology. The triumvirate also persists in a modern definition of social psychology: "an

Table 1

The Triumvirate of Social Psychology

Plato's Conception			Modern Conceptions			
Faculty	Body Locus	Social Locus	Assumption	Individual Process	Social Process	Systematic Position
Thought and Reason	The Head	The Ruling Class	Rationality	Cognition	Suggestion	Gestalt and Cognitive Theory
Action and Striving	The Breast	The Warrior Class	Egoism	Conation	Imitation	Behaviorism and S-R Theory
Emotion and Feeling	The Abdomen	The Slave Class	Hedonism	Affection	Sympathy	Psychoanalysis and Dynamic Theories

attempt to understand and explain how *thought, feeling,* and *behavior* of individuals are influenced by the actual, imagined, or implied presence of others [italics mine]."[8] Mind is held to be constituted of, and behavior originates in, *cognition, conation,* and *affection* (Table 1). When a social psychologist stresses one of the faculties at the expense of the other two in the explanation of social behavior, he is likely to emphasize, perhaps simplistically, one of three sovereign principles: suggestion, imitation, and sympathy (more on these concepts in other sections).

Depending on time perspective and criteria, the founder of social psychology might be one of the following: Plato, Aristotle, Hobbes, Comte, Hegel, Lazarus, Steinthal, Tarde, or E. A. Ross.[9] Perhaps its modern christening can be more definitively cited[10] as the publication in 1908 of the first two textbooks: E. A. Ross's approach was sociological; William McDougall's, individual and psychobiological.[11] The bifurcation was continued into the 1920s and 1930s at the two universities leading in social psychology. Chicago was clearly sociological under Burgess, Cooley, Faris, G. H. Mead, Park, and Thomas. Harvard's program remained in the general tradition of individual psychology and combined behaviorism, psychoanalysis, and purposivism, as well as Gestalt, personalistic, and cultural studies.

After the 1930s, the following three important trends in social psychology became clear: the study of group dynamics, attempts at integrating substantive content, and applications in social policy and action. Lewin's theories of group dynamics concern all the various forces that affect the behavior of members of face-to-face groups, and he introduced such concepts as cohesiveness, group decision, styles of leadership, and experimental social change.[12]

The second trend was a response to the growing body of disparate research. A number of social psychologists and their colleagues in sister disciplines attempted to structure and integrate essential concepts on a sound theoretical basis.[13] However, like historians of special periods who found Toynbee's universal model of civilizations disappointing, many anthropologists, psychologists, and sociologists found that general theories oversimplified or glossed over the complex ideas in their respective fields. Even attempts at middle-range theorizing within social psychology were found wanting; and the tendency for some systematic theorists to reorganize and change labels of familiar concepts may have been a disservice because it obscured or concealed common phenomena and past research from other scholars without bringing to bear fresh insights or new data. Allport cited a number of these changes in concept labels:

personality and culture to systems theory,
rationalization to cognitive dissonance,
friendship to interpersonal attractiveness,
pleasure and pain to positive and negative reinforcement,
maladjustment to alienation, and
character to ego-strength.[14]

The third trend was a response to the Great Depression, the rise of Hitler, and the approach of World War II. These and other factors gave impetus to research on rumor, morale, propaganda, public opinion, race relations, and to a continuing concern with applications of theory and research. Today, a growing group of social psychologists occupy academic positions outside departments of psychology, such as in schools of business, education, and medicine, as well as non-academic positions in consulting agencies, industry, business, and government.

Thus, social psychology since Plato has aggregated a vast number of disparate ideas and aspirations. While there is yet no grand overarching theory that suffices to bring them together into a unified whole, there are several systematic positions that serve to integrate clusters of central concepts. Before turning to these, consider the current content and boundaries of the field.

Boundaries and Content

Since any overview of social psychology is likely to be selective and subjective, it may be of value to present the field, if only briefly, through a content analysis of its major encyclopedic and handbook writings. Table 2 is a listing of all articles in the *International Encyclopedia of the Social Sciences,*[15] cited in the article "Social Psychology," with an indication of their citation in the articles on psychology and the other disciplines treated in the present volume. Of the 5 systematic and theoretical articles, 3 are cross-referenced with psychology, those on field, Gestalt, and cognitive theories; 2 with sociology, on Marxism and sociology itself; 1 with political science, Marxism; and none with anthropology and economics. Of all 59 articles, 20 are cross-referenced with sociology, 7 with psychology, 2 with political science, and none with anthropology and economics. Of 10 biographies, 3 are on psychologists (Allport, Hovland, and Lewin), and the other 7 are on sociologists. One is inclined to agree with Getzels[16] that because of the lack of a conceptual framework for the *Encyclopedia,* the coverage is seriously unbalanced. For example, Marxism is not a major theoretical position in social psychology; and among the 10 biographies of pre-

Table 2

Articles Cross-Referenced under "Social Psychology"
in the International Encyclopedia of the Social Sciences

	Psy-chology	Anthro-pology	Eco-nomics	Political Science	Sociology
Systematic and Theoretical Analyses					
Field Theory	X				
Gestalt Theory	X				
Marxism				X	X
Sociology					X
Cognitive Organization and Processes	X				
Concepts of General and Historical Importance					
Attitudes					
Communication					
Mass Communication					X
Groups					X
Psycho-social Identity					
Imitation					
Interaction					X
Human Motivation	X				
Person Perception	X				
Social Perception					
Personality	X				
Persuasion					
Political Behavior				X	
Social Psychiatry					
Public Opinion					X
Reference Groups					X

Table 2 (continued)

	Psy-chology	Anthro-pology	Eco-nomics	Political Science	Sociology
Psychological Aspects of Religion					
Role					X
Self-Concept					
Socialization					X
Suggestion					
Sympathy and Empathy					
Other Relevant Material					
Aggression					
Alienation					X
Coalitions					
Social Cohesion					
Collective Behavior					X
Competition					
Conformity					
Consensus					X
Decision Theory					
Mass Phenomena					
Organizations					X
Prejudice					X
Social Status					X
Stereotypes					
Methods and Techniques					
Achievement Motivation					
Experimental and Quasi-Experimental Design	X				

Table 2 (continued)

	Psy-chology	Anthro-pology	Eco-nomics	Political Science	Sociology
Interviewing					
Social Observation and Social Case Studies					
Personality Measurement					
Projective Methods					
Sociometry					X
Survey Analysis					
Biographies for Historical Background of Modern Social Psychology					
Allport					
Cooley					X
Durkheim					X
Hovland					
Le Bon					
Lewin					
Mead, G.H.					
Ross					X
Simmel					X
Tarde					
Totals	7	0	0	2	20

sumed historical significance; only 2 are included (Tarde and Ross) of the 9 cited by Allport[17] as candidates for the fathership of the field! Such is the view of the discipline by an "inter-disciplinary" committee of social scientists.

In contrast, a nicely balanced presentation of content is given by social psychologists themselves in the 1968 *Handbook*.[18] In comparing the chapter titles given in Table 3 with the titles of *Encyclopedia* articles, the differences are immediately apparent. Under

"Systematic Positions" in the *Handbook,* for example, the obsolete topic, Marxism, is omitted; two distinctively psychological positions (Freudian and stimulus-response theories) are included, as well as three leading modern positions: mathematical models, roles, and organizations. Under "Research Methods," a strong emphasis on measurement and analysis can be noted. The next two volumes (see Table 3) focus on the social psychology of individual and group behavior, and the last volume takes up applications in various contexts. The work, as a whole, offers an excellent analysis of the substance and syntax of the field, and readers who wish a broader and deeper understanding than might be gleaned from this brief chapter can do no better than refer to the *Handbook*; a note on recommended readings in Table 3 may be helpful. For the flavor of contemporary research, see the psychological journals, *Journal of Personality and Social Psychology* and the *Journal of Social Psychology*; the sociological journal *Sociometry*; and the integrative journal *Human Relations* (published in Great Britain). Also, applied journals, such as *American Educational Research Journal* and *Administrative Science Quarterly* and the popular magazines *Trans-Action* and *Psychology Today,* frequently publish sociopsychological articles.

Table 3

Sections and Chapters in the
1968 Handbook of Social Psychology

Historical Introduction
    The Historical Background of Modern Social Psychology*

Systematic Positions
    Stimulus-Response Theory in Contemporary Social Psychology*
    Mathematical Models of Social Behavior
    The Relevance of Freudian Psychology and Related Viewpoints
       for the Social Sciences*
    Cognitive Theories in Social Psychology*
    Field Theory in Social Psychology*
    Role Theory*ˢ
    Organizations*ˢ

Research Methods
    Experimentation in Social Psychology

Table 3 (continued)

Data Analysis, Including Statistics

Attitude Measurement

Simulation of Social Behavior

Systematic Observational Methods

Measurement of Social Choice and Interpersonal Attractiveness

Interviewing

Content Analysis

Methods and Problems in Cross-Cultural Research[a]

The Social Significance of Animal Studies[b]

The Individual in a Social Context

Pschophysiological Approaches in Social Psychology[b]

Social Motivation[*]

The Nature of Attitudes and Attitude Change[*]

Social and Cultural Factors in Perception[a]

Person Perception

Socialization[*]

Personality and Social Interaction[*]

Psycholinguistics

Laughter, Humor, and Play

Esthetics

Group Psychology and Phenomena of Interaction

Group Problem Solving[*]

Group Structure: Attractions, Coalitions, Communication, and Power[*]

Leadership[*]

Social Structure and Behavior[*s]

Cultural Psychology: Comparative Studies of Human Behavior[a]

National Character: The Study of Modal Personality and Sociocultural Systems[ps]

Collective Behavior: Crowds and Social Movements[*s]

The Social Psychology of Infrahuman Animals[b]

Applied Social Psychology

Prejudice and Ethnic Relations[*s]

Effects of the Mass Media of Communication[*]

Table 3 (continued)

Industrial Social Psychology

Psychology and Economics[e]

Political Behavior[ps]

A Social Psychology of Education[*]

Social-Psychological Aspects of International Relations[ps]

Psychology of Religion

Social Psychology of Mental Health[*]

---

[*]Recommended readings for a broader introduction to social psychology for students of educational administration; see especially J. W. Getzels's chapter, "A Social Psychology of Education"; for the articulation of social psychology with biology (including ethology and physiology), anthropology, economics, political science, and sociology, see chapters indicated by their respective initial letters; also see n. 1.

SYNTAX OF SOCIAL PSYCHOLOGY

Although the methods of inquiry in social psychology can be reduced to the common rational processes, induction and deduction, they are highly differentiated, complex, and abstruse. To outsiders, the voluminous journal literature appears abstract and technical; social psychologists themselves occasionally have difficulty in understanding research in unfamiliar areas of the field. Part of the difficulty is undoubtedly due to needless jargon; but, in the main, it is a consequence of necessary brevity and symbolism. Even though editors reject approximately 80 percent of the submitted manuscripts, there is limited space in the journals. And, as in the natural sciences, the primary mode of communication in psychology is the peer-referred journal paper, not independently published monographs or books. The typical paper compacts a review of related research, statement of the problem, hypotheses, a description of experimental method and instruments, the analysis, results, and discussion into generally less than 4000 words (about 15 double-spaced typewritten pages). All this contains enough detail to enable another investigator to repeat ("replicate") the study under identical conditions. Thus, the writing is terse; the logic, abstract; and the information, condensed in formulas, graphs, and tables; much of the inquiry process is symbolically coded, implicit, or assumed by both writer and reader. In this section, the essential concepts of inquiry are made explicit. As such, they are goals or standards of excellence, rather than common, easily attainable conventions. Indeed, as will be brought out later, some are extremely difficult to attain fully, and some apparently contradict one another. Hopefully, this treatment will give the reader not only a beginning understanding of the research process in social psychology but some faculty for critical evaluation as well.

Objective Critical Outlook

The social psychologist does not claim to be objective and unbiased; he recognizes that different investigators confronted with "the same objective reality" interpret it differently; indeed, this phenomenon has been the subject of much substantive research. In planning, executing, and reporting research, however, he tries to minimize subjectivity in several ways. The product of his research, the paper, can be thought of as both logic and rhetoric; the goal is to convince his scientific peers of the validity of the research, its originality, contribution to knowledge, and rigor.

Accordingly, he tries to plan a comprehensive attack on the problem, much like the lawyer outlining a brief, to answer all questions and objections that may arise. In executing the plan, he will use a number of technical strategies to avoid "rival hypotheses," i.e., extraneous causal agents. For example, injections of distilled water ("placebos") sometimes "cause" hallucinations in the suggestible and "cure" psychosomatic illnesses. Hence, the "doubleblind" experimental design is used; neither the subject nor the administrator of the injections knows who is getting various treatments or sometimes even what the treatments are. Finally, as mentioned earlier, he will report his methods and results in explicit enough detail to permit critical examination of them by his fellow scientists.

The paper will clearly distinguish between objective results and subjective interpretation of results; the limitations of the study will be noted; and the implications will be stated cautiously, if at all. To those able to follow these kinds of canons is given the title "hardnosed" (which is reminiscent of William James's turn-of-the-century distinction between "tough-" and "tender-minded" psychologists).

Yet, lurking beneath the hard shell of the "objectivist" is the seething soul of the social meliorist. Appalled by the social problems of our times and disappointed by the snippets of apparently irrelevant empiricism that seem to fill the journals, he sometimes goes far beyond the results of his work to make authoritarian judgments and recommendations regarding social problems. When he does not make clear to the public the limitations of his knowledge, he may endanger his own and the field's scientific credibility and also do disservice to the community.

An example is a recent socio-psychological experiment on teacher expectancies. School children in Southern California were given the Harvard Test of Inflected Acquisition, and their teachers were told that the test showed certain children (actually picked randomly) were about to "bloom" intellectually. When the children were re-tested later, it was found that the selected group had apparently gained more than the others in measured intelligence. Three reviewers of the book found the study so poorly designed as to be scientifically nearly worthless,[19] and a well-designed experiment failed to replicate the results.[20] But, the implication had been drawn in the book and in the press that teachers are biased against minority groups who do poorly on the tests and oppress them intellectually through negative expectations — an implication which may have aggravated the troubled race relations among community groups and teachers. Subsequent research may yet support the validity of the teacher expectancy hypothesis and its implications; the important point, however, it is that the first study did not. Had it gone through the scientific referee system of a reputable journal, it would have been nipped in the bud, and a more rigorous design for the study would have been suggested to the original investigators.

Theoretical Models

Ideally, the Kantian dictum in social psychology holds that theory without observation is play, and observation without theory is blind. Yet, the development of the two, while simultaneously maintaining their connectedness, offers great challenge. A theory is a group of general propositions used to explain a class of psychological phenomena; it specifies a number of elements, termed "constructs," and their relationships or dependencies. Its excellence may be judged by its comprehensiveness, parsimony, and capacity to generate empirical research. Lewin's formulation that behavior is a function of personality and environment or $B = f(P,E)$ exemplifies comprehensiveness and generality and, also, illustrates two levels of theory: "verbal" which often tends to be ambiguous, discursive, and intuitively stimulating, and "mathematical" which is often explicit, elegant, and over-simplified. Theories are connected to observations by "correspondence rules." Through successive iterations, the theory is modified to fit observations, and the correspondence rules are modified to bring a better match of observations to constructs. Simultaneously, theory is tested on wider classes of phenomena and constructs, and relations which are not confirmed are dropped.

This conception must be regarded as aspiration, not convention. As in physics, there are theorists and experimenters; however, in social psychology, they often pass one another like ships on a foggy sea. Even when constructs are related to referents, the connection is often tenuous and indeterminant. The experimenter often makes up ad hoc correspondence rules, adds further assumptions, and relies on intuition, rather than exact logical or mathematical reasoning.

Measurement

Social psychologists are concerned, perhaps some are preoccupied, with the empirical representation of constructs. Whether data are collected through observation, measurement, sociometric methods, interviewing, or content analysis, two concepts are crucial — validity and reliability. By validity is meant the extent to which the measure reflects the postulated theoretical construct. A measure may be simply judged valid, or it may be shown to relate to other measures as specified by theory. In the latter case, it is important that the measure correspond to other measures of the same construct (according to the correspondence rules). For example, "arousal" may be indicated by increased prespiration, as well as pupil dilation and elevated pulse rates. If the measures also forecast important acts in a manner specified by a priori theory, there is some assurance that both theory and measures are valid. If forecasts are incorrect, then the theory, the measures, or both may be invalid.

A measure is reliable if it is precise and consistent. If a construct is postulated to be stable in the individual over time, then successive measures at different points in time on the same individual should produce the same quantitative result or place the individual at the same place in the ordering of other individuals. Similarly, different administrators of the measure should produce the same quantitative results on the same individuals.

Design and Causality

Social psychologists are rarely interested in a single variable studied in isolation; for example, the rate of juvenile delinquency in a population or indications of perceived satisfaction in groups. Instead, interest centers in co-occurrences of several events or the simultaneous presence of several traits in the individual or properties in a group. Such associations are often termed "correlations," and much research employs this form of analysis. For example, delinquency has been found to correlate with defiance, gang membership, broken homes, and school behavior problems. And satisfaction tends to be negatively correlated (inversely related) to group size; that is, people in small groups tend to be more satisfied than those in large groups. In practical work, if some traits or events are found to occur before another that is socially significant, predictions and interventions can be made. For example, boys from broken homes and having certain other like characteristics are more likely to be delinquents and, therefore, might be given group therapy. A well-developed technology exists for this kind of analysis, and it characterizes much of the quantitative research in the social sciences.

However, in contrast to most other social scientists, social psychologists are likely to avoid correlations if they can, for since Aristotle, an ultimate goal of science has been to ascertain causality, to find out *why* events occur. Causality cannot be imputed from correlation even when one event, trait, or property always precedes another, for the second event may actually cause the first or both may be caused by another or most likely by many others in social phenomena. Delinquency may be a partial cause of broken homes, or both may be caused by parental alcoholism or a multiplicity of factors termed poverty. Although correlations may have practical value, they are of second priority in social psychology.

Experiments, though limited and imperfect, are the only way to establish causality in much social research. The term "experiment" applies only to those studies in which individuals or groups (experimental units) are assigned randomly to experimental conditions ("treatments"). Randomization breaks up chains of prior causality and tends to insure that the only reason a unit is subjected to a treatment is chance. Thus, differences among groups of units under various treatments at the end of the experiment are attributable to, or caused by, the treatments and chance, rather than voluntary self-selection. Unfortunately, the intervention necessary in experiments has prevented widespread applications in important sociopsychological phenomena, and it has often limited experimental research to subhuman species and college sophomores.

Probabilism and Statistics

Social psychologists note that any man is like all other men in some ways, like some other men in some ways, and like no other man in some ways. Thus, even though there are differences among groups subjected to various experimental treatments, generally, there will also be variability within each group; the highest scoring member of the lowest scoring group may exceed the lowest scorer in the highest group. A score for an individual is not determined by the experimental treatments alone but by chance factors, such as his heredity and experience prior to the experiment and measurement errors. Inferences made, then, about an individual's score or a group of scores are probabilistic, rather than deterministic, since the causal variables cannot all be specified. The role of statistics is to ascertain whether the observed differences among treatment groups could have arisen by chance alone or if they could reasonably be attributed to the treatments. Generally, inferences are creditable (termed "significant") when there is less than 1 chance in 20 (a probability of less than 5 percent) that the observed differences could have arisen by chance.

THE SUBSTANCE OF SOCIAL PSYCHOLOGY

In this section, the following three basic assumptions about the nature of man are presented: rationality, egoism, and hedonism. These assumptions parallel the Platonic three-fold conception described earlier and form the bases of three fundamental social processes: suggestion, imitation, and sympathy, as well as the starting points for three systematic positions referred to as the Gestalt and cognitive theory, behaviorism and S–R theory, and psychoanalysis (see Table 1). After treating each of these, the chapter concludes with a short assessment of the present state of the field and some speculations about its future.

Basic Concepts

Rationality. Socio–political theorists from the Greeks to Thomas Jefferson and James Madison have emphasized man's capacity to perceive, reason, and decide. Herbart's nineteenth century psychology argued that right action stems from right ideas. In this century, John Dewey, a former president of the American Psychological Association, founded his philosophy and psychology of mind and education on habit and growth, both products of rational transactions with the environment. Opinion research workers assume that people will act upon their beliefs, and nondirective psychotherapists hold that the patient can appraise his current situation and make rational decisions about his future.[21] Max Weber described the increasing cognitive emphasis and efficiency of rational organization through bureaucratic governance,[22] and today electronic computors, when they are working correctly, represent the culmination of Western rationalism.

Suggestion. Yet, much psychology speaks against reason as the source of behavior. Witness the Orwellian transformation of terms: In psychology, "to rationalize" means to invent a socially acceptable reason for behavior originating in the irrational unconscious. "Suggestion" does not imply bringing an idea into consideration for possible action, but introducing an idea while normal critical thought is suspended, such as in a post-hypnotic suggestion. Why this bias? Psychologists have been dazzled by the subtle abstractions of physics; thus, something as obvious as reason cannot be close to man's true nature. Since Watson's introduction of behaviorism,[23] many psychologists purged such terms as "thought" and "mind" from the psyche and perhaps the psyche as well.[24] Moreover, evolutionary theory stressed man's continuity with infrahuman species and his animal-like motives. Beginning with Charcot's and Freud's explorations of the unconscious and mental illness, irrationalism and abnormality have maintained leading positions in academic and popular psychology. Today, we are assaulted with irrationality; advertising is premised on presumed powers of repetition, status symbols, and sexual allurements. These are effective, one is asked to believe, because of man's egoism and hedonism.

Egoism. Egoism is the doctrine that man's nature is exhibited in his excessive love of the self, exaltation of his own ideas, pleasure, and experience, and his striving for power and status over other. Nietzsche, Spencer, and Adler each contributed to this view. Nietzsche gave primacy to the "will to power" and held that social behavior is overt or disguised power seeking. Spencer, arguing analogously from Darwin, saw society as a jungle, continuously improving the species by competitive pruning of the unfit. Adler, disagreeing with Freud's emphasis on sexual motives, believed that the wish to dominate arises from organic defects and inferiority feelings, which determines behavior. Perhaps the most extreme and grim view in this tradition, aside from Machiavelli's, is that of Le Dantec.[25] Starting with the observation that cells and organisms ultimately seek self-preservation, he developed the notion that all behavior is an all-out struggle for existence. Following from this assumption, he discounted the ostensible reasons for altruism, fellowship, and mutual aid and held that family, friendship, and nation develop out of fear and hate of common enemies. Parents care for their children to exploit them later, and leaders start wars to unify the nation and strengthen the central government. Of course, all these views of man are antisocial in that they dismiss socialization, the valid formation of individuals in the image society avows. And while social veneer and hypocrisy are perfectly evident, the egoistic view must be balanced against other assumptions.

Imitation.   Nevertheless, egoistic explanations appear to pertain to a variety of social processes, which collectively may be termed "imitation." This is the process by which a stimulus gives rise to behavior resembling the stimulus. If the individual's motive is power, the way to gain power is to band together with like minded people or to imitate a powerful individual. Thus, children imitate parental models, and adults gain status and self-esteem by conforming to fads and fashions. Impressed with the dissociation of consciousness during hypnosis, Le Bon wrote *The Crowd*,[26] the most influential book in social psychology according to Allport.[27] He held that in mobs, the individuals lose rational consciousness and regress to barbarian or primitive behavior. Following instincts and regressed feelings, they follow the crowd and are easily led by the demagogue's repetitious call to action. A related though less dramatic process is ego involvement; when confronted with the behavior of others that would imply higher status or power, the individual feels the urge to compete, to act to preserve self esteem.

Hedonism.   Theories of pleasure and pain have a long history which cannot be detailed here. Various commentators through the ages have discussed pleasure and described a number of its dimensions: the degrees of duration and intensity; its certainty following behavior; and its purity or alloy with pain. Hedonism may be linked to biological evolutionary theory by noting that pleasurable activities, such as eating and sex, make for survival of the individual and the species. Bentham and other Utilitarian social philosophers tied hedonism closely to rationalism in proposing a "hedonistic calculus." By measuring the dimensions of pleasure, one could compute the pay-off of individual behavior or social plans and maximize the greatest good (pleasure) for the greatest number. Since men ordinarily maximize their own pleasure, the best government is that which interferes the least. Classic economic laws, assuming that money buys pleasure, are founded on hedonism.[28] Hedonistic psychological theories hold that individuals continue to behave in ways they find pleasurable and avoid behavior that brings pain. Under its modern guises of "positive reinforcement" and "drive reduction" (more on these below), hedonism occupies a central position in social psychology, though it has run into difficulty in explaining martyrs and loyality, risk taking and cognitive behavior.

Sympathy. Earlier, the parallels between rationality and suggestion, and egoism and imitation were noted. However, the parallel between hedonism and sympathy (see Table 1) is somewhat forced unless altruism, giving pleasure to, or taking pain away from, others, is posited as pleasure. Though this wholesome assumption is part of our Judeo-Christian heritage, which exhorts us to do unto others as you would have them do unto you, it is not a major theoretical concept in modern psychology. Allport suggests that psychologists have overlooked altruism and have become preoccupied with hostility and aggression which are salient only because they contrast so sharply with the underlying ground of sympathy.[29] The concept has a place, however, in applied psychology, research, and action programs, especially in group dynamics; industrial and corporate management, and psychotherapy posit sympathy and the related concepts, altruism and cooperation, as central motives.

Systematic Positions

Gestalt and Cognitive Theory. An early and typical experiment in Gestalt psychology is that of Kohler who was interned on one of the Canary Islands during World War I. He gave a chimpanzee two sticks that could be joined together to reach a suspended banana. After many futile attempts, the chimp began playing with the sticks, accidentaly joined them, and immediately used them to get the banana. Thus, the primary event was "insight," the sudden realization of the pattern leading to problem solving, transfer, and from feelings of helplessness to mastery. While many psychologists, following physicists, have searched for the elements of behavior, such as stimulus-response connections, reflexes, or instincts, Gestalt psychologists have argued for a wholistic conception of the individual and his environment. William James anticipated this conception by likening consciousness to a river, and he rejected the atomistic "bucket" metaphor.[30] Gestalt psychologists focus on dynamic perception and hold that the primary data of psychology are coordinated, irreducible patterns of elements (Gestalten).

Modern inheritors of Gestalt psychology have divided their efforts on two aspects of cognition: structure and dynamics. Structure is the pattern of mental elements, such as attributes, categories, expectancies, or schemata. Developmental psychologists, such as

Jean Piaget, have attempted to discover how organizations of elements are formed and used by the child.[31] Runkel has shown that communication between "colinear" parties, those who do not necessarily agree but have similar systems of categorization in mind, is more efficient.[32] A notable contribution is Rokeach's notion of "open belief system" which refers to flexible cognitive organization receptive to external data, capable of evaluating and integrating, and acting, rather than stereotyping and rigid reflexive behavior.[33] Another role of cognition is as a dynamic impetus to emotion and action. Thus, disconfirmed expectations, such as seeing friends and enemies together, is noxious or disconcerting. The state is termed "cognitive dissonance," and the individual is likely to avoid situations that produce it. When it does occur, he will reduce it by changing existing cognitions or seeking for information.[34]

Despite its research emphasis on organization and patterns of mental activity, current work in cognition itself is somewhat atheoretical and disorganized. Although early writers, such as Kohler and Lewin, were grand theorizers,[35] modern research in the area is often not guided by systematic, logical deductions from basic postulates.

Behaviorism and Stimulus-Response Theory. The stimulus-response (S-R) theory represents the most rigorous, if not relevant, position in contemporary social psychology. Originating in Aristotelian and British associationism of ideas, the tradition has grown increasingly paradigmatic and symbolic. Much of the early S-R research was culminated in Thorndike's Law of Effect: "pleasure stamps in; pain stamps out."[36] In fact, Skinner pointed out that this law can be viewed as a special case of Darwin's Law of Natural Selection applied to individual and social behavior. One modern wing of the tradition is Pavlovian "classical conditioning" wherein an unconditioned stimulus, such as a ringing bell, is associated with a conditioned response, salivation, by repeated presentation with a conditioned stimulus, meat, until the unconditioned stimulus alone evokes the response. The other wing is Skinnerian "operant conditioning,"[37] wherein behavior emitted without the necessary presence of a specific stimulus is reinforced, rewarded. In both wings, secondary reinforcers which do not directly reduce drives, for example maternal praise, acquire reward power by association with primary physiological reinforcers, food.

Currently, S-R theorists are making concessions to cognitive theorists. This has led to the S-O-R formulation to incorporate [O]rganismic mediation, the varied behavior of different organisms.

S-R work is parsimonious and thriving theoretically and experi-mentally. Perhaps the flavor of modern conceptualizing may be best sampled in a Hullian performance equation

$$R = D \times {}_sH_R \times V \times K$$

which means that the probability or rate of response is a multiplica-tive function of 1) the strength, which is related to deprivation, of relevant drive, 2) the habit strength of the response, which is a function of the frequency of past reinforcements of the response, 3) the incentive value (for example, the magnitude) of the anticipated reinforcement, and 4) the stimulus intensity.[38]

Psychoanalysis and Dynamic Theories. Freud, in his volumi-nous works, described three subdivisions of personality. The "id," present at birth, is the seat of wishes for immediate erotic gratifica-tion; the "pleasure principle" discharges these wishes in immediate motor activity, such as emptying a full bladder or in hallucinations of desired objects. Since not all wishes can be gratified by immediate reflexes (eating requires an "object," food), the "ego" develops from the id. Through the "reality principle," it postpones immediate gratification likely to bring pain, in favor of later gratification un-alloyed with pain. To accomplish this, it makes use of familiar mental faculties: consciousness, perception, learning, memory, and reasoning. Last to be formed is the "superego," which represents social morality and arises out of parental reward and punishment patterns. Its two aspects are the "ego ideal," which sets ethical standards and the "conscience," which judges conduct, as the parents did, and punishes violations of standards through guilt and shame.

In his later writings, Freud added the death wish, the compulsion of living matter to return to the inorganic state, as in the superego's aggression toward the ego. The ego governs and mediates among the demands of external reality, the id's somatic urges, and the super-ego's socio-moral tradition. These processes are never complete nor are any of the three faculties totally gratified, since the individual is never completely socialized, and the id maintains hostility against the social order as represented in the superego and external reality. Among the ways the ego protects itself ("defenses") is "repression," the blocking of painful wishes from consciousness which results in anxiety, sometimes to the point of neurosis; errors; and slips. The resistances are likely to weaken during illness producing hallucina-tions and in sleep producing dreams. The only satisfactory defense is "sublimation," the diversion of id wishes from sexual objects to social and cultural goals. However, when a group of individuals take a leader as object, rather than, say, a task or goal; their emotions are intensified; their intellectual functions are inhibited, and they tend toward mob behavior.

THE PRESENT FIELD AND THE FUTURE

If the reader has been left with the impression that social psychology is irrelevant, fragmented, and gloomy, he may not be far from the mark. In 1935, near the end of a long, distinguished career, E. B. Holt warned that students will find any textbook "a farrago of vague, pedantic, and utterly useless abstractions." Furthermore: "The mental blindness of nearly every academic social psychologist for any fact of human nature is so unfailing and complete as almost to compel admiration."[40] And in 1968, Gordon Allport, the most eminent social psychologist of this century, recalled a question a high official in the State Department asked him. "Honestly, do you social psychologists have anything that would help me in my day to day work on the India desk?" To which he replied, "Honestly, I do not know, but I am furious with you for not using it."[41]

Allport also commented on the "jerky, nervous, and a-theoretical" work of the 1950s and 1960s, the fragmentation illustrated in "the present cloudburst of books of disjointed and astigmatic *Readings*" and other "unreadable and unread publications, crammed with method but scant on meaning."[42] Moreover, Carlson has documented the growing pessimism of general psychology in the last six decades. His content analysis of introductory textbooks showed a decline in references to pleasant emotions, among all references to emotions, from 42.5 percent in texts published before 1900 to 23.1 percent in texts published after 1960. Specifically, the number of references to anger, anxiety, and fear rose sharply, while those to joy and sympathy declined.[43]

The causes of these trends are difficult to discern. But certainly the social sciences reflect the ideology and tone of society. German psychologists gave in to the Nazis, the Russians, to Marxism. In the United States, meliorism, empiricism, environmentalism, and pragmatism greatly influenced psychology in the first two-thirds of this century, while today, we appear to have entered a period of social fragmentation, doubt, and existential anxiety. Ours has been a pluralistic society, an ideal place for social psychology to flourish. Who is to say whether it has been the two World Wars, the prospect of nuclear annihilation, the conflict of generations raised in the Great Depression and in present affluence, Calvin or Spock, or racial strife that has given pause to society and to psychology? Perhaps it is time for both to pause for self-assessment; perhaps it is a sign of progress to do so. One can be hopeful that a nation that produced the social theorists Jefferson and Madison and the psychologists William James and John Dewey can continue to solve its problems. The question is how social psychology, potentially the elemental and unifying science for understanding and helping mankind, can contribute. Let me speculate.

Social psychologists must recognize the need for studying the individual and the social situation simultaneously; when knowledge of either is lacking, understanding and prediction of behavior suffers accordingly. Cronbach[44] and Getzels[45] have argued persuasively the case for such an integration, and both have stressed theoretical models that deal comprehensively with the complexity of social stimuli and of individual differences.

Second, more experiments are needed, or a way of ascertaining causality in social research other than through experiments must be developed. The latter has appeared to be a blind alley, but much work is now being addressed to the problem. Because of experimentation, we know how to breed and nourish animals and plants so that agricultural yields have increased by many magnitudes. But we know precious little about how to raise mental capacity or increase creativity or how to prevent violence and mental disease. Until we do, we must practice hope, forebearance, and humility, carefully distinguishing the probable from the unknown and facts from value and opinion.

Last, social psychologists, without losing sight of the goal of pure science — knowledge for its own sake — must respond to pressing individual and social problems of the nation and the world. It may be more likely that schools of business, education, and social work or the newly proposed schools of applied social science might lead the way in this area. Early in this century, psychology had to struggle to break away from departments of philosophy within the university; today, scholars concerned with social policy and practice may have to break away from traditional academic psychology. Whatever the arrangement, the excellent practical work in recent years on the social psychology of attitudes, communication, education, administration, prejudice, socialization, work, and occupations must continue. Indeed, perhaps these will be the leading areas in the reconstruction of this young discipline.[46]

FOOTNOTES

1. On the relation of psychology to the social sciences, see Sigmund Koch, ed., *Psychology: A Study of Science: Volume 6: Investigations of Manás Socius: Their Place in Psychology and the Social Sciences* (New York: McGraw-Hill, 1963). For other short overviews of social psychology, see Muzafer Sherif, "Social Psychology: Problems and Trends in Interdisciplinary Relationships," pp. 30–93 in the same volume and Harold B. Gerard, "Social Psychology," in *The International Encyclopedia of the Social Sciences* (New York: Macmillan, 1968), vol. 14, pp. 459–473.

2. Thomas S. Kuhn, *The Structure of Scientific Revolutions* (Chicago: University of Chicago Press, 1962).

3. Sigmund Koch, *Psychology: A Study of a Science* (New York: McGraw-Hill, 1959).

4. See Sven Lundstedt, *Higher Education in Social Psychology* (Cleveland, Ohio: Case Western Reserve University Press, 1968).

5. For an excellent sketch, see Gordon W. Allport, "The Historical Background of Modern Social Psychology" in *The Handbook of Social Psychology*, eds. Gardner Lindzey and Elliot Aronson (Reading, Massachusetts: Addison-Wesley, 1968), vol. 1, pp. 1–80. Good historical treatments of social psychology in the context of general psychology are E. G. Boring, *A History of Experimental Psychology* (N.Y.: Appleton-Century-Crofts, 1950) and Gardner Murphey, *Historical Introduction to Modern Psychology* (N.Y.: Harcourt, Brace, 1949).

6. Allport, "Historical Background of Modern Social Psychology."

7. E. G. Boring's terms, personal communication, 1967.

8. Allport, "Historical Background of Modern Social Psychology, p. 3.

9. Allport, "Historical Background of Modern Social Psychology," p. 2.

10. Gordon W. Allport, "Six Decades of Social Psychology," in *Higher Education in Social Psychology*, ed. Sven Lundstedt, pp. 9–19.

11. E. A. Ross, *Social Psychology* (N.Y.: Macmillan, 1908) and William McDougall, *Introduction to Social Psychology* (London: Methuen, 1908).

12. See, for example, Kurt Lewin, *Field Theory in Social Science* (N.Y.: Harper, 1951).

13. A good example is Talcott Parsons and Edward A. Shils, *Toward a General Theory of Action* (Cambridge, Mass.: Harvard University Press, 1951).

14. Allport, "Six Decades of Social Psychology."

15. David L. Sills, ed., *International Encyclopedia of the Social Sciences* (New York: Macmillan, 1968).

16. J. W. Getzels, "A Review," *American Educational Research Journal* 6 (1969): 677–685.

17. See n. 9.

18. Gardner Lindzey and Elliot Aronson, *The Handbook of Social Psychology: Volumes 1–5* (Reading, Massachusetts: Addison-Wesley, 1968).

19. Theodore X. Barber and Maurice J. Silver, "Fact, Fiction, and the Experimenter Bias Effect," *Psychological Bulletin* 70 (1968): 1–29; Richard E. Snow, "Unfinished Pygmalion," *Contemporary Psychology* 14 (April 1969): 197–199; Robert L. Thordike, "Review of Pygmalion in the Classroom", *American Educational Research Journal* 2 (November 1968): 708–711.

20. W. L. Clairborn, "Expectancy Effects in the Classroom: A Failure to Replicate," *Journal of Educational Psychology* 60 (August 1969): 377-383.

21. Carl R. Rogers, *On Becoming a Person: A Therapist's View of Psychotherapy* (Boston: Houghton Mifflin, 1961).

22. Max Weber, *The Theory of Social and Economic Organization* (New York: Oxford University Press, 1947).

23. John B. Watson, *Psychology from the Standpoint of a Behaviorist* (New York: Lippincott, 1919).

24. Although a prominent behaviorist, James Deese recently wondered if 50 years of behaviorism have contributed anything to our understanding of cognition: "Behavior and Fact," *Americacn Psychologist* 24 (May 1969): 515-522.

25. F. Le Dantec, *L'égoisma: Seul Base de Toute Société* (Paris: Flammarion, 1918).

26. Gustave Le Bon, *The Crowd* (London: T. Fisher Unwin, 1896, originally published in Paris, 1895).

27. Allport, "Historical Background of Modern Social Psychology."

28. For a searching criticism of hedonistic assumptions in economics, see Herbert A. Simon and Andrew C. Stedry, "Psychology and Economics," *Handbook of Social Psychology*, eds. Lindzey and Aronson, vol. 5, pp. 269–314.

29. Allport, "Historical Background of Modern Social Psychology," p. 23. The process of selective attention to aggression in psychology may be similar to newspaper coverage of crime, war, and other such events and the lack of coverage of "insignificant" everyday acts of common kindness.

30. William James, *Principals of Psychology*, vol. 1 (New York: Holt, 1890), p. 255.

31. Jean Piaget, *The Language and Thought of the Child* (New York: Harcourt, Brace, 1926).

32. Philip J. Runkel, "Dimensionality, Map Making, and Anxiety," *Psychological Reports* (August 1963), pp. 335–350.

33. Milton Rokeach, *The Open and Closed Mind* (New York: Basic Books, 1960).

34. Leon Festinger, *Conflict, Decision, and Dissonance* (Stanford, California: Stanford University Press, 1964).

35. Wolfgang Kohler, *Gestalt Psychology: An Introduction to the New Concepts in Modern Psychology* (New York: Liverwright, 1947) and Lewin, *Field Theory in Social Science.*

36. Edward L. Thorndike, *Educational Psychology* (New York: Columbia University Teachers College Press, 1913).

37. B. F. Skinner, *Science and Human Behavior* (New York: Macmillan, 1953).

38. Clark L. Hull, *A Behavior System* (New Haven, Conn.: Yale University Press, 1952).

39. J. Strachey, ed., *The Standard Edition of the Complete Psychological Works of Sigmund Freud: Volumes 1–24* (London: Hogarth Press, 1953). For an introduction, see *An Outline of Psychoanalysis*; social-psychological works are *Group Psychology and the Analysis of the Ego* and *Civilization and Its Discontents.*

40. E. B. Holt, "The Whimsical Condition of Social Psychology and of Mankind," in *American Philosophy: Today and Tomorrow*, eds. Henry M. Kallen and Sydney Hook (New York: Lee Furman, 1935), p. 172.

41. Allport, "Six Decades of Social Psychology," p. 17.

42. Ibid., p. 18.

43. E. R. Carlson, "The Affective Tone of Psychology," *Journal of General Psychology* 75 (July 1966) : 65–78.

44. Lee J. Cronbach, "The Two Disciplines of Scientific Psychology," *American Psychologist* 12 (November 1957) : 671–684.

45. J. W. Getzels, "A Social Psychology of Education" in *The Handbook of Social Psychology*, eds. Gardner Lindzey and Elliot Aronson, vol. 5, pp. 459–537.

46. I am indebted to the work of many social psychologists beyond those cited in the footnotes, especially that of the late Gordon Allport. I thank Judith Evans of Harvard University and Maurice Each, Emmanuel Hurwitz, and Wayne Frederick for comments on a draft manuscript; any shortcomings, of course, are my own.

4

An Overview of
the Structure and
Substance of Sociology

Ronald G. Corwin

INTRODUCTION

This chapter can do no more than present the bare bones of sociology. Hopefully, even a short glimpse of the field's anatomy will provide the reader a foundation on which to build. Yet, there is at the same time the unfortunate danger that from such an abbreviated account the discipline will appear to be more fossilized and less vital than it is. Therefore, at the outset, it seems appropriate to say something about the livelier issues in the field.

There is, for one thing, some dispute about the appropriateness of treating modes of inquiry as a separate topic independently of the objectives of a particular study. It can be misleading to single out a few sociological procedures as though they represented a codified and accepted methodological base for the discipline. Sociologists disagree among themselves about the utility of statistical models, case studies, scaling, and other approaches. They have been handicapped especially by the fact that many of the more sophisticated available methodological strategies and techniques have been cultivated on the study of individuals and are not easily adapted to the study of social relationships, large scale organizations, or communities. In these latter cases, it may be more important to capture in depth the significance of the actions and opinions of a few powerful and knowledgeable leaders than it is to have a statistically balanced sample of the actions and opinions of a random sample of the individuals involved. Yet, by comparison to the probability and random sampling procedures, other procedures seem less reliable.

The stubborn fact which sociologists have not been able to accept fully is that field research situations often do not fill the requirements of the more sophisticated methodological models which often are based on the unlikely assumption that the researcher has complete control over the research process. Rather than lamenting their lack of control over respondents and the astronomical costs of collecting meaningful data on large samples of organizations and communities, sociologists are currently searching for as yet not fully explicated models more appropriate to field settings. Clearly, research must be viewed as a social process which is necessarily constrained by the same ethical principles, and which is charaterized by the same type of bargaining and negotiation between the researcher and the "subject" that characterizes any other freely contracted social relationship. Because of the complexity of the modes of inquiry in sociology, then, this topic will be treated only briefly and in context with the various concepts to be considered.

There is also raging within sociology today a dispute over an even more fundamental issue: the proper role of sociology among the brotherhood of disciplines engaged in the study of man. Having had their origins in humanities and having adopted a scientific model for disciplined inquiry, sociologists dispute what it means to be a "social" scientist. In particular, the notions that social science either can be or should be "value free" and "objectives" are being vigorously challenged by a large segment of the sociological community who propose instead a more liberal "new" sociology committed to social improvement.[1] The new breed argues that because sociology is a human enterprise needing the support of the nonscientific community and taking its leads from this community, it is, in practice, impossible for sociologists to remain neutral. And, yet, it is charged that sociologists have used the guise of neutrality to conduct research which, in fact, is calculated to support the cause of the conservative establishment at the expense of the lower status members of society. The new sociology is thus based upon an old argument: sociologists should recognize the inherently political character of social science and explicitly shift their allegiance from the establishment to the underprivileged so that they can apply their skills and knowledge to bring about needed reform on behalf of underprivileged groups.

Many administrators and other practitioners, often unwittingly, have espoused a course of action which has very similar consequences when insisting that sociologists should apply themselves more directly to problems which are relevant to practice. However, while administrators may agree with the new sociologists on the need for sociology to be more relevant to social action, ironically, they are likely to be on opposite sides of the "establishment-underdog" fence. For the argument of the new sociology is that the scholar should identify with the laymen, rather than the professional administrator.

Certainly it is difficult to argue with the general proposition that social scientists have often defined problems from the standpoint of the people who have hired them — the school boards, the administrators, and more recently the federal government.[2] However, if sociologists have been guilty of misusing science in the past by identifying too thoroughly with elite members of society, it does not necessarily follow that sociology should be deliberately converted into a political vehicle in order to be used as a front for private ideological causes, even in the interest of the underdog. In becoming so thoroughly identified with the problems and causes of certain groups, sociologists stand to lose the public's confidence. Even now the public has good reason to suspect that when sociologists undertake a study, they do so to grind their own private axe; if people refuse to participate in the research, it is perhaps for good reason.

Unless sociologists can achieve a semblance of neutrality and integrity, the enterprise will be in jeopardy. It would appear that it is no longer necessary to demonstrate the *utility* of sociology. This is not to say that sociology has in fact demonstrated its ultimate utility; it is only to observe that enough people in prominent places now believe in the practical value of the social sciences. What must now be demonstrated is the integrity of sociology as an intellectual discipline. Practitioners, who lament that social scientists have not involved themselves deeply enough in their problems and who expect social scientists to become useful and relevant for their private interests as a condition for supporting sociology, should consider the long-range consequences of what they are demanding. Hopefully, practitioners will come to judge sociology on the basis of whatever knowledge it can provide about education and not solely for its immediate and practical utility. It is on this conviction that the present chapter was written.

BUILDING BLOCK CONCEPTS

Society begins when two or more people *interact* with one another in such a way that the actions of one party influence the actions of the other(s). Sociology is the study of these patterns of interaction among people, groups, and organizations. The distinctive quality about *social* interaction is that it is normative. That is, people not only "behave"; they conduct themselves according to enforced *norms* that specify the rights and obligations of the parties involved. Any one social position, such as a high school principal, is essentially a composite of the rights and obligations associated with that position. These, in turn, determine how people who hold that position should relate to other positions — teachers, parents, the superintendent, pupils, school board members, and so forth.

Components of Interaction

Norms may take the forms of customs, or written laws and regulations. To qualify as norms, however, the rights and obligations of a party must carry some sanction(s), such as some penalty for violating the norms and/or some reward for conformity. The rights and obligations of a party and the appropriate sanctions are, in turn, determined by the situation and by the respective positions of the parties who are interacting. Norms differ in this respect from attitudes. The latter are considered to be a more integral part of the personality and, hence, not necessarily so easily conditioned by the situation and by the counter roles involved. The way people interact socially, then, does not necessarily reflect their personal attitudes.

The configuration of norms governing the relationship between two positions in a particular situation is called a *role*. A *position*, in turn, consists of various roles, which form a "role set" for that position.[3] For example, the principal has rights and obligations with respect to parents, to the superintendent, and to teachers (the parent-principal role, the superintendent-principal role, and the teacher-principal role, respectively). In a very real sense, the composite of these roles is the principal's position; for the pattern of rights and obligations literally determines the placement of the principal with respect to teachers, students, and school board members. It follows that when the rights and obligations of any of the counter positions change, the principal's position also will be affected. Therefore, the principal's position must be understood in terms of this broader context. Indeed, it must be understood in terms of the society of which he is a part.

In addition to their component roles, the positions may be comprised of broader role "segments," or in other words, norms which are found in many different positions and, hence, which are independent of a particular position. For example, the "disciplinarian" role segment is often found in the behavior patterns of principals and superintendents, as well as of teachers, and the "consideration" role segment and the professional and employee role segments are also commonly incorporated into many different positions; thus, the "professional role segment" can be understood apart from the particular positions to which it is attached. This concept facilitates comparisons among different systems and, in that way, provides a theoretical bridge between different empirical settings. There are obvious parallels, for example between the professional segments of the nurse-physician role at hospitals and the teacher-principal role in the schools.

An organization can be described in terms of the specificty of its norms, their form and consistency of enforcement, the degree of consensus on the norms, the inconsistency among them, and the behavioral conformity in them. Characteristically, norms governing complex organizations are not entirely consistent. This normative inconsistency creates *alternative* structures, and the tension among alternatives is a dynamic source of energy and charge. Alternatives are selected through a process or "role bargaining" which produces "negotiated order."

When it is necessary to choose between conflicting or diffuse norms or those on which there is low consensus, one's choice will depend in part upon the *reference group* he uses.[4] The term "reference group" sometimes refers to the norms endorsed by an actual group which is highly esteemed, such as the National Education Association (NEA); or it may refer to an impersonal standard of conduct, such as the way in which a "professional person" is expected to act. A person need not actually be a member of his reference group, and his reference groups may change under different circumstances. For example, a school superintendent may be requested by his school board to fire a competent teacher for reasons which he knows to be related to racial prejudice. As an employee, he is obligated to do what his employers tell him to do; but as a professional person, he also has another reference group, his peers or his professional association. His actual conduct will depend upon which reference group he chooses to follow, and that, in turn, will depend upon many other factors, such as the job alternatives available, his career aspirations, the basis of his self-esteem and prestige, and the support that he has from other members of the community. In this particular situation, he may choose the employee role, even though he acts in accordance with his professional reference group in most other instances.

From this example, however, it should be clear that a person's behavior is only partly determined by his personal choice of reference group. In large part, it is also determined by the influence of others over him and his *power* relative to the power of others, and in many cases, the balance of power will itself determine which reference group is invoked on a particular occasion.

Types of Relations

Power is the basis of what is perhaps the primordial relationship. The term, "power," refers to the capacity of one party to affect the behavior of another in a specified way. If the effect is maximum, it is called *control*. If it is minor, it is referred to as *influence*. If power is exercised against the other party's resistance, it is called *coercion*.[5] If the use of power is considered to be legitimate, it is referred to as *authority*. There are, however, inherent tensions in modern societies between power and authority. There may be several sources of legitimacy, and these sources may not always agree; for example, the school board and the classroom teachers' association both can serve as bases of legitimacy, but the two groups may disagree about the principal's right to remove books from the library shelves. This is the other side of the coin of what was said before; there may be several possible reference groups from which the person in a particular position may choose. In a changing heterogeneous society, the legal basis of authority is often challenged and, frequently, radically changed by contending groups. Consequently, a person may be in a position of authority without sufficient power to achieve his responsibilities, or he may gain power without necessarily having the authority to exercise it, at least insofar as some bases of legitimacy are concerned.

One of the critical but unanswered questions is whether power is a "zero-sum" quantity or an expanding quantity. In the first case, if one group gains power, another group must lose it. The latter case is more analogous to the growth of the gross national product; that is, the total amount of power in society or without an organization may be capable of expanding in such a way that all parties concerned can achieve more power without any group sacrificing power in any absolute sense.[6]

The Relative Importance of Power and Consensus

One of the key issues in sociology concerns the relative importance of power and consensus as a basis of society. The two concepts underlie different models of society. The consensus model implies a rational, functional view of society. It assumes that society is a well integrated system, held together by consensus among and between members of its various parts, each part contributing to the whole. On the other hand, the conflict model of society is based on the opposite premises, namely, that every organization is in process of ubiquitous change, with dissension and conflict among and between its parts, every part contributing to its disintegration and change; but that it is held together by the imposition of power and the use of authority.[7] The conception of conflict implied here is sociological, rather than personal, since conflict is assumed to be produced by structural differences between social positions, rather than by certain types of personalities. It should be noted that these two models point to very different types of problems for study, as well as to different approaches to the solution of these problems, as in the quest for consensus as opposed to attempts to utilize the positive functions of conflict.

Types of Sociological Variables

To fully understand the sociological perspective and the significance of some of the ensuing issues, it may help to consider the differences among different types of variables used in the social sciences. Sociological variables can be classified on the basis of their relationship to personality and social structure.[8] Beginning with the most personal variables and proceeding to the inherently structural characteristics, the following six levels of analysis, given with pertinent examples, are commonly employed in sociological research.

(1) *Personal orientations of members* — the job satisfaction of a teacher or his conception of his obligations to help motivate students

(2) *The personal behavior of members* — the number of professional conferences an individual has attended during the past year

(3) *Demographic characteristics of members* — a person's age and his level of education (there is, in fact, an entire field of social demography which focuses almost exclusively on such categories as the sex and age distribution of the members of a society, the differential fertility rates of different segments of the society, and migration patterns)

(4) *The official and formal relationships between two positions*— the number of times a principal visits a teacher's classroom or the mutual role consensus between persons in different positions

(5) *Distributions of member characteristics throughout the organization or society* — the proportion of a teaching faculty

with an M.A. degree (any of the above characteristics can
be converted into organizational distributions)

(6) *Structural properties not derivable from member characteristics* — the number of levels of authority in a school or number of departments

(7) *Contextual properties* — the size of the community in which
a school system is located or region of the country

Generally speaking, the first three categories pertain to individual
characteristics, and the last four apply to organizational ones. But
even the first three types of variables can be converted into organizational variables by treating them as distributions or percentages. For example, by averaging the individual job satisfaction of
each employee in a school system, job satisfaction becomes a property of the organization and is not possessed by any particular
individual.

The strictly organizational variables deserve more attention than
they customarily have received even from sociologists. With some
justification, it can be maintained that a group is no less real than
the individuals who comprise it and that individual personality in
itself is a hypothetical construct inferred from the consistency of
individual responses. Group properties can be inferred from individual reactions to the group just as the temperature of the sun can
be inferred from the reaction of other objects and human beings to
it. As Scott points out, "Just because an individual is used as a
source of data is no reason that the data must describe his own
characteristics rather than the characteristics of some external system to which he is . . . responding."[9]

The Issue of Reduction

Yet, there has been a pervasive tendency, among laymen and
social scientists alike, to reduce organizational problems to psychological variables. This is partly because most people feel more
familiar with psychological explanations and have been trained to
think in these terms, and, perhaps, it is also partly true because
sociological variables seem to be more difficult to control and manipulate than are those for individuals. But, even if sociological
variables can be reduced to the personal characteristics of the individuals involved, such as their age, level of aspiration or I.Q., it
does not follow that they should or must be reduced or even "controlled for" in statistical designs. To state an absolutely extreme
illustration, a theory which explains teacher militancy in terms of
the degree of bureaucratization in a school system need not be

required to demonstrate whether or not the individuals in that setting have unique personality traits, any more than it would be necessary for a psychologist to test whether people with different personality traits have different metabolism rates.

COMMUNITY AND SOCIETY

Just as a cluster of roles forms positions, so clusters of positions constitute institutions. An institution, in other words, consists of position related in stable ways governing a primary social function, such as marriage, education, or health. Institutions should not be confused with the concrete organizations commonly associated with them, however. Institutions are composed of abstract rules and sanctions, such as those regulating the conditions under which people may or must get a formal education or who may teach whom. Organizations, on the other hand, are deliberately created structures with names and definite locations. Hence, whereas education is an institution, a particular school is an organization. Strictly speaking, organizations are "associations" made up of different institutional patterns. They seldom are based on a single institution, although a particular institution may dominate. For example, a school is organized around business, leisure, political, and often religious institutions, as well as educational institutions. Organizations, then, are the stage on which these institutional spheres of the society compete for dominance and assume their form and prominence. Accordingly, the character of an organization is determined by the relative priority of the institutions in the society; as the institutional priorities change (as the priorities of this country have changed from religious to business and more recently to leisure and education), the organizations of the society also change their character and importance. Much sociological analysis has been devoted to describing the different institutional patterns and priorities within this, and other societies, at various times.

Problems of "institutional lag" develop when different institutions become relatively autonomous. They may not be well articulated and, hence, will change at different rates. Inconsistencies between different institutions are responsible for pervasive role conflicts in the society. For example, the pressures for more education in this society have infected family life. Homework competes for the time and commitment of the children; failure in school reflects upon the family status, and lack of support from the family undermines the school's effectiveness. One of the primary problems in education today, then, is to identify and describe in more precise terms the effects of changes in the relationship between education and other institutions, such as marriage, religion, and leisure institutions, and to identify the possible mechanisms for reestablishing some kind of balance between churches, playgrounds, families, and schools.

The distinction just made between institutions and associations has its parallel in a distinction often made between the concepts "status" and "office."[10] The latter concept refers specifically to a position in a particular association, whereas a status is a position within the larger institutional spheres of society. For example, the term "educator" has no specific organizational reference in the way that the term "high school principal" does. Sometimes the expectations of an official role are inconsistent with those of the related social status as, for example, when women command men in an organization, or when a younger person is promoted over older members.

Social Stratification and Mobility

The institutional system of society is organized around major social *functions*. The reward system forms still another basis of the social structure which crosscuts the institutional system. In every known society, rewards are distributed unequally and hierarchically. The arrangement of any social group or society into a hierarchy of such positions that are unequal with regard to power, property, social evaluation, and/or psychic ratification is referred to as "social stratification."[11] This reward hierarchy is so fundamental to the total life of a society that knowledge of a person's position in the reward hierarchy tells a great deal about his attitudes, values, and life style.

Social stratification is a product of the fact that different social functions are ranked and evaluated. It reflects the way in which the society rewards its members. To the extent that there is a dominant value system on which most members of the society can agree, the system of stratification functions both as a way of rewarding people for their contributions and a way of motivating members of the society to compete for the most important social roles.

However, the system at best functions only imperfectly in these latter respects because people do not necessarily agree on dominant values, because they do not necessarily rationally calculate the relative rewards in relation to the difficulty of achieving them, and most important, because in modern societies there are *competitive* ranking systems, all of which cannot contribute equally to the

society and some of which may be actually opposed to the dominant values (e.g., the criminal role). Given the competitiveness of ranking systems in complex societies, it must be assumed that the stratification system is, at best, partially based upon power and coercion, as well as upon value consensus.

Social mobility refers to the movement of individuals between different levels of the stratification system. There are several forces which produce social mobility. In the first place, social mobility rates are partly produced by changes in the distribution of higher and lower level positions in a society; the possibility of mobility increases as more white collar jobs are created. Second, it is produced by the proportion of positions which are inherited, either officially or in fact. Societies with a high proportion of inherited positions are referred to as a caste system, in contrast to a class system, but even in a class society, mobility may be "sponsored" or controlled by certain groups of people, as well as determined competitively on the basis of qualifications. Third, mobility is a product of the difference in the fertility rates between the upper and lower classes; for when members of the upper strata fail to reproduce themselves, positions in the upper class become available to people in lower classes.

There are many ways of measuring social mobility, none of which is entirely satisfactory. Mobility sometimes is measured as the number of changes which an individual makes in occupations during his lifetime or as his rate of promotion within an occupational group (i.e., the relationship between a person's age and the position that he has achieved). Another way of measuring mobility is to compare the person's present position with that of his father. However, this inter-generation index presents problems. For example, different conclusions may be reached by viewing mobility from the standpoint of the son or the father. If the father has more than one son, the average rate of mobility has a chance of being relatively high. If there are six sons, for example, and one follows in his father's footsteps, there is 100 percent inheritance. Whereas, when viewed from the standpoint of the sons, if five are mobile and one follows in his father's footsteps, the mobility rate will appear to be much different. It also depends on the points in the career curve that are considered. One gets a different perception by considering the father's occupation at the end of his career in comparison to the son's occupation at the beginning or middle of his career, than if the two are compared at the same career point. There is also the problem of changes occurring in the occupational structure between the time that the father began his career and the time the son ended his career, which together with the extreme variability of occupations within occupational classes makes measurement extremely difficult.

Dimensions of Stratification

Max Weber identified the following three fundamental systems of social ranking, which in modern societies are not necessarily correlated: the economic system (or class), the prestige system (or status), and the political system (or power).

Class. The class system in a society emerges when family relationships become subordinated to relationships based on property and on the economic division of labor in the production system. For Marx, a social class was any *aggregate* of persons (i.e., not a social community) performing the same function in the organization of production. However, it is complex and can be measured in a variety of ways. Education, occupation, and income all have been used as indicators of economic strata. Education, in particular, is a confusing factor. For while it is true that a society's level of education is closely tied to its economic progress and that the demand for education reflects the demands of the economy, at the same time, it is also possible that the educational upgrading of occupations has occurred *because* there are more educated people available. In this latter case, it is reasonable to argue that education has become the basis for a prestige system which is separate from the economic system.

Sociologists also have used occupation and income as indices of class. But here again, there is no one-to-one correspondence between either income and occupation or between one's ranking on either of these hierarchies and his function in the economy. One's occupation, for example, reflects such other rankings as his level of prestige.

Status. Prestige is the basis of a different ranking system, one which Weber and Veblen have referred to as status groupings. Just as classes are produced by the impersonal and rational processes of the marketplace, so status groups are the products of informal relations among men and of consensus within a community on the way they are to be evaluated. Rather than being based on modes of production, status groups compete among themselves to monopolize prized goods. Thus, they develop distinctive consumption patterns or complicated "life styles," and they protect themselves by refusing to bestow the honor of membership in these consumptive groups solely because someone has achieved naked power or because he has acquired goods.

Most of the studies of stratification have used occupation as a criterion of status ranking, for, as mentioned, in our society an occupation connotes as much about a person's prestige as it does about his function in the economy. However, the existing procedures for classifying occupations are not entirely adequate. For example, the famous Edwards Occupational Scale is not a scale but a ranking of occupations on the basis of median education and income (and intuition). The Duncan scale, which is based on education and income adjusted for age, is perhaps a somewhat more reliable index of occupation.

One problem with occupational scales is that a number of occupations at the same level of prestige, such as dentist, physician, and engineers, sometimes have radically different styles of life. The concept "occupational situs," which has been developed for the purpose of classifying closely related "families of occupations," offers some promise for the development of a more meaningful categorization of occupations. However, there has been little effort to rank people explicitly on the basis of their life styles (i.e., their use of leisure time), with the possible exception of Chapin's now outdated Living Room Scale, which ranked families on the basis of their home furnishings. Although recently, sociologists have begun to turn their attention to a more systematic examination of life styles among inner-city class populations.[12]

A person's occupational prestige can also be inferred from the way occupations have been actually ranked by samples of people.[13] The consensus among judges is not always high, but repetitions of the way the public rates occupations, in this and other countries, have been remarkably consistent and stable.

The occupational scales involve inferring a person's prestige from his occupational status. In addition, there have been attempts to rank individuals more directly, according to the way they are rated by other people in a community. This sampling of a community is done by asking residents to rate a list of their neighbors occupations.[14] This technique, however, is difficult to use in large metropolitan areas where people are not likely to know their neighbors well. One disadvantage of this technique has been that it is most frequently used in small communities, a fact which may have created misleading impressions about stratification in this country.

Power.   Power represents still another dimension of social stratification. The hierarchy of power arises from the competition between various interest groups for influence. It is through the political systems that differences in values are publicly reconciled and a dominant system established. Brotz sees stratification systems as substitutes for political power.[15] He maintains that the political order, since it is public, is the primary basis of public respect, but that those groups which fail to achieve the desired amount of political power turn to their own *private* standards of status and form status groups as a substitute. Status systems, in other words, are not only distinct from power structures but evolve in direct reaction to them.

Sociologists, as well as political scientists, have studied power structures. Most of these studies have been confined to local communities and to complex organizations, but there has been some attention given to regional and national power bases. There seems to be some relationship between power and economic status in the sense that the influence of certain corporate positions often carries over into the community and society.[16] However, the fact that the same may be said of some university positions indicates that the important base of power in the society is large-scale organization and is not confined to economic organizations.

A distinction must be made between locally and cosmopolitan based power structures. The locally-oriented leader joins organizations like the Elks and the Rotary Club and achieves his position from his personal relationships with other people in these organizations and the community in which he lives. The cosmopolitan leader, on the other hand, is more likely to be concerned about national and regional issues, deriving his power from his official connections and from his specialized skills.

There are a number of unresolved issues in the study of power, some of which tend to be based on differences in the methods used and the assumptions held by political scientists and sociologists. Sociologists often have used a "reputational" method by which community residents are asked to identify community influentials. This has been the subject of much criticism, particularly by social scientists who hold that "positional" or "decision making" approaches are more valid ways of identifying influential people. In the positional approach, people who hold the greatest number of positions are implicitly considered to be influentials; whereas in the decision making approach, factual decisions are studied in order to identify the persons who have an influence on their outcome. There is also some debate over whether communities typically have a single group of influentials capable of influencing most types of decisions or whether different influentials become involved in different types of decisions. In the latter case, there may be several power structures in a community, each of which participates in different spheres of community life, for example, education, political nominations, and urban renewal.[17]

Status Crystallization

Enough has been said to demonstrate the complexity and central importance of the concept of *social stratification*. Yet, it is safe to say that the average layman has been so influenced by the now outdated Warner school of stratification that when the term is used he automatically visualizes a simple six-class system. Warner and his students identified six classes in a variety of communities by asking people to rank a small sample of their neighbors. From this sample, the investigators empirically identified certain correlates of these rankings which were used as the basis for ranking the remainder of the members of the community. The primary correlates that were identified are occupational prestige, amount and source of income, level of education, and type of house and neighborhood. Every person in the community is thereby placed into one, and only one, of the classes, despite the fact that in a complex, changing society it is clear that a person's rankings on the different correlates are not likely to be highly correlated.

The concept, *status crystallization*, has been used by sociologists in recent years as a means of analyzing status incongruities. Lenski, for example, divided a sample of people in the Detroit area into two categories, those whose rankings on occupation, income, education and ethnic status were consistent; and those whose rankings on these dimensions were inconsistent.[18] He found that the two groups tended to vote differently. The concept also has been found to be associated with preference for change,[19] class consciousness,[20] and the incidence of psycho-physical problems.[21] The concept *status consistency*, then, is a potentially very useful one which merits much more attention than it has received thus far.

ASSOCIATIONS

Institutions and the demographic structure, consisting of the distribution of sex and age groups and related characteristics, together with the system of stratification constitute the basic outlines of social structure. Society assumes its concrete form from the specific formal organizations responsible for carrying out the major social functions. A formal organization, as distinguished from families or play groups, for example, is an ongoing group that has been *deliberately created*, presumably for some *purpose*.[22] Formal organizations are literally associations, of people and of normative systems, which have specific names and definite locations, membership rosters, and a calendar of events. Often, the social structure can best be studied in terms of the day-to-day behavior that goes on within associations. This is especially true in a modern, complex society where the various institutional patterns, such as marriage, religion, politics, economics, and education spawn their own distinct forms of concrete associations, such as families, churches, political parties, businesses and factories, and schools and universities. Indeed, in modern, complex societies, there may be more associations than people. A society's capacity to organize is perhaps the single most important factor determining its ability to modernize.

Complex organizations should be distinguished from simple, formal organizations. The general class of organizations include any group of three or more people deliberately established and engaged in interdependent tasks. This includes such diverse groupings as clubs, small voluntary associations, businesses, and communities. However, many of these are likely to be *complex organizations*, which are of primary importance in modern society. Complex organizations are composed of subparts, which often exist in various degrees of autonomy from the central coordinating unit. A complex organization, more specifically, may be defined as follows:

A complex organization consists of (1) stable patterns of interaction, (2) coalitions of groups having a collective identity (e.g., a name and location), (3) pursuing interests and accomplishing given tasks, and (4) coordinated by power and authority structures.[23]

Methodologies

Much of the existing knowledge about organization has been gained from case studies of individual organizations. A variety of techniques have been used in these studies, including participant observation, the use of field diaries, pretested and structured questionnaires, and open-end interviews; the physical properties of organizations also have been studied (e.g., uses of space). The records of organizations and the interaction and language patterns of their participants have been analyzed.[24] In the past few years, there also have been attempts to gather large samples of organizations drawn from a population of similar organizations. In this case, it is possible to treat organizations systematically.

However, there is no completely adequate method of studying organizations. Statistical techniques based on probability theory and development of random samples of individuals are not adequate for analyzing relationships within organizations where a person's opinion needs to be weighted in accordance with his position of influence and where his responses must be interpreted in relation to his context. The need for more sophisticated methods for studying organizations is one of the most pressing methodological problems in the field of sociology today.

Organizational Structure and Process

The sociological study of modern organizations is indebted to Max Weber, who described organizations as "bureaucracies," which refers to a particular way of organizing the administrative system of an organization. According to Weber, bureaucracies consist of several major characteristics which can be summarized in terms of a few major principles and several derivative principles: specialization of personnel and the division of labor, and their counterparts: centralization of authority and standardization. The derivatives of these principles are a hierarchy of offices based on delegated authority, a professional career, and a system of impersonal rules and records. In recent years, Weber's model has been frequently challenged and considerably modified.

The *hierarchy of authority* has several dimensions each of which can serve as a basis for classifying organizations: (1) the number of levels of authority in the hierarchy, (2) the distribution of power throughout different levels of the hierarchy, and (3) the total amount of authority exercised by the organization in comparison to other organizations.[25] The authority structure constitutes one aspect of an organization's *complexity*, which refers to the number of separate identifiable parts in the organization. *Specialization* refers to the level of training of personnel and the assignment of specialists to particular jobs (e.g., the proportion of teachers in a school with a master's degree or the number of teaching courses which they studied in college). The *standardization* of an organization can be measured in terms of the number and specificity of enforced rules and the use of standardized procedures throughout the organization.

The consistency of these dimensions represents the "structural crystallization" of an organization. This concept is analogous to the concept of status crystallization which has been used in connection with the various dimensions of an individual's status. Corwin classified twenty-eight high schools as either uncrystallized or crystallized, on the basis of the correlation among each of several dimensions of organization, such as centralization, specialization, standardization, and close supervision.[26] It was found that crystallized organizations had higher rates of conflict, as measured by the number of conflicts reported by teachers per interview.

"Structural crystallization" is a variant of the reinforcement model of organization, in which the various means of control are positively associated and mutually reinforce one another; for example, when standardization is emphasized, other dimensions of control, such as close supervision, will also be emphasized. "Structural crystallization" is only one of three primary models of organization. The other two models are the compensatory and the independence models. In the compensatory model, the various means of control are used as substitutes for one another; for example, when close supervision is relaxed, rules may be emphasized to take up the slack. These controls, in other words, may exist in a state of tension so that an emphasis on one brings about a relaxation of the others. Still a third model may be referred to as the independence model in which the various dimensions are not systematically correlated with one another.

The description of organizations has been confounded by two distinctly opposed characteristics which they are presumed to embody—bureaucracy and rationality. Rationality emphasizes competence, limited objectives, performance, and segmental participation on the part of organizational members (i.e., separation of their personal lives from their official roles), and it assumes that rewards will be based on participation in and contribution to the organization. Bureaucracy, on the other hand, consists of a higher hierarchical authority structure, specialized administrative staffs, and rewards distributed according to the office one holds.[27]

Similarly, it has been demonstrated that Weber confused two bases of authority in modern organization — knowledge and obedience to office.[28] When knowledge is emphasized in an organization, obedience to authority depends on the adequacy of the knowledge and the skills of the person in the position of authority; whereas, the official basis of authority requires obedience to the official as an end in itself. One of the primary tensions of organization sometimes exemplified in the role of the school administrator, occurs when the official in command has less specialized knowledge of the field than the specialist whom he is directing and evaluating.[29] A related tension occurs between specialists who often are more oriented to their professional colleagues outside of the organization than to their own administrative superiors. Hence, the bureaucracy's need for expertise conflicts with its need for loyal employees.

Informal Organization

The informal side of organization is a primary ingredient which often is not systematically included in the ideal description of bureaucracy and of organizational charts, but which everyone knows exists. Social science has vacillated in the importance attached to informal organization. During one period, it seemed as though the personal relations among the people in organizations were irrelevant; this has been called the "management era." Then, the focus swung to the people in organizations, as though the structure were irrelevant. This has been called the "human relations era." Currently, social scientists from many disciplines are attempting to integrate the two extremes.[30]

Informal power structures tend to be dominated by cliques of influential people who are able to gain power because of their official positions or because of outside connections with local politicians, with leaders in professional organizations, or with other acquaintances.

The term informal organization itself is a generic term that has been applied to a wide variety of organizational phenomena. One usage refers to all illegal and unofficial acts in an organization, such as a school using teachers in courses for which they have not been certified to teach. A second usage refers to behavior which is non-official but not necessarily opposed to the official norms. This includes organizational customs, ideologies, unwritten norms, and sentiments. Informal organization, in this sense, consists of two conceptually distinct parts: (1) a group of persons, and (2) a set of repetitive relationships among them. An informal *group* is based on the irreplaceable qualities of the particular people involved and dissolves when these individuals leave the group. An informal *structure*, on the other hand, is based on a commonly understood set of expectations of what people in the organization should do, which are independent of the particular people involved and which endure turnover in the membership. For example, in a particular school system, it might be understood by those in control that no superintendent, whomever he might be, would promote a Negro into the central administrative staff.

Hence, all organizations have systems of informal rules which are nowhere written down but which are commonly understood and govern the work. Moreover, even those official rules which are publicly acknowledged and written down may be interpreted passively in such a way as to reinforce the informal system. For example, Gouldner has noted a rhythmic relaxation and tightening of rule enforcement in organizations, which he refers to as their "leeway" function.[31] That is, rules are used by supervisors, like they would use poker chips, to bargain for the loyalty of employees, sometimes interpreted literally and sometimes relaxed depending on intuitive judgments about the workers' motivations and cooperation.

Organizational Conflict

Gouldner has identified two commonly used models of organization, the rational model and the natural systems model.[32] In the rational model, organizations are assumed to be goal-directed entities in which organizational goals establish the desired course of action and dominate the thinking of leaders who, in turn, are supposed to logically derive solutions for problems in view of these goals and in the light of available information. Rationality is a function of the number of alternative courses of action which leaders have considered and the amount of planning for eventualities. Hence, a rational organization is one that functions in such a way that its goals are achieved.

In the natural systems model, on the other hand, the direction of an organization depends primarily on the commitments and constraints that the organization is forced to make, rather than on its stated goals. A commitment is an obligation initiated by an organization; whereas, a constraint is one initiated by outside groups.

The two models appear to differ essentially on two points: (1) the degree of consensus on stated objectives and rational planning for the organization as a whole, and (2) the power of each segment of the organization to achieve its commitments. Rationality can be considered as a *limited* case where there is (1) complete consensus within the organization on stated objectives, and (2) each central office and sub-units within the organization has effective power to achieve its commitments. When there is less than complete consensus on stated objectives, it follows that the amount of planning that can be done is inversely related to the power of the sub-parts. Since complex organizations do not have particularly high consensus on their stated objectives and are characterized by functional autonomy of their parts, the study of organizations probably will be most fruitful if the focus is placed on the power relationships between sub-parts, rather than on the logic of decision making in the central office.

There are elements within organizational structures which promote tension and conflict as well as facilitate coordination. For example, although the social distance created by the hierarchy of authority serves to reduce the opportunities for conflict between supervisors and their subordinates, and although the division of labor and rules help to clarify roles, the segments of organizations which are thereby created to perform different functions tend to compete. Similarly, organizations exist in a degree of tension with the society while, at the same time, they depend upon that society for sustenance and support. Since organizations do depend upon the environment for resources, they must establish a degree of cooperation, but Katz also suggests that an organization can accomplish its functions more effectively if it has developed a degree of autonomy from the rest of society.[33] However, Litwak and Meyer point out that organizations sometimes also use a variety of mechanisms to reduce the social distance between them and outside primary groups; whereas, a middle-class school might attempt to increase its social distance from influential middle-class families, it might attempt to increase its association with lower-class families.[34] This tension between autonomy and dependence on outsiders is one of the key dilemmas of modern organization.

In addition to being segmentalized by official lines of authority, the internal organization is further differentiated by a variety of professions or professional groups. As organizations have bureaucratized and the pressures for more efficient decision-making procedures have increased, the gap between professional and bureaucratic norms has grown. Like other employees concerned about protecting their rights in large organizations, professionally-oriented employees are likely to encounter difficulties in attempting to work within large-scale systems.

There are fundamental differences between the professional and non-professional employee. Professional employees tend to expect decision making to be a necessary part of their jobs. To the extent that the professional is specially trained and presumedly dedicated to the welfare of his clients, he is likely to consider himself competent enough to control his own work. When he disobeys, then, it is in order to maintain professional standards. On the other hand, the non-professional employee is not likely to distinguish carefully between doing a good job and obeying his superiors. He is willing to accept the principle of supervision over his job. If he happens to be highly individualistic, he may object to any use of authority that infringes on what he considers to be his personal rights, but as an employee, he is hired to do what he is told and, hence, cannot accomplish his work without obeying the commands of his employer. Therefore, when he disobeys, he must be ready to sabotage his work.

The struggle of professional employees to govern their work has necessarily required a militant posture on their part. Hence, it can be expected that the extent of conflict in organizations will increase as the professional orientations of employees increase. It probably can be expected that, over the long run, bureaucratic organizations will become more effectively adapted to professional norms than they are at present.

Leadership

Leadership has usually been viewed in the context of large-scale organizations. One reason is that a leader in a complex society requires organizational resources if he is to be effective. Indeed, leadership consists largely of the ability to influence organizational policy and practice and manipulate organizational resources. This ability is by and large a by-product of being in certain social positions. There is little evidence to demonstrate that leadership is inherent in any special personality characteristics.[35] Nor is there reason to believe that people can be trained to be "leaders" in any generic sense. There are no "educational leaders" apart from the particular context in which they exercise their influence. The same person who is effective under one set of circumstances may become ineffective under another and the reverse. The sociological view of leadership is that it is a matter of degree, existing as a social relationship between an influential party and followers in specific settings.

Two primary dimensions of leadership have been identified as initiation of structure and consideration.[36] The initiation dimension of leadership involves the achievement of objectives or specific tasks; whereas, consideration entails morale building and supporting subordinates in other ways. People often specialize in these two roles. Some leaders are more task oriented and emphasize initiation in getting the job done. The power of these leaders inheres largely in their office, their effectiveness, and the basis of support from their subordinates depending largely on their ability to secure the necessary resources for the organization. This ability, in turn, depends more upon their relationship with their own superiors than their relationships with their immediate subordinates.[37] In this latter case, the leader's effectiveness tends to require a certain amount of social distance between himself and his followers in order to permit him to associate more freely with his own superiors and to give him enough independence so that he can maintain universalistic standards of evaluation and reward.

The effectiveness of the leaders who emphasize the consideration role, on the other hand, depends upon their ability to maintain personal relationships with their subordinates. The effectiveness of one type of leader over the other depends largely on the situation, that is, the degree of pressure, consensus on objectives, and task structure. There are, of course, some leaders who might be referred to as "formal leaders" who are competent in both the dimensions of initiation and consideration.[38]

Enormous tensions can develop in an organization when a turnover in official leaders results in a shift in leadership styles (e.g., from a consideration-oriented leadership style to a task-oriented one). Such a shift may accompany the appointment of "outsiders" to official leadership positions, since the outsider is not likely to have any strong regard for the established organizational and leadership patterns.[39]

A leader has responsibility for long-range institutional development as well as for his own organization's success. A school superintendent is responsible for the long-range goals of education as well as for achieving more resources or greater stability or a better reputation for his particular school system. Indeed, in the case of school consolidation, he may be called upon to sacrifice the organization for the sake of the institution. The same principle is involved when a principal of a suburban school neglects the problems of inner city education while working to achieve greater success for his particular school.

RELATIONSHIPS OF ASSOCIATIONS TO SOCIETY

To understand fully how organizations function, it is necessary to view them in their societal context. As composites of both people and of institutions, associations provide a strategic vantage point for the study of social structure. Organizations are related to society through their goals and their "boundary spanning roles," that is, those roles in the organization in which the primary relationships are with non-members.

Organizational Goals

"Goal" is an ambiguous term. It is sometimes used to refer to ideal states, in which case it is assumed there is general consensus in the organization. At other times, it refers to the private and often incompatible objectives of the individual members fulfilling different positions in an organization. The ideal statements often tend to be so abstract that they are not very useful, whereas, there is often little consensus on less abstract statements. Consequently, it is often difficult to say with any degree of precision what an organization's goals are. For example, is the primary goal of General

Motors to produce automobiles, to make a profit for the company, to help expand the economy, or to grow larger?

One approach to the identification of goals is to determine the amount of role consensus throughout an organization, that is, the proportion of norms that are shared by various positions in different parts of the organization. Another approach is to identify the way in which resources — money, personnel and rewards — are actually distributed throughout the organization, which will not necessarily correspond to the ideal state.[40] Still another approach, which is referred to as the functional approach, is to determine what the organization actually does for the rest of the society; in this case, it is the fact that General Motors produces automobiles, rather than the fact that it makes a profit that is crucial.

It is sometimes more useful to consider the actual direction which an organization is taking than to concentrate on its goals. Direction is a product of the commitments which an organization voluntarily makes, that is, the actual obligations to which it has pledged itself and the outside constraints on it. If abstract goal statements take the form of actual obligations, they become one of many factors that may influence an organization's direction. But the organization is also influenced by the bargains that it makes with outside groups, the way in which it responds to pressures, and by the availability of needed resources.

The character of an organization, then, is determined by the goals that it is willing to bargain away. For this reason, organizations must be understood partially as systems of exchange; they secure resources in exchange for their services.[41] Their power is derived by their ability to bargain for necessary resources and to withhold and give resources to other groups. Organizational behavior is, then, a function of the relationship between rewards and cost. A particular pattern of behavior will persist until the cost of the last unit of action is equivalent to the last unit of reward. The rewards, in social terms, consists not only of money but of esteem, friendship, and help. However, each reward involves a cost in terms of alternative rewards that one must forgo in order to achieve a particular reward. For example, an employee may find it more rewarding to assist his boss than to assist his colleague, because the boss's esteem is more valuable to him. These exchanges are, however, governed by certain norms. In the case just cited, it may not be appropriate for an employee to regard the esteem of his boss as more rewarding than the esteem of his peers.

Organizations, obviously then, are not the rationally directed creatures that they are sometimes presumed to be. Rather, they are products of bargains, commitments, and constraints. They "drift" as much as they are "goal-directed." Goals are often stated so abstractly as to provide few concrete guidelines for day-to-day behavior; daily problems tend to overshadow long-range policy, and policy is often formulated without recognition of outside pressures. For all of these reasons, abstract goals at best provide outside boundaries which have more to do with determining what an organization will *not* do than with indicating what it will do.

Organizational drift can take one of two primary forms: *goal displacement* which is the process by which primary goals are replaced by goals which have had lower priority, and *institutional lag*, which refers to the lack of responsiveness of an organization to outside demands made upon it. One of the major recurrent dramas of organization develops around the efforts of organizations to reconcile themselves to their changing environments.

One side of the dilemma is that if an organization fails to respond fully to new demands made upon it, either its objectives become outmoded or there is a failure to adapt the procedures sufficiently to perform new functions. In either case, a form of institutional lag develops, and the organization stands to lose outside support. Since organizational members typically owe their positions to the existing procedures, they tend to resist change. Accordingly, any effort to change an organization must provide ways of compensating for potential status losses. On the other side of this same dilemma, however, if an organization does adapt too readily to environmental changes and new pressures placed on it, goal displacement which can jeopardize organizational integrity and coherence is likely to occur.

One way in which organizations adapt to change is simply to take on new goals without necessarily altering or replacing the old ones. This "goal expansion" results in a comprehensiveness of objectives which the organization may not be able to handle. The problem here is that the new goals may not be compatible with the existing ones, or they may not be adequately supported by the limited resources of the organization. Unless the organizational resources are expanded accordingly, some form of compromise will be required, informally if not officially. Hence, there has been a tendency for organizations that are presumably comprehensive in character, such as the "comprehensive school," to become *informally specialized* and emphasize only a few of their total range of responsibilities while neglecting others. Hence, presumably comprehensive schools have developed "dumping grounds" while being very effective in preparing middle-class students for college.

The Interorganizational Field

An organization is related to the environment primarily through its relationships with other *organizations*. The term "organization set" has been coined to refer to the total organizational field. This term, which is analogous to a role set, provides a model for viewing the interdependence among a number of organizations.[42] An organization is dependent upon some organizations for input (e.g., resources, services and legitimacy), and it depends upon other organizations to receive its output (e.g., employers). Organizational sets may be analyzed in terms of the number of organizations involved, the degree of mutual dependence, the overlap of membership and goals, and the proportion of personnel occupying boundary roles in various organizations in the set. Organization sets also can be classified on the basis of their authority structure. For example, in a federative system of organizations, authority remains at the level of the individual organization,[43] whereas, in the corporate form of organizational set, authority is delegated to local organizational units.[44]

Organizations also may be classified on the basis of the pervasiveness of their control over their own members and the *scope* of their relationships with non-members. In general, the more pervasive the organization and the lower its scope of relationships with outside organizations, the more effectively it can maintain its boundaries.

An organization can maintain several types of relationships with other organizations. These relationships may be briefly summarized as follows:

(1) *Passive adaptation:* a form of self restraint imposed by the organization to please external groups or to avoid displeasing them; for example, a school system may review books for a library with the intent of keeping out books which might displease someone in the community.

(2) *Coalition:* an open combination between two or more organizations for a specific shared purpose; for example, business-education day in the public schools and school consolidation.

(3) *Cooptation:* the effort of an organization to control adversaries outside of an organization by incorporating them into its leadership; for instance, a principal may control parents by persuading them to become members of important committees on the PTA.

(4) *Bargaining:* negotiations between two or more organizations in which one organization forfeits some of its goals in ex-

change for the support of another organization for some of its other goals; a school board may decide to withdraw a controversial book from the library in order to maintain the support of an influential group which objects to that book.

(5) *Competition:* impersonal efforts on the part of organizations to gain the favor of the third party; for instance, when schools and hospitals compete for the favor of the taxpayer.

(6) *Open Conflict:* a direct confrontation between representatives of different organizations that may take a variety of forms from debate to open violence; teachers' strikes fall into this category.[45]

CONCLUSION

Sociology is the study of the mosaic patterns of interaction among people, groups, and organizations. Social interaction is guided by norms, which are organized as roles and as role sets, these in turn form the major social positions. Social positions exist in both the society at large in the form of age, sex, and other social statuses, and they also exist in organizations, such as schools, where they take the form of offices (e.g., superintendent or teacher). Social positions, together with the web of regularized relationships among them, form the social structure, which in turn is composed of both institutions formed around the major social functions and a stratified reward system cross-cutting institutional realms.

These fundamental elements, in varied combination, then, form a synchrony of social patterns which somehow manages to provide sufficient balance and stability for the society to hang together. The system of social stratification, for example, in establishing how members are to be rewarded and otherwise treated, is a source of stability even though at the same time it is clear that class, status, and power constitute separate and often inconsistent ranking systems. The feat of reconciling such inconsistencies is performed by a dynamic interplay between role consensus (modeled on key reference groups) and various forms of power.

Competing institutional demands are reconciled and eventually implemented through social organizations, such as the family and the school. Many organizations are formalized in the sense that they have been deliberately created for a certain purpose. And, in modern society, many of these in turn are complex organizations composed of coalitions of semi-autonomous parts coordinated via power and authority structures. The character of a complex organization depends upon the way in which specialization and standardization of work, authority patterns, and other major dimensions are combined. Inconsistency among these dimensions of organizational life constitutes a major source of organizational conflict. One of the major sources of conflict stems from the professional roles which may prescribe conduct that is incompatible with bureaucratic systems.

Organizations are related to society through a complicated system of goals and boundary-spanning roles, and they use a variety of strategies to maintain their coherence and autonomy in the face of their continued dependence upon the environment for resources and for disposing of their products. This is a precarious balance. The pressures of society may be responsible for goal displacement, whereas, to the extent an organization is able to maintain its autonomy, it may become unresponsive and subject to institutional lag.

The linkages between organizations and society provide a convenient standpoint from which to view both the society and a particular type of organization. Such linkages also are one of the fundamental keys to the way the society is organized and operates.

FOOTNOTES

1. I.L. Horowitz, *The New Sociology* (New York, N.Y.: Oxford University Press, 1964).

2. Alvin W. Gouldner, "The Sociologist as Partisan: Sociology and the Welfare State," *The American Sociologist* 3, 2 (May 1968): 103-116.

3. Robert K. Merton, "Role-Set: Problems in Sociological Theory," *British Journal of Sociology* 2 (June 1951): 106-120.

4. Robert K. Merton, *Social Theory and Social Structure* (Glencoe, Illinois: The Free Press, 1957), Chapters 8 and 9.

5. Robert L. Kahn, "Field Studies of Power in Organizations" in *Power and Conflict in Organizations,* eds. Robert L. Kahn and Elise Boulding (New York: Basic Books, Inc., 1964), pp. 52-66.

6. C.J. Tommers, "Power and Participation in Decision Making in Formal Organizations," *American Journal of Sociology* 73 (September 1967): 201 ff.

7. Ralf Dahrendorf, *Class and Class Conflict in Industrial Society* (Stanford, Calif.: Stanford University Press, 1959).

8. Allen H. Barton, *Organizational Measurement and Its Bearing on the Study of College Environments* (New York: College Entrance Exam Board, 1961).

9. William A. Scott, *Values and Organization* (Skokie, Illinois: Rand McNally & Co., 1965), p. 130.

10. Kingsley Davis, *Human Society* (New York: Macmillan, 1949), pp. 88-89.

11. Melvin Tumin, *Social Stratification: The Forms and Functions of Inequality* (Englewood Cliffs, N.J.: Prentice-Hall, 1966).

12. Herbert J. Gans, *The Urban Villagers* (New York: Free Press, 1962); Frank Riessman, *The Culturally Deprived Child* (New York: Harper & Row, 1962).

13. Paul K. Hatt, "Occupation and Social Stratification," *American Journal of Sociology* 55 (May 1950): 533-43.

14. W. Lloyd Warner, Marcia Meeker, and Kenneth Eels, *Social Class in America* (New York: Harper & Row, 1960).

15. Howard M. Brotz, "Social Stratification and the Political Order," *The American Journal of Sociology* 64 (May 1959): 571-578.

16. Floyd Hunter, *Community Power Structure* (Chapel Hill: University of North Carolina Press, 1953).

17. Nelson W. Polsby, "Community Power: Three Problems," *American Sociological Review* 24 (December 1959): 796-803.

18. Gerhard Lenski, "Status Crystallization: A Non-Vertical Dimension of Social Status," *American Sociological Review* 19 (August 1954): 405-413.

19. Irwin W. Goffman, "Status Consistency and Preference for Change in Power Distribution," *American Sociological Review* 22 (June 1957), 275-281.

20. Werner S. Landecker, "Class Boundaries," *American Sociological Review* 25 (December 1960): 868-877.

21. Elton F. Jackson, "Status Consistency and Symptoms of Stress," *American Sociological Review* 27 (August 1962): 469-480.

22. Peter Blau and W. Richard Scott, *Formal Organizations* (San Francisco: Chandler, 1962), Chapter 1. Also, Ronald G. Corwin, "Education and the Sociology of Complex Organizations," in *On Education: Sociological Perspectives*, eds. Donald Hansen and Joel Girstle (New York: John Wiley and Sons, 1967), Chapter 5.

23. Ibid., Ronald G. Corwin, p. 161.

24. Eugene Webb, *Unobtrusive Measures: Nonreactive Research in the Social Sciences* (Chicago: Rand McNally, 1966); also, W. Richard Scott, "Field Methods in the Study of Organizations," in *Handbook of Organizations,* ed. James G. March (Chicago: Rand McNally, 1965), Chapter 6.

25. Arnold S. Tannenbaum, "Control and Effectiveness in a Voluntary Organization," *American Journal of Sociology* 27 (July 1961): 33-46.

26. Ronald G. Corwin, *Militant Professionalism: A Study of Organizational Conflict in High Schools* (New York: Appleton-Century-Crofts, 1970).

27. Stanley W. Udy, Jr. "Bureaucracy and Rationality in Weber's Theory," *American Sociological Review* 24 (December 1959): 791-795.

28. Alvin Gouldner, "Organizational Analysis," in *Sociology Today,* eds. Robert K. Merton et al. (New York: Basic Books, Inc., 1959), pp. 400-428.

29. Ibid.

30. Robert L. Peabody, *Organizational Authority* (New York: Atherton Press, 1964).

31. Alvin W. Gouldner, *Patterns of Industrial Bureaucracy* (New York: The Free Press, 1954).

32. Alvin W. Gouldner, "Organizational Analysis."

33. Fred E. Katz, "The School as a Complex Social Organization," *Harvard Educational Review* 34 (Summer 1964): 428-455.

34. Eugene Litwak and Henry J. Meyer, "The School and the Family: The Use of Theories of Linkage Between Bureaucratic Organizations and Exter-

nal Primary Groups," in *The Uses of Sociology,* eds. P. Lazarsfeld, H. Wilensky, and W. Sewell (New York: Basic Books, 1967).

35. Ralph M. Stogdill, "Personal Factors Associated With Leadership: A Survey of the Literature," *Journal of Psychology* (January 1948): 35-71.

36. Andrew W. Halpin, *The Leadership Behavior of School Superintendents,"* Monograph (Columbus: Ohio State University, 1956).

37. Neal Gross and Robert Herriott, *Staff Leadership in Public Schools: A Sociological Inquiry* (New York: John Wiley & Sons, 1965).

38. Amitai Etzioni, *Modern Organizations* (Englewood Cliffs, N.J.: Prentice-Hall, 1964).

39. Richard Carlson, *Executive Succession and Organizational Change: Place Bound and Career Bound Superintendents of Schools* (Chicago: Midwest Administration Center, University of Chicago, 1962), p. 77.

40. R. M. Cyert and J. G. March, "A Behavioral Theory of Organizational Objectives," in *Modern Organization Theory* ed. Mason Haire (New York: John Wiley & Sons, 1959); also Ephriam Yuchtman and Stanley Seossbose, "A System Resource Approach to Organizational Effectiveness," *American Sociological Review* 32 (December 1967): 891-902.

41. George Homans, "Social Behavior as Exchange," *American Journal of Sociology* 63 (May 1958): 597-606. For a brief summary of exchange theory in comparison to several other approaches, see Abraham Zaleznik, "Interpersonal Relations in Organizations," in *Handbook of Organizations* ed. James G. March (Chicago: Rand McNally, 1965), Chapter 13.

42. William Evan, "The Organizational Set: Toward A Theory of Inter-Organizational Relations," in *Approaches to Organizational Design,* ed. James Thompson, (Harrisburg, Pa.: University of Pittsburgh Press, 1966).

43. Roland Warren, "The Interorganizational Field as a Focus for Investigation," *Administrative Science Quarterly* 12 (December, 1967): 396-449.

44. Sol Levine and Paul White, "Exchange as a Conceptual Framework for the Study of Interorganizational Relationships," *Administrative Science Quarterly* 5 (March 1961): 583-601.

45 J.D. Thompson and W. G. McEwen, "Organizational Goals and Environment," *American Sociological Review* 23 (February 1958): 23-30.

5

The View From Anthropology: A Perspective on Culture

Art Gallaher, Jr.

Anthropologists have long claimed "the study of man" as their special domain. This claim, viewed by others sometimes as unwarranted conceit, grows not from any view of the anthropologist that his is the only "man-study." Rather, it inheres in the perspective of anthropology, a perspective which is easily one of the most expansive in all the social sciences.[1]

THE SETTING

The viewpoint of anthropology is that man is to be understood in both his biological and cultural aspects and that understanding is to be achieved from broad perspectives in both time and space. The method is, therefore, comparative in its emphasis, seeking knowledge not only of the likenesses but also of the differences among men everywhere. This far-reaching perspective results in an emergent character unique for anthropology, a strong commitment to a holistic view of man and his works. The field is at once aligned partly with *biology*—in the study of evolution, skeletal structure, genes, muscles, functions, and other interests connected with the biogenetic inheritance of the human organism; partly with the *humanities*—in the study of culture history, the nature of human nature, and all facets of custom; and partly with the core *social sciences*, or behavioral sciences—especially with psychology and sociology in seeking generalizations on human behavior.

117

The division of labor to accommodate the sprawling and diversified interests implied above typically breaks as follows: physical
anthropologists (who study the biogenetic inheritance of man);
archeologists (who study the material evidence of man's existence
in time past); linguists (who study language and its relationship to
other forms of behavior); and cultural or social anthropologists
(who study cultures and social systems around the world). The
specialization inherent in this division of labor is causing anthropology, consonant with the other social sciences, to move toward
greater diversification and separation in its fields of study. However,
most anthropologists in the United States cling to the holistic tradition with enough stubbornness that anthropology still presents
an image of synthesizer in its "study of man." Professor Kroeber
made this point well some years ago when he said:

> It is evident that anthropology—however specific it may be in
> dealing with data—aims at being ultimately a co-ordinating
> science, somewhat as a legitimate holding corporation co-ordi-
> nates constituent companies. We anthropologists will never
> know China as intensively as a Sinologist does, or prices, credit,
> and banking as well as the economist, or heredity with the full-
> ness of the genetic biologist. But we face what these more inten-
> sive scholars only glance at intermittently and tangentially, if
> at all: to try to understand how Chinese civilization and eco-
> nomics and human heredity, and dozens of other highly devel-
> oped special bodies of knowledge, do indeed interrelate in being
> parts of "man"—flowing out of man, centered in him, products
> of him.[2]

The emphasis on the comparison, synthesis, and holistic views
of man indicated thus far does not mean that anthropologists are
mere eclectics with no real intellectual soul to call their own. It is
true, of course, that many anthropologists value eclecticism, and they
have and will, in fact, borrow freely from both the theory and the
method of fields closely related to their own special areas of interest.
However, much of what is borrowed and most of the concern and
involvement shown by anthropologists in interstitial areas relates
ultimately in some way to the concept of *culture*. This concept,
more than any other, is the master concept in anthropology, and it
remains one of the primary and more revolutionary concepts in all
behavioral science.[3]

At its more general level of abstraction, culture refers to the
feature which makes man so different from other social animals,

namely, a social life that is bio-cultural, rather than bio-social, in its origin. The latter refers to those pattern forms for social interaction that are species bound—whereas, the bio-cultural refers to those pattern forms that are learned, shared, transmitted, and, most significant of all, symbolically mediated.

At its lower level of abstraction, where the concern is not for culture but with *a* culture, the concept refers to those ideas, socially transmitted and learned, shared by the members of a human group and toward which, in their behavior, they tend to conform.[4] Culture, then, provides the selective guidelines—ways of feeling, thinking, and reacting—that distinguish one human group from another. This is true whether by group we refer to large social systems, such as nation-state societies, or more relevant for our purposes, to smaller social systems. The latter might be a community, a formal organization, such as a school system in a given community, or the small groups to be found in an organization. As a convenient way of denoting the lower levels of abstraction, the concept *subculture* is sometimes used to draw a relative distinction between a specific unit and the larger cultural setting in which it is found.

This brief introduction to the nature of anthropology as a discipline is sufficient to understand the breadth and scope of the field. We will now restrict our interest to that part of the field that is called cultural or social anthropology. More specifically, we will focus on the concept culture as one kind of understanding generated by anthropologists about specific groups.[5] First, however, we should look briefly at how anthropologists gain their understanding of *a* culture.

THE METHOD

From the beginning, anthropologists have been identified with the study of primitive peoples. This is not without some basis in fact, since before the 1930s, especially, most investigations were carried out on peoples in non-Western settings. These studies, more often than not, were of societies fairly small, relatively isolated, and not infrequently characterized by a high degree of autonomy. Since the Second World War, however, anthropologists have turned increasingly to studies in complex societies and in segments thereof. The latter might be communities or more restricted sub-cultures, such as schools and hospitals. Studies of these highly specialized groups in recent years have, in fact, become quite fashionable.

In order to understand culture and its dynamics in the settings just indicated, anthropologists traditionally have been oriented toward field research. Not only have anthropologists seen field experience as an important element in their intellectual life, but, for most, it constitutes a favorite professional activity. Thus, those who eschew field work for preoccupation with library research are somewhat looked down upon by the rest of the profession—the norm definitely emphasizes firsthand field experience.

The social or cultural anthropologist learns from people, and the way he goes about his task gives to his field a character distinct from the other social sciences.[6] Levi-Strauss makes this point succinctly when he says that "of all the sciences, it (social anthropology) is without doubt unique in making the most intimate subjectivity into a means of objective demonstration."[7] This means that the cultural anthropologist must at once be both of the "inside" and of the "outside." He must be involved enough with those whom he studies to be sure that he understands them, but he must not become so involved as to become one of them. Involvement, then, means participation but not on the order of "going native." A common myth that surrounds many anthropologists, especially those who fall into the "strange bird" or "off-beat" category among more conventional academic colleagues, is that they go native as a way of gaining understanding. An anthropologist rather participates in the unit he has under analysis to the extent that his respondents will permit, and he does this primarily so that he is better positioned to make *observations* on behavior and to *interview* people as to the nature of their intent and of their meanings. He thus seeks to get close to his sources of data, as contrasted to the sociologist, for example, whose approach to understanding more often stresses distance.

The *participant*-as-*observer*-and-*interviewer* technique of the anthropologist is used to derive data on the underlying principles of organization and the declared and undeclared meaning and functions of behavior, in both verbal and nonverbal dimensions, present in the social systems which he analyzes. The anthropologist, in this regard, is concerned more with patterned than unpatterned phenomena; hence, his method, more than that of his social science compatriots, tends to stress more the qualitative than the quantitative aspects of data. Anchored in whatever ways his hosts permit and exercising whatever means necessary to maintain ethical neutrality toward them, the anthropologist must, therefore, be sensitive to the flow of life as it unfolds before him.

The anthropologist, thus, depends heavily on observation and interviews that grow out of his marginal participation in the culture of the group being studied. And, whether his emphasis is on inter-view or observation, he strives for data from persons representing the different age, sex, and other status and role dimensions of the group. Depending on the special kind of understanding he desires, the anthropologist draws upon a wide range of techniques and pro-cedures generally found acceptable by the social sciences. Some of the more prominent of these are psychological tests and projective instruments, sociometric techniques, questionnaires, life histories, and demographic techniques.

The data generated by anthropologists are ordered and analyzed not in random fashion but according to a variety of interests made operational with reference to selected concepts. The more promi-nent of these concepts, found in the cultural anthropology sequences of reasonably well developed departments of anthropology, appear in such courses as the following: "Culture Change," "Culture and Personality," "Role Theory," "Primitive Law and Government," and a host of courses with "comparative" in the title, followed by such topical designates as "economics," "religion," "education," "social organization," etc. Through all interests, however, there runs the concern for culture. We turn our attention now, therefore, to culture as the master concept in anthropology. Our focus will be on a lower level of abstraction, that is, culture as a perspective on spe-cific human groups, rather than on the higher, more generalized level of abstraction that which is common to man.

THE CONCEPT

There exists for every human group a blueprint for the social activities appropriate for those who shall become identified as members. One is socialized into membership by having made avail-able to him for purposes of learning it, the culture of the group. Thus, as one learns the behaviors appropriate for identification, he increasingly shares in the selective orientation toward experience that is broadly characteristic of the membership. Culture, then, is internalized by the individual, and it becomes part of his environ-ment through the medium of other individuals and of cultural products.

There are, then, *regularities* in the behavior and the patterns for behavior shared by the members of any human social group. These regularities are not, however, mere caprice, but they are, in fact, interconnected through underlying structural principles. Under-standing such regularities, therefore, involves some comprehension of these *structures,* however they are conceptualized. In addition, the regularities must be understood against their *functions,* as manifest in the beliefs and intentions of the actors involved and as they lead to consequences unintended and, more often than not, unnoticed by the actors. An understanding of the regularities in a human social group must include also an awareness that regularities are, in fact, apt to *change* over time. They are, after all, adaptive for the actors who share them, and the factors which create the needs of actors are, of course, subject to change. The regularities are learned; therefore, they can be unlearned or otherwise modified.

Our understanding of culture will be organized around the conceptual devices invented or borrowed by anthropologists to explicate the ideas just indicated, that is, regularity, structure, function, and change. This approach to the phenomena of cultural anthropology is, therefore, consistent with other sciences, since they also view the nature of things around these four ideas.[8] Each of the areas of concern represents a broad spectrum of interest in cultural anthropology. However, given the purposes of this volume, breadth, in each case, will be arbitrarily compressed. I have focused only on some of the major concepts which are transferable for those with an interest in educational administration; I have made no effort, either through examples or otherwise, to effect a direct transfer for the reader.[9]

The intent is to not convey that anthropology has formulae ready and waiting for discovery, but rather that there is a perspective-culture available for those who would use it. What follows is one model for making that perspective available to you.

Regularity

In the anthropologist's analysis, the idea of regularity is expressed in one of the ways that he conceptualizes phenomena of the *explicit culture.* Explicit culture in this context refers to those regularities in word and deed that may be generalized straight from the evidence of the ear and the eye; that is to say, they are overt. This is in contrast to the *implicit culture,* which comprises "those cultural themes of which there is characteristically no sustained and systematic awareness on the part of most members of a group."[10]

Regularities in word and deed in the explicit culture are conceptualized as *culture patterns.* Thus, a culture pattern exists when any aspect of behavior, such as, thought and action, is shared overtly by more than one person. The concept does not imply that the aspect of shared behavior is necessarily rational or irrational, nor does it convey the notion of absolute uniformity. The concept rather connotes repetitive similarity in the behavior or of the ideals for behavior of two or more actors.

Culture patterns may exist as well nigh universals in the sense that most people in the total society share them. For example, most Americans will eat three meals per day, though this does not mean that the time nor the ritual for dining are adhered to by all. On a lower level of abstraction, a pattern may characterize a special interest group, or at an even lower level of abstraction, perhaps a clique within such a group. Thus, the teachers in Stonewall Elementary School verbalize the "self-contained" classroom as the *ideal* teaching situation; the fourth grade teachers at Stonewall, however, "team-teach" certain of their subjects.

It is important to keep in mind, too, that a pattern may exist in the minds of actors, such as the *ideal* mentioned above, and as defined by the anthropologist be a direct reflection of their awareness. On the other hand, it is important that we keep in mind the notion that a pattern description may reflect the scientific frame of reference of the anthropologist and, as such, not be articulated by those from whose actions and verbalizations he has derived it. For example, in the two situations just described, the anthropologist's interest may be in the *interaction* of the teachers in Stonewall School. He might, therefore, define the interaction pattern emergent in the self-contained classroom situation as one of "low interdependence," meaning that what one teacher does at a given moment has minimum direct relevance for what another is doing. In the second situation, the interaction of teachers in a team-teaching situation may be defined as a pattern of "high interdependence."

From what has been said, we can see that patterns abstracted from the explicit culture can be differentiated into those that are *normative* and those that are *behavioral.*[11] Normative patterns, thus, constitute the expressions of ideals for behavior, and they carry with them the elements of "ought" and "should." They comprise guidelines for what is correct and normal for one in a given social situation. In his real behavior in that situation, an actor may approximate the norm so closely that the normative and the behavioral patterns are essentially one and the same. In other cases, however, the normative pattern may represent a standard which, though desirable, in reality is not attainable. In still other cases, a behavioral pattern different from a normative pattern may indicate that the norm is undergoing challenge and perhaps redefinition.

The distinction drawn between normative and behavioral is more complicated than appears at first sight. It is not, for example, simply a matter of classifying regularities in culture either as one form of pattern or the other. Rather, it is possible and often desirable, to be more precise in our analysis of normative patterns especially.[12] For example, teachers in a given high school who are discussing the behavior proper for one of their number with a pedagogical problem that he cannot solve make it clear that the teacher has recourse to a number of options. Let us say the options available are to consult with a fellow teacher, the superintendent in charge of instruction, chairman of the subject-matter department, or the principal. Now, if all these options are recognized and all have equal value in the subculture of the school, we refer to them as *alternative* normative patterns. However, let us suppose that in our hypothetical situation there is but a single response recognized as appropriate. We are, then, talking of a *compulsory* normative pattern. On the other hand, of the normative responses available, let us say that consulting with the chairman of the subject-matter department is the one that is *preferred* over all others. We have, then, differentiated another type of normative pattern. Still another possibility in this situation that might be useful for analytical purposes derives from the frequency with which a pattern occurs. Thus, of the alternative patterns listed, it may be that one of them is simply more frequently expressed than are the others with no implication of value or other preference governing choice. If the latter condition obtains, then we can designate this type as a *typical* normative pattern. Finally, there is one other variation possible in the normative condition, and it reflects the prerogative, or lack of it, attached to a given pattern. For example, in our hypothetical situation, let us assume that consulting with the superintendent in charge of instruction is an option permitted only of teachers in their first year in the system; viewed another way, it could be that the option mentioned is required of teachers who experience problems during their first year of work. In either case, we can classify the pattern as a *restricted* normative pattern.

Before moving on to our discussion of structure, the reader should be reminded again that the regularities in culture, conceptualized by the anthropologist as normative or behavioral patterns, are in fact abstractions from the observed acts and/or statements of actors in given social situations. By definition, normative patterns must exist at some level of conscious awareness for actors. This does not mean, however, that actors necessarily can articulate such regularities in their abstract form. It is, however, the *business* of the anthropologist to construct *classes* of artifacts and of behaviors associated with actors and, in that way, delineate the regularities, that is, patterns of and for behavior, characteristic of the culture or subculture of specific groups.

Structure

The notion of structure conveys less the dynamic quality of human groups than does the notion of regularity. Whereas regularity connotes flow and motion, social action so to speak, structure connotes form, the arrangement of parts into some kind of framework. The advantage of structural analysis is that it enables the anthropologist to delineate the formal lines of relationship that exist among and between the parts, however such parts are conceptualized, of human groups. The disadvantage is that structural analysis might, at the same time, convey the impression of a static-like quality that does not fit reality in the human condition.

The concern for structure in social anthropology extends to both the social and the cultural aspects of human groups. In this regard, it is his interest in social structure that ties the anthropologist most closely to the sociologist.

At one level of abstraction, the anthropological concern for *social structure* is in the various groups, classes, castes, and the like, and the systems of relationships by which they are linked into the *social organization* of a total society. On the other hand, there are equally valid concerns at a lesser level of abstraction, where the focus is on age, sex, interests, and other criteria, by which people sort themselves out to get things done in specific institutional systems, such as the political, familial, legal, and the like. At whatever the level of concern, however, it is well to keep in mind that social structures are abstracted by anthropologists from data and, therefore, are to be thought of as models or constructs, rather than concrete things.[13]

The anthropological interest in social structure has developed through studies in societies that are not divided into as many groups as, for example, American society. This has enabled the anthropologist to be particularistic in his interests, that is, he can focus down on a specific institution, such as family, and within that restricted frame of reference systematically select and order certain key aspects of a social situation into a structural model.[14] Also, the kinds of societies studied by anthropologists are those in which behavior tends more toward stability and uniformity, and for that reason, one's behavior is predictable in large part from a knowledge of his *status*,[15] the position he has vis-a-vis another person or group in a social structure. Again, because of the nature of the societies in which they have done research, anthropologists are more apt than not to be concerned with the actual behavior of individuals and small groups of individuals than would be possible in studies of more complex societies. In the latter, as for example in American Society, patterns of and for behavior are often so diverse and fluid, the range of alternatives possible is so great, that the hookup between behavior and social structure is not always made.

The rights and obligations that accrue to an individual by virtue of his status in a given social structure comprise what is called a *role*.[16] Thus, in a social relationship, one's *role rights* are ideally the mirror-image of another's *role obligations*, and concomitantly, his obligations mirror the other's rights. The basic character of the reciprocity indicated here for a given social relationship derives mainly from the distribution of power, rank, prestige, and social distance between the interacting parties. The accurate definition of social relationships, as well as some understanding of their hierarchical ordering (class, caste, etc.), is, of course, essential to getting the business of a group accomplished. A focus on this point, therefore, permits the anthropologist some insight into conflict, change, and other interests that he might manifest in the culture of the group. And from a more practical vantage point, models of social structure so drawn derive their utility equally as models of communications networks.

For example, in a parish studied by the author in western Ireland, an analysis of social structure reveals a hierarchy of positions that can be conceptualized best as social classes. A model of social structure so derived has utility as it enables us to understand the nature of interpersonal relations in a number of social situations. For example, if our interest is to understand how the small farm system is being changed through the efforts of the agricultural advisory system (extension), we can look first to the nature of the social relationship that exists for one in the status of small farmer interacting with one in the status of agricultural advisor. It is soon apparent that the character of this relationship is governed to a great extent by each of the actors drawing upon his class position as a referent for behavior. The advisor, for example, is apt to show at the peasant's cottage dressed in a business suit "and maybe even suede shoes." The farmer, who "mucks" about farm-yard and fields in old clothes and "wellingtons" (rubber boots), easily gets the message. The attire and respective occupational categories of each

symbolizes the social distance between them. Translated into behavior, their positions influence the communications etiquette that
governs cross-class contacts. Analysis of this etiquette in turn shows
that direct communications flow in one direction, from superordi-
nate to subordinate status. This means that an advisor who is class-
conscious, as he relates to a peasant farmer, is apt to tell the latter
what his problems are, rather than listen to how the farmer views
them. An effective communications link is not established and,
therefore, recommendations often do not get accepted.

To reiterate a point made earlier, a focus on social structure
permits the anthropologist to freeze interpersonal or group relations
at a given point in time. He can then conceptualize the principles
which underlie such relations and utilize these, in turn, in his explanation of the regularities in custom and belief that characterize the
behavior of those who are in communication with each other.

Over the years, the anthropological concern for cultural integration has lead to attempts to view cultures as wholes. The interest
here is at a level of abstraction higher than that of pattern; it is
rather more with pattern relations, more specifically in the grouping
of many patterns into one that is characteristic of the whole culture.
This concern, which has come to be called *configurationalism*, can
be viewed in our context as a concern for the structural principles
by which the regularities in cultural behavior cohere. Our frame
of reference is the *implicit*, rather than the *explicit culture*. As in
our discussion of social structure, however, the reader should be
reminded that the configurations, principles of structure delineated
by the anthropologist, are abstracted from data and, therefore, are
to be thought of as models or constructs, rather than concrete
things.

In the beginning, the attempts at configurational analysis focused
mainly in efforts, such as that of Ruth Benedict,[17] to characterize
cultures as psychological wholes or in the view that a cultural
totality is somehow integrated by an underlying personality structure or structures. The storm of criticism that broke initially around
attempts in these directions stressed that the constructs were too
far removed from the requirements of factual science.

In later years, efforts at configurational analysis have turned on
other than personality constructs. The interests have been many,
and the attempts have been far-reaching. Here we will mention,
however, only a few of the more prominent constructs that have
been developed. For example, the integrative function of ideational,
or cognitive, aspects of culture have been stressed by both Morris

Opler and Clyde Kluckhohn. Opler, in his work among the Apaches, proposed the *cultural theme* as a construct to explain consistencies in the overt patterns of Apache culture.[18] A theme is a postulate or position, declared or implied, which predisposes people to similarly define situations. Thus, according to Opler, a theme underlying Apache behavior is that men are physically, mentally, and morally superior to women. This theme unites what otherwise seem disparate patterns of behavior in the explicit culture of the Apache. Thus, according to Opler, if a fetus has "lots of life," it is assumed to be a boy; women are considered less stable than men; they are easily tempted, especially in matters that bear on sex and witchcraft; men precede women on the footpath; men are the leaders and the tribal council functions for them; and so it goes through a number of other patterns. This theme is not, incidentally, merely male vanity that is expressed in each of the above patterns, but reflects also a view of the world concurred in by Apache women.

Kluckhohn in his work among the Navaho proposes a similar notion when he tells us that the consistencies in Navaho life can be explained as the result of *tacit premises*.[19] All such premises combine to form the world view or "philosophy" of the Navaho. One such premise, for example, is that the universe is full of dangers. Thus, one should be cautious in those areas of life over which he presumes to have little or no control; one can depend only on relatives; therefore, he should be wary of those not related to him; when in a dangerous situation do nothing, and if that doesn't work then seek safety in flight. According to Kluckhohn, tacit premises, such as the one delineated, explain consistency in the patterns for behavior which make up the explicit culture of the Navaho.

Other configurational constructs have stressed the action, or conative, and the emotional, or affective, aspects of cultural systems. Ralph Linton, for example, proposed the notion that in every culture certain *interests* are of primary importance, that these taken together constitute an integrated system.[20] In his analysis of Commanche culture, he noted that many interests converged on young men in the warrior class. These interests appeared not only in the activities of the warriors themselves, but also in a variety of other activities, such as familistic, economic, and in the subcultural aspects of comparable age-grades among the young women of the tribe. Dominant interests, such as the one indicated, would then, according to Linton, provide an *orientation* for Commanche culture.

Clyde Kluckhohn and others began a project in the late 1940s which had, among other goals, the development and refinement of concepts and methods for the study of *values*.[21] Out of this project, which compared five cultures in the American southwest, there has emerged one of the more promising and methodologically sound constructs for configurational analysis, *value-orientations*. The basic premise involved is that the value aspects of a cultural system have to do with the selecting, regulating, and goal-discriminating processes of the members of a group. Value-orientations are conceptualized as meaningful clusters of associated values. Furthermore, they are thought to occur in "patterned arrangements and that these arrangements may add as much to the unique qualities of a culture as the presence or absence of given values."[22] We can illustrate by drawing upon an example from Homestead, one of the cultures studied in the project.[23] Homestead is a rural community of Texas and Oklahoma migrants who moved to New Mexico during the dust-bowl era of the 1930s.

Evon Vogt, who has reported most extensively on the Homestead phase of the project, reports that the value-orientations for Homestead were abstracted from three kinds of empirical evidence. These were a Cultural Orientations Questionnaire administered to a random sample of the community; intensive interviews with a selected sample of informants who represented strategic positions in the economic and social structure of Homestead; and observations of recurring situations as these emerged in all general field notes accumulated during the project. These three kinds of data yielded the identification of

> ... the major value-orientations, which are conceptualized as general value-statements summarizing the patterned relationships which the Homesteaders strive to achieve and maintain with key aspects of their total life situation: relations to other men, to nature, to time, to work (i.e. the allocation of activities from day to day), and to other cultural groups.[24]

An example of one such value-orientation is what Vogt calls "individualism." This particular value-orientation rests on the following "associated values." One should have his own farm; one should be his own boss; each man should have equal voice in community affairs; one should keep up with his neighbors, and one should be free of the law. Vogt demonstrates how each of the associated values is, in turn, incorporated into a number of patterns for behavior in Homestead.

The above mentioned constructs represent for our purposes some of the more important attempts by anthropologists to account for pattern relations. The strategy is to derive structural principles which enable us to explain the broad consistencies in group behavior. Whether the construct springs from personality, or from the cognitive, affective, or conative characteristics of cultural systems, the result is perceived as very much the same — threads, however conceptualized, interlace patterns in the explicit culture and tie them into larger, integrated wholes.

Function

The distinction between structure, as just discussed, and function is mainly that between form and process. However, it will become apparent in the following discussion that in anthropology the two are not unrelated.

The concern for function in anthropology breaks along two axis. There is, on the one hand, a long-standing interest in the interdependence of parts that make up a given system, and, on the other hand, there is concern for the orientation of such parts, however conceptualized, toward given ends.[25]

The concern for interdependence began with an organic model applied to social systems. And so long as anthropologists confined their research to societies not yet under the full impact of European contact, the model worked reasonably well. As opposed to a historical approach, which asks the question of how an element of culture, such as pattern, came to be what it is at a given point in time, the "functionalist" approach questions how an element of culture works.

In seeking answers to the question of how, functionalists concentrate not only on discovering connections between things that otherwise seem to be quite unrelated but, also, on the meaning and the implications of such connections for the working of patterns. For example, it is not enough to know that the custom of *lobola* in South Africa is ostensibly payment made in compensation to a girl's family for her loss upon marriage; rather it also fixes the social position of the children born of a marriage. Thus, if a proper *lobola* payment is made, the children of a marriage belong to the father's family and take their proper place in the social and religious life of that group. However, if no *lobola* is paid, then the child belongs to the mother's family, and its status is then irregular.[26]

The organic model referred to above, combined with the experience of intensive research in small scale societies, lead many anthropologists to an equilibrium model of social systems, that is, one harmoniously integrated by a set of smoothly interacting and remarkably self-adjusting social institutions. In this scheme of things, less than total integration was not "healthy," and changes that did occur were generally seen as having an external origin. The homeo-stasis implied in this approach, though enabling the tracing out of consequences of external intrusions, obscured not only tensions and strains within the social system but, also, the concomitant variable probabilities for innovation as their consequence. However, as anthropologists have moved toward the analysis of more complex, highly differentiated societies in the West, where change is a more normal state of affairs and where there is growing sensitivity to the need for planning change, they have given over the equilibrium model to one that enables recognition of conflict and strain as nor-mal consequences of social life. This is, in fact, a major current trend in anthropological analysis.[27]

The second concern for function, that of the orientation of ele-ments of culture toward given ends, has received more attention by anthropologists than the concern for interrelations just dis-cussed. There is, on the one hand, the long-standing interest in how an element of culture, such as a pattern, serves or fails to serve the needs of the individual in a group. On the other hand, there are those who seek to understand how an element of culture functions to meet the needs of the group itself. The latter concern has led to a pairing of structure and function, with function viewed by some as a consequence of structure. Thus, one hears of "structural-functional" analysis. The logic of the latter proceeds from the delineation of the functional requirements for the operation of a given social system to relating these requirements to a given structure.

In doing functional analysis of the kind indicated here, the re-searcher must keep in mind, then, that a given pattern for behavior may function to meet the needs of individuals, as well as the group. Furthermore, needs can be conceptualized at two levels of abstrac-tion. There are those that are recognized and intended by the actors themselves, and the patterns that lead to their satisfaction are, therefore, said to have *manifest* functions; there are others that are generally unrecognized by the actors, and generally unintended, and the patterns that lead to their satisfaction are said to have *latent* functions.[28] The latter are meanings derived through scien-tific analysis and are assigned by the analyst to behavior.

An example will help to clarify some of the points just made. In a rural Ozark community, that I once did research in, the manifest function of membership on the school board for an individual was to work with the superintendent on budget and other policy matters. From the standpoint of the community a similar manifest function would be attributed to the school board as a unitary body.[29] However, a latent function of membership on the board was the acquisition of a kind of political power that had nothing whatsoever to do with education, but which, when exercised by an individual, could be detrimental to the school and its purposes. The power in question had to do mainly with decisions that involved the allocation of economic rewards, and for some board members, the temptation for self-aggrandizement was too great to resist. At the same time, the school board performed the latent function of supporting anti-intellectual sentiment in the community in ways that were detrimental to the educational program. Examples that come to mind are occasional forays of the board into curricular matters and the kinds of judgments made about the competence of professionals. There were times, in fact, when the school board operated as though its mandate was to protect the community from an intellectual elite made up of the teachers.

Change

Of the four conceptual lenses through which we are examining culture, the anthropological interest in change has produced the greatest variety of ideas and concepts. The following discussion will, therefore, be selective in its emphasis.

Anthropologists see, in any culture, forces that make for both stability and change. However, since culture is socially transmitted and learned and since what is learned can be unlearned or otherwise modified through experience, anthropologists have long accepted the inevitability of change in culture. Their view on this score is given support on two other counts, one of which grows from the knowledge that culture is the major adaptive mechanism available to a group. Since there are strong arguments for the notion that man's adjustment to the non-human aspects of his environment alone is never fully complete — what Wilbert Moore calls the constant environmental challenge — change in some aspect of culture is, therefore, always immanent. Furthermore, the knowledge that no known group is free from social deviation gives added strength to the argument that change in culture is inevitable.

Anthropologists perceive change in culture as involving three, rather broadly conceived processes. These are (1) *innovation*, the process whereby a new element of culture or combination of elements is made available to a group; (2) *dissemination*, the process whereby an innovation comes to be shared; and (3) *integration*, the process whereby an innovation becomes mutually adjusted to other elements in the system.[30]

If we look at the concern for innovation in anthropology, we find that interest centers mainly in whether innovations are internally or externally derived. If they are internally derived, then the processes are those of *discovery* and *invention*. Discoveries constitute unique additions to knowledge and because of that do not occur often. Inventions, on the other hand, are new combinations of knowledge already in existence and are, therefore, much more common. A discovery might be the principle of the wheel; whereas, the almost infinite variety of applications derived from the principle constitute inventions. There has been some concern in anthropology for delineating sociocultural and psychological variables which underlie the latter,[31] but most of the interest in innovation has centered on the stimulus for change generated by groups in contact.

The process which accounts for the transfer of culture elements from one group to another is known as *diffusion*;[32] if, however, the researcher is interested in the processes of change in the culture of one group as a consequence of innovations diffused from another, the concept utilized is that of *acculturation*.[33] Out of the diffusion and acculturation research, there emerged the distinction between non-directed and directed change in culture.

By directed change is meant a structured situation in which an advocate interferes actively and purposefully with the culture of potential acceptors. In this situation, the advocate consciously selects elements in a target system, that which is to be changed, and by stimulating the acceptance of innovations, inhibiting the practice of prior patterns of behavior, or, as is frequently the case, doing both of these things simultaneously, he manages the direction of change. The success with which this is done depends mainly on (1) how the advocate plays his role, and (2) the behavior of those who make up the target system. To understand the latter, we shift our emphasis to dissemination, the conditions which influence the acceptance and rejection of innovations by potential acceptors.

Anthropologists generally accept the premises that (1) people more readily accept innovations that they can understand and which they perceive as relevant; and (2) that acceptance is made easier if people have had a hand in planning their own future. This means that the *structure of contact* between two groups bears importantly on the elements of culture permitted to pass between them.[34] So far as directed change is concerned, the task of an advocate is made easier if he is *prestigeful* in ways that are valued by the target system. In this regard, related to the matter of prestige and very often a function of it, is the more important variable of the *dependence upon authority* that is shared in the target system.[35] For example, in the Ozark rural community mentioned earlier, technological innovations in agriculture were acceptable to most people if they were first accepted by men who were established as successful. In this case, the *authority* of success and prestige combined to make them emulative models. Viewed in a different way, the matter of authority assumes added relevance. If, for example, we view authority as the control that some members in a group have over the activities of others, it follows that those with rank and power in the group can exercise sanctions. This means, in effect, that those in authority can sometimes effect change by manipulating rewards. In this regard, however, it is important to distinguish between genuine and spurious change. The former is effected only if an acceptor comes to value an innovation, whereas the latter may be accommodative to real or presumed threat, desire for rewards, or other variables that accompany an innovation.

Another variable that affects dissemination, whether the change is directed or non-directed, is the *expectation of change* shared by the members of a group.[36] In directed change especially, it is important to know those aspects of culture where people value change and where they have come to expect it. These are channels into which innovations can be fed with the greatest chance of success. On the other hand, it is equally important to know the *margins of security* within which potential acceptors must weigh decisions. It may be that one accepts the idea behind an innovation, what Kroeber calls *stimulus diffusion*,[37] but his margins of security, as measured by money, prestige, power, or other relevant criteria, are such that he cannot afford to assume risks. Irish peasants whom I know, for example, are conservative in assessing agricultural innovations because of the fear of their neighbors ridicule should they experience failure.

A number of other variables that influence the acceptance and rejection of innovation involve the general matter of scale. For example, what is the extent of the group's *felt need* for change? Is the *time* factor right; that is, is the system already undergoing change, or is there apathy induced by previous innovative failure? What is the *fit*, not only of form, but also in meaning and function between an innovation and the host system? There is also the matter of the *extent* of change being induced. Finally, it is especially important for those who attempt to direct change to keep in mind continually the perspective embodied in what has been said before. That is, any element of culture has the properties of form, meaning, and function, and in a situation of change, these are not to be considered as necessarily intrinsically bound together.[38] In other words, change can occur in one property but not in the others, and so on.

Many of the variables just mentioned as influencing the dissemination process anticipate the concerns of anthropologists for understanding the integration of innovations into a host system. There are three subprocesses employed to explain integration. These are *replacement*, in which the innovation is substituted for a prior pattern of behavior, as in the case of "new math" for conventional math; *alternatives*, in which the innovation is accepted as an alternative to a prior pattern, with the latter continuing in existence; and *syncretism*, as when the elements of an innovation are fused with elements of a prior pattern. For example, a peak into the teacher's *cell*, classroom, will surely reveal that more than one innovation intended to be a replacement has ended up as an alternative not being utilized or, perhaps, has been modified by fusing with traditional practices. For those who would plan changes in the culture or subculture of others, it is important to know which process offers the best chance for success with minimum disruption in the system undergoing change. The importance of this caution cannot be stressed too strongly. Problems encountered during the integrative phase of culture change can easily lead to collective negative response. Important triggering mechanisms in this phase are the sensitivities of potential acceptors to discrepancies between normative and behavioral patterns, manifest and latent functions, and the functional interdependence of parts in a system, all referred to in our earlier discussion.

POSTSCRIPT

The temptation is great to tie off the above perspective on culture with a long list of postulates. I shall, however, resist the temptation in favor of a much shorter list, one that hopefully will, therefore, command greater attention. The following postulates, though simply stated, are complex in their implications for understanding human social life at whatever level of abstraction. First, the culture perspective is that the significant differences in behavior that differentiate human groups are understandable as *learned* cultural

Core Content from the Social Sciences

patterns, rather than biologically derived characteristics. Second, the cultural patterns characteristic of a group are *adaptive* for conditions both internal and external to it. Third, the patterns of and for behavior are interrelated so as to form a system which, given the beliefs of the members of the group, has an *integrity* of its own. Fourth, an understanding of the regularities in cultural behavior in a given group must take into account not only the explicit beliefs and intentions of its members, but also the unintended and largely unaware (for them) consequences of their beliefs and actions. Finally, the patterns that comprise the culture of any group are subject to change not only in their content but in the ways in which they are interrelated.

FOOTNOTES

1. An easy-to-read general introduction to anthropology is Clyde Kluckhohn's *Mirror For Man* (New York: McGraw-Hill, 1949). See also Pertti J. Pelto, *The Nature of Anthropology* (Columbus, Ohio: Charles E. Merrill Publishing Co., Inc., 1965).

2. A. L. Kroeber, ed., *Anthropology Today* (Chicago: University of Chicago Press, 1953), p. xiv.

3. For a brief overview of the concept culture see Ernest L. Shusky and T. Patrick Culbert, *Introducing Culture* (Englewood Cliffs, New Jersey: Prentice-Hall, Inc. 1967).

4. See A. L. Kroeber and Clyde Kluckhohn, *Culture: A Critical Review of Concepts and Definitions,* Papers of the Peabody Museum of Archaeology and Ethnology, Harvard University, vol. 47, no. 1, 1952, for an analysis and classification of some 160 definitions of the concept culture.

5. Rachel Sady, *Perspectives from Anthropology* (New York: Teachers College Press, Columbia University, 1969) is a readable account of what anthropology is all about, with particular focus on the significance of anthropology for education.

6. Benjamin D. Paul, "Interview Techniques and Field Relationships," in *Anthropology Today,* pp. 430-451, is a good statement on anthropological method and techniques. In the same volume see also, Oscar Lewis, "Controls and Experiments in Field Work," pp. 452-475.

7. Claude Levi-Strauss, *The Scope of Anthropology* (London: Jonathan Cape, 1967), p. 26.

8. A similar conceptual framework is used in John Bennett and Melvin Tumin, *Social Life: Structure and Function* (New York: Alfred A. Knopf, 1949). The viewpoint expressed here is, of course, the "naturalistic" view of the world as articulated in western science over the past four hundred years.

9. For more direct application to education see George Spindler, ed., *Education and Culture: Anthropological Approaches* (New York: Holt, Rine-

hart and Winston, 1963). See also *Social Education* 32 (February 1968), a special issue devoted to the same topic.

10. See Clyde Kluckhohn, "The Study of Culture," in *The Policy Sciences,* eds. Daniel Lerner and Harold Laswell (Stanford: Stanford University Press, 1951), pp. 86-101.

11. The classic statement on the concept culture pattern is by Clyde Kluckhohn in his "Patterning as Exemplified in Navaho Culture," in *Language, Culture, and Personality,* ed. Leslie Spier (Menasha, Wisconsin: Sapir Memorial Publication Fund, 1941), pp. 109-130.

12. The discussion of patterns here follows closely the material in Kluckhohn, ibid.

13. The anthropological literature on social structure is indeed vast, and much of it is highly technical. A reasonably concise and not too technical overview of anthropological concerns in this area can be gotten from a good introductory text in social anthropology, such as Paul Bohannan's *Social Anthropology* (New York: Holt, Rinehart, and Winston, 1963).

14. The greatest attention to structural models in social anthropology has been in kinship analysis. In fact, kinship and social organization are considered by many anthropologists to be virtually synonymous. A non-technical introduction to anthropological perspective in this area is Ernest L. Shusky's *Manual for Kinship Analysis* (New York: Holt, Rinehart, and Winston, 1965).

15. For an excellent analysis of the concept status in anthropology, see Ward Goodenough, "Rethinking Status and Role: Toward a General Model of the Cultural Organization of Social Relationships," in *The Relevance of Models for Social Anthropology,* ed. Michael Banton (London: Tavistock Publications, 1965), pp. 1-23.

16. A good introduction to the concept of role as it is used in anthropology is Michael Banton's *Roles: An Introduction to the Study of Social Relations* (New York: Basic Books, Inc., 1965).

17. See her well known *Patterns of Culture* (Boston: Houghton-Mifflin, 1934). Benedict reflects the influence of Edward Sapir.

18. See his "Themes as Dynamic Forces in Culture," *American Journal of Sociology* 51 (November 1945): 198-206.

19. See, especially, his "The Philosophy of the Navaho Indians," in *Ideological Differences and World Order,* ed. F. S. Northrop (New Haven: Yale University Press, 1949).

20. Chapters 24 and 25 in his *Study of Man* (New York: Appleton-Century-Crofts, Inc., 1936).

21. For a description of the project see, especially, the Preface by Clyde Kluckhohn to Evon Z. Vogt, *Navaho Veterans: A Study of Changing Values,* Peabody Museum of Harvard University, Papers, vol. 41, no. 1, 1951.

22. Evon Vogt, *Modern Homesteaders: The Life of a Twentieth-Century Frontier Community* (Cambridge: The Belknap Press of Harvard University Press, 1955), p. 7.

23. Ibid.

24. Ibid., p. 191.

25. For an excellent summary of the concept function, see Raymond Firth's "Function," in *Current Anthropology,* ed. W. L. Thomas (Chicago: University of Chicago Press, 1955).

26. This example is drawn from A. R. Radcliffe-Brown, *Structure and Function in Primitive Society* (London: Cohen and West, Ltd., 1952), p. 30.

27. As examples see the following: Max Gluckman, *Custom and Conflict in Africa* (Glencoe, Ill.: Free Press, 1955); Victor Turner, *Schism and Continuity in an African Society*, (New York: Humanities Press, 1957); Robert A. LeVine, ed., "Anthropology and the Study of Conflict: An Introduction," *Journal of Conflict Resolution* 5 (March 1961): 3-15; and Alan R. Beals and Bernard J. Siegel, *Divisiveness and Social Conflict: An Anthropological Approach* (Stanford: Stanford University Press, 1966).

28. The distinction between manifest and latent functions was drawn first by the sociologist Robert Merton. See his *Social Theory and Social Structure*, (Glencoe, Ill.: Free Press, 1957).

29. Art Gallaher, Jr., *Plainville Fifteen Years Later* (New York: Columbia University Press, 1961).

30. For a fuller discussion of these concepts, see Ralph Linton, *Acculturation in Seven American Indian Tribes* (New York: Appleton-Century-Crofts, Co., 1940), last three chapters.

31. See, especially, Homer Barnett, *Innovation: The Basis of Culture Change* (New York: McGraw-Hill Co., 1953).

32. The most complete synthesis of diffusion research is by a sociologist Everett Rogers. See his *Diffusion of Innovations* (New York: The Free Press of Glencoe, 1962).

33. Acculturation is one of the major concepts used by anthropologists in their studies of change process. One of the first attempts to systematize the concept was by a Social Science Research Council Sub-Committee on Acculturation, composed of Melville Herskovits, Robert Redfield, and Ralph Linton. The results of the seminar were published in 1937 and were recently made available again under the original title, *Acculturation: The Study of Culture Contact* (Gloucester, Mass.: Peter Smith, 1958). The bibliographic reference is to Melville J. Herskovits. Another Social Science Research Council Seminar grappled with the concept in 1953. The results of that seminar are reported as "Acculturation: An Exploratory Formulation," *American Anthropologists* 56, 6 (December 1954): 973-1003. Another useful publication is Bernard Siegel, ed., *Acculturation Abstracts*, (Stanford: Stanford University Press, 1955).

34. See Edward H. Spicer, "Types of Contact and Processes of Change," in *Perspectives in American Indian Culture Change*, ed. E. H. Spicer (Chicago: University of Chicago Press, 1961).

35. Barnett, *Innovation: The Basis of Culture Change*, Chapter 3, for a discussion of this variable in connection with innovation.

36. Barnett, *Innovation: The Basis of Culture Change*, Chapter 2.

37. A. L. Kroeber, *The Nature of Culture* (Chicago: University of Chicago Press, 1952), pp. 344-358.

38. The concepts of form, meaning, and function are clarified in Linton's *Study of Man*, Chapter 23.

6

Political Science: An Overview of the Discipline

David W. Minar

There are few fields of scholarly endeavor, perhaps none, with such ambiguous legacies and such high levels of internal conflict as political science. The study of politics, of course, is an ancient enterprise, and it has been a continuous preoccupation of men through the ages. Yet, we are still far from agreement even about what the subject matter is, to say nothing of the appropriate questions to ask about it and how to ask them.[1] Any attempt to deal with the discipline as a whole must be qualified, therefore, in various ways. It is certain not to elicit consent among all political scientists, and it is sure to reflect in some degree the values and experiences of its author. These are caveats that the reader should keep in mind.

What follows has a two-fold purpose: It sets out, in brief, the main questions at issue in the discipline, and it presents an approach to them. It is not, however, an effort to survey or summarize or to provide a guide to the field of political science in its entire scope. Nor is it a historical account of the way the study of politics took its present form. In substance, it is intended to discuss the study of contemporary politics as many political scientists pursue it.

POLITICAL SCIENCE — THE STATE OF THE DISCIPLINE

Aims of the Study of Politics

Some of the ambiguity of the discipline of political science may be revealed by an examination of the aims of the study of politics as they are viewed by those who engage in it. At the outset, it strikes a rather strange note, perhaps, to talk about the "aims" of a scholarly discipline. Presumably, the disciplines are dedicated to the collection, ordering, and dissemination of knowledge. In fact, however, there are few, if any, of them that could stop with such a description and satisfy all interested parties, and the dissents, exceptions, and qualifications to this delineation·of the aims of political science would ring loud and clear. These would reflect a variety of intellectual and action perspectives on what the study of politics is supposed to be about.

One version of political science, the one with the greatest currency in the discipline, would start with the general position mentioned above, that the generation of knowledge is the basic aim, and move beyond this only to elaborate on the nature of meaningful knowledge about politics. We refer to the view that it is possible to develop more or less generalized systematic explanations of political phenomena.[2] This is an outlook that tends to take its cues from natural science, and one that sees political science as one of the "behavioral sciences," though it does not necessarily take individual behavior as its primary object of analysis. It emphasizes explanation, as distinct from understanding or description, searching for regularities of condition or variation — asking what state accompanies what other state, what difference in phenomena makes differences for other phenomena. The ultimate objective of such effort is the depiction of cause, though most social scientists are diffident, for one reason and another, about actually claiming to develop generalized causal explanations. "Why" questions are the ones whose answers are sought through this approach: Why are there revolutions? Why wars? Why are some policies developed and not others? Why do some modes of political activity flourish in some environments, other modes in others? This approach to politics deals mostly in relationships, and it emphasizes the generation and testing of theory (i.e., abstract statements with some degree of generality) about them.

An explanatory political science necessarily involves description; the collection of facts about phenomena to be compared in the testing of theory. Description may also be an aim in itself; some political science, through the conscious choice of those who practice it or otherwise, does not move beyond this kind of activity. A large proportion of the work done by American political scientists in this century falls in this category. Some descriptive efforts deal with a broad sweep of events and institutions, some with highly specific, particularized situations. Some represent a kind of reflective journalism; some show the heavy influence of a historical outlook. All tend to treat the field as if its goal were to provide a chronicle of what is happening in politics.

A third tendency in the study of politics seeks understanding, rather than explanation or description. The line that separates understanding from other modes of dealing with politics is sometimes obscure, and there is no firm point of reference around which it is oriented. This outlook rests on one or a combination of propositions about politics that we might summarize as follows: (1) The most significant aspects of politics are too subtle to capture merely through systematic explanatory networks or descriptive statements; (2) politics has important qualitative, as well as quantifiable dimensions; (3) there are few, if any, significant regularities in human behavior, at least as far as political life is concerned; and (4) the study of politics is inextricably bound up with politics as action, study itself being a form of action that projects itself into its material. Political action is choice-making behavior, and choice-making involves the development and application of standards; hence, the study of politics is, in some sense, a process of evaluation. One of the prime problems of political science is to consider this intricate action-value-scholarship nexus in insightful ways.

Finally, some political scientists are committed to evaluation, to the judgment of political acts, arrangements, and policies. From its early manifestations in ancient Greece, Western political thought has been much concerned with the moral dimension of politics, and this interest remains active. It reflects, no doubt, the tremendous importance of politics to social life and the capacity of political organs to affect men's outlooks. Thus, thinking about the workings of political systems has often turned to questions about whether they ought to perform the way they do, what goals they ought to seek, what limits they ought to observe.

The standards of evaluation utilized by students of politics are as various as the imaginations of men. Some work in this field first seeks principles, some the explication of principles set out in classic sources, and some the application of standards to existing or imagined systems and policies. Some has sought modes of evaluation beyond the invocation of a priori principles. Thus, interest in evaluation ranges from the thoroughly philosophical examination of the abstract relationships between politics and other aspects of life to the critical examination of contemporary institutions. Evaluation also points toward the activity of prescription, the development of guidelines for future action in politics.

This neat set of categories should not be taken to mean that any given piece of work in political science can be placed in one or the other. In fact, a great deal of the work in the field overlaps two or more. Description and evaluation, for example, often go hand-in-hand. At the same time, it must be said that these images of the aims of the discipline do form focal points for controversy among scholars about what it can and ought to try to accomplish. We will not attempt to review the substance of these arguments here, but it should be understood that these differences are of great importance in the collective life of the political science profession. The remainder of the chapter is written chiefly from the point of view that takes explanations as the goal of political inquiry.

The Boundary Problem

It will have been noted that these paragraphs about the aims of political science have begged a critical question, namely, what it is that students of politics study. Whatever the aims of the discipline, presumably, it is about *something*. The matter of defining politics is by no means a simple one, and here again perspectives differ. What we are seeking, however, is not a definition by essences but a useful, agreeable verbal tool to help us set the field in order.

Politics is variously defined in terms of the institutions that carry it out, for example, government, in terms of functions that it presumably fulfills, such as, reducing conflicts among men, in terms of the purposes it seeks, insuring justice, or in terms of the kinds of human acts it comprehends. Most commonly, perhaps, people think of politics as simply the "active" aspect of government, but many students of politics regard this definition as unduly restrictive for two reasons: (1) it is hard to tell where government-related activities end and others begin, (2) the definition excludes a range of activities not strictly oriented to government but very similar to the type of things we commonly call political.[3]

These problems illustrate the difficulties one confronts as he attempts to set out specific boundaries for the political domain. Consider, to take the matter further, the fourth approach to a definition of politics listed above. This is probably the most inclusive and most fertile outlook on the discipline, the one that takes political science farthest along the way toward explanation. Human acts are observable, describable, recordable, and they exhibit discernible regularities. What is it, then, that makes them political?

The first step in answering this question is easy to take; politics is clearly social activity, hence, the kind that involves interactions among people. It also has something to do with their capacity to live together in groups and arrive at joint courses of action in respect to some matters of common concern. It does not, however, always involve the application of some kind of coercion, nor does it always result in agreement. From this standpoint, it does not always flow through given kinds of institutions, that is, through certain regularized patterns of interactive behavior. Thus, the going soon gets hard. We are left with the vague position that political acts are all those through which people attempt to settle their relationships with others.

Some students of politics have suggested such phrases as "the authoritative allocation of values" to delimit the kind of activity properly labeled politics.[4] While suggestive, this phrase does not have much boundary-setting power, for it raises in turn the equally vexing question of what authoritative ought to mean, a problem we will discuss at greater length below. Still, politics is a sphere of social interaction very much intermingled with other aspects of life.

What these comments suggest is the difficulty of finding a clear boundary between political acts and others. The interaction of people to settle their relationships with one another is to be found in couples, in families, in clubs and groups of various kinds, in clusters of people casually thrown together, as well as in formally governed states. The family, for example, may have highly regularized means of dividing labor, apportioning resources, and doing other things that affect its life together. Consider, for another example, a gathering of people waiting on a downtown corner for a bus; most of them will never have seen each other before, and they probably will not consult with each other about how to board the bus when it comes. Nonetheless, boarding the bus is something they will do in relationship to one another. They may do it in an orderly way, women and children first, by mutual understanding, or they may push and shove and, perhaps, even fight. Their behavior will probably grow more interactive as the thing they seek is more valuable, for example, as space on the bus becomes more scarce. Is there not an element of politics in this situation?

No, some would reply, for politics implies command and obedience. Yet, if we compare the social scene described above with one that is clearly political, we may doubt whether such a distinction helps much. We may say, for example, that when the government tells people to pay taxes, they obey, but this does not always describe what happens, for some conceal income; some refuse to pay, and so on. We might also say that the distinction between a political relationship and others is that sanctions are levied against those who disobey a political command; again, the point is doubtful, for sanctions are evident in many social situations. The person who cheats on the bus queue may be called names. Is the child denied approval by the family or the lover denied affection any less punished than the tax dodger fined or the felon incarcerated? Yet another answer might be that a political command *ought* to be obeyed, but likewise, many would say that able-bodied men ought not to elbow old ladies aside when the bus stops.

These comments do not reach all the potential distinctions between politics and other social activities, but they illustrate the problems of setting boundaries for political science. This need not, however, be a critical deficiency, for it is not clear that boundary definitions are essential to the pursuit of a scholarly discipline. The position we may take is that just as the substance of politics is intermingled with other kinds of social action, the study of politics is intermingled with sociology, economics, anthropology, social psychology, whatever fields are interested in the systematic treatment of society. The social sciences may be fuzzy at their borders just as biology and chemistry or physics and astronomy tend to run together at spots. Such an admission does not compromise scholarly effort but awakens it.

Further, to doubt that boundaries are important to the study of politics does not condemn political science to an aimless formlessness. Whether we can recognize the boundaries of politics or not, there are recognizable nodes of political activity around us, identifiable institutions, processes, and modes of behavior that can anchor the efforts of the student of political life. Thus, he may center his attention on the way public decisions are made or the way attitudes about politics are formed or the common meanings of political symbols, and he may examine the relationships among these facets of social life. These inquiries may take him into the domains of the family, economic motivation, culture, or personality. What marks his role is the fact of his inquiry, not the boundary within which he works. Some of these nodes and directions of political inquiry will be reviewed in pages to follow. For the present, the important point is that political science shares its subject matter with its sister social sciences.

Methods

As the preceding pages might seem to suggest, it is difficult to describe the methods of political science with concision. The following two points are apparent: one, that the techniques of inquiry vary with the aims and focus of the investigation; the second, that the techniques of political science have much in common with those of other social sciences. A few further comments and illustrations may be helpful in highlighting some of the problems of method in the study of politics.[5]

As interest in the political science discipline has turned more toward systematic inquiry and toward explanation (a trend that may be dated roughly from the time of the Second World War), increasing attention has been paid to the use of appropriate techniques. Where formerly a great deal of the scholarly treatment of politics was based on speculation, intuition, and casual observation, recent work has emphasized the collection of evidence grounded one way or another in sensory perception, sometimes direct and sometimes indirect. The ultimate tests of such methods are whether they accurately reflect the phenomena to which they are applied, whether they react with the phenomena to contaminate what is being observed, and whether they can be utilized in different places and at different times to provide comparable observations. At the optimum, they yield measurements of a quantitative sort that may be submitted to sophisticated statistical techniques of analysis. Such techniques may show, for example, differences in magnitude, direction, trend, and so on, among phenomena being compared. Some of the materials of importance to the political scientist, however, do not readily lend themselves to very concise quantitative depiction or analysis, and much current work in the field hovers between systematic inquiry and impression.

One quality of the current political science that merits special attention is that it is in some sense comparative; that is, it relies on measuring its subject against some standard, either another "natural" subject or a model or invented standard. Traditionally, comparative politics dealt with the gross characteristics of nation states. However, it has more recently been recognized that all sorts of political study involve comparison. A question about the effects of a given structure of local government is approached by comparing towns of that structure with others of a different kind. The relationship of environment to the development of political attitudes would be assayed through the comparison of attitudes in different environments.

The techniques in common use in the study of politics today are many. Perhaps the best we can do in limited space is to enumerate and briefly explain some main sources of data and associated techniques in current use.

(1) Aggregate data. A considerable variety of information on politics and matters related to politics is summarized in statistical data readily available in the society. Most of this is collected by government and private bodies and is, thus, accessible to the scholar at low cost. Census data, election returns, economic statistics, legis-

lative rollcalls, trade data, budgets, and tax information are among the obvious sources. They have been employed in studies of all levels of government, from local to international. Aggregate data do have shortcomings: they are collected chiefly in large units and on subjects often not related to the needs of research; thus, they tend to be inflexible, to leave gaps, and not to get to many of the problems of interest to the discipline.

(2) Interviews. Interviews are among the most productive data sources for all social science, political science included. They may range from in-depth explorations of behavior and attitude with a few subjects to large population opinion-polling ventures. Systematic interviews are expensive to administer, and they collect the information respondents tell the interviewer; hence, for some research purposes, they are simply not relevant. But the range of problems they do reach is great, and they provide well-focussed and manipulable data.

(3) Observation. Observation can mean a variety of things in political science research. Just as much of the political writing of the past was based on casual interviews, a good deal was also based on casual observation. In more recent years, some success has been achieved in systematizing observation, though the problems involved in getting comparable data from observations are many. Observational techniques have been particularly effective in the study of group decision-making processes.

(4) Content analysis. Content analysis is a means of recording symbols of communication, in newspapers, documents, speeches, and so on. Its utility is linked to the relevance of such symbols to the problems of politics.

(5) Group experiments. The use of experimental methods in political science is essentially an adaptation of approaches used in social psychology and organizational science. Experiments and related small-group exercises, such as simulations, have been used to explore basic social processes with some of the elements that confound them in natural settings held constant. The strength of experimental technique is also its weakness; it hides much of the subtlety and richness of actual political processes. Nonetheless, in such fields as the study of decision making, experiments are in active use and appear to hold much promise for the future.[6]

(6) Case studies. Case study methods are not really comparable to the others mentioned here, for they may utilize one or an amalgam of special techniques. Usually, however, a case is a descriptive account of a process or event put together from a variety of data sources, often unsystematic. A vast amount of the political science literature is based on case study material. Case studies are without doubt valuable in illustrative and heuristic ways, and they have given us a reservoir of information about what has happened in political life. They are, however, seldom comparable, seldom cumulative, and, hence, not often a basis for generalization.

Problems of Theory

The two preceding sections have stressed the difficulties of finding boundaries for the discipline of political science and the multiplicity of research methods being used in it. These comments may have conveyed an impression of formlessness about the contemporary study of politics, and such an impression is not entirely amiss. The very nature of creative and exploratory activity dictates that no scholarly field can be in perfect array; political science is doubtless somewhat less in array than many others. Nonethelesss, there is more coherence, at least in the work of individuals and subdisciplines, than the foregoing may suggest, and much of the coherence is ascribable to the element of theory in political scholarship. The role of theory is to focus the inquiry process and to link together concepts, ideas, and discrete pieces of work.[7]

"Theory" has meant, and still means, a variety of things in the political science discipline.[8] Undergraduate courses and graduate training in political theory have tended to concentrate heavily on the history of political ideas, on "classic" works of well-known figures from the time of the ancient Greeks to the early twentieth century. Approaches to this material differ. To some, it is simply worth studying for its own sake; some have thought it a source of wisdom, insight, or moral guidance; some have concerned themselves with the role of ideas in shaping political action; some have gone to the classics to seek propositions suggestive for empirical or logical work on contemporary politics. Thus, the work of people concerned with conventional political thought cannot easily be described in general terms. Much of it, however, has had heavy overtones of evaluation and much has been dedicated to the goal of acculturating people to the dominant Western liberal condition.

Out of the classics of political thought has come a variety of deterministic theories of politics, usually embedded in perspectives on other aspects of life. These ideologies or world views have been of tremendous importance for political action and for the study of politics. Each carries its own implications about purpose, order, method, value, and about the epistemological foundations on which political knowledge can be based. Examples readily spring to mind. Outlooks on these things are commonly identified as Platonist, Marxist, Thomist, Hegelian, existentialist, liberal, conservative. In-eed, in this ideology-laden world, perhaps nothing is more important to politics than the fact that men so readily submit to such pre-patterned ideas.

Recent work in political theory has turned in the empirical direc-tion. The empirical study of social phenomena need not, and most of its devotees would say should not, be disconnected thrashing around with whatever evidence or whatever subject happens to be at hand. Theory is at least as important to empirical research as the gathering of evidence, and in a critical sense prior to it. The term theory used in this sense means generalization, the statement in explicit terms of expected relationships. It sets out problems for inquiry and points to the methods through which they may be ex-plored. It constitutes a connective web among the concepts in which a science deals. Out of a body of theory, hypotheses are drawn, and these define the subject of investigation. Theory is an attempt to hang ideas together in a network of interrelated explanations; an attempt to state why relationships are as they are. In an ideal sit-uation, theory and research go hand in hand, as the latter provides tests of the former and leads to the rejection or revision of the theoretical version of how the world works. The process of develop-ment of knowledge is one of give and take between the two levels.

Many critics find deficiencies of theory the main weakness of empirical political science. Some bodies of theory have been devel-oped or adapted by the discipline and gained rather widespread influence.[9] At the level of theory, as in research techniques, political science has often shared with and borrowed from other social sci-ences, notably sociology, social psychology, organizational science, and economics. The theory of political science at present tends to deal with relatively small segments of political life, to constitute what Harold Guetzkow has called "islands of theory" relatively discrete from one another.

The following shortcomings of political theory reflect a variety of difficulties in the study of politics: the complexity of political phenomena; the predominance of ideological modes of thought; the sensitivity of political questions; the rapid pace of social change;

the explosion of research technologies. The activities of politics are so tangled with each other and with the variety of aspects of social life that the intellectual task of capturing them in adequate theory is immense. They are so intimately related to the satisfaction of aspirations and desires that it is difficult if not impossible to approach them objectively. The whole field of political scholarship, like others, is so swept up in accelerating change as to discourage efforts to reduce it to manageable theoretical terms. Such factors as these have sometimes impelled political scientists to focus their work on the more obvious problems. The critics of systematic social science have accused their science-oriented colleagues of preoccupation with trivia and ignorance of the significant. Such criticism doubtless reflects both concern for the onrush of social events and impatience with the slow, tedious, additive social process of building a firm body of knowledge. If political theory is in disarray after centuries of effort, we cannot be much surprised, given the nature of the subject matter and the environment in which the enterprise of scholarship must proceed. Some of the problems of political theory should be more apparent in the discussion of some substantive aspects of politics that follow.

SOME BASIC CONCEPTS

One of the ways of getting a grasp on a field is by surveying its concepts, examining the labels it applies to the sets of phenomena with which it deals. To a substantial degree, a discipline is defined by the concepts it commonly uses. They are the moorings to which its intellectual apparatus is fastened; theory can be thought of as the attempt to specify the relationships among concepts.

It goes without saying that we cannot provide a directory of the concepts of political science here, nor do more than note briefly some of those that figure prominently in current work in the field. Our choice is necessarily arbitrary. It omits some of the terms long in use to deal with political life, including, for example, state government, sovereignty, and justice. While these, and other exclusions, are not accidental, they do not in every case reflect judgment of the utility of the excluded items for the expansion of political knowledge. Like so many other aspects of political science, the varying use of concepts is a matter of difference of perspective and emphasis, and it is a rare political scientist who self-consciously and effectively uses all the concepts discussed below in the course of his work. They tend to be identified with systems of theory, approaches to research, and particular kinds of political subject matter, and to be employed according to the needs and outlooks of individuals or research groups. In the paragraphs that follow, a variety of concepts have been lumped into several categories, categories that might themselves be challenged. The categories are a matter of convenience, the concepts, a sample from a large universe.

Institution, System, and Process

These are all, of course, terms familiar in the everyday language of politics. They refer to settings or sites of political activity, not in a geographic but in a social sense. They identify kinds of interactive patterns among people, patterns that are involved with the political side of life.

The idea of institution is probably the simplest of the three. It suggests concrete, steel, and bricks, buildings and grounds in which things happen. In the social sciences, however, it usually is used to designate regularized, repeated patterns of behavior. Thus, an institution may be an established way of getting things done, not necessarily in the sense that it was created for that purpose, but in the sense that things happen to happen in that way. The family and school are institutions in which socialization of the young goes on. The legislature is an institution out of which social policy issues, the party being the one that recruits political leadership.

Much of the literature of politics is devoted to institutional description, to accounts of the activities of a genus or species of institution. Institutions are identifiable, relatively easily affixed with a name and ascribed a substance. Because many institutions are "formal," that is, develop or are given sets of stated rules and procedures, they are particularly likely to attract attention and, hence, to seem all the more important. It is clear, however, that the formalities often do not describe in any important way the workings of an institution, even though they may be mistaken for the institution itself. Growing awareness of this fact accounts for a turning away from institutions as a central focus of analysis by many political scientists.

System is a more complex term, one with highly sophisticated connotations that we cannot explore here. It has widespread use in social and natural sciences and engineering, uses that have had influence in developing theoretical structures in political science.[10] A system, as the term is commonly employed in social science, is a set of interrelated behaviors with some measure of stability. The concept of system stresses the element of interrelationship. As a tool of analysis, system posits equilibrium in a set of interrelationships, the equilibrium being a quality imposed by the mind of the analyst. A systems approach is, then, one that is interested in the conditions of equilibrium, the influences that upset it, and the means by which it rights itself. A political system may be the set of interrelationships through which a society authoritatively allocates values, as David Easton puts it.[11] This system is "open," that is, subject to influences from its environment, in this case both intra- and inter-societal. These impose stress on the operation of the system, rearranging its parts and eliciting response; stresses are threats to equilibrium which may bend the system to a new equilibrium. The political system is constantly subject to "demands" from its environment which it may accommodate through policy "outputs" and which may change the set of interrelationships through which claims on social values are handled.

This approach to politics obviously raises questions for inquiry, which is what it is supposed to do. It leads directly to such problems as what influences from the environment are stressful, what stresses bring about what changes in the system, how these stresses are handled, what changes in input modify the nature of the equilibrium, how policies feed back on the environment, and so on. The system idea affords an elaborate framework for comparison of political situations. It is not without problems, however, for some of its main assumptions, especially concerning equilibrium, are difficult to grasp, and its elements are more easily translated into research problems than into operational units and categories.

Process is a term perhaps even more familiar in everyday use and, also, more difficult to assign precise meaning. Process implies movement and change and a relationship between interactions and objective things acted upon. "Political process," however, is a very broad term that embraces a good many things; perhaps its only persistently distinctive characteristic is that it denotes activity, rather than the regularity emphasized by the concept of institution. Unlike "system," it does not usually suppose equilibrium, stress, and their necessary impact on the political interaction set itself.[12]

Power, Conflict, Authority, Decision

This set of concepts, like the preceding one, is a rather loose collection. All of these terms refer to modes of political activity; each of them is thought by some scholars to convey the defining quality of political action, and each has been the subject of a considerable amount of controversy in the discipline.

Power is usually used to refer to a capacity to induce desired behavior by others.[13] It is essentially a relational concept, that is, one that refers to a characteristic of the relationships among people. More than most social science concepts, however, power is often left very ambiguous, one of the reasons being that it is commonly treated as a characteristic of persons and not of relationships. Thus, we say, "that person (or that group) *has* power," without specifying that the power is with respect to some other person, situation, or subject. Further problems arise from difficulties in making the concept operational, in devising consistent and objective means of detecting and measuring it. While to some scholars politics is the use of power in social situations, others feel the concept is so vague and subject to ambiguity that it is best avoided altogether. It is a term with enormous common sense appeal, but one that tends to break down under systematic scrutiny.

Authority is a term with similar connotations and similar problems to those of power.[14] However, authority is usually said to carry with it recognition of the legitimacy of the rules made by the person or institution exercising it. In other words, authority is a recognized capacity to make legitimate rules or standards for behavior. This concept evokes classic fundamental questions about the justification of rule and the grounds of obedience. Some think authority is the quality that distinguishes political relationships from others. It seems clear, however, that authority is not confined to "public" or state-related interactions, but it is present in the spheres of "private" life as well, for example, in the family, the work-group, and so on. Like power, authority raises difficult problems of detection and measurement, but it is also very much a part of the conceptual equipment of the field.

Conflict is again a common sense ingredient of political life; according to many of the classic theories, it is the reason for the development of political relationships. Government is the consequence of the tension conflict creates in men, and it finds its justification in its capacity to reduce conflict. The study of politics, given such assumptions, may be organized around questions about the sources, circumstances, routines, and results of conflict and attempts at conflict resolution.

The concept of decision is one with wide applicability to social phenomena, but it is particularly attractive to students of politics.[15] The political process is presumably aimed toward a rearrangement of standards of behavior or resources through the development of policy, for example, toward, in Easton's terms, the allocation of values. Hence, it would appear to involve points at which decisions are made in response to political stimuli. Decisions imply focused, identifiable actions with significant consequences. Decision making is a way of describing the activity of the institutions of politics most familiar to us in common sense use, legislatures, judges, boards, commissions, councils, and the like; and many of their actions proceed in understood routines and issues and specific pronouncements subject to decision-making analysis. Work in decision making has given rise to several schemes of categories which, when applied to the process, provide frameworks for comparison. Richard C. Snyder, one of the leading theorists of this approach, suggests three significant variables: "spheres of competence," "communication and information," and "motivation," as sufficient to explain the political process.[16]

The decision-making approach aims essentially at accounting for differences in the outcomes of decision-making processes. These outcomes are the policies, rules of behavior, and so on, set by the organizations under examination. Thus, it may seek, for example, answers to questions about the effects of aspects of the environment on the decisional products of organizations' work. For reasons suggested above, most political science research on decision making deals with the business of formal government agencies. Though decision making can be applied to informal "mission-oriented" groups and to suborganizations, and though it does not restrict itself to the formal aspects of the political process, critics of this approach have suggested that its tendency to push in this direction leads to an over-emphasis on formalities and structures. Decision-making studies have dealt with both crisis or one-shot decisions and with on-going policy-making processes.[17]

Change, Development, Integration

In recent years much attention has been fixed by all the social sciences on the analysis of change. The sources of this interest are apparent; the world has surely never before experienced such radical alterations in technology, outlooks, and conditions and ways of life. While the entire Western tradition has been concerned with ideas like progress, the compulsion of change is more obvious now, given the sensitivity of contemporary society and the dramatic quality of the events it experiences.

Approaches to the study of change have not found agreement among political scientists. Some have taken cues from the deterministic theories of history, and these, of course, differ among themselves. Some have concentrated on the shifting nature of political processes themselves, some on changes in political systems as consequences of socioeconomic changes, and others on politics as an agent of change. The analysis of change presents problems on the levels of both theory and technique, especially when it attempts to deal with gross phenomena and complex societies, for the untangling of variables comes to seem as nearly impossible. Attempts to treat change are thus likely to come off either obviously over simple or so vague and grand as to offer little substantial ground for prediction. Despite the importance of problems of change, much of the work of political science deals, in fact, with statics, cross-sectional pictures of political phenomena. Even some work that has a prima facie orientation toward the dynamics of political life turns out, in the end, to treat differences over time but not the elements, processes, or agents of change themselves.

Some kinds of change have been matters of particular attention in the recent political science literature, again, for reasons directly related to the condition of the contemporary world. One is the phenomenon of "development," of the alteration of social, political, and economic relationships in the non-Western world. The subject is complicated both by its scale and by some attitudes of mind through which Westerners ordinarily approach it. Thus, "progress," the movement toward Western ways, has long been a subject of interest to social scientists, as has "evolution," the movement toward "higher" states of being. Both terms assume a Western norm of desirability and/or naturalness and imply that movement in some other direction is deviance. Some of the same connotations attach to "development" and to terms like "underdeveloped areas" and "developing areas."

The range of studies directed toward questions of development is vast.[18] Some are descriptive and some self-consciously comparative; some are large in scope, and others deal with particular institutional segments of societies. Politics may be treated as independent or dependent variable, considered from the standpoint of its effect on other aspects of society or from the standpoint of their effects on it. A good deal of the political scientist's interests in development has revolved around the roles of such forces as technological change, industrialization, economic system, urbanization, and ideology. Attention has also been paid to the influence of colonialism, external powers (especially the U.S. and U.S.S.R.), and the general international system on the non-Western countries.

A second focus of interest has been "integration," the development of political identity out of formerly fragmented societies.

Integration is a concept applicable to various levels of political organization and hence, one that facilitates comparison of basic processes. It has been used as a key in the study of change in local governments, traditional societies, nations, and international communities.[19]

A PARADIGM OF POLITICS

To this point, our discussion has dealt chiefly with current issues in the study of politics and current approaches to the discipline, but it has said little about how the political system fits together and how it works. This section will attempt to add some substance of the latter kind. It is impossible in this setting, however, to do more than touch the subject lightly here and there, and what follows should be considered a sort of paradigm of politics, an occasion to point out some of the questions in which students of politics might be interested. What we have said before should make it clear that this represents one perspective on the field, with points of emphasis selected accordingly. It is by no means a complete guide to the problems of the discipline.

We should perhaps take note at this point that political science tends to organize itself by categories somewhat different from those used here, and that most specific work in the field is identified by its relationships to those categories. They have gained acceptance through use, though they have little coherence and show little coordination. Thus, graduate programs, professional meetings, and such tend (though less with the passage of years) to be organized into such lumps as American government, foreign governments, international relations, public administration, state and local government, political behavior, public law, and political theory. These "fields," as they are commonly called, are variously defined by geography, function, and institution; and, despite occasional pretensions to the contrary, they do not describe all the points of focus political scientists pursue in their work.[20]

Politics and Social Life

Political systems — we use the term here in a loose and nontechnical way — may be large or small, "public" or non-public, short- or long-lived, more or less complex. In any case, they have some characteristic features through which they can be analyzed and compared. While the discussion that follows will draw more illustrative materials from some kinds of units than from others, the questions it raises can substantially be asked of all kinds of systems. This is not intended to be exclusively an examination of the American democratic polity, though it may have something of that appearance as a result of the chief interests (and, perhaps, to be perfectly candid, the biases) of the author.

Each political system works in an environment that does much to shape its processes and influence its policy. The environment works on politics and, in turn, is worked on by it; politics as a mode of social activity has to do with such things as the resolution of conflicts and redistribution of resources in its social sphere. Politics operates on cues from the society, signals about strains that require adjustment, and signals about means by which such strains may acceptably be resolved.

The relevant environment has three aspects: a social structure, a culture (or cultures), and a set of external elements, all of which play these context roles for the political system. By social structure, we mean the objective aspects of the society, that is, such matters as the distribution and characteristics of sub-populations, and the technology, and structure of economic relationships. Urbanism, both in the sense of concentration of population and in the sense of heterogeneity, interdependence, and division of labor, is a structural characteristic of many contemporary societies that is clearly salient to politics.

Culture, as we use the concept here, refers to subjective elements of the society, to its established ways of doing and looking at things. Thus, it comprehends manners, usages, customs, ideologies, and institutions, whatever terms we use to depict social regularities that bridge the past with the future. In recent years, the concept of political culture has come into use to designate those aspects of culture with special political content. "Political tradition" is an idea closely related to the concept of culture, and a constitution, including that of the United States, can be thought of as a kind of codification of the culture in which it is established.

By external environment, we refer to two general sets of influences on the system. They are those from the natural setting and those from other systems. The former obviously includes the natural resource base and physical geography of the system. The latter includes influences from "foreign" sources, other systems that are jurisdictionally separate from the one in question. If the system under examination is a local system, other local governments and governments at "higher" levels are external; if it is a nation state, other nations and inter-nation organizations are external. If the global political system is the subject, other worlds may conceivably play external roles.

These contextual elements create and give form to "demands" on the political systems, pressure from within or without for response. Foreign nations may exert threats, or internal groups may make claims. The environment in this large sense also puts limits on the extent and form of response the system may make. As was noted above, cultures define some modes of political action as acceptable, others as not so. "Liquidation" as an instrument of government policy and assassination as a form of citizen political action, for example, are not usually thought acceptable to American society. The context and effect of the relations between environment and political system are, of course, empirical questions and problems for political theory. Political scientists have been interested, for example, in such matters as whether an advancing level of urbanism does stimulate the political system to greater activity and, if so, in what structural and cultural circumstances.

The Political Process

The political process is the activity through which these influences from the environment are made manifest, felt, sorted, and (some of them) translated into authoritative policy. This process encompasses most of what we commonly call politics and government, and it is clearly too complex to treat in any detail here.

An aspect of this process is the development of political beliefs and attitudes and the acquisition of information about political matters. This "political socialization" is a portion of the broader function of acculturation of young and old. The beliefs and attitudes held by the people of a society are variously translated into political messages by ways the culture prescribes — in the American society by the voting process (albeit indirectly by voting for decision-makers), through the power to petition, through a variety of petition and "pressure" type activities, through demonstrations, and now and then through violence. These activities are generally accompanied by efforts to spread points of view so as to increase the scope and intensity of pressure for action. They are also given form and effect by organization, notably in some systems through political parties and voluntary associations, which become media for political demands.

Thus, political stimuli are projected into the portion of the system where decisions are made. This may include a variety of institutions, offices, and groups, visible and invisible, official and unofficial, depending on the form of the system. Legislatures, executive agencies, and courts are the kinds of bodies where these functions are most commonly carried out in the American system, but other systems show greatly divergent ways of processing political pressures. Even within the United States these differ from sub-system to sub-system and even from issue to issue within the same system. Much of the research of political science deals with the causes and consequences of such differences.

The activities of decision making may be broken down in various ways. They include, for instance, such functions as follows: (1) the interpretation of political messages received from the environment; (2) the determination of agenda, for example, the selection and formulation of items of business for consideration; (3) the development of information about the nature and costs of possible policies; (4) the choice of a course of action or policy; and (5) the transmission of that policy into the society or its relevant parts. Each of these stages has substantial importance for the operation of the system; agenda making, for instance, has much to do with what messages from the environment get response and what do not. A given system may omit some steps but not without consequences. The problems of the political scientist run all the way through this system, from those having to do with why it takes the form it does to its consequences for the policies it develops. Political science is interested in who carries out the various aspects of decision making, the atmosphere in which they are performed, the responsiveness they show to political stimuli, and the effects they have on the society and its relationship to other societies. Both normative and empirical questions may be involved in the analysis of this aspect of politics as may such classic concepts as leadership, power, and authority.

The Products of the Political Process

The culmination of the political process, the reason for its existence, lies in its outputs or the products it creates. These may be rules of behavior, standards by which the people of the society are expected to live, or they may be allocations of resources. They may be classified according to a variety of principles.

For example, one approach would distinguish those outputs that relate to the structure and activity of the political system itself from those that have a "substantive" impact on the society. The former are the provisions a system makes for the life of its political element; they include such things are governmental reorganization, taxation to sustain governmental activity, arrangements for voting, and the like. Substantive outputs are those that distribute values, provide guidelines for the resolution of conflicts, proscribe kinds of behavior, and so on. Thus, criminal law, redistributive taxes, and policies for welfare, health, education, economic stability or adjustment, and the like are all among the ends of political action of this type. Measures to provide for the peaceful or violent conduct of relations with other systems may be cast in this category or made the subject of a separate one.

The gratifications and deprivations that are provided people by the political process are both material and symbolic. Politics has to do with such questions as how well people may live and what kinds of activity they may carry on. It also has to do with their sense of security and with their capacity to develop loyalty and commitment to their community. Politics may have integrative effects, raising the sense of identity and common purpose among the people, or it may indeed have the opposite consequences, contributing to the disintegration of whatever societal attachments they feel.

Another aspect of the political system is comprised by the activities of carrying out policy — the activities commonly called administration. Most policies do not execute themselves but need tending by people designated to do the job, such as policemen, tax collectors, inspectors, soldiers, clerks, and the host of auxiliary and supervisory personnel of government. The treatment of administration as a particular segment of the political process may suggest some misleading conclusions. Administration is an enormously complex set of activities and is not a set easily distinguished from many of the other aspects of politics, for administration and the people involved in it are intertwined with the whole fabric of the political process. Administrators play roles in the creation and communication of demands; they put pressure on the process for the revision of policy; they supply information for decision makers. Furthermore, as administrators interpret policy and carry it out, they make decisions; there is much in the way of judgment involved in the administrative process. Even the clerk doing supposedly routine administrative functions can materially affect the outcome of policy by his decisions about the order in which business will be handled, the literality and rigidity he will use in interpreting rules, and the tone he will impart to his contacts with the public and his co-workers. The same is true, but in greater degree, of high-level administrative functionaries. Thus, administration becomes an important contribution to the outputs of the political system.

The end of the political process is not, of course, simply policy but the effect of that policy on the social material with which it works. It was suggested earlier in this action that politics acts on signals about tensions in its environment, and decision making systems may also respond to their own internal tensions. These actions may be slow, irrelevant, or negative in effect. Signals are often misperceived, and the entire process of government may be fraught with inefficiencies and efforts to use public power for private gain. Nonetheless, politics is finally directed toward adjusting through policy the social settings and routines in which people interact.

Hence, to use a term from the vocabulary of systems analysis, the activities of policy "feedback" on the environment. As policies are developed and carried into effect through administration, they may alter relationships so as to relieve tensions, or they may indeed enhance them. Whether a given policy has one effect or the other or no effect at all is an empirical question. In most cases what actually happens is probably some of each; that is, some aspects of the situation are changed and some are not. The total environment, itself undergoing constant alterations, may then be expected to generate new signals about new needs and wants. The processes of politics are thus constantly kept in motion, though the pace and substance of political business change.

THE FUTURE OF THE DISCIPLINE

Given the state of political science today, it would take a brave man indeed to predict with confidence where the discipline will go in the course of the next few years. We will confine ourselves here to a very brief discussion of a few of the problems and opportunities that political science faces, supposing that this will indicate some potential routes of development.

Many of the needs and deficiencies of political science as it is now practiced are apparent in what has been said above; most political scientists would probably agree that the field is still in a rather primitive stage as a body of systematic knowledge about regularities of political life. It has no agreed framework of theory, and even the limits of the subject matter are in dispute. While the volume of evidence about politics is growing, it still shows great gaps; a good bit of what there is is non-comparable, and some of it is trivial. Research techniques relevant to some basic political problems are undeveloped, and modes of analysis, though they have advanced rapidly toward sophistication over the last few years, still show deficiencies. One can expect with confidence that a substantial portion of the efforts of political scientists over the next period of time will be dedicated to remedying these shortcomings, to further work in theory, on techniques, and on the gathering and analysis of evidence about the variety of political systems. It seems probable that as these activities proceed the political science discipline will grow closer and closer to the other social sciences, perhaps, to the point where the present artificial and dysfunctional distinctions among them will disappear.

Such developments in political science, which represent improvements in the present modal activities of the field, are not likely, however, to be the only changes that come over the discipline in the near future. At present, there are ample signs that more attention is being drawn toward evaluation, recommendation, and reform.[21] These are, of course, activities long practiced by members of the profession. Students of political philosophy have been interested in questions about the grounds and standards of authority and obedience, and, in much more immediate ways, political scientists have advocated reforms in the specific structures and policies of governments. Much of the administrative and electoral reform of American government during the past three-quarters of the century, for example, has been influenced by work and people in the academic political science field.

It seems unlikely, however, that the role of the discipline will be in the future quite what it has been in the past. The swing toward the systematic empirical study of politics has brought, in perspective and technique, some new materials to the evaluative capacity of the field. Where evaluation, in the past, has often been a matter of invocation of received authority, such as, the old classics or of untested "principles," especially, in such fields as public administration, it is now influenced by the theory and evidence of empirical research. Hopefully, the future lies in the convergence of empirical and normative interests, not in an imperialist war between them. This is not to suggest that conflicts over methodology and purpose are likely to disappear, but that the variety of activity in the discipline may come to be seen as complementary parts of a complex field of study.

Political science is likely, in other words, to turn increasing attention to the ills and tensions of (and among) the societies in which it flourishes. Among the goals of such a political science (all of them now carried on at least in minor degree), we may find the following:

1. The examination and clarification of social values

2. The detection and examination of stress-creating social problems

3. The analysis of the consequences of the use of various forms and processes of politics

4. The examination of the impact of policies on the societies at which they are directed

5. The development and translation of information on the subjects mentioned in points one through four as back-up for the decision-making process

6. The analysis of the relative costs (in dignity, time, money, other resources and values) of alternative social policies

7. The continued comparison and exposition of modes and standards of judgment of political acts

8. The development of materials and techniques of education for political sensitivity

These activities will be variously judged by different people. They rest on assumptions that the environment is dealt with best by people who know it and that the open exchange of ideas, information, and points of view will best assure felicity and creativity in social life. They point directions through which knowledge may be put in the service of freedom, dignity, and equality. Whether that will, in fact, be the consequence of expanded knowledge of politics probably will depend on the openness and sense of community of the societies in which such knowledge is generated.

FOOTNOTES

1. For general treatments of the development and present scope of the discipline, see Albert Somit and Joseph Tanenhaus, *The Development of American Political Science from Burgess to Behavioralism* (Boston: Allyn and Bacon, Inc., 1967); Albert Somit and Joseph Tanenhaus, *American Political Science: a Profile of a Discipline* (New York: Atherton Press, 1964); Charles Hyne-

man, *The Study of Politics* (Urbana: University of Illinois, 1959); Bernard Crick, *The American Science of Politics* (Berkeley and Los Angeles: University of California Press, 1959); Herbert Storing, ed., *Essays on the Scientific Study of Politics* (New York: Holt, Rinehart and Winston, Inc., 1962); Roland Young, ed., *Approaches to the Study of Politics* (Evanston, Ill.: Northwestern University Press, 1958).

2. See, especially, Heinz Eulau, *The Behavioral Persuasion in Politics* (New York: Random House, 1963); Vernon Van Dyke, *Political Science: a Philosophical Analysis* (Stanford: Stanford University Press, 1960); Austin Ranney, ed., *Essays on the Behavioral Study of Politics* (Urbana: University of Illinois Press, 1962).

3. Several of the works cited above discuss definition. See also Vernon Van Dyke, "The Optimum Scope of Political Science," *A Design for Political Science: Scope, Objectives, and Methods* (Philadelphia: American Academy of Political and Social Science, 1966), pp. 1-17.

4. See David Easton, *The Political System* (New York: Alfred A. Knopf, 1953).

5. Discussions of method in political and other social sciences abound. For a recent essay see Karl W. Deutsch, "Recent Trends in Research Methods in Political Science," *A Design for Political Science*, pp. 149-178. More generally, see Fred N. Kerlinger, *Foundations of Behavioral Research* (New York: Holt, Rinehart and Winston, Inc., 1964).

6. On simulation in social science, see Harold Guetzkow, ed., *Simulation in the Social Sciences* (Englewood Cliffs, N.J.: Prentice-Hall, 1962).

7. On the role of theory, see Abraham Kaplan, *The Conduct of Inquiry: Methodology for Behavioral Science* (San Francisco: Chandler Publishing Co., 1964); Ernest Nagel, *The Structure of Science: Problems in the Logic of Scientific Explanation* (New York: Harcourt, Brace and Co., 1961); Thomas Kuhn, *The Structure of Scientific Revolutions* (Chicago: University of Chicago Press, 1965).

8. See the survey by Neil A. McDonald and James N. Rosenau, "Political Theory as Academic Field and Intellectual Activity," in *Political Science: Advance of the Discipline,* ed. Marian D. Irish (Englewood Cliffs, N.J.: Prentice-Hall, Inc., 1968). For differing points of view (representing by no means the entire range) see Fred M. Frohock, *The Nature of Political Inquiry* (Homewood, Illinois: Dorsey Press, 1967); Eugene J. Meehan, *Contemporary Political Thought: A Critical Study* (Homewood, Illinois: Dorsey Press, 1967); George Kateb, *Political Theory: Its Nature and Uses* (New York: St. Martin's Press, 1968); Ithiel de Sola Pool, ed., *Contemporary Political Science: Toward Empirical Theory* (New York: McGraw-Hill Book Company, 1967); and David Easton, ed., *Varieties of Political Theory* (Englewood Cliffs, N.J.: Prentice-Hall, Inc., 1966).

9. See, for example, Karl Deutsch, *The Nerves of Government* (New York: Free Press, 1963); Robert A. Dahl, *A Preface to Democratic Theory* (Chicago: University of Chicago Press, 1956); James M. Buchanan and Gordon Tullock, *The Calculus of Consent: Logical Foundations of Constitutional Democracy* (Ann Arbor: University of Michigan Press, 1962).

10. There is relatively little literature on institution as a concept, much on system. On the latter, see David Easton, *A Systems Analysis of Politics* (New York: John Wiley and Sons, 1965); Oran R. Young, *Systems of Political Science* (Englewood Cliffs, N.J.: Prentice-Hall, Inc., 1968); D. P. Eckman, ed., *Systems: Research and Design* (New York: John Wiley and Sons, 1966); and the annual editions of *General Systems,* published by the Society for the Advancement of General Systems Research.

11. Easton, *The Political System.*

12. Two books about process that focus on politics as group transactions are Arthur Bentley, *The Process of Government* (Chicago: University of Chicago Press, 1908), and David B. Truman, *The Governmental Process* (New York: Alfred A. Knopf, 1951). For discussion of a more general process approach based on cybernetics, see Karl Deutsch, *The Nerves of Government* (New York: Free Press, 1963).

13. The literature on power is vast. See Harold Lasswell and Abraham Kaplan, *Power and Society* (New Haven: Yale University Press, 1950); Harold Lasswell, *Politics: Who Gets What, When, How?* (New York: Mc-Graw-Hill Book Co., 1936); Robert A. Dahl, "The Concept of Power," *Behavioral Science* 2 (July 1957): 201-215; Edward Banfield, *Political Influence* (New York: The Free Press, 1961); Hans Morgenthau, *Politics Among Nations* (New York: Alfred A. Knopf, 1961).

14. Much of the literature on power also deals with authority as a concept. See, also, Herbert Simon, *Administrative Behavior* 2nd ed. (New York: Macmillan and Company, 1957); James G. March and Herbert Simon, with Harold Guetzkow, *Organizations* (New York: John Wiley and Sons, 1958); Robert L. Peabody, *Organizational Authority* (New York: Atherton Press, 1964); Carl J. Friedrich, ed., *Authority* (Cambridge: Harvard University Press, 1958).

15. See especially Richard C. Snyder, H. W. Bouck, and Burton Sapin, *Decision-Making as an Approach to the Study of International Politics* (Princeton University, Foreign Policy Analysis Project, 1954); Richard C. Snyder and James Robinson, *National and International Decision-Making* (New York: Institute for International Order, 1961).

16. Richard C. Snyder, "A Decision-Making Approach to the Study of Political Phenomena," in *Approaches to the Study of Politics,* ed. Roland Young (Evanston, Ill.: Northwestern University Press, 1958), p. 24.

17. For critique, see James N. Rosenau, "The Premises and Promises of Decision-Making Analysis," in *Contemporary Political Analysis* ed. James C. Charlesworth (New York: Free Press, 1967).

18. Again, the literature of the subject is so great as to permit mention only of a few leading examples: Gabriel Almond and James S. Coleman, eds., *The Politics of Developing Areas* (Princeton: Princeton University Press, 1960); David Apter, *The Politics of Modernization* (Chicago: University of Chicago Press, 1965); Edward Shils, *Political Development in the New States* (The Hague: Mouton, 1962); there is also a large number of studies of specific developing countries and comparative studies of functions and institutions.

19. Philip E. Jacob and James V. Toscano, eds., *The Integration of Political Communities* (Philadelphia and New York: J. B. Tippincott Co., 1964).

20. A discussion of the literature chiefly organized by traditional fields may be found in Marian D. Irish, ed., *Political Science: Advance of a Discipline.*

21. See Harry Eckstein, "Political Science and Public Policy," and Robert A. Dahl, "The Evaluation of Political Systems," in *Contemporary Political Science: Toward Empirical Theory* ed. Ithiel de Sola Pool (New York: McGraw-Hill Book Co., 1967); George Kateb, *Political Theory: Its Nature and Uses,* James C. Charlesworth, "Some Thoughts Relating to the Present Dimensions and Directions of Political Science," in *A Design for Political Science: Scope, Objectives, and Methods,* ed. James Charlesworth (Monograph 6; Philadelphia: American Academy of Political and Social Science, 1966); Harold D. Lasswell, *The Future of Political Science* (New York: Atherton Press, 1963).

7

The Syntax and Substance of Economics

André Daniere

ECONOMICS AMONG THE SOCIAL SCIENCES

There is no better way to locate economics on the intellectual map than to list, in order of visibility, the elements that give it a distinct personality among sister sciences in the "social" family. Needless to say, the family link is more than a matter of shared universe: There is a substantial overlap of data, concerns, and methods, and the family resemblance grows sharper as the sciences get older. But economics exhibits features that, at least in the chronology of their appearance, place it in a special — and not altogether dismal — position.

A. *Empirical Investigation of Quantitative Models*

Most evident of all is the heavily quantitative and numerical component of a great deal of economic analysis. One aspect of this quantification is the expression of most economic variables as numbers representing concrete units, such as bushels, ton-miles, employees, days, dollars, and soon, all of which are easily identified and counted. But, quantification goes much further than simple enumeration. The particular dimensions of physical and human behavior which economists have carved out as their own have lent themselves to a successful sequence of "scientific" investigations.

The author is grateful for comments on earlier drafts provided by his colleagues at The Institute of Human Sciences, Boston College. The greatest critical contribution, however, was that of Professor Edward Kane, of Boston College's Economics Department. He is the least to blame for whatever obscurities or misrepresentations remain in the present version.

These have produced statements of ever increasing sharpness and usefulness concerning quantitative stochastic *models* of the "real" world which economists wish to control or understand.

Fundamentally, an economic model specifies the probability distribution of certain "dependent" or "endogenous" variables, given the values taken by some "control" or "exogenous" variables. It can be expressed as a single relationship equating the dependent variable to some function of the control variables *plus* a distributed "error" term; or as a *system* of similarly structured equations and/or other conditions to be fulfilled by the variables, such that endogenous variables and their error distributions are determined once exogenous variables have been fixed. The relationships may refer to such "transformation" units as industrial processes, individuals, organizations or systems, and the set of variables may include material objects (e.g. consumption goods), persons (e.g., trained manpower), claims (e.g., money), signals (e.g., prices), behavior patterns (e.g., supply curves), levels of satisfaction (on some specified scale), and various indices serving to simplify analysis and communication.

The basic element of the research sequence is the specification of a class of stochastic models thought to include a "true" model, and the systematic use of newly marshalled empirical evidence to narrow down the range of compatible models by checking actual outcomes against those predicted under each model in the class. The original class is usually described as a single a priori model, certain parameters in its structure and/or its error distribution remaining unspecified; the "narrowing down" consists in a partial specification of the initially free parameters, including their "likelihood" distribution, tests of specific hypotheses concerning their magnitude, "confidence" intervals, and so on. These inferences are incorporated in the next round of economic decisions, explanations, and predictions; for some purposes, they are translated into "estimates" of the a priori model, the value of each parameter being selected by a "least squares" or other criterion of general relevance.

This outline of scientific methods does not, as such, distinguish economics from other social sciences, except that it has been pursued longer and more systematically in economics than in any of the sister disciplines. In spite of much wastage and wild shooting, the sequence of economic investigations does build up toward constantly more accurate and more useful instruments. Enough is learned at each stage that the next a priori model subjected to new evidence is more likely than before to (1) include a "true" alternative, (2) be testable by reference to the evidence gathered, and (3) generate useful statements. Orderly progress on the second front has been of special importance in a science which cannot engage in controlled experimentation but must rely on data generated by the complex interactions of the real world. Whatever the "sample design" accidentally produced, it must be well enough understood that probability distributions of sample outcomes under alternative models in the class tested can be accurately predicted; and a valid evaluation of sampling conditions requires reference to an already sophisticated model of the system that generates the data. Similarly, each new specification of an a priori model and each new collection of evidence benefit from earlier tests in the same or related areas and are likely to permit "tighter" and/or more relevant inferences. Finally, the order of relevance of alternative structures becomes better known as the systems in which they will enter (whether for "decision" or "understanding" purposes) reach higher levels of definition and acceptance.

Without disparaging the efforts of quantitative researchers in other social sciences, it is difficult to escape the impression that most social disciplines are still short of the "take-off" point in the progressive sequence just outlined. While much is being done in the way of survey sampling and survey analysis, an inordinate amount of energy goes into the building of indices, the determination of useful class boundaries or summary variables[1] and, at the limit, the testing of parameters in simple linear models for their acceptance as non-zero. In other words, each investigator still appears to stand on his own in the face of a confusing universe with very little support from previously "certified" knowledge.

B. *Emphasis on Interdependence Systems*

As already suggested, economists find it possible to link individual relationships between variables into complex systems that are meant to represent the operation of some identifiable portion of the universe. The resulting models are so built that "everything depends on everything else," except for some exogenous variables which the analyst views as generated outside the system and whose values, through the whole set of interactions described in the model, *determine* the distribution of other variables of interest.

The non-stochastic part of the model is normally represented by a system of simultaneous equations between functions of overlapping subsets of the variables, although the initial structure may describe various types of behavior (e.g. maximization under constraints) which eventually translate into additional equations. The individual relationships constituting the model may have been subjected to separate quantitative analysis and subsequently "stuck together" or first linked into an a priori large model and jointly constrained by relevant empirical evidence. The second approach is often mandatory as a way of ensuring that sampling conditions implicit in the data base are compatible with the a priori model, that is, conditions justify specific probability statements concerning sampled elements for alternative values of the model's parameters.

In any case, the profession is bringing out models of increasing size and complexity (several hundred equations is an accepted order of magnitude) with fully estimated parameters, together with a wealth of probability statements concerning some or all of their parts. Their ability to predict (explain) past or future events in a quantitative way, once exogenous variables have been specified, is vastly superior to that of sociological models. Many of the models are "dynamic," meaning that variables observed at one point of time (and treated as exogenous magnitudes) allow prediction of subsequent states of the system in a probabilistic but unconditional form. For instance, the two large models of the American economy in use since World War II both predicted the downturns in economic activity occurring in 1945, 1958 and 1960,[2] and they have an excellent record of predicting GNP and its major components over the last six years.[3]

C. *Liberal Use of Simplifying Assumptions*

This is not to say that the empirical record of economics is perfect. The empirical evidence is not so constraining that many conflicting models cannot live side by side and feed noisy controversies between various schools of thought. Many systems subsist with large error variances, and many more still are eventually found biased when used in predictions. Furthermore, it is common for economists to ignore the error component of individual relationships and to operate strictly in terms of point estimates of their model's parameters. Disturbing as these observations may be, two particular areas of methodological weakness deserve special mention.

(1) It is not at all clear that the most effective use of empirical evidence is always promoted. At one end of the spectrum, some economists are attracted by tight, elegant models dealing with large aggregates or indices. Such models are relatively easy to manipulate and lead to a variety of intellectually exciting and potentially use-

ful generalizations; but the building of aggregates and indices involves a frightening waste of information, as well as a large volume of implicit—and generally intuitive—analysis. At the other end are those who wish to operate close to raw measurements and make full use of whatever they have identified as "good" information; since, however, models of many variables entering sophisticated relationships are not yet amenable to computation, they are forced to specify very simple structures which contradict some elements of a priori knowledge but can accommodate large quantities of data. No one is quite sure where the ideal lies, but there is a suspicion that the choice of one or the other extreme by so many does not average to an optimum strategy.[4]

(2) While emphasizing rigor in their use of statistical instruments when they do resort to quantitative analysis, economists put heavy reliance on behavioral assumptions that are only subjected to loose and infrequent tests. The richest of such assumptions has been that of *maximization* of utility by individuals and of profits by business firms. When this assumption is combined with empirical elements of information concerning preference patterns and industrial technologies, it allows the analysts to predict the outputs of a broad range of input combinations without the need for specific empirical investigations. While introspection strongly suggests the validity of utility maximization and various observations of behavior are consistent with it, it is by no means clear that maximization is pursued systematically and, hence, that a "logical" decision model gives a satisfactory account of consumer behavior. While, again, business managers keep affirming an objective of profit maximization and much observation is consistent with it, the rise of corporations and giant corporate structures has forced successive revisions of the profit concept, and some are now denying that profit maximization in any sense is adequate to describe modern corporate behavior. Yet, much modern analysis relies on such traditional postulates concerning the objectives and attitudes of various economic units.

D. *Theoretical Investigation of Formalized Models*

Whatever the quantitative flavor of the discipline, much model building and model manipulation in economics remains far removed from empirical measurements and quantitative statements. Two major deviations occur in this respect. Most familiar to the layman are books in the "political-economy" tradition devoted to relatively simple restatements of central economic propositions, but with new emphases and a new outlook on the long-term evolution of major variables (population, wealth and power distribution, technology, social-class identification, and so on) which the ordinary economist handles rather shyly. The outcome of such efforts is generally instructive, sometimes entertaining, and, on occasion, explosive.[5] The other common deviation from hard empiricism has generated its share of instruction and entertainment but more strictly to the benefit of economists. It has taken the form of extensive mathematical or logical model building on the basis of relationships *specified only* to the extent of some of their mathematical properties. Foremost among those is the "convexity" assumed by mathematical functions, for example, the fact that, as consumers have more of one good, they are ready to exchange more of it for a unit of any other. When this type of information is added to "maximizing" assumptions and to some fairly general institutional and physical constraints, an amazing wealth of conclusions can be drawn concerning all levels of the economy.

Both the volume of literature and the impact on public policy produced by either form of qualitative analysis have been far greater, to date, than those attributable to strict empirical research. In addition, the a priori models subjected to the constraints of empirical evidence owe a great deal to the qualitative theoretical work carried out by reference to "lean" morphological and behavioral assumptions. It is apparent, however, that qualitative models cannot, as such, satisfy the requirement for quantitative explanation and prediction which modern clients of economics are putting forward. It is also true that some practitioners of the art are caught at their own game: They can no longer resist the exhilaration of pure reason and proceed to build models for the sake of their logical richness with little concern for the empirical relevance of their basic assumptions.

E. *Independent Development of Statistical and*
   Mathematical Tools

While all social sciences have made substantial contributions to general statistical methods, impressive advances have been scored by econometricians, especially in dealing with empirical evidence that is generated raw by a world in motion, rather than harnessed under carefully controlled experimental conditions. *Econometrics* has, in fact, become an independent body of knowledge unrelated to the "economic" nature of the variables originally considered, and it is now part of the required intellectual baggage of any "quantitative" social scientist.

Other methodological breakthroughs of relevance beyond the confines of the discipline can be traced to the more mathematically inclined economists. Traditional mathematical tools and standard theorems did suffice in the early stages of model building, but increasingly modern techniques had to be incorporated as more ambitious systems were contemplated. Eventually, economists had to charter their own course, adding to the mathematical literature in such cases as game strategies,[6] growth paths of multivariate systems, general properties of constrained maximum solutions, maximization techniques,[7] and so on. Even if, as some would have it, economists are truly a sect of third-rate mathematicians fully engaged in impressing one another with occasional second-rate achievements, it remains that the profession distinguishes itself among other social scientists by the extensiveness of its mathematical commitment.

F. *Search for Optimum Solutions to Decision Problems*

While economists derive some satisfaction from "explaining" or "accounting for" past developments, most of them find this exercise less than fully rewarding. More than any other social scientists, they are willing and eager to *use* their models toward practical ends. At the very least, they will offer conditional and unconditional predictions of the path of certain variables which decision makers in various areas must incorporate in their plans. The most visible and most publicized of their outputs take the form of projected series of employment, gross national product, interest rates, gross investment, consumer purchases, and so on, to which government units, interest organizations, business corporations, and others jointly or selectively refer.

At the next level, economists will provide their "client" with predictions of "objective variables" of specific interest to *him*, for each of several policies (or sequences of actions) he may be contemplating. If, in addition, the client is willing to communicate his "preference" or "value" system, they will translate their findings in "cost-benefit" terms, providing, in effect, a desirability ranking of policy alternatives. The schedule of client preference goes by the name of *objective function*. In its more sophisticated forms, it does, indeed, take the shape of a mathematical function linking the client's index of satisfaction to values jointly taken by objective variables of interest. In practice, it is often expressed as a weighted sum of the objective variables, each weight measuring the independent value (positive or negative) of a unit of the variable.

Once he has gone that far, however, the economist sees more exciting possibilities. His inclination will be to go one step further and to engage in a systematic search for the *best* policy available to his client. The alternatives originally contemplated may not include that optimum, and special skills are required to scan all possible variations quickly and efficiently. These are, par excellence, the skills of the economist. Not only does he have on hand a bag of "optimization" techniques applicable to several types of situations, but he is past master at fitting complex realities into simpler models to which available techniques are applicable.

The clientele of economists ranges all the way from business firms to national governments, taking in interest groups and all types of collectivities. The problems they handle can be as narrowly technical as the determination of an optimum inventory policy and as broadly political as the discovery of optimum schemes of income redistribution. They may concern the choice between single actions, repetitive actions, or sequences of actions; the term "planning" being used if contemplated actions are relatively independent of contingent events and "policy" if actions are conditioned by future events. The area of choice may cover the whole set of integrated activities of the client (the total operation of the firm or government unit), or it may be limited to a subset of such activities. The problem is essentially the same in all situations, and the set of techniques available at any point of time is fairly standardized.

Decision models have never been fully identified with economics, and they are becoming less so as time goes on. Optimization is, of course, quite familiar to engineers, and the science of decisions, especially in its probabilistic extensions, is by no means an economist's monopoly. Systems analysis and operations research have expanded the scope of the methodology and made it accessible to areas of the social universe untouched by traditional economics. Looking into the future, it is apparent that economists will have to share even more with other disciplines (e.g. control theory). Nevertheless, the complex of methods and empirical information which they can bring to bear on decision problems is far more powerful than what other social sciences can, or are willing to, offer.

G. *Progress Toward a Formal Theory of*
   Decentralized Decision Making

One of the more difficult problems faced by economists is the determination of optimum decisions when the model linking actions to relevant outcomes is incomplete. An economist may, for instance, be requested to perform a cost-benefit analysis of federal aid programs in education, without knowing what policies are to be simultaneously pursued in such complementary areas as health and welfare, employment, urban development, federal taxation, and so on, or what competing federal activities will be cut as more budget dollars are drawn to education. The more appropriate approach would be to let a central team develop a comprehensive policy-decision model covering all federal activities and crank out a complete federal plan in which all elements fit neatly toward a general optimum. The trouble is that all central decision makers, and especially those dealing with federal policy, must live with constantly changing conditions and objectives and, mostly, with serious constraints on the information they can absorb or process in any time period. Partial decisions must, somehow, be made, without the benefit and burden of a simultaneous determination of best policies for the whole complex of interrelated activities.

A good deal of the ingenuity which the economic profession so lavishly dispenses has been devoted to finding ways of making such decentralized decisions in a manner compatible with overall maximization of the organization's objective function. The main prop of this operation is an initial determination that actions within the reach of the individual unit have a negligible impact on a majority of related variables, so that proximate outcomes of its decisions can be calculated approximately within an independent subsystem of relationships. This narrowing of the decision model does not, however, obviate the necessity for relating outcomes of the unit's actions to the objectives of the organization—for these hold the key to the valuation of costs and benefits. This is where economists have on hand a trump card in the form of *marginal valuations* or *shadow prices*—a set of numbers that carry "value" information down to all levels of the system and provide instant criteria for decentralized decision.

The determination and use of prices in decentralized decisions can be briefly described as follows. Given the constraints operating on the whole set of related decisions facing a given organization (e.g. the Chief Executive), a complete solution of its "maximization" problems puts a so-called "shadow price" on all constraining factors; that is, it generates measures of their marginal values in terms of index units of the organization's objective function. Similar shadow prices (marginal value productivities) can be calculated for the outputs of all activities in the system; their relation to "factor" prices depending on the morphology of available processes. If shadow prices are used to measure "costs" and "revenues" of individual activities, a fairly obvious property of the maximum solution is that no "profit" is obtainable from expanding or reducing any activity in the system. For if it were possible to increase the "value" produced in the form of some output by more than the "value" absorbed in the form of corresponding inputs, some net addition to the ultimate index of satisfaction would be possible, and the solution would not, therefore, represent a maximum.[8] Given a position of the system that is off the optimum, marginal valuations can also be calculated for a maximum solution under which some of the variables are constrained to remain at their initial level. These valuations can then operate as signals for reaching the "true" maximum solution: that solution is approached by pursuing "profitable" expansions or reductions of activities, the costs and benefits being measured in terms of the calculated "marginal valuations". The signals, however, only have directional value—a given expansion or reduction may either undershoot or overshoot the mark.

This suggests, although it does not prove, that continuous adjustments toward optimality (when the system is given to slowly shifting objectives, constraints, and information) can be achieved through an alternation of decentralized "profit maximizing" decisions within the restricted scope of each unit, and centralized "pricing" decisions reflecting estimated shifts in marginal value productivities. The new set of prices at each stage is obtained from the solution of a simplified comprehensive decision model in which "lower-order" choices have been settled in accordance with preceding decisions.[9] More ambitiously, the central decision maker may set up a market system among decentralized decision units in his organization, or play market with the help of a computer. The market is organized by (1) placing independent decision units in control of each constraining factor and instructing them to maximize revenue consistently with their selling the whole supply; and by (2) placing independent decision units in control of each output and instructing them to maximize profit consistently with their price not exceeding marginal cost. If the central maker acts as a "consumer", balancing his purchases (out of a fixed budget of internal monetary units) to maximize his satisfaction, all activities in the system will eventually stabilize at the "optimum" level from the standpoint of his objective function.

H. *Interpretation of the Social System as a Decentralized Organization*

Economists do, therefore, have models for the efficient decentralization of decisions. The fact of the matter, however, is that no organization below the level of the national economy is known to decentralize decisions by reference to its own internal prices. Subunits of business firms and government agencies are asked to develop cost-effective solutions in terms of "outside" resource prices (in response to omnipresent budget constraints), but eventual decisions on the form and magnitude of programs are made centrally or through a consensus process that bears little resemblance to the market model. For all the fuss generated around new concepts of program planning and budgeting, large government organizations continue to initiate program proposals at all levels of their bureaucracy without the benefit of any quantitative signal (except arbitrary budget limitations) from the central authority. The pressures placed on existing organizations by uninterrupted demands for decision and action are, apparently, too strong for new structures to be tried out and established. It is only at the level of the national economy that conscious steps toward the use of a managed price system seem to have occurred, and this in socialist countries. Even they, however, have inherited a mechanism not of their making and can only claim to have "taken hold" of it for national planning purposes.

For it is obvious that "prices" and "markets" did not spring out of any social thinker's imagination. With some essential qualifications, economists have found the decentralized market model in full bloom at the very center of the competitive-free-enterprise economies they are trying to explain. Members of the social "organization" in control of each scarce factor—if they are numerous or regulated enough—compete in such a manner that revenues are maximized consistently with disposal of the whole supply. Intermediate decision makers, in the form of business enterprises, do not individually follow the appropriate expansion rule, but their competition for profits or power, helped by government regulation, leads to an industry behavior consistent with the rule. While no central policy maker acts as final purchaser for the nation, private consumers and governments do compete for the purchase of goods and services in the light of their individual objectives. Economists are, thus, in possession of a working market model, with the peculiarity that it maximizes no specific objective function but rather responds to the competing objectives of individuals and collectivities. It is easily shown, however, that something *is* maximized. The end result is such that no one's economic welfare could possibly be increased further, except in ways that would take from some and give to others. It also turns out that the relative market prices of any two items measure the relative contributions to economic welfare of an additional unit of each.

The regulated free-enterprise economy does more than suggest a model for decentralized decisions in other types of organizations. Reliance on prices obviously simplifies individiual economic decisions, since many of these can be made in terms of aggregate money costs and revenues with a known equivalence in marketed goods and services. It also provides a "natural" valuation system for the making of independent decisions or evaluations when the objective or standard is defined in terms of social welfare. Such decisions and evaluations must be made by professional economists and well meaning governments because many areas of activity, especially the provision of collective services, are not subject to market determination, and because many markets operate very imperfectly. Referring again to the cost-benefit study of federal aid to education, suggested earlier, it is apparent that the analysis requires something more than information on competing and complementary programs under federal auspices. The benefits, for instance, must be measured by reference to some model of the economy showing what goods and services will be generated over time as a result of larger or differently distributed college graduations. If so, the analysis, and any other analysis in support of government decisions, would seem to require processing of a full-scale model of the economy in thousands of equations, a bleak prospect indeed. This is where the availability of a standing price system tied to some implicit social optimization provides invaluable assistance. Rather than predicting and measuring ultimate outcomes, it is enough to refer to the "price" which the market puts on graduates, that is, their expected earnings over time,[10] in the secure knowledge that it measures the relative contribution of an additional graduate to economic welfare.

Clearly, current market prices can only be used safely as long as the proposed (or observed) changes are of small enough a magnitude not to affect the price structure in a drastic way. It must also be recognized that all social objective variables of interest are not subject to market valuation, so that market prices may be biased measures of ultimate values. Finally, actual markets do not always behave in the proper "optimizing" way. All in all, therefore, economists may be making too much of a good thing, and they can legitimately be accused of using market prices irresponsibly in a good deal of the cost-benefit analysis they provide. Nevertheless, it is probable that the existence of market prices interpretable as measures of marginal social value is the main advantage which economists have enjoyed over their colleagues in other social sciences. This is a handicap that cannot be fully bridged through better research, and there are obvious impediments to restructuring all social transactions along market lines.

I. *Policy Advocacy Toward Social Welfare*

Finally, economists exhibit a traditional weakness for adopting whole nations as their willing or unwilling clients. While a good deal of their applied work is contracted and paid for by business firms or government units with relatively identifiable objective variables and value systems, much of what they publish and become famous for represents a gratuitous admonishment to nations (or to the world) concerning policies they *ought* to pursue. In other words, economists are political philosophers, and they are prone to reminding themselves and their readers that the science used to be known as Political Economy.

In their more cautious moods, practitioners of the art take great care to specify the social value system under which proposed solutions have an optimum quality. In their least guarded moments, their conclusions take the aspect of prophetic pronouncements in which value postulates, if at all identifiable, are implicitly the result of divine inspiration. Except for the recent generation of social cost-benefit analysts, however, those imbued with scientific rigor feel uncomfortable with value systems of less than universal validity. They will not affirm a system (theirs) as *the* socially valid one, but neither will they fall into relativism and generate findings that are less than general.

They compromise by strictly limiting the range of acceptable social welfare statements: A situation is called better than another one if it gives some individuals or groups a higher level of satisfaction without reducing the satisfaction level of any one; and a higher level of satisfaction is characterized by a capability to consume more of some goods and services without sacrificing any. This so-called "Pareto" criterion avoids value judgments concerning distribution of welfare among economic participants, while making it impossible to compare two situations in which some get more and some get less. The result has been a peculiar form of intellectual exertion known as Welfare Economics, the practitioners of which seek the most general welfare statements deducible under the criterion. Of particular significance was the conclusion, already noted, that a properly regulated competitive market system would be Pareto-optimal. More and more, however, it is recognized that emasculated value systems will not do. The explicit incorporation of welfare distribution and other social concerns does specialize the relevance of conclusions to those who share in the proposed values, but partisan conclusions are preferable to universal truths if the latter are weak and incomplete.

It should not be concluded that economists, bent on optimum social solutions, represent a constant revolutionary threat. As already suggested, their attitude toward institutional arrangements is fairly conservative. In the West, the mainstream of the profession takes for granted all major features of the competitive free-enterprise system, as it does central economic control in the socialist world or did mercantilist structures in pre-industrial nation-states. Their present tools are, in fact, inappropriate for systematic study of institutional variations. But they have gone one step further, proving that both a perfectly competitive system and a decentralized socialist system receiving appropriate signals would, in some sense, offer a maximum of social welfare. The demonstration, built on the kind of general problem formulation discussed earlier, fails on many accounts, but it does reassure that economists are accommodating fellows.

Nor should anyone accuse economists of intellectual arrogance and incipient tyranny. Their independent formulation of social values and objectives is not entirely unsolicited. The fact of the matter is that most governments and government agencies are unclear about social goals. If the economic consultant or advisor is bold enough to require a statement of the prevailing value system, his is likely to be viewed as part feebleminded and part subversive, with foreseeable consequences on his career. If his recommendations are presented as a mathematical function of alternative value weights on outcomes, he will be called undecisive and unfit for policy work. The inescapable conclusion is that economists have no choice but to trace the path of human fulfillment, and the suggestion that they would do so in any case is perceptive but irrelevant.

* * *

If economics stands apart from other social sciences on so many scales, the phenomenon requires some explanation. A science historian would no doubt build a voluminous record on the subject, but a modest inquiry produces a few fairly obvious lines of differentiation, some having to do with the subject matter and others with the historical role of economists.

The relative solidity of empirical relationships in economic models and the sophistication of their mathematical representation owe a great deal to three factors. First of all, the economic domain is as much in the physical world as it is in the human or social. Technological relationships, themselves reflecting well-grounded laws of the physical sciences, constitute a substantial portion of most economic models, whether they come in the form of detailed "production functions" efficiently linking the inputs and outputs of a firm, or in the guise of fairly general characterizations, such as the famous "law of diminishing returns." Secondly, the number of behavioral and, until recently, social variables which economists manipulate is a very small fraction of those of concern to sociologists and social psychologists. The social universe of economists is one of households, business firms, and governments which produce, consume, stock up, capture, give away or exchange goods, services, and claims by reference to known technologies and predictable behavior patterns of others, to maximize some simple criterion. This is thin indeed, even if the activities covered are a central and consuming social concern. Not only is the universe sparse and simplistic, but many of the most relevant questions can be answered in terms of large group behavior with attendant benefits in empirical estimation. Third, the models that fit economic systems exhibit highly desirable mathematical properties from the standpoint of discovering optimizing social interventions; moreover, most economic systems are built around market structures that guarantee an approximation of Pareto optimality and generate prices which can serve as marginal measures of "social utility." This provides economic analysts with an invaluable shortcut to the cost-benefit evaluation of partial or decentralized interventions, as long as the outcomes of interest are all priced by the market.

How heavily the success of economists rests on those three pillars is well brought out when excessive demands are made on the profession. Economists share with electronic computers the dubious privilege of arousing infinite expectations among the uninitiated. If a question must be answered in terms of quantities produced and consumed, and, more particularly, if dollar figures must be quoted, it is assumed that economic analysis will deliver the solution. Such assumptions were made, for instance, by administrators and planners of education, when they called on economists to determine optimum schedules of resource allocation at all levels of the education sector. That economists either failed or begged off is traceable to one peculiarity of the situation: the dismal state of technological information concerning education processes and the need to refer to "non-economic" social models in estimating some crucial benefits of education. There is some magic to economics, but it can only go so far. The props must be provided before a tolerable show can be put on.

Historically, the relative manageability of economic models has attracted scientific intelligences from an early date, thus giving the discipline a methodological handicap which others have been slow to bridge. It is commonly recognized among adepts of the other social sciences that not only more scientific, but also better brains, have been drawn to the economic profession—a belief which economists hold with equal conviction but never voice openly unless by inadvertence. Whatever these advantages may be, it is likely that they will not survive much longer. As economists are forced by popular demand to deal with "soft" technologies in human and social development, to incorporate new ranges of behavior, and to be concerned with additional social criteria, pure intellectual satisfactions will no longer be so freely available. Those willing to meet the challenge will have to be ready for a less tractable and less pliable universe several steps further removed from that of the physical sciences. Once in that state of mind, they may find the other social sciences to be no less congenial than economics.

The greater willingness of economists to formulate and resolve policy problems is grounded, in part, in the greater confidence they can place in their models and, in part, in the sustained demand to which they have been subjected. These two aspects are, in fact, reinforcing. Statesmen and, later, businessmen might have gained an earlier awareness of sociological and psychological realities, thus making earlier demands on the associated professions, had the latter developed along more rigorous and more empirical lines. The process of adjustments is a slow one, especially on the part of the professions. While governments and corporations are more than willing to incorporate social science findings in their decision models, non-economists remain reluctant to move away from a certain scientism which allows both the rigorous pursuit of empirical findings and the loose explanation of past matrices of events but frowns upon attempts at linking available generalizations into predictive models and, even more so, attaching any kind of value system to outcomes.

The ethical foundations of this reluctance are legitimate up to a point: no one should predict who cannot, in fact, predict. Economists and meteorologists do so with great abandon and view discrepancies between observed and predicted events as just other pieces of useful information, but this may be saying little for their integrity. On the other hand, no opprobium should ever attach to the evaluation of outcomes by reference to value systems as long as such systems are carefully and openly specified. That many do, and will, abuse the privilege is obvious; the needs are too pressing, however, for social scientists to respond negatively. Better that some mislead than all seek escape into social sterility.

ECONOMICS IN THE HISTORICAL PERSPECTIVE

Viewing economics against the background of the social sciences brings out the essentials of the syntax and some of the substance of the discipline. Of all possible ways to fill in the canvas, the most effective is a chronological review of professional concerns and achievements over the last century. The record is a bit heavy for a six page summary, but major thrusts can be identified without too much difficulty.

While the early classicists (Adam Smith,[11] Malthus, Ricardo, and later, Marx) had been true political economists bent on tracing and redressing the course of human institutions, economists in the second half of the nineteenth century had turned into full-time analysts of the detailed mechanisms of industrial capitalism. The broad historical models linking population growth, capital accumulation, institutional evolution, power distribution, and the like were all but abandoned in favor of more "scientific" efforts sheltered from the winds of political reform. The less analytically inclined applied Germanic thoroughness to minute compilations of the historical record or built impressive expertise in the functions and structures of economic institutions. The dominant neoclassical school, however, centered on developing logical models of individual markets and drawing the social welfare implications of their interrelated operation.

In the neoclassical competitive model, each good service, or claim has its market with suppliers lined up on one side and potential users on the other. Each individual member (firm or household) is a maximizer (of profit or "utility") and, as such, schedules the amounts he will buy or sell at different times for different constellations of relevant market prices. As long as the reigning price in any market fails to equilibrate amounts offered and demanded, competition among sellers to get rid of goods in surplus or among users to appropriate goods in shortage shifts the price in a self-correcting way. Thus, through all the movements brought about by population growth, inventions, discoveries, random upheavals, and the slow process of capital accumulation; the economy tends, at all times, toward some general equilibrium in which all markets would exactly be cleared. In the longer-run perspective, capital accumulation is itself determined by the market, and the path of economic growth tends to some final equilibrium of either the "stationary" or "balanced growth" variety.

The competitive model provided the general background for analysis in a variety of directions. With increasing sharpness, "general-equilibrium" theorists could describe the system of interrelated markets as one of simultaneous equations which, given certain initial or exogenous values, would determine the path of prices, productions, consumptions, exchanges, investigations, and so on over any time horizon. Rather than describing the full path, many preferred to deal with the stabilized equilibrium, emphasizing some of the conditions holding in such a state, especially the equality between prices of production factors and the value of their "marginal product" or the proportional relation between prices of goods and their "marginal utility."[12] All conclusions were based on very sketchy descriptions of the technical and behavioral relationships involved centering almost exclusively on their slopes and curvatures. The models, therefore, could not supply quantitative measures of the outcomes of alternative policies; at best, they identified directions and limits of expected change. But their main contribution was in the field of institutional choice: Increasingly rigorous proofs were offered that the marginal conditions holding when production, consumption, and investment had been stabilized under pure competition were precisely those which independent calculations (in a social "decisions model" constrained only by available resources and technologies) showed to be necessary for maximization of a social-welfare index. Not only, therefore, could the competitive profit system be defended as an overall form of economic organization, but localized deviations from its ideal performance could be identified and corrected.

The bulk of the neoclassical literature found itself concerned with the partial equilibrium implications of the general model or with some "aggregative" versions oriented to specific problems.[13] Partial-equilibirum studies took for granted the establishment of competitive conditions in the system as a whole and analyzed the adjustment of smaller units (firms, groups of firms, households, communities) to various conditions, with special emphasis on local deviations from marginal criteria of social welfare maximization.

Those could originate from individual attempts at monopolizing markets, from unwise taxes or controls on the part of governments or from unfortunate imperfections of the institutional framework.[14] In aggregative versions, large chunks of economic activity were regrouped and treated as a single entity so as to analyze certain mechanisms (e.g.; the monetary system, capital accumulation) in a simpler context. Whether aggregative or not, however, the analysis remained dominated by the competitive model. Not only were most problems to be solved by enforcing a more competitive behavior, but recognized shortcomings of the free enterprise system were to be accepted as a small price to pay for the virtues of competition. Business cycles, in particular, had to be taken as an unfortunate, but mostly unavoidable, feature of long-term competitive adjustments.

This orthodoxy, of course, was never fully accepted, and critics became increasingly articulate after the turn of the century. Enforcing competition in one sector of the economy would perhaps enhance social welfare if other related sectors were themselves competitive; if not, and if nothing could be done about the latter, enforcing competition in the first would simply deliver it to exploitation by others. In any event, the case for full competition was far from established. In many industries, the level of production at which individual firms ceased to enjoy increased efficiency (reduced unit cost) through large-scale operation represented a substantial proportion of the whole market. To insist on a large number of firms for the sake of competitiveness meant that the small production share of each would prevent the achievement of minimum unit costs. Some form of oligopoly[15] was, therefore, necessary, and the best one could do was to enforce reasonable levels of profit on the few controlling members of the industry. In still other industries (e.g., most public utilities), a single firm could fill the whole (localized) market and still be capable of lowering its unit cost through further expansion. Not only was competition then out of the question, but the unit cost at which the market was supplied would keep falling as the latter expanded. This contradicted a fundamental assumption of the model under which "marginal rules" for maximum social welfare had been established; with decreasing-cost markets, welfare conditions became far more complicated and far less general, and their enforcement in the market was clearly to be achieved by means other than competition.

More fundamentally, the proposed "maximization" of social welfare was strictly relative. In line with the welfare-economics approach outlined earlier, the only guarantee concerning an equilibrium meeting the marginal rules was that no possibility remained of improving the well-being of all participants.[16] No social optimum could, indeed, fail this so-called Pareto condition, but it happened to hold for an infinite number of situations other than the particular equilibrium achieved. Without even considering alternatives to competition, it was clear that different initial endowments of capital among economic participants would lead to different competitive equilibria, each meeting the Pareto condition. Not only was there a problem of choosing between such relative optima, but the introduction of more specific value judgements could make a "non-optimum" equilibrium preferable to an "optimum" one. For example, the enforcement of a minimum-income policy might so distort work incentives as to prevent a fully efficient allocation of the labor force, yet the resulting income distribution could be found preferable to that evolving under strictly competitive conditions. In other words, insistence by orthodox economists on avoiding value judgments had led them to leave distribution problems to take care of themselves. Clearly, a more realistic approach was required if economists were to assume fuller responsibilities in this area.

It was not, however, until the last decade that distribution as such became a central concern of the profession. The world depression during the early thirties brought about renewed interest in business cycles. This interest, eventually extended to problems of long-term economic growth, soon polarized energies to the point where, shortly after the second World War, economics became identified in the public mind with the science of sustained growth and full employment. The analytical substratum was provided by J.M. Keynes, a British economist, in the form of an aggregative model linking national employment, gross national product, aggregate savings, aggregate investments, government taxes and expenditures, interest rates and the money supply. By denying the validity of some traditional models of behavior, concerning saving, the holding of liquid assets, and responses to unemployment, he concluded that uncontrolled economic systems could remain stabilized for long periods in a state of drastic unemployment. On the other hand, full employment and continued growth could be achieved by the simple process of sustaining aggregate demand for goods and services, and this, in turn, only required that Government adjust its own contribution to demand to make up for shortages or excesses of private demand. The new theory held the center of the economic stage right into the sixties, and the huge literature it generated ranges all the way from econometric works to institutional studies. It also opened the way to sophisticated multisector models of the economy, in which more attention was paid to empirically measured behavior and less to postulates of the the competitive model. Most important, it has now gained general acceptance, both within and without the profession.

The same period saw enormous progress in theoretical understanding, research methodology, and empirical discovery. New light was thrown on a variety of market structures, with a better appreciation of non-price instruments available to participants.[18] Most significantly, the whole theoretical apparatus was refined and consolidated into clean mathematical models.[19] The limitations of calculus in solving complex maximization problems were partly overcome through their respecification in "programmatic" form and use of relatively standard solution methods. The new specification does entail some simplification of the original model, mostly linear approximations, but practitioners soon learn to keep the damage within bonds. Not only is a full solution obtained, in the sense that magnitudes required for a maximization of the "objective function" are all determined, but "shadow prices" (or values of marginal products) can be calculated quickly and elegantly. Other major advances were registered in the handling of dynamic structures and in the specification of decision models. New emphases in the latter area included the rational treatment of probability elements, the investigation of "game" situations in which interacting agents develop contingent "strategies," and the analysis of "collective" decision under agreed sets of rules.

The most prominent gainer, however, was the field of econometrics, so much so that a Ph.D. thesis lacking in quantitative analysis is now viewed with great suspicion by most economics departments in our universities. On the one hand, progress was realized in eschewing fancy intellectual constructs and in adjusting multisector models of the economy to the available data base. On the other hand, brilliant additions were made to statistical methodology, with main emphasis on estimation problems in non-experimental situations, that is, situations in which the information base consists of measures thrown out from day to day by a complex system whose structure is not accurately known.[20] The theoretical framework developed by econometricians is still being built upon and represents a major gift of the profession to other social sciences. Within economics itself, it has supported, and continues to support, a large crop of quantitative inferences that promise new orders of magnitude in the efficiency of economic models.

While much of the economic output in recent years can be viewed as occurring near boundaries reached two decades earlier, several new trends are discernible. Most important of all, economists have fully accepted their role as builders of policy decision models at all levels of business and government. Cost-Benefit and optimization have become the pass-words, and there is hardly any area of the social universe which economic analysts are not ready to tackle. The old reluctance to deal with anything but broad policy principles or, later, high-level fiscal and monetary decisions of the central government has been overcome. Those engaged in the new enterprise do not hesitate to specify social objective functions and to classify policy alternatives in their light. They recognize that a clear reading of consequences is the first requirement of increased rationality in political decisions.

The change has been accelerated, if not induced, by new political concerns affecting income distribution, human-resource development, economic opportunities, and social-welfare components other than the private consumption of goods and services. Distribution problems, in particular, have assumed a central role, forcing value judgments into the open. Value questions crop up again in the consideration of collective costs generated by pollution, congestion, defacing, and other evils of the industrial system, or collective benefits expected from education, conservation, environment planning and all efforts toward humanizing social structures. This is where traditional economic models begin to burst at the seams, not only because personalized welfare criteria are inadequate to the task, but because relevant social outcomes must be pursued far beyond the usual confines of the economic universe.

Finally, cost-benefit analysis is arousing a new awareness of the structural limitations of standard economic models. Variations on the theme of the competitive market are no longer sufficient. Policy, especially on the part of governments, is exercised through a variety of instruments which include far more than the fixing of prices and production levels. Objectives are pursued through enforced regulation, suasion, complex bargains, and other modes of controlling behavior, with special emphasis on the establishment of appropriate organizations. While available economic methodology allows for the systematic search of "best" parameter values, once basic structures have been specified, the comparisons it can make between alternative frameworks of organization and modalities of control are still guided by intuition and constrained by tradition. The next task of economics, therefore, is to develop new modes of describing large classes of alternative actions including more than parametric variations and new optimizing methodologies capable of scanning such alternatives efficiently. The answers expected from that effort concern all levels of social decision, from the broad reform of our economic institutions to the determination of state subsidization schemes in education, through the reorganization of planning and budgeting functions in federal departments and the redistribution of fiscal powers among levels of government. This is an impressive challenge and one that economists are sure to meet, even if, in the process, they must acquire new identities or join hands with colleagues in the other social sciences.

FOOTNOTES

1. A good touchstone of a science's empirical maturity is the extent to which it can do without "factor" or "principal-component" analysis. By this standard, economics is way ahead of the game although it can be argued that the technique is unduly, and somewhat carelessly, neglected by economists.

2. University of Michigan Research Seminar in Quantitative Economics and Econometric and Forecastic Unit of the Wharton School of Finance.

3. The Forecasting Unit of the Wharton School of Finance has had the following record on one-year predictions of changes in GNP, demand for consumer goods and services, and capital investment:

	GNP		Consumer Goods and Services		Capital Investment	
	Actual Change	Predicted Change	Actual Change	Predicted Change	Actual Change	Predicted Change
1963	$30.0 bil.	$31.0 bil.	$18.2 bil.	$16.7 bil.	$3.2 bil.	$ 4.9 bil.
1964	38.7	40.9	23.5	20.1	5.6	7.7
1965	42.9	39.0	28.8	26.8	5.4	5.9
1966	59.3	55.4	32.8	29.3	9.1	10.6
1967	45.5	48.0	26.7	27.0	3.2	4.7
1968	75.6	56.9	42.1	32.4	7.5	3.5

Considering that year-to-year changes constitute less than 10% of the total, the results are impressive indeed.

4. The aggregative approach is well illustrated by recent work on the contributions of "Capital," "Labor," and the "Third Factor" to economic growth. For instance, see Robert Solow, "Technical Change and the Aggregate Production Function," *Review of Economics and Statistics* (August 1957), pp. 312-320.

The "down to earth" school is best represented by "input-output" analysis as originally developed by Wassily Leontief. See W. Leontief, *Input-Output Economics* (New York: Oxford University Press, 1966).

5. Cutting across styles and history, the list of authors in this category would include Malthus, Marx, Schumpeter, and John Kenneth Galbraith. For a sample of their books, see: Thomas R. Malthus, *An Essay on the Principle of Population*, first published in London in 1798, now available from (New York: Dent, 1952); Karl Marx, *Capital*, 1st German edition, 1867, recent English edition (New York: International Publishers, 1967); Joseph A. Schumpeter, *Capitalism, Socialism, and Democracy* (New York: Harper, 1942); John Kenneth Galbraith, *The New Industrial State* (Boston: Houghton Mifflin, 1967).

6. The fundamental work in the field was produced jointly by a mathematician (Von Neumann) and an economist (Morgenstern). See, therefore, John Von Neumann and Oskar Morgenstern, *Theory of Games and Economic Behavior*, 2nd ed. (Princeton: Princeton University Press, 1947).

7. Linear programming was developed by George B. Dantzig in 1947 as a planning technique for use by the U.S. Air Force. His pioneering paper circulated privately for several years, and it was eventually published as G. B. Dantzig, "Maximization of a Linear Function of Variables Subject to Linear Inequalities" in *Activity Analysis of Production and Allocation*, ed. T. C. Koopman (New York: John Wiley & Sons, Inc., 1951), pp. 339–347.

8. In the case of activities where output can only be expanded by repeating the same fixed combination of inputs, a zero profit on "additional" output at the given prices implies a zero profit on the whole output. This insures equality of price and cost; that is, the shadow price of an output is the cost of associated inputs measured at their shadow price.

9. To the extent that "activities" organize themselves on several levels (the outputs at one level entering as inputs in higher-level activities), decisions can proceed in a downward sequence: the decision unit responsible for one output simply attempts to produce the quantity demanded at minimum cost and, in the process, determines some of the demand for lower-level outputs. The quantity demanded should be reduced by the amount generated as a by-product of the activities of other decision units in the previous round, and the value (positive or negative) of by-products generated by the decision unit should be subtracted from costs.

10. If the value of graduates is compared with the cost of their production, expected earnings over time must be discounted to the present by reference to the rate of return on alternative investments.

11. Smith is considered the Father of Economics for his book, *The Wealth of Nations*, first published in 1776. A recent edition is that of the Modern Library, New York, 1937.

12. The first rigorous representation of a general equilibrium competitive model was supplied by the Swiss economist Leon Walras in *Éléments d' Économie Politique Pure* in 1874. For a recent edition see *Elements of Pure Economics* (London: Allen and Unwin, 1954).

13. The neoclassical school flourished from the mid-nineteenth century through the first third of the twentieth, with main centers in Austria and England and later major contributions from the United States and Sweden. It culminated in the writings of the British economist Alfred Marshall. See Alfred Marshall, *Principles of Economics*, 8th ed. (London: Macmillan, 1920).

14. International trade adjustments were the object of partial-equilibrium analysis in the context of a worldwide economic system.

15. A situation in which a few firms supply the major portion of the market.

16. More precisely, no other feasible arrangement could improve the well-being of some or all individuals without hurting others.

17. John Maynard Keynes, *The General Theory of Employment, Interest, and Money* (New York: Harcourt, Brace and World, 1936).

18. The major contribution in this area came from Edward Chamberlin. See: Edward Chamberlin, *The Theory of Monopolistic Competition* (Cambridge: Harvard University Press, 1932).

19. The celebrated textbook author, Paul Samuelson, was in the forefront of this movement with his book: *Foundations of Economic Analysis* (Cambridge: Harvard University Press in 1947).

20. The breakthroughs were provided by a group of economists working as the "Cowles Commission for Research in Economics." See Tjalling Koopmans, ed., *Statistical Inference in Dynamic Economic Models*, Cowles Commission Monograph 10 (New York: John Wiley and Sons, Inc., 1950).

Part Three

Case Descriptions of Content Selection and Use

This part draws upon the actual experience of professors in preparatory programs who have responsibility for preparing educational administrators. The chapters seek to illuminate issues associated with social science content selection and use. Most of the chapters describe the experiences of individual professors in seminars or courses. Chapter Eight, however, examines the problems within the two institutional contexts of Harvard University and The University of Chicago.

In writing the chapters, the authors were requested to specify the criteria they used in selecting social science content and to clarify the relationships between the criteria used and the content selected. They were also asked to provide information on the students taught and, if courses or seminars were involved, to indicate where in programs these experiences were placed.

The cases were chosen for their relationship to the differing perspectives of relevance which provide the basic framework for the book. Chapter Eight is designed to illuminate the career-based concept of relevance. Problem-based relevance is treated in Chapter Nine, while Chapter Ten is written from a discipline-based perspective. The two final chapters are designed to shed light on the theory-based approach to relevance.

Since the various perspectives are not entirely discrete and since professors seldom use one framework only in content selection, the cases presented are not pure illustrations of given perspectives. However, they represent systematic examination of the questions of "how," "why," and "what" in relation to social science content selection and use.

8

The Social Sciences and the Preparation of Educational Administrators at Harvard and Chicago

Joseph M. Cronin and Laurence Iannaccone

Both Harvard University and the University of Chicago, for more than twenty years, have drawn heavily on social science and social scientists in planning and implementing doctoral programs in educational administration. A.W.K. Kellogg Foundation report in 1961 found the two universities shared a common commitment: integrating contributions from social science disciplines in the preparation of educational administrators.

> At the University of Chicago, the Department of Education is part of the Division of Social Sciences, and the social sciences at that institution have played a part in the training of educators for many years. In the sequence of basic seminars and courses which constitute the core of the doctoral program in educational administration, insights from sociology, psychology, political science, and other disciplines are integrated into the work.
> Somewhat similar to this approach is the plan followed at Harvard University, where the social scientists are ultimately related to the total program rather than merely teaching discrete courses, and where these teachers are members of the Faculty of the Graduate School of Education. This method seems to provide an integration of relationships and a continuity of point of view which might not be possible if the students simply took courses in other disciplines.[1]

Although the general aspirations of professors in the universities were similar, they developed very different kinds of programs to fit very different kinds of objectives. Their students "consumed" social sciences for diverse reasons; therefore, their subsequent career patterns also differed. Since both universities paid special homage to the social sciences, it would seem useful to retrace the steps which led to the development of their differing programs. Such a retracing should illuminate the rationale underlying the selection and use of the social sciences in preparatory programs at each of the universities.

The reader needs to be informed of two explicit caveats:

1. Neither university has used the social sciences simply as sources of "concepts;" methods of analysis and modes of inquiry have been considered as significant as concepts. One course taught at Harvard was named Cases and Concepts in Educational Administration, but the use of social sciences was quite broad. The faculty at the University of Chicago sought to develop various kinds of "administrative theory;" for them, concepts were the bricks and mortar of larger constructs and the search was instead for comprehensive theory possibly useful for research and, in some instances, for action.

2. Neither university has finished trying to determine the appropriate use of social scientists. Committees have planned program revisions at both universities at frequent intervals, and shifts in emphases have reflected both the appearance of new personalities and the recognition of new sets of problems or priorities. The following descriptions and evaluations of the efforts must account for the shifting sands of educational administration, most spectacularly a shift from the growth problems of the suburbs in the 1950s to the present urban crisis. Neither program was static; neither program will be the same in five years.

Some differences may be seen between the Harvard and Chicago statement of their plans from the start. The Chicago emphasis includes a concern for adding knowledge and understanding to the field of school administration. This kind of concern one would expect from scholars with an orientation towards training other scholars, although this was not initially the University of Chicago's major goal. Secondly, the University of Chicago's plan was to continue a Ph.D. program within the structure of the university's social science division. This implied a context and from that context constraints which would tend to maximize a concern for the production of knowledge and understanding in school administration. At Harvard, the situation was initially different to some extent. The Ph.D. at Harvard is under the control of the faculty of Arts and Sciences. The Harvard Graduate School of Education, by strengthening the Ed.D. rather than developing the Ph.D., would be able to move away from the often ritualistic demands for scholarship of the faculty of Arts and Sciences and emphasize a concern for the immediate utility of the social sciences to the clinical practitioner. It was in their contribution to the practitioners' work that the role of the social sciences was found for the Harvard program. The implications probably not seen at the very early stages of the two programs were that, in the case of Chicago, the role of the social scientists in the program (within the context of the social science division of the university which controlled the Ph.D.) would be dominant, whereas in Harvard the role of the social scientists would be that of junior partners in the program. But initially, on paper at least, the differences between the two programs did not appear to be great. In time, the divergence of the operations of the training program in each school was to grow further and further from each other until now, twenty years later, they seem in some ways to be almost 180 degrees apart.

This has led to what is an oversimplified point of view: Harvard trains practitioners and works on school improvement in the field directly; Chicago trains professors and is committed to the production of knowledge about schools as an indirect means of improving schools. Specifically, the explicit commitment of Harvard was that "students will be encouraged more strongly to work with the problems of educational administration rather than *merely contemplate them*."[2] The Chicago plan emphasized, "understanding the purposes and functions of educational administration. . . ." Looking back, one can now identify two competing views on administration as an object of study. Yet leaders of both programs worked with the field much of the time, and both incorporated courses seeking to impart an understanding of administration.

What grew from these seeds diverged even more, given the soil of each institution and the significant effect of the context. The key decisions which determined the context of each program seem to have rested primarily on Chicago's program remaining in the university's social science division while Harvard's grew in the increasingly policy- or problem-oriented education school as it developed under Francis Keppel. As significant as the differences in the context for each of the programs may be, the differences of the key actors brought into the program may have been just as significant. Philip Selznick's work suggests the complex reaction between initial program design and the subsequent changes required because of the people involved.[3] To leave out people while discussing ideas and the effect of the interjection of the social sciences by the universities in their programs in educational administration is meaningless. Each program made a different use of its social scientists and was dissimilarly influenced by these. Selznick placed emphasis upon the significance of bringing potential supporters into the organization as participants in decision making. Even with Kellogg financial support, both administration programs needed the resource of key personnel to carry out their mandate, and, inevitably, these participants shared in redefining the mandate, ideology, and content of the programs.

The central influences first of Alfred Simpson and then of Herold Hunt at Harvard and of Frank Chase followed by Roald Campbell at Chicago are clear. But the role of social scientists, Jacob Getzels in particular at Chicago, and Neal Gross and Charles Benson at Harvard, differed from the outset. The informal influence of the social scientists in each program was crucial. Their contributions to each program seem to have increased the divergence between the two programs.

This chapter will be divided into four parts: background on the basic program ideas and changing formats, a close look at the courses and other ways social sciences were used, examination of the ultimate careers and other by-products of the programs, then an assessment of what happened at each.

Harvard University: 1950–1970

Professor Alfred Dexter Simpson, in 1949, developed a Center for Field Studies in the School of Education with a policy committee drawn from the graduate schools of business, public administration, design, public health, as well as education, and with representation also from the social relations department.[4] The Center provided a coordination of efforts to improve educational practices through school system surveys. The Center could accept other opportunities for "cumulative research" which also had instructional value. Although Simpson founded the Center essentially to serve school systems, it later assumed the responsibility for research and training activities. Between 1949 and 1953, the Center, while conducting twenty-one studies of school systems, accepted responsibility for Russell Sage supported studies of what community factors contributed to making "good schools." It also became responsible for the W. K. Kellogg Foundation grants which were designed to improve the training of educational administrators.

During the 1949–1953 period, several social scientists joined the faculty of the Center: Alfred De Grazia, Peter and Alice Rossi, John Lieper Freeman, James Shipton, and Neal Gross. The Rossis, Freeman, and Shipton conducted a three year research study of Bay City, a middle-sized municipality with several large ethnic groups. Gross began his long-term school executive studies. Everyone conducted his own research, but was based in a center of essentially applied research and school surveys of immediate use to school boards.

The W. K. Kellogg Foundation grant to Harvard stipulated efforts to change both the pre-service and in-service education of school administrators in New England. The existing doctoral program at Harvard did not require full-time study (one could study for four or five summers and part-time during the year) and culminated in a doctoral dissertation for the Ed.D. degree.[5] Many of the dissertations were quite scholarly — Norman Boyan on the informal organization of schools, James Laurits on faculty morale, Cyril Sargent on state fiscal policy, Owen Kiernan on state education law. At the time the grant was made (1951) many students and a few faculty questioned the appropriateness of the research model for training men of action. Social scientists criticized the tendency of many students to focus on the nuts and bolts of school management. Dissatisfaction with education in administration was conveyed to the education faculty in January 1952, after more than a year of debate and planning. The following excerpt sheds some light on why the social sciences were seen as relevant to administrator preparation:

> In one respect, past thought and practice has conceived administration too narrowly. It has often been viewed as a technical task of executing the precise commands of superior authorities. In fact, however the administrator of school systems, like other executives, is always a judge of values and frequently a determiner of policies. He therefore needs education in the study of his own values, of the values of the community, of the values of persons with whom he must contest his policies, and of the values argued and transmitted from history. He needs, furthermore, an education going beyond the techniques of carrying out the orders of others into the procedures by which he may capably assist the makers of public policy.

In another respect, administration has been shown not to have done well enough those tasks it has admitted as its own. A cursory glance at the literature and research of the various fields of administration will readily reveal how new findings and methods are emerging from the various social sciences. Psychologists, sociologists, political scientists, and specialists on administration are discovering that certain older theories about morale, productivity, leadership, and organization are inadequate in the face of many new studies on those subjects. Few graduate schools have adjusted their faculties and curricula to remedy such deficiencies in the traditional theory of administration. The program under consideration here revises the study of administration in favor of subjects and methods that contemporary social sciences hold to be basic to the understanding of administrative behavior.

Together with the two major types of change described above stands a third proposed change of a pedagogical nature. Besides broadening the perspectives and skills of future administrators, and increasing the contribution of the social sciences to their development, the program is designed to foster creativity. Students will be encouraged more strongly to work with the problems of educational administration rather than merely to contemplate them. A fact of administration, they will learn, does not have an isolated existence, alongside innumerable other facts similarly detached. The arrangements in the program that provide for group work, case method of instruction and field research, together with immersion in the theory of school administration, are intended to develop total and complete meanings of facts and to teach their application in real life. The students will learn their facts contextually and operationally.[6]

The faculty was then asked to approve for a five year period a new experimental program, one to prepare "those 'action' or 'practising' administrators who will assume key positions in the actual administration of school systems." The proposal urged acceptance of a new program different from that of "those who will go on to research careers or engage in university teaching." The latter would continue, but the revised program would imply an additional orientation towards the "master practitioner," a phrase borrowed from the medical profession. The proposal maintained this emphasis on careers in the field would also increase the graduate schools' impact on the profession. Men in the schools were needed to direct younger men to advance studies and provide laboratory situations for research and training.

The new program would recruit both experienced and inexperienced administrators, the latter with at least one year of school system experience and with an Ed.M. or equivalent. The faculty would admit an equal number from each category at the outset, but shift gradually to a 16:4 ratio of inexperienced to experienced candidates by 1956–57. Although the older men might be less familiar with "recent appropriate social science literature," the younger candidates would profit from relationships with the men of recognized competence (who might later help place their juniors and recruit others.)

The actual program assumed three needs:

1. for increased emphasis on the social sciences in administration programs. The administrator, in a sense, is a social science generalist.

2. for a core — a series of multiple experiences — centered on the development of the administrator . . . (yet) blocks of time . . . for guided electives selected from course offerings both in the school and elsewhere in the university.

3. for increased guided experiences in field or clinical situations. This together with more extensive use of the case method of instruction, can hope to serve the function of integrating for the student in realistic fashion his necessarily more knowledge-and-theory-oriented classroom experience.

Inexperienced candidates would in their first semester engage in a field experience in a community observation post (city hall or community service agency) as well as in a school system. They would also complete an eight week internship with some administrative responsibility, typically during the summer between the second and third year of study. All candidates in the Ed.D. program for practising administrators would take one course in "Problems of Administration and Related Research Methods," and then take field work of both the "contractual" and "social science research" types. The former would be a school survey with a strong service orientation; the latter would be a community study, perhaps such as the Bay City studies of public opinion and political leadership. All candidates would take a course entitled Cases and Concepts for half of the second semester and one quarter of the second year. Two or more elective courses would be chosen. The final semester would be spent in an individual administrative project.

The course in administration and related research methods was designed:

1. to appraise critically administrative problems previously familiar to the participants, using the frames of reference and conceptual tools of administrative analysis as developed by such writers as Follett, Urwick, Drucker, Mayo, and Barnard.

2. to offer training to the student in social science research methods pertinent to the analysis of the administrative problems considered and to the field research program in which seminar members would be later involved.

For the experienced administrator, a basic purpose of this course was to "loosen attachment to outdated or overly formalized views of administration" already acquired. For all candidates, the methodological portions of the course might include training in participant observation, interview and scaling techniques, and sociometric methods. The inexperienced administrators would receive separate emphasis on how schools were organized and what administrative practices were currently recommended by authorities.

The cases and concepts sequence was spelled out in considerable detail and subsequently will be analyzed in this chapter. The cases would represent specialized "aspects of administration such as personnel relations, supervision, budgeting, programming, or public policy." Cases would be selected not only from educational problems but from business, public, and other kinds of social service administration. The concepts would relate to the cases and would require a "critical examination of scholarly learning." In the social sciences students "would partake heavily of significant works in sociology, anthropology, and psychology." From the humanities, history, biography, critical letters, and philosophy might contribute a breadth of outlook. This course would be chaired by a professor from educational administration, but with assistance from one faculty resource person in social science and another long on administrative experience. Other faculty and guests from other graduate schools might be invited in as discussants.

Two kinds of field work would be required: one quarter of one semester devoted to some comprehensive or specialized field study for a school system, and one quarter of another spent with a social science research team to gain "some first-hand insight into rigorous social science problems and procedures."

Each student would carry out an individual administrative project for most of the second semester of the final year. An administrative problem would be analyzed, and then a student would be assigned considerable responsibility for a course of action. Many projects could grow out of the organization of relationships with laymen as well as educators, the relating of philosophy or theory to a problem, and then the recommendation of suitable action or policy. The social sciences might be helpful in diagnosing the problem or the setting in which the student would work.

Elective courses could be taken anywhere in the university. Those wishing further study of administration could take courses in supervision with William Burton, school building with Homer Anderson, finance and business management with Simpson, or work in curricular development. The faculty projected that the school plant planning course might eventually be offered with the School of Design, that the finance course might lead to a new course offering in economics, and that technical aspects could be dealt with in less than the usual four-unit time blocks for a regular course.

The 1952 program proposal represented a dramatic shift away from conventional courses in the technical functions of administration — school supervision, business management, school buildings, personnel management, school law, and elementary and secondary school administration. Instead, the faculty proposed that blocks of time (a favorite Kellogg project idea) be used in different ways, that a more conceptual approach be developed, with social sciences providing the "frames of reference." Two rather global courses would be required—the problems and methodology courses, and the sequence in "cases and concepts." The rest of the program would stress systematic immersion in communities through (1) observation, (2) a school survey and a research study, (3) a summer internship, and (4) an administrative project. The focus was clearly on applied problem solving.

Herold Hunt, recruited from the Chicago school superintendency in 1953 as the "outstanding action administrator" needed to represent the viewpoint of experience, recalls that the program design emphasized learning the kinds of behavior men would be expected to have when employed in the field. The stress was on the application of conceptual knowledge and skill to real problems.

At the same time, the program would exploit social sciences in all of the required courses and would expect of students that their analysis of problems incorporate the appropriate methods of scholarship. Most dramatic was the shift away from a research-oriented thesis requirement to a reliance on actual performance on some administrative project. The faculty felt that the adviser should read not chapters, but instead a series of short clinical reports or working papers on the plans for action. At the end, the Dean, some of the faculty in education, and a representative from the Policy Committee of the Center, would conduct an oral examination of the candidate — again, the kind of appropriate evaluation for an action administrator.

Instead of a qualifying examination, the faculty proposed oral examinations each year on cases and concepts and a comprehensive review of each candidate's performance in both seminars and field work. Meanwhile, research-oriented candidates would continue to follow a program organized around the research thesis. To differentiate from the usual doctoral format which led to a research career, the new program was called the Administrative Career Program (ACP).

By the fall of 1953 the faculty reported "it has been increasingly difficult to distinguish clearly between various activities of the Kellogg Project, the Center, and the Administrative Career Program. Many of the faculty members were supported by Kellogg, worked on studies contracted by the Center, and taught in the ACP.[7] Students in the ACP gathered at the Center for seminars, for faculty consultation, for work on field studies built into the program by the faculty of the Center. Rapid growth, multiple field studies, and the development of totally new courses added up to intense pressure on the several instructors which the faculty later judged "could scarcely be considered optimum,"[8] but the program was working, the field study approach was in some ways too successful, and the faculty made changes as they identified problems.

The central problem was the success of the field study which in 1952–53 so powerfully attracted the students that most of their time was devoted to solving Boston's school building problem; other studies were neglected. In fact, the experience "led them to ask why the social science disciplines represented by the faculty in Spaulding House cannot be 'taught' by involving the total faculty in those aspects of the contract study which might draw upon the various disciplines."[9] It was also clear that faculty-student relations were less formal and based more on mutual contributions than they were in the usual course offerings. The faculty recognized that the roles played by students as university field workers threatened the sharply differentiated status lines which characterized the rest of higher education. Solving real problems in the field created a few at the university.

Obviously the students had a point, one not so different from the ideas of learning through experiences advanced long ago by John Dewey and others. Yet the field study was too insatiable a master; it could consume all faculty and student time allowing no time for reflection, for generating knowledge of social science that might not rise out of a specific setting. So the faculty decided to set aside the first and last six or eight weeks for formal course instruction and to conduct a field study of Lawrence, Massachusetts, between November 15th and March 15th, with any course meetings clearly subordinate during this time. Such was the pattern from 1954 through 1960. Formal course work in the social sciences simply had to stay out of the way of the contracted study.

Although the faculty wanted a two-year program, student time and scholarship aid allowed for only one year of residence for most students, and one year and one summer for the less experienced. This meant much less time for the social science research courses and experience. In 1952–53, the students took part in a research seminar on the Bay City study. They collected some data from the field through interviews before and after school elections with a random sample of 900 voting-age citizens. Peter Rossi's report of research on the Bay City schools indicated that the seminar was "of significant value" in understanding survey research.[10] But the activist students, understandably, committed much more of their energy to figuring out how to close down several dozen of Boston's dilapidated mid-nineteenth century schools than to survey research on voter attitudes.

These were years of furious activity:

1. The Rossis, Freeman, and Shipton were deeply involved in the Bay City studies between 1951 and 1955.

2. Simpson, his former student Cyril Sargent, and others were deeply involved in twenty-one field studies.

3. Neal Gross and his associates, Ward Mason and Alexander MacEachern, were starting the sociological research called the School Executive Studies.

4. Herold Hunt, Oliver Gibson, and others were planning the administrative project phase.

5. Sargent and Eugene Belisle asked Russell Davis and several case writers to develop more than 100 cases for the cases and concepts course.[11]

Could such a program give equal weight to social science disciplinary research and the more problem-oriented school surveys? By 1954 the faculty concluded:

> We fell into an error in separating too sharply community studies designed by social scientists to obtain knowledge relevant to the understanding of communities and their attitudes towards education from contractual studies entered into by the Center for Field Studies with communities which sought the aid of the university in solving problems defined by the communities themselves as a result of the real and pressing issues of a going school system.[12] The belief in social science remained undiminished, but the solution was to try to merge the two types with more than a leaning towards the contractual relationship with "actual responsibilities for an actual set of recom-

mendations." The faculty felt fewer studies of greater depth over large periods of time (several years, if possible) would allow more use of social science resources. But the studies would not be those "more logically . . . undertaken by a unit whose primary function is social science research rather than educational administration."

The new program, in summary, represented a sharp break from the traditional approach to preparing school administrators. Instead of courses leading to written exams leading to a thesis, the ACP required field observations, a brief internship, and a broad "cases and concepts" survey — all leading to an individual administrative project. Time constraints prevented either much formal social science course work or more than a token participation in social science research. Yet sociologists and political scientists were part of the Center for Field Studies staff and took part in the surveys.

President Nathan Pusey, in 1957, called for a careful and impartial investigation of the program and its accomplishments. He asked Ralph Tyler, Arthur MacMahon, and Lester Nelson to visit the school, question faculty and students, and review the program. The Tyler Committee felt that the preparation of school superintendents was a worthy task for a great university, given the unique and profound responsibilities of this role in the United States educational patterns. In the first five years, 129 students were enrolled, 66 received the doctorate, and most of the student responses were highly favorable. The Tyler Committee cited positive features, such as the broader range of disciplines, the focus on relating theory to practice through the case course, the school system study, and the culminating project. In courses the evaluation found a minimum of memorization and an emphasis on analysis and problem solving. Given the "significant contribution to the education of school administrators, this Committee recommends that the program be continued even though no improvements are made in it."[13]

The ACP faculty, however, eagerly responded to the suggestions offered for improvement. The Tyler group urged focus on recruitment of the younger students, age twenty-five to thirty.[14] More permanent faculty and the use of resources outside the program were among the recommendations. The committee approved of a shift from studying "sick school systems" to helping systems willing to develop a collaborative school-university relationship (such as Lexington, and Concord, Massachusetts). But a more varied and comprehensive research experience was recommended, including work with a faculty member engaged in research. The several recommendations and student criticism of the limited time led to another suggestion — that the program add a second year and systematically place third year students in school system internships.

During 1959 the American Association of School Administrators voted to require two years of graduate study in the university program for school administrators as a condition for membership starting in 1964. The faculty considered this still another reason for moving to a two year program. New courses in educational issues and administrative analysis (theory) were approved. Students could take up to six electives. The 1960–61 academic year was spent in a major planning venture with the assistance of Willard Spalding, a visiting professor. Each of the social scientists would offer a required course in their field — sociology, economics, and government. The field study was deferred until the second year, the project then to a third year.

Professor G. Ernest Giesecke, associate dean of the Graduate School of Education, University of Chicago, led a 1962 NCATE evaluation team of Harvard. The report called the ACP field work "probably the most complete, the most 'total program integrated' to be found anywhere. If one accepts Harvard's philosophy of strong emphasis upon applied theory in administration, then one must be impressed with the ACP field experiences."[15]

The NCATE team noted "a heavy orientation toward social science understanding and the conceptual aspects of administration with consequent reduced attention to the technical aspects of administration."[16] It also mentioned, in several places, the exclusive career focus on preparing superintendents of schools, especially for major city school systems. The team reported the faculty in educational administration included three social scientists, one each from economics, political science, and sociology, with each offering one or more courses of his own. The faculty in administration was found "united in its devotion to the preparation of practitioners as contrasted with preparing scholars for teaching and research in educational administration."[17] Among other observations, the team commented on the relative absence of formal hurdles in the doctoral program (only a special paper with a "research flavor" was required of all doctoral candidates at HGSE; significantly, at various points in time the ACP sought to do away with this requirement, offering instead oral exams on clinical problems).

In 1962 the Center for the Study of Education and Development was established to carry on research concerned with problems of educational planning in the developing nations, and in 1964–65, a doctoral program in educational administration planning was begun. Initially, the latter program concentrated on preparing personnel who would be concerned with manpower resource planning, especially at the national level. By 1966 the need for qualitative national planners concerned about teacher training, curriculum, and the relationship between centralized and local agencies was identified. An almost entirely separate group of social scientists, planners, and administrators were needed for purposes first of research, but also for training. The program was quite different from the ACP but the rhetoric of the rationale was quite similar:

> The type of skill demanded for educational planning is not simply a series of techniques, but a new fusion of understanding of a variety of factors at the levels of both individual and society . . . We are certainly engaged in work from which are beginning to emerge a number of new concepts relating to education, economics, sociology, and other specific disciplines, but which are centrally concerned with the process of change in society, of which the work of planning is the practical aspect.[18]

Between 1965 and 1968 the Research Career Program grew active. Dean Theodore Sizer used it as a device to individualize a program for several students concerned about problems in higher education, independent schools, or public policy in general. Joseph Cronin recruited students for a Danforth Foundation Study of educational decision making in urban school systems, including Boston. Several other advisers urged students to consider the "thesis option" rather than a project.

The Administrative Career Program was again evaluated by the faculty in 1967 and 1968. A grant from the Educational Professional Development Act provided resources for a reorganization, with the following features:

1. A year long introductory course on educational administration for first year students, stressing problems of the city, bureaucracy, planning, and both public and nonpublic schools.

2. Observation of a role in a metropolitan or city agency, with a seminar.

3. Selection of an elective in the areas of government, economics of education, and sociology or organizational behavior.

4. Choice among alternative field studies, led by professors of administration.

5. The option of advanced courses in administration on such general problems as "organizational development" and "dispute settlement and educational reform."

Other clinical experiences, such as observations in a ghetto and seminars taught by community leaders and practitioners, were proposed. The new format which formerly required courses in curriculum development, educational policy, and administrative theory — in addition to an introductory course and two case courses — provided for more electives and for individual study.

Social scientists in 1967 gathered around a new center for social research on policy problems, such as school integration, decentralization, and poverty. They proposed a new program in educational policy relying heavily on the social sciences, but with careers in policy institutes or special agencies in mind.

Thus, by 1970, the programs multiplied, as had the number of social scientists. The faculty debated the issue of "one degree — one program with many options" versus multiple programs and specialization. The original coalition and focus on the superintendency opened up as faculty members were added in response to international agencies and foundational support of national planning in Asia, Africa, and South America. The "policy thrust" was very much a response to the opening of various nongovernmental centers for the generation and evaluation of public policies, and recognition of the limits of existing structures and solutions. So the school's use of social scientists grew varied, as did the kinds of courses: on urban social policy, on economics and educational technology, on the politics of development, on urban and metropolitan government, etc. It was hard to realize that in 1952 a graduate school might have to create its own courses in community sociology or urban politics. In the 1970s the alternative specialized courses could provide students with many more options. The pendulum swung again to the offering of elective choices rather than detailed specification of most of the theoretical work and clinical applications.

Meanwhile, the trend towards increasing the investment in sound research and policy evaluation gained momentum. This was a very different way to use the talents of social scientists from the earlier notion that social scientists would *help out* in the applied field studies. The social scientists could insist on greater student investment of time on methodological concerns, on social science readings, and on the collection of data not for immediate problem solving, but to gain knowledge of how the social science discipline could be used to engage the problem. Several dozen faculty members, for example, participated in a faculty seminar wherein the Coleman Report was reanalyzed. Economists quarreled with sociologists about the way in which the multiple regressions were run and interpreted. They felt, properly, that their audience was a mixture of other social scientists and perhaps the White House and Congress where key decisions about resource allocation were being made. The challenge was to understand which policies, e.g., compensatory education or school integration, could be made workable under what circumstances. The new breed of social scientist had only passing interest in the problems of an individual school superintendent or principal, and was not generally available for work on field studies.

The Social Sciences — Harvard

The ACP faculty agreed to a review of social sciences disciplinary courses in the Administrative Career Program in 1960–61. Sociologist Dan Lortie assisted Willard Spalding in that phase of the staff discussions. Lortie asked his colleagues for a review of course offerings including the history of the course and its contents and methods.

Benson, the economist, inherited a course in school finance taught by the late Alfred D. Simpson. Student papers indicated that "intergovernmental relations" was a major topic in that course in the early 1950s. Benson brought a background in public finance to the course. He used Paul Mort's texts for many years, while he gradually developed many readings and eventually wrote his own text which drew heavily on economic reasoning. Benson tried to teach the differences between school system problems and major problems in the economy and emphasized the corrective factors inherent in education grants-in-aid. He also stressed tax theory, economics of salaries, capital outlay, debt finance, and other problems on which he worked.[19]

Marden reported on the course which placed the inexperienced administrators in communities for a semester of observation, much of it in city hall or nonschool agencies. Marden insisted on journal accounts or "logs" of these often vivid encounters with reality to force students to reflect on their observations. He himself was a political scientist who had worked at the state level on civil defense policy and later had run successfully for a school committee. Student field observations were shared and critiqued in a companion seminar led by Marden which introduced the competing analyses of city and suburban politics of Floyd Hunter, Robert Dahl, Robert

Wood, and others to help students understand what they were seeing.

Lortie inherited a seminar on "The Social Organization of the Community and the School," which had previously been taught by a series of sociologists, including Burton Clarke who stressed the study of different types of social organization. Lortie wanted students to learn about "the structure and functioning of communities and organizations." He also cultivated the methodological approach common to many empiricists — the suspension of moral judgment, the careful look at the relationships of people, etc. Students read Hollingshead on human ecology, Blau on bureaucracy, and others on class, society, and community structure. In 1959–60 Lortie added Olmstead's review, *The Small Group*, and in 1960–61, he tried to give students more examples of good community studies and organizational studies. His comments revealed a predictable frustration at trying so much in one course; his suggestions included a core course in social science the first year or a double course for the semester with some more effective use of studies in a local community. Lortie wanted the students to use sociological analysis in their field experiences.

The social scientist also reacted to other features of the program. Lortie found himself dissatisfied with student performance in a community field study where students "did not apply sociological methods to their work." This persuaded him to add more examples of community studies to his course. He also felt a need for more sustained study of social science methods and actual experience in their use, as a prerequisite in subsequent applications by administrators.

Benson felt the program lacked an adequate technical preparation in the superintendency, especially in topics he preferred not to teach: accounting, school business management, payrolls, inventory control, school planning, population projection, and school law. He urged a full year course other than the field study; later, the rest of the staff asked him to supervise a noncredit course taught largely at clinic meetings by architects, lawyers, and school business specialists who agreed to help.[20] The "technical phase" was later managed by Vincent Conroy until his death in 1967. Conroy arranged to have a full-time architect and much of the time of a lawyer on the field study staff; he thus used the evening meetings for new dimensions of regional education, educational parks, the future of nonpublic schools, etc., and other aspects of school planning, his special interest and responsibility.

Later in the 1960s, Harvard had as many as three economists on the faculty. Students could study with Andre Daniere, work in "economics and the technology of education" with Sam Bowles, delve into the study of social indicators or cost-effectiveness with Martin Katzman, or study human resources development and practical school business management problems with Manuel Zymelman. These options were possible since the other centers each hired their own economists.

When Marden left in 1964, Dean Sizer asked James Q. Wilson in the government department and Edward Banfield from the Joint Center for Urban Studies to include ACP students in their urban politics course. No longer did it seem necessary for the School of Education to offer its own course in urban politics. A former teacher and Boston City Councillor, Thomas Sullivan, led a supplementary seminar. Martha Derthick and, still later, Daniel P. Moynihan taught other "politics of education" seminars which considered issues such as race and decentralization.

Bud Khleif took over the Lortie course and led students through a rigorous treatment of sociology from Max Weber and George Simmel to Everett Hughes and Howard Becker. Nancy St. John then taught courses with a focus on socio-economic status and race. Neal Gross taught seminars on role theory; Nathan Glazer's broad courses in urban social policy in many professional fields were popular with ACP students, as the electives grew.

Harvard students chose social science electives at an average of two in the program prior to 1960 and four afterwards. Data prepared for the Tyler Committee revealed:

1. In 1952–53, six students took Human Development: Introduction of Educational Anthropology; two took educational psychology; three took human relations courses at the business school; eight took a social relations seminar on community structure.

2. In 1951–54, twenty-one students took one or more government courses in the Graduate School of Public Administration on the planning process, the administrative process, public policy, and American political thought.

3. In each subsequent year, numbers fluctuated and the elective pattern reflected larger enrollments in courses in elementary or secondary school organization. But in 1956–57, six took work in the social relations department, including work on family roles and American social structures.

After 1960, individuals had more electives which meant they could sample many fields or develop a special strength. Several students took four or more courses in state and federal policy and later accepted positions in state departments of education. After 1965, more students took courses in labor relations either at the Harvard Business School or the Department of Economics. Student interests varied; some pursued themes such as "metropolitanism" while others sought skills in race relations or data processing. Within the School of Education, several students each year took work in the psychologies, research, or human development fields. But many of these courses reflected not a disciplinary orientation as much as an interest in a problem or policy area.

Much of this study culminated in the special or doctoral qualifying paper, roughly equivalent to a sample chapter in a thesis and often a review of the literature or position paper on a problem. Some students researched the passage of an education law or studied an educational innovation as an effort at introducing change. Some papers were of the case study genre, but with analysis either logical, social scientific, or eclectic. In the late 1960s, many of the papers were on the problems of race, poverty, collective negotiations, innovations, federal programs, higher education, and other topics which required review of some social science literature. This paper came the closest to that of a formal research effort, yet students could, instead, simply critique the existing knowledge or advocate a new approach. Thus, social science knowledge could be applied or could be ignored, depending on the topic and the training and inclination of the student.

One of the boldest program innovations was that of the new course called Cases and Concepts in Educational Administration. The case approach to the study of professions was largely developed in other Harvard graduate schools, especially the law school and the business school, both of which rely almost totally on case methods of instruction.

The Graduate School of Education planned first one, then a second course in "cases." Unlike the other graduate school case courses, the first course for administrators was to be an omnibus course in a variety of substantive areas — school personnel problems, plant planning, supervision, superintendent-school board relations, etc.

Planning responsibilities of the course fell to Cyril Sargent and Eugene Belisle, both very active in the field relationships — Sargent in the field studies, Belisle at the Advanced Administrative Institute. Between 1952 and 1955, 130 cases were prepared with the help of a special case-writing staff.[21] Thirty-five of them were subsequently published in book form.

Use of the case method reflected a basic criticism of categorizing administration as "finance," "budget making," "school plant" without consideration of the human context, "the attitudes, the behavior, the relationships of people." Sargent and Belisle felt that the close analysis of cases allowed students both to test generalizations, yet witness and discuss the unique aspects of a real situation. They were skeptical about treating administration as a science when individual cases required of a man both knowledge and skill in acting upon the data.[22]

Sargent and Belisle held strong convictions about public school administration. They felt schools lacked sufficient numbers of administrators (vividly termed "administrative deprivation") compared to other large enterprises, but that education had to point the way by exerting "creative leadership," by defining clearly both the needs of education, the remedies, and the plan to cope with school boards and citizens of varying competence. Quite early this team recognized the school administrator as "essentially a special kind of public administrator" acting simultaneously as a member of a "relatively undeveloped professional discipline and *as a pragmatist in the arena of political forces.*" They even saw risks in becoming *too professional,* i.e., isolated "from those currents of political behavior that ultimately sustain and determine the directions of educational policy" as well as in becoming too "realistic" politically.

They also felt strongly that students examining cases needed help in organizing ways of thinking about life. The study of concepts served the function of furnishing the conceptual resources of each student and then in reordering one's conceptual system in response to administrative situations and roles.

No one definition of concepts prevailed. The word was used in its several meanings: idea, term, or sociological or philosophical label for a phenomenon. Some emerged with specialized meanings attached by social scientists: value orientation, status, role, communication, group, personality, culture, avoidance, and maturation. Others came from research on industrial and military organizations: span of control, delegation, discipline, coordination, group dynamics, and supervision. Some reflected the objectives and aspirations of education: role of public education in a democracy, equality of educational outlook, prognosis, progress, policy, and planning.

Attempts to link the concepts to the cases failed quite early. The authors report ". . . we imagined the possibility of relating specific cases and specific concepts very closely, in a kind of contrapuntal scheme. We imagined a pattern which would move sometimes from a case to the study of related concepts and sometimes from an area of concepts to a case or series of cases. We soon discovered various errors in our idea."[23]

The instructors thought they knew which concept was illustrated by any one case. Packaging quickly became too tidy, given the complexity of a case. Furthermore, students felt they would be rewarded for verbalizing the notion rather than in probing the case. The instructors decided the administrators rarely verbalized the concepts they used, and that the role of the teacher was to guide a student towards his own systematic way of sorting experiences.

As a result, concepts were left largely to individual reading and reporting on the usefulness of the readings. Instructors counseled each student, or referred him to another source. The Sargent and Belisle book lists the kind of readings recommended:

1. In administration and subtopics, the works of Elton Mayo, Luther Gulick, Chester Barnard, George Homans, Herbert Simons, and others published in the 1940s and early 1950s.

2. In organization and specific concepts such as "interactions" and "group dynamics," readings in the social sciences "based largely on bibliographical references supplied by our colleagues from these fields."

3. In planning, readings from Mumford, works on ecology, human societies, and forecasting.

4. In personality and awareness, readings from Moreno, Riesman, Allport, Cattell, Fromm, Rogers, and various authors in vogue at the time.

5. In value orientation, F.S.C. Northrop, Sorokin, Toynbee, Robert Ulich, other philosophers, and Mumford again — two more of his works.

No sequel to the general case book ever appeared. Carl Dolce and Roderick McPhee developed cases from some of the field studies in cities where school integration was an issue. Joseph Cronin developed six cases on collective negotiations which were distributed through the Connecticut and New England school development councils. Robert Binswanger conducted a series of "case development" seminars and considered new media such as kinescopes and taped cases. Again, the cases were assembled more around policy problems rather than social science disciplines.

The use of cases influenced Francis Keppel and others who taught a course called The American School (an introductory course on educational and related social and political issues). McPhee and Dolce's Advanced Cases course in the 1960s experimented with the use of novels and other sources of data on human decision making. Herold Hunt, in his courses, made frequent use of NEA reprints of the various commission reports on personnel and other serious professional problems in U.S. school systems. Cronin, in a course that evolved from administrative theory to organizational development, used cases from Matthew Miles' *Innovation and Education*, and asked students to either write a case with some social science analysis, or read several and write on one or more ways of thinking about planned change.

In the late 1960s, the original "case course" was very popular with MAT, Ed.M., and doctoral candidates outside of administration. The year-long seminar in administration used some cases along with other approaches (in 1968-69 the students attended a play aptly titled *Riot*; the Whitman and Madison school "in-basket" materials were used as elaborate cases, and students played variations of the Collective Bargaining Game to understand the complexity of negotiations).

Thus the case method made some impact on other courses and other teachers. But in no sense did it become the single most prevalent mode of instruction. One side effect of the cases and concepts course was the subsequent avoidance of course labels such as "personnel relations," "school-community relations," and other course labels familiar to state certification technicians often baffled by the vague Harvard transcripts.

Concepts taught in administration courses more heavily emphasized the political and economic concepts, as those kinds of social science research appeared in education — with Charles Benson, John Vaizey, Jesse Burkhead, Steven Bailey, Robert Dahl, Robert Salisbury and others as major contributors to the repertoire of analytical approaches. But never did the systematic selection of concepts become a fetish, or even a preoccupation of the staff. Various ways of thinking about administration, e.g., management by objectives, the dynamics of planned change, maximum feasible participation, flashed into view along with shifts in public policy or emphasis within the profession. Educators found it essential to learn the differences between mediation and arbitration; James Coleman pointed out the variety of ways of defining equal educational opportunity; the White House prescribed "program, planning, and budgeting systems," and social scientists found cumulative deficits and cultural deprivation as problems to remedy. Many of these concepts demanded more precision in definition and skill in program evaluation than hitherto expected; thus, the need for a Center for Educational Policy Research. None dispensed with the need for educational administrators in roles including, but ranging beyond, the superintendency, and for men and women for public and non-public agencies who could draw on social science research and ways of thinking about problems — or at least could learn what to expect or not to expect from the emerging social sciences.

Both the field study and the individual project provided opportunities to apply some of the social science perspectives and methodology. Given the pragmatism and "action" orientation of the program, these may not be fair tests of social science! On the other hand, the program design called for the continuous interaction of theory and practice and the application of knowledge to real problems.

Virtually all evaluators (CPEA, NCATE, and Tyler et al.) found the field study generated unusually high motivation among students. Social science knowledge rarely takes the form of normative prescription. A 1954 discussion of the 1951-54 experience suggested that the problem was *more* than one of differences between pure and applied research. CPEA reviewers found "no satisfactory basis for reconciliation ... at present, between the neutral role of the 'pure' social scientist and the change agent role of the 'participant' researcher."[24]

Most of the field studies required work on pupil population projections, a very applied kind of demographic analysis. In the late 1950s, a series of studies towards implementing racial integration policies (Englewook, Hartford, and Pittsburgh) added the factor of projection by racial residential trends — no simple task. Vincent Conroy, then director, found very few social science resources in these studies.

The field studies often involved surveys of community opinions and aspirations about the schools. The staff sociologist usually worked with student "community committees" on the design, data collection, analysis and interpretation of the data. On a 1963 study of Brockton, Massachusetts, the "Task of Public Education" instrument developed at the University of Chicago was used to survey public values and expectations. In many other communities, students under faculty direction tried to discover a "community power structure" as a source of insight on how much the study could recommend — how and why. Not much of this analysis appears in the text of field studies; but a few reports couch the arguments for greater investment in education on such grounds as economic development, industrial growth, and increased individual economic returns.[25]

An individual's solo test was performance in an administrative role and the design and implementation of a project. Committees of at least three faculty members, with one or more social scientists, conducted oral examinations at the outset and conclusion of each project. At the outset, candidates were expected to write a proposal in which they described the role, situation, and problem, and also reviewed the relevant literature. Sometimes social science insights offered implications for the planning and execution of the project. A social science point of view was not, however, a required feature — depending on your advisor and committee.

What was a "good" project? The faculty in 1960-61 voiced dissatisfaction and found many problems: criteria for success or failure, the inequities of the job market, the "safe" projects students tended to submit, and the failure to render full or frank accounts of mistakes. Many students wrote projects on such manageable and usually low-risk (although useful) topics as "Developing a Written Manual of Policies and Procedures" or "Establishing a Faculty Council on Instruction." During the 1960s the faculty asked students to make more explicit the criteria by which their work could be evaluated, and ruled out confidential project journals and progress reports. Students then began work on such concerns as "Planning a Teacher Training Program for the Peace Corps," "Waging a Local War on Poverty," and "Improving Race Relations in a Northern City School System." ACP projects were completed on such sensitive problems as school desegregation and state tax reform. A larger percentage of the students took on major programs or staff reorganizations which required attention to the literature on the planning of social change. Projects such as "New Facilities on Tax Levies" requiring voter approval meant review of the research on voter behavior and communication with various publics, some of which came out of the Bay City study.

The NCATE report in 1962 summarized ACP staff concerns about the project, such as whether "the former requirements elicited high enough intellectual requirements on the part of candidates. There was a failure of candidates to make a sufficient application of social science understandings. The old requirement seemed to give too much advantage to a person with verbal facility." No candidate ever failed a project once the faculty approved the idea and the reports were submitted.

In the 1960s, the faculty tightened the project procedures somewhat. The same committee members attended both the initial and final oral examinations, and read all the journals. The project topics were often more social science-oriented (political or sociological problems at least). A few students failed — and either withdrew or had to complete additional analyses. Faculty members still wrestled with the problems of quality control, but the project format at Harvard spread gradually from administration and guidance across to reading, curriculum development, supervision, teacher training, and planning.

The Impact of the Harvard Program

In a 1954 request to a foundation, the Harvard faculty discussed the problem of evolution of the program. "Over a long time, presumably, the impact of the men trained and of the publications can be roughly assessed. Presumably the number of young men who take positions of leadership in school systems and colleges is one index. Another is the extent to which the program influences programs in other institutions. Finally, we think, a detached observer, studying our present situation and returning five years later, could assess the degree to which this program is integrated into the university structure, thereby both drawing and giving strength."[26]

Obviously the program content is no more important than the quality of candidates admitted or the care with which graduates are placed and later recommended for other positions. But the leadership patterns are well worth studying.

By 1970 almost 300 students were admitted to the Administrative Career Program. Of the first 221, a total of 47 were superintendents of schools and another 41 were employed in school district central offices. There were 49 principals, and 11 assistant principals. So two-thirds were in elementary and secondary education. Higher education claimed 37, more than half in administrative capacities; 17 were on the staff of state departments of education, 2 were in business, and 16 in other agencies, including foundations.

In the late 1960s, graduates held the superintendents of Philadelphia, New Orleans, Dallas, Portland (Oregon), Minneapolis, Fairfax County (Virginia), Springfield (Massachusetts), Berkeley, New Haven, Newton, Princeton, and a dozen other significant communities. Graduates included the director of a regional educational laboratory, a school of education dean who had served as city school superintendent in Pittsburgh and New York City, several community college presidents, and a former U.S. associate commissioner of elementary and secondary education. Another graduate founded a highly innovative Nova University in Florida. Alumni served in the Peace Corps and Office of Economic Opportunity in administrative positions. Two were state commissioners of education; four took a turn as director of New England School Development Council. One served as an executive in the American Educational Research Association, another as an associate executive secretary of the NEA; still others served on the Education Commission of the States and as state association officials. Four of the Ford Foundation education staff in 1969 were ACP graduates.

Black urban educators included top assistants in Chicago, a board member in New Orleans, a district superintendent in New York City, the superintendent of Compton, California, assistant superintendent of West Chester, Pennsylvania, director of the New Lincoln School in New York City, and foundation and AID project leaders.

The scholarly output of the program consists of more than two dozen published field reports and several volumes including Sargent and Belisle's, Herold Hunt's *Principles of Educational Administration,* R. Oliver Gibson and H.C. Hunt's, *The School Personnel Administrator,* and chapters of Roald F. Campbell, Luvern Cunningham, and Roderick McPhee's, *The Organization and of Control American Schools,* which drew on special papers and projects. Benson's works on the economics of education have had a major impact, as cited, and grew out of his teaching and field studies as later did *The Cheerful Prospect.* Forthcoming are research reports by sociologists Nancy St. John (on the effect of integration) and Bud B. Khleif (on the schooling career of military department children — with Herold Hunt). Work on collective negotiations, including three qualifying papers and two projects, will be reflected in a volume on *School Board-Teacher Negotiations,* by Joseph M. Cronin. Various papers and cases have been published, such as Thomas Minter's on the P.S. 201 Community School controversy in New York City.

The Bay City studies never appeared in one volume, but portions appeared in NESDEC publications. Neal Gross's school executive studies were reported in two volumes, *Who Runs Our Schools?* and *Explorations in Role Analysis,* with Mason and MacEachern.

Harvard has sponsored interuniversity seminars on the case method in educational administration and on urban education and the American Negro. Faculty members appear often at AASA, UCEA, and other forums and take part in cooperative research such as the Whitman School Decision-Making Studies or the Danforth Study of City School Boards.

Several states have approved the program for certification purposes. Other universities have not adopted the ACP format in toto;
many have adopted one or more features such as the courses on
economics or the case course. Of course other universities have developed case books and more recent cases; Harvard was simply one
of several leaders. Several other schools of education have adopted
the project option. The field study or school survey is a familiar
university service, but still unusual as a major component of a doctoral program staffed by an interdisciplinary team.

The program "drew strength" from the business school and the
Kennedy School of Government where some students took electives.
Daniel P. Moynihan, director of the MIT-Harvard Joint Center for
Urban Studies, was also a professor of education whose seminars
on urban politics attracted administration students. In the period
1963-66, the integration field studies were monitored by a presiden-
tial committee on the educational and legal aspects of school
integration, with four law school professors. In 1969, a Law and
Education center developed, partly because two lawyers were then
on the faculty (both working closely with the ACP) and four students in the 1960s came with LL.Bs already in hand.

Several ACP staff members lectured at the Harvard Divinity
School in a course on religion and education; a conference at HGSE
several years earlier had paved the way. ACP staff gave lectures in
a business school course entitled Business, Society, and the Individual and at the Eastern Academy of Management. One course in
planning was taught collaboratively with a faculty member in the
Graduate School of Design. The dean and faculty established joint
appointments with other graduate schools, including Arts and Sciences. As of 1969-70, plans to extend relationships with the Sloan
School of Management at MIT and other faculties were being considered.

A program does more than prepare a man; it develops tastes and
values as part of a "socialization" process. More than that, it makes
a man or woman visible to the field. The Harvard faculty decided
not to prepare a program for junior college administrators, nor did
it from 1952-1965 try to develop professors of administration. ACP
graduates have filled both roles — from California to New Hamp-
shire. Until CSED was established, no formal training in education
and development was available; ACP graduates accepted AID and
Peace Corps administrative assignments in the United States and
Africa. The career choice of graduates responded to the demands
of the field; fortunately, the breadth of program offerings never

constricted a man. The focus on administration, "broadly conceived" by Al Simpson, precluded narrow specialization and allowed graduates to apply their wisdom in newly created roles.

The coalition of social scientists and educational administrators was in no sense permanent. Willard Spalding in 1961 noted the problem of replacing untenured social scientists at the end of a few years. He found this practice defensible financially but not conducive to the long-term goal. "Each social scientist must work with at least one eye upon the chance for advancement elsewhere, shaping his writing and research to this end. Since his next post is far more likely to be in an academic department than with a school of education, each social scientist must be guided more by the expectancies of his academic colleges than by those of the Administrative Career Program. Commitment to the preparation of school administrators is not likely to occur frequently under these circumstances."[27]

By 1970 it was clear that social scientists could find significant positions in schools of education, such as at Chicago and Berkeley. Harvard also chose several eminent social scientists for tenure positions — Daniel P. Moynihan in urban politics and Nathan Glaser in urban social policy. Spalding's judgment cuts both ways; men who have achieved high recognition for their research or policy ideas may be less committed to the training of men to implement policies and more committed to the organization of new social agencies and institutions.

Of course, Spalding also urged that the specialized ACP social sciences courses be replaced eventually by elective offerings in the several social sciences. As Neal Gross has suggested, the appropriate function of social science for an administrator is not to develop specialized skills, but rather to "sensitize" a potential practitioner to the viewpoints, perspectives, and ways of thinking about a problem. When Harvard began to hire more social scientists concerned about urban issues, the choice of electives and the variety of perspectives almost automatically increased.

The issues of generalized versus specialized training by and large has been resolved by students. ACP candidates who wanted to develop specialties in race relations, labor-management problems, or group dynamics have so arranged their electives and made these topics the focus of other courses and the special paper. Many of the candidates suspect that they may encounter challenges in many areas of social concern and, therefore, allocate their electives in such a way as to develop further several social sciences. In a formal thesis program, this eclecticism could create problems. But the project format is such that the would-be generalist can draw on the skills and knowledge appropriate at the time of planning or decision making. The "action program" in effect acknowledges the different life style of the agency decision maker. The Research Career Program, the doctorate in planning, and eventually the policy students, follow the more familiar format of methodological and substantive concentration in one area with a special focus on one problem in depth. Quite possibly the several programs at Harvard may move closer together — in staffing if not in format — but each will exploit the social or "policy sciences" for their uniquely appropriate ends.

One issue perplexing the faculty in 1954, that of the dichotomy between objective research and subjective participation, no longer worries the faculty in the same way. Most of the social sciences now have strong camps of scholars advocating "policy-oriented" research, that is, research which tests out solutions (such as school integration, compensatory education, and system decentralization) and guides the decision maker. Social scientists such as Daniel P. Moynihan and Thomas Pettigrew have become advocates of positions buttressed by social science research data. So the cleavage between research, policy, and action appears to have diminished. Of course to have shaped a policy is not to put it in operation. The various steps between policy planning and program evaluation include rather central problems of logistical resource allocation, organizational design, contingency planning, and other less visible tasks of negotiations and adaptation. Social scientists in fields not emphasized in the Harvard program, particularly organizational or social psychologists and anthropologists, share many of these concerns.

The program at Harvard has stressed the use of social science, never for very long as discrete "disciplines," rather lightly as a source of "theory," but mostly for the purposes of solving applied or policy problems. The greatest investment of resources has been made in preparing men for careers as action administrators-principals, superintendents, and agency officials. In recent years the career options of planners, researchers, and policy evaluators have been advanced as equally appropriate career objectives. Harvard's use of the social sciences has begun to shift to accommodate this broader spectrum of career objectives and policy applications.

THE UNIVERSITY OF CHICAGO—RELEVANCE OF SOCIAL SCIENCES

The recent history of educational administration at the University of Chicago begins with the founding of the Midwest Administration Center in August 1950. The W.K. Kellogg grant to the university identified Chicago as the center of a twelve-state region in which more than thirty colleges and universities concentrated upon preparing educational administrators for all levels.

Not an old university even by land grant college standards, the University of Chicago was born in the 1890s. It was a child of the Rockefeller fortune and of the Germanic scholarship of the genre which a few years earlier had spawned Johns Hopkins University, as essentially a research institution.

At Chicago, education from its early days was a department of social sciences. Students of education were expected before 1950, and to this day are still expected, to take very seriously the rigor of the several academic disciplines, especially sociology in which Chicago has always been strong. Doctoral candidates, then and now, have but one option for the doctoral degree: to pursue the Ph.D. with the time-honored and scholarly dissertation, albiet with much leeway in the selection of a topic.

The first of four objectives of the Midwest collaboration was "to improve the calibre and basic preparation of educational administrators." The other objectives stressed growth in "understanding the purposes and functions of educational administration . . . ," increase in the "effectiveness of consultative services for the improvements of administration, instruction, and school-community relations," and cooperative study . . ." (for) better organization and administration of education."[28]

Faculty members at the University of Chicago thoroughly revised the program for preparing educational administrators. In the process, assistance was given by administrators in the area, graduate students, and consultants from public administration, economics, sociology, and psychology. The new program provided an increased emphasis on the human relations aspects of administration, a greater provision for field experiences, and review of procedures for selection of candidates and evaluation of progress.[29] Less directly, changes in courses were made by professors who were conducting workshops, interviewing practicing administrators, and "learning to tap the special knowledge and insight of business executives, public administrators, economists, political scientists, and social psychologists."[30] The Center's Executive Committee reflected the broadening search for useful knowledge from the social sciences. Chaired by Maurice Seay, chairman of the Department of Education, the committee included: Frank Bane, director, Council of State Governments; Herbert Emmerist, director, Public Administration Clearing House; Theodore Schultz, chairman, Department of Economics; Ralph Tyler, former Dean of Social Sciences—newly appointed director for the Center for Advanced Study in the Behavioral Sciences; and Leonard White, professor of public administration. In subsequent years the committee would shift away from the public administration emphasis to one on the separate and basic disciplines within the social sciences.

From the outset the Center sponsored many clinics, conferences, and publications, from which the *Administrator's Notebook* would serve as a monthly vehicle for research and commentary. The Center also sponsored research on administration. But, for the first three or four years, the ideas for this research came not from the social sciences but from problems suggested by state and local administrators. For example:

1. Reorganization of school districts

2. Improvement of the effectiveness of boards of education

3. Development of sound finance policies for schools

4. Development of public understanding of education

5. Improvement of consultative services to schools, especially from state departments of education

6. Leadership in the improvement of instruction

The University of Chicago staff members (Center Director Chase, William Savage, and Professor Rehage) assessed the leadership of the three latter programs, sponsored studies, held conferences, and otherwise disseminated the findings.[31]

Thirteen research assistants of the Department of Education worked on the research, the conferences, and on publications along with the senior staff. In April 1951, twelve of the thirteen responded to questions about the value of their work. The students reported gains in "understanding the problems of administration," of the chance to observe "administration in operation in the Center, in school systems, and educational agencies," and in learning about "human interaction in administration."[32]

The students were learning mainly from what was called "cooperative studies," ones in which "hundreds of administrators and board members are learning more about how to conduct investigations to gain the facts and understanding necessary for wide policy decisions."[33]

Chicago professors realized the hazards of action-oriented research and as early as the 1951-52 report stated a new need for testing, for "a few central hypotheses regarding the processes and leadership roles . . . (in instruction)", for identifying the "new concept . . . as to the respective roles of school boards, administration, teachers . . . productive human relationships . . . the effects produced by various kinds of leadership in different types of situations." They asked, "How can we examine our data so as to be sure of their import? Can we draw more heavily on the insights of psychologists, political scientists, sociologists, and other scientists in deriving and testing hypotheses?"[34]

By 1953, the Midwest Administration Center was moving away from more action-oriented research in a quest for more basic kinds of knowledge:

> New concepts and techniques are being applied to the study of administration. Progress is being made in developing a theory of administration which will focus on the elements of human interaction in planning and cooperative activity for the accomplishment of purposes . . . to clarify role functions and role expectation. Particular attention is being given to the effects of various kinds of communication and various types of leadership on understanding, morale, and effectiveness of operation.[35]

Also mentioned was the use of research techniques developed by psychologists and sociologists, instruments such as "critical incident" studies, the "Q" sort, interaction analysis scales, and projective tests.

At least one faculty member wanted students to move beyond the quest for social science "insights" and methods to a more fundamental training in social science research. His indictment of much of what passed for research would later reach all the major departments of educational administration around the country.

Toward a Theory or Theories of Administration

Jacob Getzels was an assistant professor of educational psychology and one of several social scientists invited to consult with the Midwest Administration Center. Getzels was very dissatisfied with the lack of systematic research in educational administration and the lack of theory to guide what was being called research. He developed this criticism in an article published in the *Harvard Educational Review* in the fall of 1952, and prepared the beginning of a theory based both on sociology and psychology.[36]

Getzels' outline of a theory dealt with the nature of the leader-follower relationship in institutions. He looked at the sources of a leader's authority and the kinds of interaction between those in the two roles. The article appealed to Arthur Coladarci, a psychologist at Stanford University. Both Getzels and Coladarci addressed the National Conference of Professors of Educational Administration in Denver in 1954 and decided to collaborate on a monograph elaborating their concerns about the need for an administrative theory, its utility and practicality. That paper aimed directly at removing the semantic confusion that seemed to prevent administrators from using theory as underpinning for research and other decisions of an empirical nature.

Meanwhile, the Center entered its fourth year and arranged for an external review by three experts on the practice of administration—Editor Walter Cocking of the *School Executive Magazine*, Wayne Reed, assistant U.S. commissioner of education; and H.I. Willett, Richmond, Virginia superintendent and AASA president-elect. After discussions with staff, students, and others, they delivered an evaluation which was supportive, yet firm in pushing for a more interdisciplinary tack. They praised the primary focus on research and the new techniques used, but called for "new and better research procedures than are now employed in education."[37] They found the use of graduate students wise, but urged "slightly fewer" of them and a mix of students from administration, anthropology, sociology, and other fields led by more full research specialists. Their interviews led them to recommend a "team approach," inviting representatives of related social science disciplines on an equal basis. They subtly raised questions about the six facets of study urged on the Center by administrators and recommended other areas for research, such as "the whole field of personal relationships."[38] These practitioners were, in effect, urging a problems-based orientation while acknowledging the contribution of the disciplines.

At the evaluation conference the graduate students themselves testified on the experiences they found of value—the work in social science courses in various other departments of the university, and the chance to apply theoretical concepts developed in course work. They reported that departmental courses had been changed as a result of Center activities and mentioned a new course in research design.[39]

The Next Five Years: Theory and Research

Director Francis Chase and his staff responded to their own as well as the external evaluations with a new set of purposes. They began by acknowledging the need for a "theory of administration which will guide both practice and research."[40] Such a theory would recognize administration as a process, the school as a social structure, and productivity as a function of motivation of the persons involved. Research on the morale and motivation of persons would be needed, "to test emerging theories." The new theory and research must then be effectively communicated and translated into practice.

Chase himself was also questioning the basic educational structure, the grouping of pupils, and the organization of schools. He proposed the creation in each school of instructional teams, an idea that others also advocated later in the 1950s.

Still another focus was to be on the selection and preparation of professors of administration in leading colleges and universities. The staff voiced dissatisfaction with "the prevailing pattern . . . (of) differentiated preparation for specific positions:" the principalship, the superintendency, and director of guidance. They also were not pleased with the emphasis on techniques rather than "concepts of society, the school and administration."

The Center staff decided to select each year six or seven students, either doctoral or post-doctoral, to be administrators but would "possess an unusual interest in theory and research."[41]

Getzels, Egon Guba, and Proctor Thomas (education and economics) served as Chicago faculty consultants along with James Harlow, Herbert Schooling, Robert Snider (an audio-visual expert) and Robert Ohm, principal, Chicago Laboratory School. William Savage was associate director, and H.T. James was assistant director. The Advisory Committee was the old Executive Committee plus the university hospital superintendent, a vice-president emeritus, and Professor Leonard White of political science.

The Center added a seminar with a special focus on administrative theory with wide readings and psychological and sociological interpretations of administration. Another objective of instruction (Getzels, Guba, and others) was a volume of social science readings by 1958.

Staff associates were given opportunities to engage in "studies designed to test emerging theories of administration," especially on morale, motivation, administrative functions, roles and relationships."[42] They could also help evaluate other university preparation programs and help plan a new round of clinics and conferences, including one for faculties in administration of other universities.

The nature of the research studies began to shift. Senior staff members wrote summaries of the Center's projects, such as the school board studies and Consultative Services Project, and cleared the Center agenda for theory-based research. The new research begun in 1955 and 1956 required staff and students to develop a conceptual framework and a research design to examine administrator-teacher relations.[43]

By 1956, the staff associates in their second year of study were assisting in the teaching of courses in administration, human relations, supervision, and finance. The Chicago faculty conveyed the explicit expectation that many "in the field may be expected to assume professorships in educational administration."[44]

Thus, a major revolution had taken place, not in the Chicago commitment to research which was already substantial, but in the more sophisticated approach to research on administration. The ideal of theory-based research supplanted in a few years the kinds of status surveys and tabulations that previously characterized administrative research around the country. The new research was planned not only with the assistance of social scientists, but also conceptualized and designed with a theoretical framework derived from one or several of the social sciences. Graduate students in administration were expected to learn how to use a theoretical framework in planning their own dissertation. This approach prevailed, although the Center would continue to conduct other kinds of administrative "studies," but independently, not as the center of a consortium.

An example of the new type of Center research is a cooperative research project on the satisfaction and effectiveness of teachers. Initiated in 1955-56, this research was based on a theory of staff relations and examined teacher-principal expectations concerning teacher performance. In 1956, Francis Chase launched a study of teacher morale and school administration. Egon Guba and Charles Bidwell were research consultants to the associates working on this research."[45]

In 1957, Roald Campbell became the new director and Andrew Halpin joined the faculty as an assistant professor and research professor. Halpin's book on the *Leadership Behavior of School Superintendents*, had been published in 1956. Halpin and Campbell came from the Ohio State University faculty where major research on leadership was underway.

One of Halpin's early contributions was the editing of a seminar report on "Administrative Theory in Education." The conference was sponsored jointly by the Center and the new University Council for Educational Administration. Halpin, Getzels, and Campbell of Chicago made presentations as did Daniel Griffiths of Columbia, James Thompson of Pittsburgh, Dr. Carroll Shartle of Ohio State University, and John M. Hemphill of Educational Testing Service.

From Harvard, Talcott Parsons presented a paper, and Cyril Sargent gave a summary and critique of the meetings. The November 1957 seminar papers were subsequently edited by Halpin in a paperback entitled *Administrative Theory in Education.*[46]

Halpin defined theory, using the psychologist Herbert Feigl's discussion of the search for scientific explanation. Halpin told of the many difficulties, especially in searching for a single theory when alternative explanations ought to be considered. He also warned that people would debate each other on the issues of what "is" and what "ought" to exist, not realizing their interdependence when one tries to predict what may take place in the future under specified circumstances.

Getzel's paper on "Administration as a Social Process" explained his model of organizational behavior and reported the research of several staff associates, two being Ferneau and Moyer, who had written dissertations on administrator-teacher expectations. Other dissertations, those of Congreve, Moser, Prince, and Sweitzer, also bore the imprint of social psychological theories.[47]

The Center in 1958 prepared three alternative training programs:

1. A two-year "associateship for doctoral students," as preparation for the professorship in administration or important posts in schools and colleges.
2. A combination associateship and internship in school systems.
3. A post-doctoral research program for young faculty.

The first and the third clearly identified a growing interest in improving preparation for the professorship. The focus on the line administrator was given less of an emphasis, and it took from 1959 to 1962 to launch a two-year Masters program in school administration to prepare prospective principals.[48]

Research at the Center was reviewed by a research panel consisting of Getzels, Philip Jackson, and Peter Rossi of sociology, Schultz of economics, Herbert Storing of political science, and J.D. Lucas of the law faculty. A new research theme stressed the ecology of schools and administrator's personality variables. In 1959, a conference on "Administrative Theory as a Guide to Action" led to a publication of the same title edited by Roald Campbell and James Lipham.

In 1960, the second Kellogg grant expired. It was a logical point at which to assess progress. The Midwest Center had had the resources to train a new cadre of research-oriented professors of administration. New money from the U.S. Office of Education was obtained to train others for the professorship with "even greater attention to the relationship between administration and the social sciences."[49] Approximately half of the Center graduates were accepting university teaching positions in the late 1950s. In 1960 and 1961 a total of seven graduates became professors; an eighth went to work for UCEA; one became a principal; and one a superintendent.

Several program variations were added. In 1961, the Center accepted two Chicago School Board internships in administration. From 1963-1967, the National Institute for Mental Health sponsored a program with an administrative residency in the third year. The proposals stressed the applicability of social science theories to research and training in educational administration.

The Center continued to sponsor research, but the subjects grew quite diverse: for example, Roald Campbell and students examined nationalizing influences on American schools. Luvern Cunningham, new director under Dean Cambpell, studied team teaching and community school board decisions. Donald Erickson's work was on nonpublic schools and J. Alan Thomas, the new director, conducted research in 1967, on educational productivity and school finance. Students worked not only on these topics, but with psychologists and sociologists such as Herbert Thelen, Morris Janowitz, Robert Havighurst, and Dan Lortie, formerly of Harvard. Some worked at the law school, as did Arthur Wise, who in 1969 was named an assistant professor and assistant dean. Social science remained the base but faculty interests were clearly problem-oriented.

In the late 1960s, the urban crisis created a concern on the part of the faculty as a whole. Summer workshops were conducted in the Chicago ghetto schools. Research on big city school boards were conceptualized and support obtained from the Danforth Foundation. Attempts to recruit activist students from minority groups and the innercity were successful by the end of the 1960s.

Thus, the faculty decided that the need was for urban educational administrators, especially black administrators. The University of Chicago Department of Education, Committee on Administration, in 1968–69, decided to recruit and train from twenty to thirty individuals for high-level leadership positions in urban schools. Eight to ten new students a year, starting in 1969-70, would be supported with federal funds under the Education Professions Act. Chicago would train a "sizeable number of outstanding black administrators" in a three-year program.

Students and faculty both developed the new program. Urban geographers, and historians, as well as the sociologist Janowitz, contributed suggestions. The Graduate School of Business, the

Center for Urban Studies and the Industrial Relations Center each would contribute ideas and staff assistance.

In July of 1969, Director J. Alan Thomas outlined the major change in the doctoral program. The highly individualized programs and variety of courses selected had been successful in the past. But the new programs would require a more unified and integrated approach. The city would be viewed as a "social and ecological system within which the schools are subsystems."[50]

Therefore, the school leader must be aware of the other agencies and the exchange between school and society, especially in accounting for results.

> This conceptual scheme calls for a new kind of training program. Administrators in training must develop the ability to communicate with parents, community representatives, and students, as well as with increasingly militant teachers. They must know more than ever about the role of the welfare agencies, the city planning departments, the police, and the various organizations involved in manpower development. They must be thoroughly trained in the politics of urban education, urban geography, and labor relations. They must have a good grounding in the nature of school systems as social organizations, and they must have some understanding of the economic aspects of education. In addition, they must have specific training in some practical aspects of administration, including the use of newer technologies.
>
> This way of thinking about school systems makes clear that a more specific program is needed in the future than in the past. Accordingly, we have begun to develop a program addressed to the following areas:
>
> School-community relations
> The politics of education
> Systems analysis, including the economic aspects of education
> Urban geography
> Labor relations
> The organization of urban education
>
> This work will be placed within a context which continues to stress analysis of problems, sound planning, and the ability to use existing knowledge for the improvement of education.[51]

Chicago thus expanded the scope of concerns. The faculty would continue to instill a high regard for the rigors of research and the life of inquiry. The use of theory for action never won many advocates outside the Midwest Center. The prestigious career was one of research, teaching, and writing. Theory was one of the ingredients of research and, for social science type research, one of the expected by-products. It might provide some useful generalizations, if not predictions about behavior, but only with a proper caveat from the researcher.

At the same time, the Midwest Center had outgrown its regional label. Its publications and alumni (its constituency) became nationwide. Its research concerns were on national issues; the staff grew less willing to look at practical problems such as the "intermediate unit" between the state and local school district.

The Social Science Content of the Chicago Program

The phase of the doctoral program at Chicago 1950-1969 that counted most of all, was a man's doctoral dissertation. Midwest Center's annual reports devoted up to three pages summarizing each dissertation for the benefit of those who had left, and maybe for those coming up from below. Very little was reported on coursework; the development of theory usually involved research, and a man's doctoral dissertation could further the research interests of the Center.

Dissertations in educational administration, as in other fields, often grow out of a faculty member's research. Seminars often form around that research: such was the case at Chicago.

As noted earlier, the research in the early 1950s was "cooperative," i.e., cosponsored with state agencies, school board associations, and local school districts. As such, the design was usually pragmatic and atheoretical. In several instances, theoretical approaches were developed along the way at the suggestion or insistence of a social scientist. As early as 1954, some of the dissertations show the influence of Getzels and others defining administrative interpersonal perception. Before that time, most of the studies were the more familiar surveys which relied on checklists and interviews seeking opinions on the problems identified by administrators.

The Ph.D. at Chicago in all departments follows a standard format:

1. The first year culminates in a departmental preliminary examination and foreign language test.
2. The second phase of study, one or more years, leads to an individual's work on a doctoral research proposal under faculty supervision.

After the preliminary examination, a student's course work normally builds the technical skills and substantive knowledge needed to work on a dissertation.

Early in the life of the center, students took traditional courses in school finance, school laws, school planning. Psychology and sociology courses were offered in the Department of Education. As the pressure for a theory of administration grew, first mentioned in 1953—the need for course revision in the Department of Education was recognized. One approach was the addition of new courses. In 1955, a Midwest Administration Center seminar was organized for "the extension and clarification of administrative theory."[52] Although the focus was largely psychological and sociological, resource persons from anthropology and political science were also invited to the session. Several times a week the faculty and staff associates met for discussion and critique of the literature in the several disciplines.

The 1956 report adds detail and cites the contribution of economists, and industrial and business administration as well. Francis Chase conducted the seminar with the help of Guba, Bidwell, Herbert Schooling, H.T. James, and James G. Harlow. One seminar activity was the design of research on the administrator-teacher relationship, starting with a conjectural framework and moving into the collection and analysis of data.[53]

Also, the seminar reviewed books and articles on the nature and function of administration. Guest discussants included Jacob Getzels, Peter Rossi, Morton Grodin of political science, Henry Toy of the Citizens' movement, and Walter Cocking of *School Executive Magazine*.[54]

Starting in 1956, students in the second year group helped teach the courses in school finance, human relations and supervision.[55] They also attended and planned professional conferences and helped to edit the *Administrators' Notebook* and other publications. Each associate also helped conduct the research and administrative surveys led by the faculty.

Especially the teaching was recognized as "particularly important in the training of individuals who aspire to professional positions in institutions of higher education."[56] This gradual immersion into the professional roles of teaching, research, and survey assignments was later identified as a significant professional socialization process by Roald Campbell in an essay in the "Professorship of School Administration."[57]

Dissertations completed in 1957 reflected the new emphasis on theory-based research: Congreve's study of administrative behavior and adult social systems in the secondary schools; Moser's study of administrator-teacher interactions; and Sweitzer's study of role expectations and teacher morale. As of 1958, the Center staff could look back with satisfaction and say, "In a very real sense, the work of the past eight years has helped define the problems for study and has produced some pioneering approaches to the development of theory and of training programs. The actual development of a generation of administrators who have been influenced by recent research findings and reconceived training programs is a task that still remains and one to which the Center hopes to contribute.[58]

The staff associates that year helped design and develop a research study on administrative organization. The group worked out a conceptual framework, each member evaluated an actual school system, and reported their research in a mimeographed document. The Center sponsored a series of staff courses on research which invited many guest speakers from psychology, economics, sociology, political science, and other disciplines.

The major publications of Chicago faculty show the kinds of social science theory stressed at Chicago in the mid-1950s. Halpin's *Administrative Theory* includes the chapter by Getzels which views administration through socio-psychological lenses. Leadership was viewed in terms of the exchange between a main personality and his role, the latter defined in expectations and perceptions. Students were encouraged to identify the interpersonal perceptions of teachers, principals, and superintendents.

In 1959, the staff associates began to work in the St. Louis County study by participating in a summer quarter study of "the basic discipline of demography, economics, political science, and sociology in order to obtain insights concerning the relevance of these disciplines to the solution of educational problems that have arisen with the current trend toward metropolitanism."[59] This exercise provided field training in the use of the social sciences.

The staff categorized research efforts into four major problem areas:

1. The ecology of administration, "metropolitanism," demography, the economics of land use, and governing boards.
2. The sociology of administration, the roles and goals of social systems.
3. The personal variables in administration, especially of leader behavior and interactions.
4. The selection and training of educational administrators, especially as the staff tried to decide how to consider the sex, age, and experience factors.[60]

The 1960 staff associate seminar led by Roald Campbell with Conrad Briner, R. Jean Hills and Dr. Philip Jackson as resource persons examined socio-psychological variables among schools (cohesiveness, adaptability, status differentiation, etc.).[61] A seminar led by Luvern Cunningham studied educational government, as a stimulus for group inquiry and individual research.[62]

Faculty members extended their research into other areas—for example, Roald Campbell's inquiry into various forces "nationalizing" American education was the focus of a research seminar in 1961. In 1961 Luvern Cunningham and Donald Erickson, a second year staff associate, later a professor, conducted a seminar on non-public schools. Several dissertations grew out of their studies. The seminar on psycho-social variables continued to lead to exploratory research activities.[63] Dissertations themselves most properly represent the extent of the Chicago commitment to social science research.

Lazarsfeld and Sieber, in their survey on educational research, identified the Midwest Center as especially interested in concepts and theories. Their field study on the center revealed that "the very first dissertation under its guidance was entitled 'Consultant Services Offered by Three State Departments of Education to School Administrators' (1952) . . . 11 of the 13 dissertations completed through 1955 were of this more traditional variety, while less than half of those completed between the end of 1955 and the end of 1960 were of this type. Today, one reads of reference groups, role conflicts, role expectations, vertical mobility, value orientations, congruence of expectations, the social system model, and need-dispositions."[64]

The additions of Dan Lortie and Donald Erickson to the Center staff in 1963 were described as part of an interest in urban settings. J. Alan Thomas, assistant director of the Center, brought a background in school finance and economic concerns. Seminar guest speakers included Charles Benson, Harvard economist of education, in 1963.[65] Dissertations that year ranged widely from studies of role conflict and teacher satisfaction to analyses of teacher organizations and the social liberalism of suburban dwellers.

The 1960s witnessed a gradual increase in the scope of scholarly concerns. By 1967, students were researching the Teacher Corps, the courts and inequality, teacher migration, the NAACP, and other topics. The staff concluded that "the goal of a unitary theory of educational administration has to some degree been replaced by multiple theories, each of which deals with some aspect of the administrative process."[66]

As of 1969, Director Thomas spoke not of the uniformity of the program, but of the diversity of individual programs. The program did not consciously select social science concepts, but instead encouraged students to pursue the tools of the discipline most related to the problems they wished to study. Students of the economics of education worked with Mary Jean Bowman. Students of organizations could work with Bidwell, Janowitz, David Street, and others. Dissertations under Getzels, Jackson, and Herbert Thelen would continue to use the approach of social psychology. Professor Paul Peterson's interests were in urban politics and policy making. Faculty members in law, the business school, and other departments of the university, would each contribute theories, points of view, and methodologies as needed.

The program in the 1970s was to change, however, as Chicago turned its attention to the need for black city school administrators and the preparation of practitioners to deal with urban problems. Specialists in labor relations and urban geography were consulted. Systems analysts and "urban studies" generalists might help.

The Productivity of the Chicago Program

Between 1953 and 1967, the Midwest Administration Center granted ninety-three doctorates. Although large numbers taught in universities, many served as principals or superintendents at some point in their career. Some moved from a university post to the field and back, or in the reverse order. William Wayson took leave from the Syracuse University faculty to head a difficult innercity school. Roderick McPhee worked in AASA, taught at Harvard, was superintendent at Glencoe, and then headed for the Punahoe School, Hawaii.

Between fifty and sixty graduates, at any moment, were in higher education, usually in teaching and research on educational administration. Chicago men became department chairmen in many university schools of education such as Syracuse, Alberta, Calgary, George Peabody, the University of British Columbia, and the University of Wisconsin, Milwaukee. Its graduates became deans — Harlow and Ohm at Oklahoma, James at Stanford, McCarty at Wisconsin, Hencley at Utah, Ferneau at Tulsa, and Heywood, President at Eastern Montana.

Professors Bidwell, Erickson, Rippey, Congreve, and Wise subsequently taught with the Chicago faculty, or held other major assignments. David Levine helped direct Metropolitan Studies at the University of Missouri.

In each case, this meant a man could continue his research whether at Chicago or elsewhere. For example, Bidwell continued research of the sociological aspects of administrative decision making. Erickson became one of the nation's most informed and influential commentators on the nonpublic schools. Congreve and Levine led urban projects, the latter in collaboration with Robert Havighurst who sharpened his concern for innercity and metropolitan research.

At Syracuse, Chicago alumnus Samuel Goldman developed a new research-oriented program with the help of federal funds and the Maxwell School of Public Affairs. McPhee at Harvard, in the early 1960s, initiated a course in administrative theory. At Stanford, H.T. James directed three major school finance research projects which, as by-products, trained more than a dozen researcherprofessors for as many universities. In each region of the country, other Chicago alumni introduced or elevated the importance of theoretically-oriented research.

Half a dozen graduates worked in the Chicago schools as principals or directors. One headed innovations in Philadelphia public schools. One each headed an Upward Bound program, worked for Ford Foundations overseas, taught at Annapolis, presided over a college, and directed supermarket personnel program.

One important measure of the Chicago impact is the number and quality of publications, most of them research-oriented. A large number of staff associates edited and contributed to the *Administrators' Notebook* over a twenty-year period. Many wrote one or more articles for new journals such as *Educational Administration Quarterly*, edited first by Roald Campbell. Many continued to conduct research or build theory.

A few thought theory developments an especially significant part of their subsequent careers. One Chicago graduate wrote in the introductory pages of a monograph that problems of measurement "... are far less exciting to me than are problems of theoretical conjecture."[67] Hills traces to his Chicago appointment concerns about Parsonian theory and application to the study of organizations. He devoted six years of his professional life to trying to explicate the utility of Parson's model of social action to organizational analysis.

Many felt it worthwhile to use social science theory as a base for their subsequent research in educational administration. The Midwest Center published a number of monographs which had their origins in dissertations and studies at Chicago. Several which represent the Chicago contribution would include:

> Egon C. Guba and Charles E. Bidwell, *Administrative Relationship*
>
> Lawrence W. Downey, *The Task of Public Education*
>
> Roald F. Campbell, Gerald E. Sroufe, and Donald H. Layton, *Strengthening State Departments of Education*

Two major volumes which collect numerous studies made by Chicago faculty and students are:

J.W. Getzels, J.M. Lipham, and R.F. Campbell, *Administration as a Social Process: Theory, Research and Process*

Roald F. Campbell, Luvern L. Cunningham, and Roderick F. McPhee, *The Organization and Control of American Schools*

Both works drew heavily on the dozen or more dissertations on administrative behavior and role perceptions. The second volume drew also on the Midwest Center studies of the task of public education, nationalizing influences, interest groups, and nonpublic schools. More than three dozen Chicago monographs and staff associates' dissertations are cited in the Campbell book. Most of all, the central theme of the book demonstrates the eclectic disciplinary viewpoint of the Midwest Center that schools are subsystems of the larger society and knowledge of the behavioral sciences are vital to the effectiveness of a school administration.

The *Organization and Control* book demonstrates still another point: Chicago graduates brought new ways of looking at the field of study within education. Chapter 15 discusses financial resources according to the cluster of variables which James and his students developed to study educational expenditures. His Stanford studies, one authored by a student later named director of the Midwest Center, are reviewed along with Downey's summary of Chicago research and three other Chicago Ph.D. dissertations. Two chapters on community pressure and interest groups prepared by McPhee cite special research papers prepared by three of his Harvard students and two colleagues, Neal Gross and Robert Marden.

One side effect of Chicago was the impact of men who taught at the Midwest Center and then moved on to other positions. Egon Guba headed the Bureau of Research at Ohio State University and later moved to Indiana where he continued to analyze the problems of educational change. Luvern Cunningham was named Dean at the Ohio State University where he led a national research project on school board decision making begun while at Chicago. One of his associates in that study was Conrad Briner, chairman of Education at the Claremont Graduate School. Andrew Halpin directed research at Utah and worked at Claremont, Washington University, and the University of Georgia. His long-term research on organizational climate influenced more than a score of dissertations and replication studies elsewhere.

Thus, Center staff, faculty, and associates created a kind of ripple effect in research and teaching educational administration. As a focal point for research-minded professors, Chicago lured Rossi and Lortie from the more activist policy-oriented Harvard. Whether the program in the 1970s turns away from the pursuit of theory, the impact of the previous twenty years would remain profound. One chairman of a growing state college even complained, "No one is training teachers of school plant planning anymore; all the new doctorates around the country want to teach administrative theory, organizational behavior, or the politics of education." Chicago provided the seminal thought in these areas or reinforced the inclinations of those who wanted these new specialties to flourish in schools of education.

However, the 1970s seemed to present a major test to the apostles of theory. Were their theories useful and relevant to the innercity education? Could administrative theory really generate research that would make schools more responsive and innovative? Hills, in a concluding chapter to a monograph on Talcott Parsons' model of organization reports the difficulty of convincing others of its utility. He quotes several pre-publication readers saying, in effect, "It's interesting, but I don't know what to do with it. It doesn't make any difference in the way I think about organizations, or provide me with any research ideas."[68] This may be too harsh a criticism of the theory movement as a whole. Halpin has complained of the gap between the enthusiasm of the mid-1950s and the actual yield from researchers in the next ten years. Chicago's decision to turn to more direct ways of wrestling with urban education is not a repudiation of the past, but rather recognition of the validity of claims for a problem-oriented approach to the preparation of innercity administrators.

SUMMARY AND CONCLUSION

The framework identified in the introduction of this chapter suggests that certain crucial decisions about the social sciences are made quite early in the life of a program and affect the role and subsequent contributions of social scientists. At Harvard, the case studies and field study provided for students a problem-based perspective during the 1950s. Implicit was a commitment to breadth, to an interdisciplinary series of social sciences, rather than to concentrated depth in the study of one or a few of these. This is in sharp contrast to programs for those who are going into research careers to continue the study of administration. The view of the admininstrator, coming from this very beginning of the program, is that of a social science consumer *generalist*, a professional who would use social science findings in an action career rather than generate findings in a research career.

Consistent with that option came the selection of Herold Hunt, an experienced and successful large city school administrator, as the leader and central figure in the program for almost twenty years. At the same time, the social scientists, the galaxy which includes names in the forefront of those contributing to the understanding of educational organizations and educational administration, came to the Harvard program as junior faculty. This is implicit in the fundamental shift from the emphasis on the thesis to the emphasis on field work and an applied action project as the ultimate test of competence. Such a shift could well have meant that the social scientist concerned with field data and theories concerning field data selection, operations, and analysis would dominate the program. The shift at Harvard was away from that research which a social scientist would do, to that which centered on a contracted study with a school system, and to performance in an administrative role.

One needs only to read Callahan or Lazarsfeld to realize the extent to which field studies that are contractual in nature usually lack in depth in the application of the social sciences and, hence, minimize the training in use of the social sciences. This may yield more practical results for the client. It may help produce better-trained school administrators. But it reduces the significance of the social sciences as an element in the program.

It is difficult enough to apply the social sciences well to a field study where the problems are determined by the contract. There are also great difficulties in determining how much of the conceptualization and methodolgy should go on paper in the final report. But above all else, the problem of allowing sufficient time simultaneously to train people, collect data with them, make the difficult decisions (including value judgments) that must be made in such surveys, and then work effectively with the client may indeed preclude the possibility of using the field study as a major and central vehicle in a program. One alternative is a field study carefully preceded by intensive work both in the concepts to be used during the course of the study and in the methodologies of field data collection, hypothesis formation, change and development, and, finally, analysis of field data. There was no room for this in the Harvard program as it developed.

Given these difficulties, the junior role of the social scientists, the turnover due to the lack of tenured positions on the Harvard faculty, the dominant concern for the generalist administrator, and the program's concern for action over inquiry are understandable. During the latter 1960s, a wider range of social sciences and social scientists became available to the students. In short, fragmentation and evidence of the need for new direction appeared during the last few years of the Harvard program. This fragmentation is accented by the development of the Policy Center and its priority on the invention and evaluation of educational programs.

In summary, the Harvard program has produced an important and impressive group of school administrators operating in particular in urban settings. Its contribution to the intellectual understanding of school administration is considerably more modest. Except for the by-products, for example, the work of Neal Gross, Peter Rossi, and Charles Benson, Harvard did not stress the contribution of the social psychological approaches to school administration. Nor did it lead the way in the contributions of anthropology or sociology within the Administrative Career Program. Little of the pioneering work on the politics of education at Harvard was published. Charles Benson's major work in the economics of education was done mainly in applied settings, given the format of the program. This reflects the early choices in the program—to grow rapidly in size, and to use the social scientists as auxilliaries and associates. The concern at Harvard now, and throughout the period, might best be summarized as a concern not with development of knowledge, nor even with answering the question, "What are the concepts which are most useful for understanding a problem?", but instead on how to deal with the social problems of our society. The social sciences help to an extent in sharpening the questions, but not necessarily in identifying appropriate action.

At Chicago, the early commitment to research and theory was reinforced later by the interdisciplinary approach. The retention of the Ph.D. program and the centrality of the thesis was also a major factor in that program from the beginning. Social scientists, especially Jacob Getzels and Andrew Halpin, were permitted to influence deeply the way in which the social scientists contribute to the program. Explicitly, Getzels carried with him a social psychologist's reinterpretation and application of Talcott Parsons, which dominated so much of the research and thinking in the school administration at the University of Chicago for most of the last twenty years. In fact, the influence of Getzels has extended to other university programs and to social service professions, such as nursing, as well.

The search for theory at Chicago became social science-based by 1955 and expanded the earlier commitment to research. In more recent years, Chicago program leaders deepened their concern for policy making, politics, economics, systems analysis, and elements which would not have come out of Getzel's framework itself. As problems in the field multiplied, theories from other social sciences were found useful.

As noted, the Chicago program led to a development of students who went into higher education and became professors of school administration, some of them moving into the administration of higher educational institutions. These graduates have an influence out of proportion to their numbers, as the ripple effect between their work and their students may be seen. Chicago, on the other hand, unlike Harvard, has had less direct impact on as many large city administrative situations. The search for new direction with its program suggests, perhaps, that the twenty years effect of the Kellogg work both at Harvard and at Chicago is coming to an end, and that the seventies requires something new of both programs.

Both Chicago and Harvard now search for new directions. Chicago manifests a concern for urban affairs and for the development of administrators for school systems, particularly the urban systems. Much of the stirring looks similar to that which occurred at Harvard in the early sixties. At Harvard students request more administrative theory in the program, reflecting a need for intellectual understanding of educational administration. It is almost as if each institution, having worked out the logic of the divergence that began at the beginning of the Kellogg era, has now gone so far one from the other that the reality of the situation demands that each begin to move back somewhat closer to the ground occupied by the other a decade ago.

FOOTNOTES

1. *Toward Improved School Administration* (Battle Creek, Michigan: The W. K. Kellogg Foundation, 1961), p. 19 — The Kellogg Foundation invested

seven million dollars in educational administration programs, of which Harvard received $576,864, Chicago $898,967.

2. *Proposal for a Revised Doctorate Program in Educational Administration*, submitted to the faculty, Harvard Graduate School of Education, January 1952, mimeographed, 21 pages.

3. Selznick, Philip. *T.V.A. and The Grass Roots* (New York: Harper Torch Books, 1966).

4. At Harvard, the term social relations links sociology, anthropology, and social psychology. The social relations department is part of Harvard College and the Graduate School of Arts and Sciences. Public administration at Harvard stresses the study of economics and government.

5. The Ph.D. at Harvard is under the control of the faculty of Arts and Sciences. Each of the professional schools is autonomous and offers a distinctly different doctorate (M.D., J.D., D.B.A., Ed.D., D.D., etc.) unless the doctoral program is jointly sponsored (e.g., History of Education Ph.D.).

6. *Proposal for a Revised Doctorate Program in Educational Administration*, op. cit. Prophetic of current interests, the faculty speculated, "Perhaps the university of the future will offer an advanced professional program in administration per se, with the various specialized graduate schools supplementing the administration core of the university-wide program." p. 3.

7. *Five Year Report*, Center for Field Studies, HGSE, 1954.

8. Ibid., p. 28.

9. Ibid., p. 32.

10. *Seen in Review*, The Corporative Program in Educational Administration, 4th Annual Report, Center for Field Studies, Cambridge: Harvard University, 1954, p. 36.

11. *Five Year Report*, op. cit., p. 43.

12. Ibid., p. 41 — One of the costs may have been the departure of Peter and Alice Rossi to the University of Chicago, and eventually to the National Opinion Research Center, the other kind of "unit." Neal Gross stayed at Harvard, but withdrew from the program to carry on his research and train sociologists of education.

13. Report of the President's Committee to Review the Program for the Preparation of School Administrators at Harvard, September 1958, page 11, Ralph W. Tyler, Chairman.

14. A criticism of graduates was "the preponderance of students from the larger cities and from the New England area." The former represented Herold Hunt's recruiting and visibility as a big city superintendent; in the 1960s, this became recognized as an asset, especially since minority groups were represented in most ACP groups. Harvard's Kellogg money was for New England, although the faculty insisted on national recruiting.

15. Report to the National Council for Teacher Accreditation of Teacher Education on Harvard University, Camb., Mass., October 22-24, 1962, mimeographed p. 29.

16. Ibid., p. 31.

17. Ibid., p. 40 — Despite earlier disclaimers that the Research Career Program would falter, no more than half a dozen students in administration between 1952 and 1965 wrote theses.

18. Center for the Study of Education and Development, Annual Report, 1965, Howard Graduate School of Education, p. 2.

19. Benson, Charles S. *The Economics of Public Education* (Boston: Houghton Mifflin Co., 1961) (1st edition), and *Perspectives on the Economics of Education* (Boston: Houghton Mifflin Co., 1963).

20. Benson's perspective on the course was fascinating. "I fear they leave here under a disadvantage . . . in the view of experienced board members . . . I don't want to create a group of automatons . . . It is possible to have the course without the students coming to feel that its content is the center of school administration." Harvard's program for activists never suffered from excessive technical detail.

21. Sargent, Cyril G., and Eugene L. Belisle, *Educational Administration* (Boston: Houghton Mifflin Co., 1955), p. 6.

22. Ibid., pp. 30–37.

23. Ibid., p. 461.

24. Cooperative Program in Educational Administration Report, Harvard Graduate School of Education, p. 12.

25. The studies went through various phases from 1952 to 1956. All were of the older industrial cities (Lawrence, Pawtucket, Chelsea). From 1956–1960, the Cooperative Study of "good" suburban systems, from 1963 to 1965, studies of Northern School segregation, 1968–1970, back to very political Massachusetts cities — Watertown, Lowell, Boston.

26. Five Year Report, p. 45.

27. W. B. Spalding memo to ACP Faculty, Harvard Graduate School of Education, June 14, 1961, p. 4.

28. *The Midwest Moves Forward*, Annual Report, University of Chicago, Midwest Administration Center, 1951–52, p. 3.

29. Ibid., p. 4.

30. Ibid., p. 4.

31. *The Third Year of CPEA in the Midwest*, Annual Report 1951–52, University of Chicago, Midwest Administration Center, 1953.

32. Ibid., p. 35.

33. *The Midwest Moves Forward*, op. cit., p. 5.

34. *The Midwest Moves Forward*, op. cit., p. 24.

35. *The Third Year of CPEA in the Midwest*, op. cit., p. 39.

36. Getzels, Jacob W. "A Psycho-Sociological Framework for the Study of Educational Administration," *Harvard Educational Review* 22 (Fall 1952): 235–246.

37. *Fourth Annual Report*, 1953–54, Univ. of Chicago, Midwest Administration Center, 1954, p. 32.

38. *Fourth Annual Report*, p. 35.

39. *The Midwest Administration Center: A Review of Its Programs*, May 27, 28, 1954, The University of Chicago, the Center, 1954, p. 11.

40. *Fifth Annual Report*, University of Chicago, M.A.C., 1955, p. 1.

41. *Fifth Annual Report*, op. cit., p. 2.

42. Ibid., p. 4.

43. *Annual Report*, 1956, Midwest Administration Center, University of Chicago, 1956, p. 6.

44. Ibid., p. 11.

45. Ibid., pp. 12–20.

46. *Administrative Theory in Education*, edited by Andrew W. Halpin, Chicago, Midwest Administration Center, University of Chicago, 1958. The book documents the exchange of ideas between men at major universities. Getzels acknowledges his intellectual debt to Parsons; Parsons and Halpin both refer to the role studies of Neal Gross; and Roald Campbell quotes Shipton's findings from the Bay City study. This suggests a wholesome communication network among the social scientists at both universities.

47. Annual Report, 1957, pp. 22–24.

48. Annual Report, 1959 and 1961.

49. Annual Report, 1960, p. 5. The Federal grant was under the National Defense Education Act.

50. "A Training Program for Urban Administration," J. Alan Thomas, Committee on Administration, University of Chicago, July 1, 1969, mimeographed.

51. Ibid., pp. 12–13.

52. Fifth Report, op. cit., p. 3.

53. 1956 Report, pp. 6, 7.

54. Ibid., p. 8, 19.

55. Ibid., p. 11.

56. 1959 Annual Report, p. 13.

57. Ibid.

58. Annual Report, 1958, p. 42.

59. 1959 Report, p. 12.

60. 1959 Report, pp. 20–47.

61. 1960 Report, pp. 34–35.

62. Ibid., p. 37.

63. 1961 Annual Report, pp. 47–50.

64. Lazarsfeld, Paul F., and Sam D. Sieber, *Organizing Educational Research* (Englewood Cliffs, N. J.: Prentice-Hall, Inc., 1964), pp. 89–90.

65. Annual Report, 1963.

66. 1967 Report, p. 29.

67. Hills, R. Jean *Towards a Science of Organization* (Eugene, Oregon: Center for the Advanced Study of Educational Administration, 1968).

68. Hills, op. cit., p. 114.

9

Social Science Concepts and Collective Negotiations

John J. Horvat

THE SETTING

The purpose of this chapter is to describe the selection and application of various social science concepts in a two-week workshop on collective negotiations in educational settings. The specific workshop experience which provides the basis for this chapter was sponsored as a regular summer course by the College of Education at Boston University. The workshop met for eight hours a day for fourteen days during the months of June and July, 1968.

Participants included twenty-six practicing school administrators (largely superintendents and assistant superintendents of schools) and six individuals who were officials in various school district teachers' organizations. About one half of them had experienced limited involvement in face-to-face negotiations prior to their enrollment in the workshop, but none could be considered to be experienced negotiators.

The major purpose of the workshop was that of preparing practicing school administrators for engagement in collective negotiations with representatives of teachers' organizations.[1] While the entire phenomenon of collective negotiation in education was considered in some detail, the major focus was on the processes and techniques of face-to-face negotiating,

It should be noted that Massachusetts law relative to negotiation in public employment had been changed only a few months prior to the time of the workshop. The new law, in effect, mandated that boards of education (school committees) engage in collective negotiations with properly designated representatives of local public school teachers' organizations if such organizations so requested. Because of this change in the legal basis for negotiations, the workshop participants were highly process-oriented; this orientation precluded a highly theoretical or long-range outlook emphasis within the workshop.

THE WORKSHOP ACTIVITIES

Four major types of activity comprised the substance of the workshop: (1) readings; (2) lectures and discussions; (3) simulation of face-to-face negotiations; and (4) detailed analysis of participant behaviors in, and substantive outcomes from, the simulated negotiations activities.

The key element of the workshop activity involved the simulation of face-to-face negotiations. Approximately 60 per cent of workshop time was devoted to simulated negotiations and the subsequent analysis of behavior exhibited within the simulated sessions. The device, the Negotiation Game, created by Horvat was utilized as the basis for simulation.[2] This device is designed to assist in the training of students and/or practitioners of educational administration in the theory and practice of collective negotiation with particular emphasis on the face-to-face, across-the-table aspects of negotiating. The device provides the following:

1. Methods and materials for selecting and placing trainees on teams for the purpose of engaging in simulated negotiations.

2. Background materials which set the context of the simulation and which serve to prepare the trainees to engage in simulated negotiations.

3. Substantive issues to be negotiated in simulation, and negotiating guidelines for the negotiators (trainees).

4. Materials and methods for use in the analysis of the outcomes of the simulated negotiation sessions—so that feedback on negotiating behaviors and outcomes can be provided to the trainees.[3]

A critical phase of the simulation technique utilized in the workshop involved the analysis of negotiating behaviors and outcomes exhibited in the simulated negotiation sessions. Various techniques were used to analyze such behaviors and outcomes. The major analytical tool incorporated a modification of the Bales interaction analysis process to analyze the verbal behaviors and interactions of workshop participants during the simulation sessions.[4] By this means participants were led to a self-confrontation of their behaviors and the effects of their behaviors in the negotiations context.

PROBLEMS PERSPECTIVE

The instructional situation of the negotiations workshop was, by its very nature, highly problem-oriented. The participants, for example, viewed the entire area of collective negotiations in education as a problem which they little understood, and in which they were unprepared to function with success. "The problem," as the participants viewed it, was simply that of learning to function and survive as spokesmen for their (board-administration) negotiating teams.

While the problem in negotiations, as seen by the participants, was one of a rather clear-cut, "how to do it" type, the instructor's perceptions of the instructional problems involved was rather more complex. Generally, three major instructional problems were seen to be inherent within the workshop situations:

1. The problem of providing general familiarization with the broad arena of negotiations in education to the workshop participants.

2. The problem of providing workshop participants with reality-oriented experience in negotiation processes and procedures.

3. The problem of providing workshop participants with, at least, rudimentary understanding of the social, economic, and behavioral manifestations which are inherent in collective negotiation contexts.

The first two problem areas listed above were susceptible to relatively straightforward instructional treatments. General familiarization relative to the broad arena of negotiations was provided by straight didactic methods, such as direct provision of information through assigned readings, lectures, and discussion. The provision of reality-oriented experience in negotiation processes was accomplished by simulating face-to-face negotiation processes, including prenegotiation activities, negotiation activities, and post-negotiation session procedures (contract writing and grievance handling procedures). Adequate response to both of these instructional problems was essential to the success of the workshop. However, an *adequate* response here did not require heavy emphasis or reliance on social science concepts.

The problem of providing workshop participants with understanding of the social, economic, and behavioral aspects of negotiations was, of course, another matter. Such understanding, however limited, could be gained *only* by reliance upon content derived from the social sciences. The remainder of this chapter will be devoted to a description of the means by which social science concepts were selected, organized, and presented so that some of these basic understandings might be gained by the workshop participants.

PROBLEM DIMENSIONS OF COLLECTIVE NEGOTIATIONS

The processes of collective negotiations were analyzed by the instructor so that the major elements within these processes could be identified. As mentioned earlier, the specific processes involved in face-to-face negotiation activity formed the major focus of the workshop. The fundamental assumptions which provided the framework for the analysis of negotiation processes follow.

Negotiation is a process which encompasses four major subprocesses.[5] These subprocesses include:

1. *Distributive bargaining*—a subprocess comprised of competitive behaviors that are intended to influence the division of limited resources. The function of this subprocess is to resolve pure conflicts of interest. It is the type of activity which is most familiar to students of negotiations and is referred to by game theorists as fixed-sum games.[6]

2. *Integrative bargaining*—a subprocess comprised of activities that increase the joint gain available to the negotiating parties. These activities are problem-solving behaviors which identify, enlarge, and act upon the common interests of the parties. It is the type of activity which is closely related to what theorists call varying-sum games.[7]

3. *Attitudinal structuring*—a subprocess comprised of activities that influence the attitudes of the parties toward each other and affect the basic relationship bonds between the social units involved.[8]

4. *Intraorganizational bargaining*—a subprocess comprised of the behaviors of negotiators that are meant to achieve consensus within their own organization.[9]

Specific problem dimensions of face-to-face negotiation processes were developed by analyzing the commonly recurring events under the four major negotiation subprocesses listed above. A large proportion of the social science content of the workshop focused on events which are most common to the distributive bargaining subprocess. The workshop participants were most concerned with this particular subprocess; that is, they were concerned with survival in the immediate conflict (adversary) situations. The integrative, attitudinal structuring, and intraorganizational aspects of face-to-face negotiations were not as crucial or compelling to the participants as were the conflict-distributive elements. This attitude is not surprising since the most visible, spectacular, and concern-inspiring elements of negotiation do in fact evolve from distributive bargaining activities. Distributive difficulties can ultimately lead to strikes, sanctions, and other unpleasantries which make headlines, while difficulties within the other three subprocesses typically do not.

The instructor, in accepting the immediate motivations of the participants, emphasized distributive bargaining problems in an approximate three-to-one ratio over problems of attitudinal structuring, and integrative, and intraorganizational bargaining.

The Major Problem Dimensions

The major problem dimensions inherent within the four bargaining subprocesses were identified and selected as follows:

A. Distributive Bargaining Problem Dimensions
   1. Problems of conflict
   2. Problems of power, threat, and commitment
   3. Win-lose decision problems
   4. Utility function problems
   5. Problems of decision-making in conditions of competition

B. Integrative Bargaining Problem Dimensions
   1. Problems of information processing in decision-making

    2. Problems of intergroup cooperation, collaboration, and
       joint problem solving
C. Attitudinal Structuring Problem Dimensions
    1. Problems of promoting attitudinal change
D. Intraorganizational Bargaining Problem Dimensions
    1. Problems of role conflict and ambiguity[10]

Obviously, factors other than those listed above inhere in the
processes of face-to-face negotiation, but these were seen to be the
most common, most salient, and most generally comprehensive of
all identifiable problem dimensions. Obvious, also, is the fact that
there is considerable overlap of problem dimensions between and
among the negotiation subprocesses. Negotiations in the real world
(and in simulation) seldom present any *purely* distributive bargaining issues, but rather involve significant elements of conflict *and*
considerable potential for integration of common interests.

Given the major problem dimensions listed above, the task of
instruction was reduced to that of selecting various social science
concepts with which to illustrate and amplify each dimension. The
criteria used for the selection of social science concepts were the
same for all problem dimensions and were very simple indeed. The
following criteria were used:

1. The instructor had to be acquainted with the concept(s).

2. Concepts had to apply to problem dimensions in a direct and
   fairly obvious manner.

3. Concepts had to be amenable to relatively unsophisticated
   presentation, since the social science capabilities of the participants and the limited instructional time precluded extensive or rigorous study of any one concept.

Concept Applications

The need to gain skill in understanding and resolving conflict is
probably the critical problem for the would-be negotiator. Certainly, if the conflict elements of negotiating can be handled well,
the other problems inherent in negotiations will become much more
amenable to resolution.[11]

There is a fairly large body of literature in the social science field
which deals specifically with the concept of conflict. The work of
Boulding,[12] Schelling,[13] and Kahn and Boulding,[14] provided the

major concepts relative to conflict which were utilized in the work-shop.

Concepts Related to Conflict

1. Conflict is defined as "a situation of competition in which the parties are aware of the incompatibility of potential future positions and in which each party wishes to occupy a position that is incompatible with the wishes of the other."[15]

2. The total range of possible conflict involves a spectrum from pure and complete antagonism to pure and complete common interest. Between the extremes, there is both conflict and common interest. In negotiations, the extremes never occur (except possibly for rare cases involving specific issues), but specific negotiation situations can and do exist at all the points on the spectrum.[16]

3. The nature of conflict situations is such that an act or move-ment on the part of one party so changes the field (situa-tion) of the other that it typically forces an act or movement on the part of the other, which, in turn, changes the situa-tion of the first, forcing a move, and so on. Movement can generate either more or less conflict.[17] This concept was pre-sented in order to provide a basis for understanding the behavior of the typical offer, counter-offer, counter-counter-offer, and so on, in the negotiation process.

4. Differences in value systems are among the most important sources of conflict. While one might wish to conduct nego-tiations solely on the basis of facts which can be validated and about which agreement in principle can always be found, much of negotiating conflict rests upon judgments of value which cannot be validated and which provide no sure roads to agreement.[18]

5. Group conflict can be of positive value if it eventually serves to advance constructive efforts. "What is inherently evil within conflict is its resolution through violence and destruc-tion. . . ."[19] In another sense, task-oriented conflict may ultimately be productive whereas personality or non-task-oriented conflict is usually dysfunctional, if not destructive. This concept helped the participants to understand the major difference between rational and nonrational conflict and to explore ways of avoiding nonrational conflict.

6. Hostility may be caused by a number of factors. However, "the evidence is clear that hostility depends less on how

strongly the person feels about an issue than on whether he has received the weight he expects for his point of view."[20] The implications of this concept suggest that the negotiator should make every attempt to take seriously the comments, requests, and demands of the other side's negotiators. Even if such demands are repugnant or clearly ridiculous, they should be treated seriously or else needless hostility may be generated.

7. "Rational conflict exists whenever two or more value systems, *apparent to both parties* [emphasis added], are in juxtaposition."[21] This concept was used to illustrate the need for negotiators to attempt to discover the problem which caused the other side to make a particular request or demand.

It was emphasized that attempting to deal directly with a particular demand or request would very often lead to nonrational conflict; whereas, attempting to determine the problem (or values) which precipitated the demand was a means to promote rational conflict behaviors.

Concepts Related to Power, Threat, and Commitment

The consideration of conflict in negotiations leads rather naturally to problems of power, for ". . . the more prevalent conflict . . . becomes, the more keenly will the need for power be felt and the more ardently will it be sought."[22]

Power is operationally defined as the ability of one individual or group (A) to cause another individual or group (B) to behave in a manner in which it otherwise would not have behaved. In short, A is able to influence B's behavior.

In the context of distributive negotiations, power appears to be largely a function of the ability of one party to influence the behavior of the other by means of various threat and commitment behaviors. In the workshop, the following concepts pertaining to threats and commitments were considered:

1. Threat was defined as "the expression of an intention to do something which is detrimental to the interests of another."[23]

2. Commitment was defined as "the act of pledging oneself to a course of action."[24]

3. The threat differs from the commitment in that it makes one's course of action conditional on what the other party does. While commitment fixes one's course of action, the

threat fixes a course of reaction or of response to the other party.[25]

4. The concept of "settlement range" in negotiations was introduced so that concepts of threat and commitment could be explicated. The two relatively simple illustrations shown below were used to describe positive and negative settlement range situations in negotiations.[26]

A. *Illustration of Positive Settlement Range on a Salary Increase Issue*

	B_i	T_m	B_m		T_i
Salary Increase	$100	$200	$300	$400	$500	$600

Positive Settlement Range

B_i = ideal settlement point for board of education

B_m = minimum settlement point for board, i.e., worst acceptable position

T_i = ideal settlement point for teachers

T_m = minimum settlement point for teachers, i.e., worst acceptable position

B. *Illustration of Negative Settlement Range on a Salary Increase Issue*

	B_i		B_m		T_m	T_i
Salary Increase	$100	$200	$300	$400	$500	$600

Negative Settlement Range

Code: Letters equivalent to those of illustration A.

From the above illustrations, it was made clear that agreement was possible under conditions of positive settlement range and that the negotiating problem is largely one of gaining agreement at a point which is most favorable to a particular side's point of view. Thus, in Illustration A, the board negotiators would attempt to discover the T_m point and to get agreement at or near that point. Under conditions of negative settlement range, it is impossible to achieve an agreement unless shifts are made in the minimum points of one or both parties. Negotiators in this situation would attempt to force the other party to shift its minimum point. It should be noted that the minimum points described in the illustrations are almost never known with any degree of certainty. Most of the ritual of negotiating is devoted to the discovery, and the shifting, of the other party's minimum points on the various issues to be negotiated.

5. Threats and statements of commitment are a major means by which the parties reveal their preferences to each other and influence the preferences of the other. The successful use of a statement of commitment is a strategic move which induces the other party to choose in one's favor. It limits the other party's range of choice by affecting his expectations and reducing the possible range of settlement points.[27]

6. If one can make an irrevocable commitment to a position near the other party's minimum point, then one has narrowed the settlement range down to the points most favorable to himself. This, of course, applies only when a positive settlement range exists. If the settlement range is negative, one would attempt to make a commitment near his own minimum point but below it so that a counter-concession by the other party, if one is forthcoming, is a major move toward one's minimum point.[28]

7. To be effective, both threats and commitments must be credible to the other party. Credibility usually depends upon the costs and risks associated with fulfillment for the party making the threat or commitment. Credibility occurs only if the action or reaction threatened would cause worse damage to the threatened party than to the party making the threat.[29]

8. "Threats are not only the most dangerous, but usually the least effective form of indicating strength. As often as not, people who make threats find it necessary to do so because they are bluffing. An experienced negotiator will tell you that if you have the strength, you don't need to make threats; if you haven't the strength, when the showdown comes you must choose between taking some suicidal action, or eating your words. When you hurl a threat, you buy some militancy, but often at too high a price. . . . You have served notice on the other party that if he yields to you, he openly acknowledges himself in retreat. You may have scared him a bit, but in all likelihood you have made it impossible to accede to you. . . ."[30]

The concepts related to power, threat, and commitment listed above were all interwoven into an examination of negotiating behaviors during simulation. The effects of participants' threat and commitment behavior were examined. It should be noted that extensive literature exists relative to threat and commitment and that these concepts are related to others, such as concession and convergence strategies, flexibility, firmness, promise making, and promise or concession hinting.

Game Theory Concepts

Game theory has been described thus:

> . . . a method for the study of decision making in situations of conflict. It deals with human processes in which the individual decision unit is not in complete control of other decision units entering into the environment. It is addressed to problems involving conflict, cooperation, or both, at many levels.[31]

As such, game theory offers many insights to the student of collective negotiation processes. Because of the time constraints of the workshop situation and because game theory is complex, only a few rudimentary concepts were used. They included the following:

1. The general concept of fixed-sum, strictly competitive games was used to depict pure win-lose situations.[32]

2. The elementary concepts of two-person, variable-sum, co-operative games were used to depict the typical nonstrictly competitive situation which occurs in bargaining. For example, the simple payoff matrix shown below was used in explicating possible strategies on the simulation issue relative to exclusive recognition of the teacher's organization. The utility to teachers (T) of gaining exclusive recognition was arbitrarily set at 5 and of failing to gain recognition at −5. The utilities were reversed for the board (B). It was assumed that the "reject-stand pat" combination would lead a strike which had utility of −10 to B and −5 to T. The visual representation of this hypothetical situation is shown in Table 1.

Table 1

Teacher's options on recognition demand

Board options	Stand Pat	Yield
Reject	−10, −5 (strike)	5, −5
Accept	−5, 5	+5, +5 (?) *

*In this situation, if T yields before B accepts, the payoff is 5, −5. If B accepts before T yields, the payoff is −5, 5.

The above example was used to show that the teacher's best strategy was to stand pat; that is, insist that the demand be met, since the −5 payoff of the "stand pat-reject" combination is no worse than the −5 payoff possibilities of the "yield" positions, and the −10 payoff of the "stand pat-reject" combination for B would probably force B to select the "accept" option. Questions drawn from this matrix were: (a) what is the likely outcome if the "stand pat-reject" combination has utilities of −10, −10? (b) how does B attempt to change T's perceptions of the utility of the stand pat-reject combination? and (c) what is the importance of timing of commitment to options? Other elementary illustrations of this type were used to depict hypothetical bargaining situations.[33]

3. Game theory illustrations were related to concepts of threat and commitment as described earlier in this chapter.

Concepts of Utility

The game theory and/or economic concepts of utility, utility function, and marginal utility have great relevance for the process of negotiation, particularly for the distributive aspects of the process. However, since these concepts in their full explication are complex, the depth of their treatment in the workshop was limited.

Utility was described as a quantity which

> . . . is experimentally determined (hence operationally defined) by an *act of preference*: if a subject chooses alternative A in preference to alternative B, A is said to have greater "utility" for this subject than B. More precisely, it should be recognized that the "utility" is associated with those characteristics and/or consequences of the alternatives (and the probabilities of their occurrence) that the subject *expects and considers* when making the choice. In the [negotiations] realm, where the consequences of choices are so complex and intuition plays such a large role, it is clear that utility thus defined is unlikely to remain stable during the course of negotiations.[34]

It was noted that game theory assumes that utility is stable for a player throughout the game and that each player knows, at least, his own utility. In negotiation, however, utilities are generally unknown and unknowable. Utilities in negotiation are, in fact, formed by and during the process. Support for this concept is provided by Walton and McKersie who write:

A . . . serious deficiency of game theory is the assumption that participants act as if they attached constant numerical values to the possible outcomes. The fact is that evaluations of the outcomes are not constant during the course of negotiations. *Indeed, apart from the final single power of the two negotiators by which they make a choice and conclude negotiations, the negotiators' bargaining activity serves primarily to estimate these utilities and to alter them.*[35]

The above concept, in conjunction with the so-called Bernoulli Norm, provided the basis for the general application of utility concepts to the processes of negotiation. The Bernoulli Norm, is stated by Marschak:

Unless your tastes are of a peculiar character, utilities are not proportional to money amounts (and moreover they can and should be attached to many other objects of choice besides money!), and one must be careful to state that the consistent decision-maker maximizes his expected utility, not his expected monetary wealth.[36]

Through the use of these concepts, the problems of manipulating the utility parameters of the other party in negotiations (which is the key tactical act of negotiation behaviors) were considered. The general propositions provided by Walton and McKersie relative to this form of manipulation were followed in this area of consideration.[37] These propositions include the following:

1. In contract negotiations, objective knowledge virtually never becomes complete in the sense that the true nature of all factors is accurately understood by both sides. Thus, it is only necessary to change the other's perceptions in order to alter his bargaining position.

2. The first need of the negotiator is to assess the other party's utilities. The following two general means are available for meeting this need: (a) indirect assessment of the factors which underlie utilities on various issues, for example, estimates of importance of and commitment to a particular demand which are based on "grapevine" information, and (b) direct assessment based on clues provided by the other party's behavior during negotiations; for example, off-the-record conferences, outbursts at the table.

3. A second tactical need is to conceal or misrepresent one's own utilities, at least during early stages of negotiations, so that information can be gathered from the other party to test the appropriateness of one's own utilities. This can be accomplished by minimizing clues; that is, talk little and listen a lot, and by conveying deliberate impressions of one's utilities which are somewhat overstated so that "bargaining room" is created. Care must be taken not to engage in gross exaggerations, or one's credibility is lost.

4. A third tactical need is to modify the other party's perceptions of his own utilities. This may be accomplished by either changing the other party's view of the utility of its own demands to itself or by changing the other party's view of the unpleasantness of one's proposals. Specific procedures involved all operate to bring to bear the right information at the right time to influence the other party. Examples of the ways in which this can be accomplished include: (a) informing the other party of the consequences to be faced if it maintains its original position (threat or straightforward enlightenment), and (b) minimizing the advantage to the other party if its position were to be accepted (perhaps even showing it to be inherently disadvantageous).

These concepts were illustrated by specific examples drawn from the participants' own simulated negotiation behaviors. They were extended somewhat by considering utilities as they are affected during impasse, sanction, and strike situations.

One other important, albeit simple, concept relative to utilities was presented. "The exchange of labor for money looks very different from the side of the employer, or buyer of labor, from the way it looks to the worker or seller of labor."[38]

This concept was used to make the point that in certain phases of negotiations the utilities of employees are measured in terms of human life while the utilities of employers are measured in terms of a service or a commodity. The depth of feeling on the part of the employer's utility tends to be impersonally oriented. Lack of sensitivity to the human aspect of employee utility (the exchange of life for income) in such cases can lead to bitter misunderstandings.

Concepts Related to Decision Making
in Conditions of Competition

One of the major points which the instructor emphasized during the workshop was that of the dysfunctionality of excessive competition in decision-making situations. Several simulated negotiation sessions were contrived (rigged) to create highly competitive negotiating teams, and these sessions were analyzed in order to illustrate (1) the lack of progress in reaching agreement, that is, poor decision-making potential, and (2) the virtual absence of joint problem-solving behaviors. In addition to these illustrations taken from the simulation context, references to concepts to be found in the literature of competitive decision-making situations were provided. The key concepts relative to the undesirability of excessive competitive decision-making behaviors included the following:

1. "In intergroup relations, win-lose conflict distorts realistic judgment. Heightened disagreement tends to obliterate objectivity, Yet, . . ., objectivity is a primary condition of intergroup problem solving. When win-lose competitive attitudes reach such a degree that the parties are unable to make realistic appraisals, then the possibilities of future cooperation have been reduced or eliminated."[39]

2. When contacts between two groups are competitive and mutually frustrating, the interactions of groups . . . lead to strong stereotype formations. Members of each group develop negative attitudes. They express hostility toward members of the opposite group. "These hostile expressions, in turn, have an accelerating and provocative effect. The stereotypes are saturated with negative emotions. The consequence of provocation tends to be counter provocation. This, in turn, leads to the further intensification of conflict. The end result is erosion of mutual respect and confidence in the constructiveness of the other's intentions."[40]

3. ". . . commonalities tend to be overlooked and disparities increased when groups are in competition. Consequently, needless barriers to understanding and agreement are created."[41]

4. Experimental studies indicate that competitive groups, as compared with groups which behave cooperatively, exhibit: (a) less achievement pressure, (b) less communication to one another, (c) less attentiveness to fellow members, (d) less mutual comprehension of communication, and (e) poorer quality of product and discussion.[42]

The shift from consideration of *distributive* bargaining to consideration of the *integrative* bargaining and *attitudinal structuring* aspects of negotiations required utilization of a different realm of concepts. Concepts dealing with competition and conflict were replaced by those concerned with cooperative, collaborative, and joint problem-solving behaviors.

The key concept relative to integrative bargaining and attitudinal structuring was that, for negotiations of this kind to occur, the prime prerequisite is simply that of mutual trust and respect between the negotiating parties.[43] The methods by which mutual trust and respect could be generated from what is inherently a situation which mitigates against such behaviors comprised the major substance of this element of the workshop. The following concepts were used to achieve this purpose.

Concepts Related to Communication within the Bargaining Situation

1. One of the major barriers to cooperation in negotiations contexts and to development of mutual trust and respect among the negotiators is defensively-oriented behavior. Defensive behavior is simply "that behavior which occurs when an individual perceives threat or anticipates threat in the group."[44]

2. Defensive behavior creates several undesirable consequences within the decision-making (i.e., negotiating) group. These include, in part, (a) distortion of received messages, (b) inability to accurately perceive the motives, values, and emotions of message senders, (c) reduced attention to the group task, and (d) general loss of efficiency in communication.[45] Once the points relative to defensive behavior had been made, Gibb's twelve categories of behavior characteristic of the supportive and defensive climate in small groups were used to illustrate techniques for reducing defensive behavior within the negotiation context.[46]

Concepts Related to Problems of Intergroup Collaboration, Cooperation, and Joint Problem Solving

In order for negotiations to move away from competitive, largely win-lose behaviors, relatively large degrees of trust, cooperation, collaboration, and joint problem-solving activity must exist. To create such behaviors within the negotiations context is no small task because, generally speaking, negotiating is inherently a competitive process.

The great body of literature in the social sciences related to group cooperation and problem solving deals with monolithic groups with roughly similar goals and objectives. That is to say the literature deals with intragroup, rather than intergroup processes. However, the following social science concepts were found to be useful in dealing with the intergroup cooperation and problem-solving processes.

1. "Intergroup problem solving must emphasize solving problems and not the accommodation of different points of view. Causes of doubt, misunderstanding, and reservation must be explored rather than the relative merits of the parties' stated positions.[47]

2. Conditions which must exist for successful intergroup problem solving include: (a) problem definitions must be developed by and through intergroup contact — the parties must search out the issues that separate them, (b) a full review of the basic definitions of the problems, (c) development, and joint understanding, of a range of possible alternatives for dealing with each of the defined problems, (d) non-structured debate of the alternatives by the entire negotiations group, and (e) joint searching for the evaluation of solutions.[48]

3. A fundamental key to collaboration is based on avoiding impulsiveness that leads to win-lose pitfalls, through sensitivity to "win-lose" signals and cues that elicit conflict. This means that each action and every assumption underlying a reaction that feels "natural" must be deliberately screened for win-lose dynamics in order to avoid the pathology associated with it.[49]

4. When problem identification is achieved by *joint* action on the part of the groups involved and where it is based on shared fact finding rather than on in-group perceptions, a substantial foundation is provided for obtaining mutually satisfactory resolutions of differences."[50]

After the above concepts were presented, selected workshop participants were encouraged to apply them in simulated negotiation sessions in order to determine if cooperative, joint problem-solving behaviors were enhanced. The agreements attained during such "integrative" simulation sessions were compared with agreements attained in the earlier "distributive" sessions.

Concepts Relative to the Promotion of Attitude Change

The matter of producing changes in the attitudes of human beings, be they involved in negotiations or in other endeavors, is so highly complex that only limited attention could be given to this problem within the workshop. The instructor did not attempt a comprehensive or rigorous treatment of attitude change in the negotiations process, but rather presented a limited number of selected concepts including the following:

1. Fundamental attitudes, relative to the other party, which are brought to the table by negotiators may be the critical factor affecting the success of negotiation activity. Often, negotiators are selected only if they are highly identified with the group they are to represent. "Selection of negotiators who are hostile to the opposed group is not uncommon. The result of selecting such representatives is negotiators who are not able to understand and appreciate the problems of the other side, communicate with one another, or evaluate one another."[51]

2. One means by which attitude change can be caused to occur in others is by demonstrating attitude change within one's own group. "By permitting ourselves to be influenced by others, we make them willing to accept reciprocal influence from us."[52]

3. Once a person commits himself to a position, that commitment itself becomes a barrier against change, however immediately counter influences are brought to bear. The more a person is emotionally involved in his beliefs, the harder it is to change him by any argument or propaganda — that is, through an appeal to intelligence — to the point of virtual impossibility in cases of deeply felt matters.[53]

4. If the bargainers' primary orientation is competitive, communication from any source which is not directed at changing this orientation is unlikely to be effective.[54]

5. Experimental evidence suggests that one method for causing attitude change to occur in the negotiations context is that of having each party air its internal differences in the course of negotiations with its adversary. "Although it is not uncommon for negotiating teams to be internally divided, it is uncommon for them to air their disputes publicly in the presence of their adversaries."[55]

If the bargaining strategies of *both* negotiating teams are guided by the principle of dissent [open discussion of internal differences], there may well be a greater probability not only of a resolution of the conflict but also of a "creative" or an "integrative" type of resolution than if negotiations are guided by the principle of unanimity.[56]

6. Blake and Mouton suggest several means by which attitudes can be changed within the negotiations process. These means include, for example, (a) joint examination of the consequences of win-lose warfare against the background of anticipated consequences of collaboration, and (b) the use of norm-setting conferences in which actual participants talk through their own attitudes, reservations, doubts, hopes, and so on, concerning cooperation as an orientation to a former adversary.[57]

7. Finally, the following caveat relative to attitude shaping was provided. "To a surprising extent, the quarrelsome in this world are manipulated into peace by the peaceable simply because the peaceable control their own reactions where the quarrelsome do not."[58]

Most of the concepts relative to two-party negotiations presented above apply as well to intraorganizational bargaining. The major difficulties which the administrator is likely to face in this realm of bargaining relate to problems of role conflict and ambiguity. These problems apply to high-level administrators who may be engaging in face-to-face negotiations with representatives of teachers' organizations, as well as to so-called "middle management" administrators, for example, elementary principals who must, under many contracts, serve as the first step in the grievance procedure.

Problems of role conflict and ambiguity stem from two major sources. First, the generally "adversary" nature of negotiations creates role conflict and ambiguity because administrators (professionally and traditionally) perceive themselves as rather benevolent, democratic leaders of teachers and of the educational program. This "trained-in" self-image is simply not compatible with the role which administrators-negotiators must play in "adversary" situations.[59] The second source of role conflict and ambiguity is the new relationships between boards of education and chief administrators which negotiation causes to occur. Negotiation is, from the point of view of administration, a radically new method for policy decision making. Many administrators, and even more board members, find it very difficult to accept the fact that negotiated agreements are relevant operational policies — perhaps the most relevant policies. Boards of education and chief administrators have been in the habit of creating policies and directives unilaterally. When it is recognized that policy is no longer simply "made," but that it is negotiated, great intraorganizational (board-administrator) role conflict invariably occurs.[60]

Concepts Related to Role Conflict and Ambiguity

In presenting social science concepts relative to the problems of role conflict and role ambiguity to the workshop participants, the work of Kahn and others served as the primary reference.[61]

The concepts of role, role expectations, and role pressure were presented and the causes and effects of role conflict and role ambiguity were examined. These concepts were related to the processes of intraorganizational, that is, administrator-board, bargaining and to the processes of administering negotiated agreements, particularly grievance procedures.

Major points brought to the attention of the workshop participants included the following:

1. Role conflict is a result of lack of agreement among top-level decision makers (board and superintendent) relative to role expectations of the holder of an office.

2. Particularly strong role conflict is apt to occur when the board, because of the nature of the negotiation process, must delegate rather broad powers to its chief negotiator so that he has freedom to "wheel and deal" at the table.

3. Conflicting expectations, in terms of traditional administrative behavior and negotiations behavior exist, and their force is strong because both teachers and higher-level management impose expectations which are logically and operationally incompatible. Simply stated, the man-in-the-middle is subjected to mutually contradictory sets of role expectations.

4. Ambiguity is an inherent element of the negotiator role and cannot be avoided. For a role to be unambiguous, one must know what activities and behaviors will fulfill the responsibilities of office and how these activities can best be performed. Greatest ambiguity occurs when one does not know about the immediate consequences of one's actions. None

of these ambiguity-reducing conditions is available in the context of face-to-face negotiating.

5. Role ambiguity is reduced by valid feedback on performance and progress. In negotiations, such feedback is extremely limited and typically is available only when final agreement is reached.

6. Role conflict and ambiguity are costly for the role incumbent in terms of emotional stress. One who would negotiate should have high tolerance for ambiguity and stress.

7. High levels of intraorganizational role conflict and role ambiguity are particularly costly in the negotiations context, for in this process intragroup coordination and collaboration are important strengths.

8. In a bureaucratically oriented organization, a role (such as chief negotiator) which demands innovative, creative solutions to nonroutine problems is likely to be confronted with high role conflict and role ambiguity.

SUMMARY

There is little question that many, many more social science concepts could be brought to bear in any course of instruction in the area of negotiations. The processes of negotiation, the human behaviors involved, and the interaction of behaviors, situations, and environmental factors make negotiation a rich topic for the application of social science facts and concepts.

The extreme richness of opportunity to apply social science concepts to the negotiations process was, in fact, the basis of the major frustration experienced by the workshop instructor. Virtually any one of the concepts presented could have been explored in much greater depth, and many additional concepts could have been used to good advantage. However, the desire to provide additional useful information from the social sciences had to be balanced by the need to provide the trainees with basic negotiations vocabulary, reality-oriented experiences, and general "how to do it" information. The instructor's need (or compulsion) to cram a great deal of varied information and experience into a relatively short training period no doubt led to a degree of superficiality of treatment of social science concepts. Given the needs and constraints of the workshop situation, the instructor was unable to avoid this possibility.

FOOTNOTES

1. The workshop, of course, was not billed as a means by which the participants could become expert negotiators in just two weeks. It was merely a means by which the participants could gain detailed knowledge about the processes, tactics, strategies, and so on of negotiating.

2. John J. Horvat, *Professional Negotiations in Education: A Bargaining Game with Supplementary Materials — Instructor's Manual* (Columbus, Ohio: Charles E. Merrill Publishing Company, 1968).

3. For a detailed description of the simulation materials and the methods of the simulation see John J. Horvat, "The Collective Negotiations Game," in *The Use of Simulation in Educational Administration*, ed. Dale L. Bolton (Columbus, Ohio: Charles E. Merrill Publishing Company, 1971), Chapter 8.

4. Robert F. Bales, *Interaction Process Analysis: A Method for the Study of Small Groups* (Cambridge: Addison-Wesley Press, Inc., 1950).

5. The author has borrowed freely from the conceptual work of Richard E. Walton and Robert B. McKersie in their book, *A Behavioral Theory of Labor Negotiations* (New York: McGraw-Hill Book Company, 1965) in describing the four subprocesses of negotiations.

6. Ibid., pages vii and 4.

7. Ibid.

8. Ibid., p. vii.

9. Ibid.

10. The selection process was nonempirical; that is, the instructor selected particular problem dimensions solely on the basis of his experience in the arena of collective negotiation.

11. Because of space limitations, the concepts utilized in the workshop are presented here in very limited form. Detailed explication of the concepts and extensive commentary relative to application are not presented.

12. Kenneth E. Boulding, *Conflict and Defense: A General Theory* (New York: Harper and Brothers, 1962).

13. Thomas C. Schelling, *The Strategy of Conflict* (Cambridge: Harvard University Press, 1960).

14. Robert L. Kahn and Elise Boulding, eds., *Power and Conflict in Organizations* (New York: Basic Books, Inc. 1964).

15. K. E. Boulding, *Conflict and Defense*, p. 5.

16. See Schelling, *The Strategy of Conflict*, p. 11.

17. See K. E. Boulding, *Conflict and Defense*, p. 25.

18. Ibid., p. 295.

19. Daniel Katz, "Approaches to Managing Conflict," in *Power and Conflict*, eds. Kahn and Boulding, p. 113.

20. Murray Horowitz, "Managing Hostility in the Laboratory and the Refinery," Ibid., p. 77.

21. Herbert A. Shepard, "Responses to Situations of Competition and Conflict," Ibid., p. 128.

22. Ibid., p. 3.

23. Deutsch and Krauss, "Studies of Interpersonal Bargaining," *Journal of Conflict Resolution* 7 (March 1962): 54.

24. Walton and McKersie, *Behavioral Theory of Negotiations*, p. 50.

25. See Schelling, *The Strategy of Conflict,* pp. 123–124.

26. Adapted from Walton and McKersie, *Behavioral Theory of Negotiations,* p. 43.

27. See Schelling, *The Strategy of Conflict,* p. 122ff, and Walton and McKersie, *Behavioral Theory of Negotiations,* pp. 49–116.

28. See Walton and McKersie, *Behavioral Theory of Negotiations,* p. 83.

29. Schelling, *The Strategy of Conflict,* p. 6 and pp. 123–24.

30. Edward Peters, *Strategy and Tactics of Labor Negotiations* (New London, Conn.: National Foreman's Institute, 1955), p. 44.

31. Martin Shubik, ed., *Game Theory and Related Approaches to Social Behavior* (New York: John Wiley and Sons, Inc., 1964), p. 8.

32. For a technical description of such games see: R. D. Luce and H. Raiffa, *Games and Decisions* (New York: John Wiley and Sons, Inc., 1957), pp. 56–87. For a less formal treatment of such games see: Anatol Rapoport, *Fights, Games and Debates* (Ann Arbor: The University of Michigan Press, 1960), pp. 135–150.

33. The situations are considered to be hypothetical, not simply because they were contrived for the workshop, but also because in actual bargaining one party can only estimate, rather than know, the payoff utilities of the other party on an issue or a combination of issues.

34. F. C. Ikle, "Negotiation: A device for Modifying Utilities," in Shubik, *Theory and Approaches to Behavior,* p. 245.

35. Walton and McKersie, *Behavioral Theory of Negotiations,* p. 48.

36. Jacob Marschak, "Scaling of Utilities and Probability," in *Theory and Approaches to Behavior,* p. 107.

37. Walton and McKersie, *Behavioral Theory of Negotiations,* pp. 59–82.

38. Boulding, *Conflict and Defense,* p. 210.

39. Robert R. Blake, et al., *Managing Intergroup Conflict in Industry* (Houston: Gulf Publishing Co., 1964), p. 23.

40. Ibid., pp. 24–25.

41. Ibid., p. 26.

42. Morton Deutsch, "An Experimental Study of the Effects of Cooperation and Competition upon Group Processes," *Human Relations* 2 (July 1949): 231–232.

43. Robert R. Blake and Jane S. Mouton, "The Intergroup Dynamics of Win-Lose Conflict and Problem Solving Collaboration in Union-Management Relations," in *Intergroup Relations and Leadership,* ed. M. Sherif (New York: John Wiley and Sons, Inc., 1962), p. 106.

44. Jack R. Gibb, "Defensive Communication," in *Interpersonal Dynamics,* eds. W. E. Bennis, et al. (Homewood, Ill.: The Dorsey Press, 1968), p. 606.

45. Ibid., pp. 606–607.

46. Ibid., pp. 606–612. See also Jack R. Gibb, *In Search of Leaders* (Washington: American Association for Higher Education-NEA, 1967), pp. 55–66.

47. See Blake, et al., *Intergroup Conflicts in Industry,* p. 87.

48. See Ibid., p. 90–92.

49. Blake and Mouton in *Intergroup Relations and Leadership,* ed. Sherif, p. 112.

50. Ibid., p. 115.

51. W. E. Shurtleff, "Union-Management Relations: Cooperation or Conflict?" *Personnel Journal* 27 (March 1949): 385–386. See also C. H. Weaver,

"The Quantification of the Frame of Reference in Labor-Management Communication," *Journal of Applied Psychology* 42 (Feb. 1958), pp. 1–9, and J. J. Horvat, "A Quasi-Experimental Study of Behavior in the Professional Negotiations Process," (Ph.D. diss., The Ohio State University, 1968), pp. 163–164.

52. Elise Boulding, "Further Reflections on Conflict Management," in *Power and Conflict*, eds. Kahn and Boulding, p. 150.

53. B. Berelson and G. Steiner, *Human Behavior: An Inventory of Scientific Fndings* (New York: Harcourt, Brace, and World, Inc., 1964), p. 575.

54. W. Deutsch and R. Krauss, "Studies of Interpersonal Bargaining," *Journal of Conflict Resolution* 7 (March 1962): 76.

55. W. M. Evan and J. A. MacDongall, "Interorganizational Conflict: A Labor-Management Bargaining Experiment," *Journal of Conflict Resolution* 2, 4 (December 1967): 399.

56. Ibid.

57. Blake and Mouton in *Intergroup Relations and Leadership*, ed. Sherif, pp. 109–111.

58. K. E. Boulding, "A Pure Theory of Conflict Applied to Organizations," in *Power and Conflict*, eds. Kahn and Boulding, p. 139.

59. Often in the negotiation context, administrators find themselves in the position of arguing against that which they have been arguing for during most of their professional career. Examples include the superintendent as "board negotiator" who must, because of his role as prime negotiator, fight against teacher salary increases and smaller class size.

60. It should be noted that the lack of clarity of statutes in many states and the lack of *any* statutes on negotiations in most states adds to the ambiguity of the administrator's position. It should also be noted that new negotiation statutes in some states conflict with older ones relative to the legal responsibility for the governance of public education, and this frequent incompatability lends additional ambiguity to the negotiations arena.

61. Robert L. Kahn, et al., *Organizational Stress: Studies in Role Conflict and Ambiguity* (New York: John Wiley and Sons, Inc., 1964). Also see Robert L. Kahn and Donald Wolfe, "Role Conflict in Organizations," in *Power and Conflict in Organizations*, eds. Kahn and Boulding.

10

Discipline-Based Content: The Economics of Education

Harry J. Hartley

The major purpose of this chapter is to identify the criteria used to select content from the discipline of economics for a course entitled the Economics of Education. More specifically, the objectives are sixfold: 1) to outline the instructional goals for a graduate course in economics of education; 2) to relate this course to a total preparatory program for administrators; 3) to specify ten assumptions that influence the design of a course; 4) to identify 20 criteria used to select and organize the most relevant content from the entire warehouse of economic knowledge; 5) to examine elements in the instructor's decision process vis-a-vis content selection; and 6) to present an illustrative outline for a course in the economics of education based upon fundamental, compelling ideas that have emerged from both economics and educational administration. This chapter is intended to serve as a point of embarkation, rather than a final destination.

It is beyond the scope of this chapter to consider the diversity of approaches in designing program objectives, content development, instructional and organizational patterns, and value constraints. Objectives vary greatly from university to university. However, it is suggested that one might consider the Five-Year Plan of the University Council for Educational Administration as a generalized statement of program ideas and first order goals for universities that wish to formulate curriculum plans.[1] The UCEA Plan specifically recommended the development of a Gestalt conception of preparatory programs in order to: 1) synthesize the results of the last 15 years of experimentation; 2) describe needed knowledge or content in program; 3) examine emergent societal factors; and 4) describe needed learning situations.

Educational administration courses fall under at least three categories: 1) *task-oriented*, for example, supervision of instruction; 2) *position-oriented*, for example, secondary principalship; and 3) *discipline-oriented*, for example, politics of educational governance. Economics may be viewed as satisfying the requirements for each of these categories, although most likely it should be placed in the third category. To illustrate, economics may be used in instructing students how to prepare a budget under the first category. It may also focus upon the position of school business administrator in the second category. Economics may be conceived in the third category as a systems discipline, or social science, that contributes analytical tools to the study of education as an economic system. As such, economics assists in the reconciliation of the complex, multiple goals of education.

GOALS FOR ECONOMICS OF EDUCATION

Why should students of educational policy be exposed to a discipline that has been called the "dismal science?" It may be that the very factor that prompted Carlyle to issue his charge of "dismal," that is, that economics begins with the pessimistic assertion that there is *scarcity* in the world and is devoted to the study of individual and collective choices in the allocation of scarce resources for the satisfaction of human wants, is exactly the reason why economics is appropriate for education. Economic systems are confronted with the problem of infinite wants and finite resources. So are educational systems. In the 1970s, school finance replaced student discipline and racial integration as the number one problem confronting local schools. Most, if not all, of the problems that currently confront school officials have economic implications. Thus, solutions based upon the guiding principle of economic efficiency may be stated either as maximizing satisfactions from given resources or as minimizing the resource costs of a given level of aspiration.

The immediate purpose of a course in the economics of education is to introduce immediate purpose students to economic reasoning. Such a course provides a framework for systematic thinking about educational issues and solutions that have economic roots. One of the objectives is to inculcate economic habits, that is, the sensitivity to, and practice of, identifying the economic aspects of educational problems, as well as the cost implications of their solutions. If the course is successful, it will enable students of administration to reach independent, rational judgments respecting economic matters.[2] As many economists have noted, the theory of economics does not furnish a body of settled conclusions immediately applicable to educational policy. It is more a *method* than a *doctrine*. Economics is an abstraction, or apparatus of the mind, that helps its possessor to draw logical conclusions. Of course, abstraction is the common characteristic of all science, inasmuch as the aim of science is to find systematic order and regularity in the facts, experiences, and observed phenomena of the real world. Observable uniformities in economic behavior can be expressed as generalized theories that possess explanatory and predictive value.

Perhaps the most important abstraction to be learned by the student is the economic system itself. No one has ever "seen" an economy. But the concept of an economic system is essential to a comprehensive understanding of an educational system. The existence and nature of a system are conceptualized and inferred from the mass of data relating to economic activities. Otherwise, school finance courses might consist of little more than statistical rodomontade derived from sophisticated ignorance. If the initial purpose of a course is to increase economic reasoning, then the means for accomplishing this consist of providing representative tools and methods for analyzing economic problems in education. Specific content to achieve this purpose is discussed in subsequent sections of this chapter. Table 1 contains a list of ten instructional goals that support this basic purpose.

Within each of the ten goals shown in Table 1, it is possible to identify specific topics that enhance the overall objective of economic reasoning. For example, the goal of *analysis* might include the following topics:

Benefit analysis — identify economic benefits to education;

Cost analysis — enumerate economic costs of education;

Revenue analysis — examine sources of funds;

Expenditure analysis — examine patterns of spending;

Fiscal analysis — conceptualize intergovernmental relations;

Budget analysis — formulate budget process, format, and content;

Equalization analysis — review principles of state aid; and

Equilibrium analysis — relate demand-supply to price determination.

If the notion of spillover is in effect, then these goals which enhance economic reasoning would also enhance reasoning in general.

Table 1

Instructional Goals Intended to Enhance Economic Reasoning in an Economics of Education Course

---

1. REASON — Stimulate economic reasoning and logical thinking; abide by rules of logic as a mode of inquiry.

2. ANALYSIS — Exercise objective powers of analysis by encouraging detachment and ethical neutrality in the study of current economic problems.

3. ADAPTATION — Examine old problems with new tools; relate analytical concepts of the "new economics" to perennial problems of education.

4. SYSTEMIZATION — Encourage economic model building and the design of administrative content via the "systems" perspective.

5. ACCURACY — Use economic language carefully; avoid misinterpretations of abstractions; try to redefine imprecise educational objectives.

6. RESEARCH — Generate innovative thinking that leads to significant research on economic problems of education.

7. VALUES — Describe normative dimensions of economics; examine economic proposals that contribute to human betterment in urban schools and racial relations; provide frameworks for reordering priorities.

8. PRAXEOLOGY — Examine emergent economic planning strategies that are designed to improve educational policy and decision-making; portray "practical" aspects of economics.

9. RESOURCES — Familiarize students with current references of economic, financial, and statistical data that pertain to education.

10. LIMITATIONS — Portray crosscurrents of economic ideology and political feasibility; describe limitations of economics in the context of education.

ASSUMPTIONS

In designing a graduate course, a professor makes a number of assumptions about general content and specific conditions in his institution. A number of assumptions are made for the economics of education course, ten of which are described below.

Prerequisites

It is assumed that most of the students have had no previous formal graduate study in economics. Although it would be desirable for the students to have studied economics previously, the course is planned so that the first several sessions will emphasize essential foundations and bring all students to nearly equal starting points.

Student Clientele

Students will be educators, for the most part, who are preparing to be administrators, supervisors, or professors. Most of the students will hold the master's degree and will be pursuing certification, sixth-year diploma, or the doctorate. For many of the students, this course is an elective, and it will not be the basis for their dissertation research.

Length of Course

This one-semester, three-credit course consists of fifteen class sessions. In some universities, it may be expanded into a two-semester course. At some institutions, after a student completes the economics of education course, he may take a seminar in the economics of education that examines in greater depth specific topics, such as systems analysis, information systems, and program budgeting. The concept of modular instruction could be used to encourage greater variety in the topics that students may study.

Breadth vs. Depth

Emphasis is upon breadth rather than depth.[3] The reason is that there is insufficient class time to probe deeply into each of the many major topics that should be presented. Students are encouraged to study in depth specific topics for class reports, term papers, outside readings, or dissertation development. A number of professors of economics appear to believe that economic life furnishes merely the concrete examples from which abstraction into mathematical models begin. However, many educational administration students are not prepared to study in depth a number of areas of specialization within economics.

Course Sequence for Total Program

It is assumed that this course is offered in a department of educational administration, rather than in a foundations of education department. The course is open to students from any department but is particularly relevant for administration students. Administration students are encouraged and, perhaps, required to study the basic course, "Fundamentals of Administration," prior to taking economics of education.

Philosophy of Education

Content selection and methodology reflect the subjective factors inherent in an instructor's philosophy of education. My preference is the radical conservatism of Hutchins' perennialism. I believe education is the deliberate, organized attempt to help people become intelligent. Education is preferable to training. The latter implies an ad hoc, vocation-oriented approach; whereas, the former includes the classic goals of the liberal arts. I do not equate innovation with improvement. On the positive side, I look forward with Hutchins to a "learning society" in which every man is educated not to fit into a system but to discover the richness of life and ". . . to understand his experience and reflect upon it in such a way as to be wiser than he otherwise would be."[4]

Conceptual-Analytical Emphasis

If a distinction can be made between courses that have a conceptual-theoretical emphasis and those that rely on an operational-applicative orientation, then this course falls in the former category. It is almost a cliché to assert that the most practical education is the most theoretical one, but the statement is appropriate here. Basic concepts will be related to theoretical models prior to their application to specific school finance problems. The intent is to show how particular issues (such as the state aid computation for a given school district) are dependent upon concepts (such as equalization and wealth) that are related (such as in the state aid formula) at a high level of generalization. Theory implies practice, and the basic difference between the two is the degree of abstraction.

Evaluation

If the university requires grading, student evaluation is based upon some combination of the following: class participation, term papers, critiques of readings, oral reports, quizzes, and examinations. The exams include both objective and essay items. Economics is perhaps the most precise of the social sciences and is well-suited for objective test items. Students should be given the opportunity to criticize the course after its completion. In fact, at some universities instructors are evaluated and rated by students, and the results are printed and distributed. Evaluation of students is desirable, but a cult of testing is not.

Training of Instructor

The instructor should possess at least a master's degree in economics and have some formal study in educational administration. In several UCEA institutions, instructors in schools of education possess earned doctorates in economics. But generally, the doctorate would be in the field in which the professor is housed departmentally in the university, in this case educational administration. Formal training is less crucial than competency. The instructor should be familiar with economics literature and be able to contribute published scholarship and research to his field. Disputes over the issue of whether the instruction of such a course should be conducted by economists attached to liberal arts departments or by professors of educational administration ". . . seem somewhat pedantic, if not unexpected. The attention given to questions of this sort appears to stem in part from concerns with status maintenance. The main point is to get the work accomplished with ample measures of scientific competence and imagination."[5]

Nature of Economics

It is assumed that the nature of economics, as described in Chapter 4, will influence the criteria for organizing and selecting content for the graduate courses.

The discipline of economics contains numerous areas of specialization which have grown almost like Topsy. The American Economic Association identified 21 areas but did not provide a taxonomy which would be desirable for content selection and criteria identification. Table 2 contains a listing of these fields.[6] However, such a list is not all-inclusive. Areas which are omitted from Table 2 include national income accounting, Soviet economics, economics of technological changes, operations research, economic statistics, and urban economics. Each of these major areas can be subdivided into many categories. Public finance, for example, can be broken down into more than 20 sub-areas including compensatory finance, stabilization policy, incidence of taxation, expenditure analysis, and fiscal administration.

It is apparent that only a very small portion of the total fabric of economics may be woven into a course entitled the economics of education. Intuitive decisions about relevance must be made by the instructor. What factors does he take into account in designing such a course? Some of these factors are discussed in the section that follows.

Table 2

Areas of Specialization Within Economics

1. General Economic Theory
2. History of Economic Thought
3. Welfare Economics
4. Econometrics and Mathematical Economics
5. Economic History
6. Economic Development and Planning
7. Comparative Economic Systems
8. Money, Credit, and Banking
9. Business Cycles
10. Public Finance
11. Business Finance: Investment and Security Markets
12. Business Administration and Managerial Economics
13. Marketing and Accounting
14. Industrial Organization: Government and Business
15. International Trade and Finance
16. Labor Economics
17. Agricultural Economics
18. Economic Geography
19. Economics of Location and Transportation
20. Economics of Population and Migration
21. Welfare Programs and Social Security

CRITERIA FOR SELECTION OF ECONOMIC CONTENT

The interests of economists in education have centered on a number of the topics shown in Table 2, and there is no uniform structure for a course in the economics of education. Thus, it would seem to be desirable if each of the contributors to this emerging field of specialization would identify those criteria that he used to select content and organize a course. A variety of approaches have been taken in teaching a course in the economics of education, and each approach was indicative of the selection criteria used by the professor. Twenty criteria are identified below. The objective is clarification, not necessarily settlement, of issues about which more professional dialogue is needed. Perhaps this is the most valuable part of a description of the development of any course, for it answers the question of "why" an instructor arrived at a particular outline. In other words, he must specify his assumptions and make explicit the controlling criteria upon which he placed the greatest priority.

The 20 criteria, which are different in their nature, origins, and implications, fall under five general categories: 1) nature of the discipline of economics; 2) nature of the professional field of education; 3) interests and competencies of the professor; 4) background and expressed interests of the student; and 5) environmental spheres of influence. In an uncharacteristic display of courage, these five categories are listed according to my order of priority. The dangers in exposing one's values are both numerous and obvious. For example, in this era of student power, a professor should be a bit reluctant to admit that student interests rank only fourth among his priorities. However, it can be argued that student interests are best served after the first three factors have been considered. Those who disagree with the criteria listed in Table 3 are urged to formulate different ones. In this way, greater clarity in the usage of social science content will evolve and the objectives of this book will have been achieved.

Table 3

Twenty Criteria Used in the Selection of Content
for a Course in the Economics of Education

Categories	Controlling Criteria
A. Nature of Economics[a]	1. Principles of economic reasoning
	2. Historical perspective from OIKONOMIA to economics
	3. Current interests and scholarships of economics
	4. Availability of economic instructional-research materials

[a]See also Table 2 for the nature of economics.

Categories	Controlling Criteria
B. Nature of Education	5. Educational planning and economic benefits of education 6. Revenue analysis in educational finance 7. Expenditure analysis in educational finance 8. Normative prescriptions of economics and administration
C. Nature of Professor	9. Formal training and experience of professor 10. Orientation in research and published scholarship 11. Lecture competencies and instructional media 12. Current interests and personal preferences
D. Nature of Students	13. Background and competencies of students 14. Deficiencies and expressed interests 15. Professional goals and research orientation 16. Criticism of course offered by previous students
E. Nature of Environment	17. Type of current funded research projects 18. Emergent career positions in education 19. Trends of national economic-education policy 20. Spheres of influence (university constraints, current problems, pressures, and innovations)

The first two categories pertain to the published scholarship available in economics and education. In this regard, the current pace at which professors of economics and educational finance are adding to the printed pages on the economics of education is "stunning," according to Professor Bowman, former editor of the *Journal of Political Economy*. Six years ago, she stated that

> . . . it was still possible to give a reasonably adequate picture of what was happening in "the economics of education" by

classifying work under a few main headings, ignoring odd items scattered here and there. However, this will no longer suffice. Furthermore, with the building up of empirical-analytical work done close to the cores of theoretical economic systems, the economics of education itself takes off from such cores. Or restating the same point, the economics of education is genuinely economics, rather than a collection of techniques of estimation and special isolated investigations, only to the extent to which it is geared into a systematic body of economic thought.[7]

Instructor's Decision Process Vis-à-Vis Content Selection

It might be helpful to show how an illustrative concept meets the criteria chosen and how it was chosen by the instructor. Instead of choosing a concept that would be universally included in such a course, I have selected one that seems to require the justification of the selection criteria: PPBS.

Planning-Programming-Budgeting System

PPBS is a concept that comprises several sessions in my course, economics of education. The unholy trinity of planning, programming, and budgeting has been described in detail elsewhere,[8] so we shall concentrate here on relating the criteria listed in Table 3 to this concept. PPBS is a prototype of economic reasoning because it includes the following: consideration of alternatives; setting of economic priorities; establishment of explicit objectives; time-phased strategic planning; identification of evaluation criteria; cost-effectiveness analysis; curricular systemization; comparison of costs with accomplishments; personal accountability; and optimum usage of scarce resources. Each of these characteristics reflects a principle of economic reasoning. Thus, PPBS meets the criterion listed as A-1 in Table 3.

PPBS also meets the criterion listed as A-2, "historical perspective from Oikonomia to economics," because it includes preservation of past approaches to economic planning and budgeting. The evolution of PPBS parallels the development of budgeting through historical stages covering different doctrines. Budgets were developed to: 1) prevent administrative abuses; 2) maintain central control of spending; 3) identify objects-of-expense; 4) assess work efficiency; 5) emphasize scientific management, unit cost analyses, and efficiency; 6) identify function-object expenditures; and finally, 7) formulate policy and plan expenditures on the basis of programs. The study of PPBS provides an historical perspective to the evolution of economic thinking, including the Keynesian impact on national income accounting and full employment budget planning.

There is no need to belabor the obvious. PPBS satisfies the controlling criteria A-3 and A-4 in Table 3, based upon the increasing interest of professors and growing volume of literature devoted to this topic in the early 1970s. In the second category of Table 3, Nature of Education, PPBS satisfies each of the criteria. It contains planning models that measure educational benefits. It relates sources of revenue for programs to expenditure analysis in educational finance. It serves as a basis for decision making in a normative sense. PPBS, as a course topic, satisfies all four criteria under category 3, Nature of Professor. The fourth category, Nature of Students, provided much assistance in the revision of an existing course and was the key determinant in devoting more class time to PPBS. The expressed interests of students and the criticism of the course by students after they completed the course originally led to the preparation of a number of handouts and several lectures on PPBS. The final category, Nature of Environment, is more indirect and subject to interpretative judgment. However, PPBS appears to satisfy these four criteria.

The Ford Foundation and the federal government have supported PPBS research projects. Emergent career positions in the U.S. Office of Education, state departments of education, and an increasing number of local school districts include systems analysts, program specialists, budget analysts, and others who would benefit from an understanding of PPBS. Public policy in a number of city and state governments, in addition to the federal government, is being made with the assistance of a PPBS format. Approximately 20 states have mandated PPBS in various forms by 1972. Finally, PPBS is an innovation that is included among the spheres of influence for an economic course in educational administration. In addition to the rather brief coverage of PPBS in this course, a second course, which is a seminar in the economics of education, is devoted entirely to the planning-programming-budgeting system in education.

In the decision process, it was determined that PPBS was more relevant to the course than other topics, such as operations research or economic growth, to cite two diverse examples. How was this decision made? It was arrived at by listing a number of topics that might be included and then applying the criteria of Table 3 to each topic. For the original design of the course, the present ranking of the five categories of Table 3 represented the order of priority. However, for purposes of revising the course each semester, the five most important criteria in my order of priority are: D-4 (criticism by students), C-4 (current preference of professor), A-4 (availability of instructional materials), E-4 (spheres of influence), and B-4 (normative uses of economics in urban-racial problems of education). Using these five criteria, it was decided that neither operations research nor economic growth and development should be included as required topics at the present time in the economics of education. Topics that did satisfy the selection criteria are included in the course outline that follows. A summary of the elements in the decision process to choose content is contained in Table 4.

Table 4

Elements in the Decision Process Vis-À-Vis Economic Content Selection

Element	Procedure
Program Goals	1. Establish academic-professional goals for a preparatory program
Course Objectives	2. Establish academic-professional objectives for a course in the economics of education (Table 1)
Major Topics	3. Identify the interests of economists in the field of education according to major topics
Specific Concepts	4. List the various economic concepts that might be studied under each of the major topics
Criteria Formulation	5. Identify criteria for selection of content in order of priority
Content Analysis	6. Relate each topic and concept to the controlling criteria
Content Selection	7. Select those topics that are most relevant according to the criteria
Pilot Course	8. Prepare a course outline and offer the course on an experimental basis
Course Review	9. Analyze the results of the course each semester in terms of written evaluations, students' criticism, and subjective factors
Course Revision	10. Revise the content, methodology, and materials according to specified selection criteria (Table 3)

Content analysis, the sixth element listed in Table 4, is especially important for the overall purpose of this book. At least eight distinct steps were employed in the analysis of economic content:

1. Formulate instructional objectives (Table 1)
2. Identify all major areas in which specific content from economics may be selected (Table 2)
3. Establish controlling criteria for selecting content (Table 3)
4. Relate 21 major areas (Table 2) to criteria (Table 3) in order to determine those areas of economics which are most relevant to the proposed course (public finance, general economic theory, managerial economics, and labor economics)
5. Select concepts from the four appropriate areas and compare their worth on the basis of the five categories of 20 criteria which are presented in order of priority (Table 3)
6. Prepare a written list of concepts, models, and procedures from economics that satisfy the controlling criteria
7. Allow for intuitive judgment in analyzing content
8. Plan for the next step, which is selection of content

An example of a concept whose worth was deemed high in this process is assessed valuation (selected from the area of public finance). On the other hand, the concept of right-to-work law (from the area of labor economics) was not judged sufficiently valuable to be considered in the selection of content for the proposed course.

PROBLEMS IN APPLYING COURSE SELECTION CRITERIA

The attempt to be systematic in relating criteria to content is grounded in the mode of thinking known as systems analysis. One aspect of systems thinking is the development of procedural logic in program planning and model construction. The purpose is to simplify and bring order to numerous activities or complex phenomena that otherwise would be unrelated. Systems analysis is "common sense by design." The application of systems modeling in this chapter involved consideration of monitoring procedures so that a course may be planned, set in motion, evaluated, and revised as necessary.

However, in all fairness to rational planning, there may be a number of intrinsic difficulties in this process that prevent it from being widely used in actual university courses. The key obstacle would appear to be faculty unwillingness to devote the time needed to establish instructional goals, identify assumptions, and formulate criteria for content selection. Even though our field is one in which we professors take ourselves pretty seriously, there have been very few written attempts to identify course criteria. Goldhammer observed that the content for the entire field of educational administration "... has never been clearly delineated, in spite of a proliferation of college courses, and its practices in the field have emerged in response to social exigencies rather than from a commonly accepted theoretical base or a specific body of information which delineated the application of specific strategies for the achievement of desired consequences."[9]

A second major limitation pertains to the difficulty in setting fairly explicit instructional objectives. During the early development of systems analysis, the standard requirement was that the initial requisite is a clear, specific definition of objectives for a person or organization. This simplistic, delusive doctrine was put forth by many quantitative analysts who seemed to believe that "if you can't count it, it doesn't count." It led to a subtle change in the role of a systems analyst in organizations. Where formerly the analyst told the client first to state objectives, the analyst now actually helps to determine the organizational objectives as the final step, rather than the first step of system analysis. After analyzing the system carefully, he then determined what the objectives should have been in order to achieve the activities he observed. Similar implications may exist in the statement of criteria for selecting course content. Perhaps the course will have to be taught several times in order to determine what the criteria will be. At any rate, the limitations of trying to plan systematically are far outweighed by the potential advantages to be gained.[10]

ILLUSTRATIVE COURSE OUTLINE

The dynamic character of economics is such that it is difficult to prescribe a fixed course outline. Thus, the outline that follows is presented for illustrative purposes to indicate how the criteria presented earlier can lead to an actual course. Of the 21 possible areas of specialization within economics (Table 2), the course below includes content from the following four areas that are listed in order of perceived relevance:

1. Public finance (class sessions 3,5,6,7,8,9,10)
2. General economic theory (sessions 1,2,4)
3. Managerial economics (sessions 11,12)
4. Labor economics (sessions 13,14)

The assumption is that the course will consist of 14 class sessions, in addition to the final evaluation session. It is likely that not all of the topics listed for each session will be covered in class. The course covers five general topics, each of which can be described by a question:

Topics	Questions
1. Education in an Economic Setting	How may education be viewed as an economic institution?
2. Revenue Analysis	From what sources are school revenues derived?
3. Expenditure Analysis	How are the resources allocated and utilized?
4. Systems Analysis	What systems concepts are useful in educational administration?
5. Value Dimensions	How can economic rationality contribute to human betterment?

Benson noted, "In recent years economists have suggested that education should be moved to a higher place at the banquet table of the public sector. This is encouraging news. However, we still need to be concerned about equity of provision of school services, equity in support, and related to both of these concerns, efficiency in the spending of money."[11] It is with these types of subjects in mind that this course outline is designed. The topics for the 14 sessions follow:

I. Introduction to Economic Analysis
    A. The Discipline of Economics Viewed as a Social Science
        1. Structure, scope, and methodology of economics
        2. Areas of specialization within economics
        3. Theoretical propositions and the predictive value of economics
    B. The Relationship of Economics to Educational Finance (overview)
        1. Public finance conceived as the basis for educational finance

2. Allocation of limited resources within the public sector
3. Education, public policy, and political economy

II. Essential Economic Concepts and Principles—Foundation and Equalization Sessions (The purpose is to provide for students a common base upon which more technical concepts are founded. Since most students will have no graduate training in economics, the objective is to explore selected relevant economic concepts and analytical procedures, with emphasis upon breadth, rather than depth, in order to bring all students to common starting points in their study of contemporary school finance problems.)

A. Economic Institutions
   1. Education conceived as an economic institution
   2. Public education in the American economy
B. Economic Objectives and the Role of Government
   1. Responsibilities and limitations
   2. Allocation, distribution, stabilization, and growth
   3. The "new economics" and public policy
C. Macro-economics and Micro-economics
   1. Macro aggregates of income, employment, and price levels
   2. Micro emphasis on price determination for particular goods and services
D. Economic Sectors and the Traditional Factors of Production
   1. Consumers, businessmen, government, foreign trade (GNP)
   2. Land, labor, capital, entrepreneur
E. Various Authors and "Schools" of Economic Thought (optional)
   1. Adam Smith, Karl Marx, J.M. Keynes, Paul A. Samuelson, Milton Friedman, Walter Heller, *et al.*
   2. Mercantilism, Classical School, Socialism and Keynesian economics
   3. Emphasis upon diversity of thought in the discipline of economics.

III. Essential Economic Concepts and Principles (continued)
   A. National Income Analysis
      1. Definition and components of Gross National Product
      2. The relationship of gross national product to economic policy

        3. Keynesian and neo-Keynesian economics (macro models)

        4. Potential GNP, actual GNP, the GNP gap

    B. Characteristics of a "Mixed" Economy

        1. Market vs. planned economy

        2. Free private enterprise; competitive capitalism

    C. Business Cycles

        1. Causes of instability

        2. Economic stabilizers: institutional and automatic

        3. Government regulation, such as wage-price controls

    D. Fiscal Policy

        1. Economic principles underlying government spending, taxation, and debt management

IV. Essential Economic Concepts and Principles (continued)

    A. Equilibrium of demand and supply

        1. Elasticity and inelasticity

        2. Utility and indifference concepts

    B. Models of Economic Growth

        1. Capital formation and changes in population, natural resources and technology

        2. Economic indexes which are relevant to educators

        3. Productivity concepts

    C. Inflation

        1. Analysis of selected theories of inflation

        2. Effects on public education

    D. Urbanization and Metropolitanism

        1. Changing population trends and effects on the schools

        2. The "spread city"

    E. Economic Theory vs. Political Feasibility

        1. Economists may suffer from "illusions of adequacy"

        2. Politics of resource allocation and distribution

V. The Economic Magnitude of Public Education

    A. Educational Expenditures; Revenues; Personnel Data; Projections

        1. Financial status of public schools for the current year

        2. Short-range and long-range projections

    B. Selected Topics in Public Finance

        1. Welfare economics and public education

        2. Financing the public economy

    C. Human Capital
       1. The return on educational investment (individual and social)
       2. Reproducible and nonreproducible capital
       3. Social implications and policy

VI. Governmental Structure and Federal–State Taxation
    A. Functions of Government in an Exchange Economy
       1. Review economic objectives and tools of government
    B. Federal and State Taxation
       1. Criteria of a just tax
       2. Types of taxes and distribution of payments
       3. Shifting and incidence
       4. Distributive aspects
       5. Compensatory fiscal policy as a tool of economic stabilization
       6. Expansionary vs. restrictive policy
    C. Principles of Taxation: Tax Base, Structure, and Incidence
       1. Progressive, proportional, and regressive rates
       2. Benefits received vs. ability to pay
       3. Marginal tax rate vs. average tax rate
       4. New tools for fiscal analysis
    D. Tax Reforms
       1. Erosion of the tax base; shifting
       2. Proposals for improvement
       3. The tax system and economic growth
    E. Government Expenditure Patterns
       1. Federal budgetary expenditures by major purpose
       2. State budgetary expenditures by major purpose

VII. Local Taxation and School Revenues
    A. The Property Tax
       1. Advantages and limitations
       2. Court rulings against the property tax
    B. Assessment and Tax Practices
       1. Full valuation and assessed valuation
       2. Tax rate determination
    C. Inadequacies in Opportunity, Ability, and Effort
    D. Tax-exempt Property and Erosion of the Tax Base
       1. Government owned, religious exempt, secular exempt
       2. Lack of coordination of tax efforts at the state-local level

E. Trends and Prospects in Local Government Finances
   1. Increased services and growing expenditures
   2. Sales, income, and payroll taxes
   3. Population growth and demographic changes; "unbalanced" communities
   4. Statewide school taxes
   5. State Lotteries
F. State Grants-in-Aid, Local Effort, Equalization, Foundation Programs
   1. Emphasis upon New York State programs

VIII. Local District Financial Issues

A. Revenue Estimates and Estimated Expenses
B. Definition of Terms Relevant to School Finance
   1. Valuation, R.W.A.D.A., state aid ratio, current expenditures, ratio of assessment, debt service, capital funds, austerity budget, equalization, serial bonds, ability and effort, expenditure per pupil, state budget code classification, etc.
C. Expenditure Patterns of Local Schools

IX. Local District Financial Issues (continued)

A. Computational exercises in school finance (state aid)
B. Capital financing
   1. Borrowing powers of local districts
   2. Debt service
C. Review of recent school budget and bond referendum results

X. Analysis of Local School Budgets

A. The Class Will Critically Review Budgets from Local School Districts
B. The Processes of Public School Expenditures
   1. School business management (brief)
   2. Salaries of personnel; non-instructional expenditures
C. The Budgetary Process
   1. Preparation, presentation, adoption, execution, appraisal
   2. Definition and legal requirements of a budget
   3. Staff and lay participation
   4. Administration of conventional budgets

XI. Systems Analysis and the Program Budget

A. Systems Analysis to Assess the Efficiency of Alternative Input Combinations

    B. The School Viewed as an Economic System
1. Also, as a social, political, cultural, socio-psychological system
2. Conceptually distinct, interdependent parts of a unified whole system
3. Economic tools of analysis: operations analysis, input-output analysis, management information system, cost-benefit analysis, program evaluation, etc.
4. Systems analysis portrayed as a mode of thinking

    C. The Program Budget
1. Conceptual approaches to budgeting
2. Advantages, characteristics, limitations
3. Applications in government and industry
4. Planning-programming-budgeting system (PPBS)

XII. The Program Budget in Local School Districts

    A. Present applications and completed projects
    B. Identification of Program Elements in a Program structure
    C. Function-Object Budget vs. Program Budget
    D. Research Needed on this Concept
1. Measures of educational productivity
2. Explicit objectives for curricular programs
3. Computer-based analytical models
4. Optimum organizational structure
5. Determination of "power centers" for budgetary decisions

XIII. Economics of Metropolitan Areas

    A. Determinants of Educational Expenditures in Large Cities
    B. Trends in Total Population of Cities vs. School-Age Population
1. For example: New York City's total population declined 1%, but pupils increased 20% in last decade.
    C. Factors Contributing to Financial Crisis in City Schools
    D. Factors Affecting the Budget Process of City Schools
    E. Property Valuation, Tax Trends, Municipal Overburden
    F. Fiscal Dependence vs. Independence
    G. Unique Problems of New York City
1. Revenues and expenditures
2. Collective negotiations
3. Current statistics

        4. Erosion of tax base

XIV. Economic Priorities and Social Values
    A. White racism and urban school crises
        1. Colonial status of blacks and functional illiteracy
        2. Economic priorities and institutional racism
        3. Co-optation of black leaders and coalition politics
    B. Black Power and Self-determination
        1. Community control of local school governance
        2. Removal of the racial "Maginot Line"
        3. Political-economy of liberation
        4. Decentralization and community control
    C. Economic-Educational Implications of Civil Disorders
        1. What has happened?
        2. Why did it happen?
        3. What can be done?
        4. Who is best able to provide remedies (federal, state, city)?
        5. What are our national economic priorities?

CONCLUSION

Ever since the historic passage of the Employment Act in 1946, the major economic goals of the United States have been those stated in the Act: Maximum employment, production, and purchasing power. The major problem of the 1970s in economics involves a simple goal that has eluded most industrial nations; namely, how can we combine high employment with stable prices? The economics of education, as a hybrid derivative of the discipline of economics and the professional area of school finance is based on the methodology of economics, but has as its main focus the acquisition and utilization of funds for our system of education. The major purpose of this chapter was to identify criteria that are used to select content from economics for a course in the economics of education.

Ten years ago, there was hardly such a subject as the economics of education, but in 1972 it was one of the most rapidly growing branches of economics. The subject falls rather neatly into two categories: 1) analyses of the economic value of education; and 2) analyses of the economic aspects of educational systems. Blaug distinguished between the two categories, "The first is concerned with the impact of schooling on labour productivity, occupational mobility, and the distribution of income. The second deals with the internal efficiency of schools and with the relations between the costs of education and methods of financing these costs."[12] The course described earlier was based largely on the second category.

Robert S. McNamara once defined a realistic mind as one that is restlessly creative, free of naive delusions but full of practical alternatives. This chapter was directed toward readers possessing such realistic minds. A number of alternatives were put forth in the hope that they may be of some value to persons interested in the economics of education. The knowledge revolution has created an education industry, and it is possible that organized intelligence is becoming a more decisive resource in contemporary society than conventional capital itself. Unfortunately, many professors may turn out to be the servants of old values refurbished, rather than creators of new values. This chapter examined both new and established values in the context of course development for the economics of education. A deliberate attempt was made to maintain balance between rigor and relevance in the study of economic facts, concepts, principles, and modes of inquiry.

SELECTED REFERENCES

Benson, Charles S. *The Economics of Public Education.* 2nd ed. Boston: Houghton Mifflin Co., 1968.

Economic Report of the President. Washington, D.C.: U.S. Government Printing Office, annual.

Heilbroner, Robert L. *The Worldly Philosophers.* 3rd ed. New York: Simon and Schuster, 1967.

Martin, Richard S. and Miller, Reuben G. *Economics and its Significance.* Columbus, Ohio: Charles E. Merrill Publishing Co., 1965.

National Education Association, Committee on Educational Finance, *Financial Status of Public Schools.* annual.

Review of Educational Research. Two issues each devoted a chapter to the economics of education: vol. 37, no. 1 (February 1967), Chap. 8; and vol. 37, no. 4 (October 1967), Chap. 2.

Robinson, Marshall A., et al., *An Introduction to Economic Reasoning.* Garden City, N.Y.: Anchor Books, 1967.

Samuelson, Paul A. *Economics: An Introductory Analysis.* 8th ed. New York: McGraw-Hill Book Co., 1971.

FOOTNOTES

1. *Toward the Development of a 1969-1974 UCEA Plan for Advancing Educational Administration* (Columbus, Ohio: University Council for Educational Administration, 1968), pp. 65-96.

2. Rationality, of course, is a term that is universally approved but only rarely defined. I have attempted to follow Santayana's general definition of reason ("a harmony of impulses") in applying it to education. See Harry J. Hartley, "Santayanan-Weberian Reason in Administration," *Journal of Educational Administration* 7, 1 (May 1969): 45-56.

3. The issue depth vs. breadth in economics of education is not new. It was discussed at three conferences in Columbus, Ohio by the University Council for Educational Administration in May 1965, January 1966, and March 1967. Discussants included Professors Ernest Bartell, Charles S. Benson, Andre Daniere, Walter Hack, Harry J. Hartley, R. L. Johns, Meno Lovenstein, William P. McLure, Gordon Mowat, Devoy Ryan, John Sokol, and J. Alan Thomas. The participants agreed that they disagreed on this issue.

4. Robert M. Hutchins, *The Learning Society* (New York: Frederick A. Praeger, Inc., 1968), p. 28.

5. Donald J. Willower, "Review of *Handbook of Organizations,*" *Educational Administration Quarterly* 3, 1 (Winter 1967): 26.

6. These areas are used by the American Economic Association to describe current graduate training in economics. See Millard F. Long, ed., *Graduate Study in Economics* (Evanston, Ill.: American Economic Association, 1965), p. 17.

7. Mary Jean Bowman, "The Human Investment Revolution in Economic Thought," *Sociology of Education,* no. 2 (Spring 1966), p. 112.

8. Harry J. Hartley, *Educational Planning-Programming-Budgeting: A Systems Approach* (Englewood Cliffs, N.J.: Prentice-Hall, Inc., 1968).

9. Keith Goldhammer, "Knowledge Needs in Educational Administration and Teacher Education in the Decades Ahead," in *Educational Information System Requirements: The Next Two Decades,* eds. John W. Loughary and Murray London (Eugene, Oregon: College of Education, University of Oregon, 1967), p. 78.

10. Harry J. Hartley, "Limitations of Systems Analysis," *Phi Delta Kappan* 50, 9 (May 1969): 519. See also Hartley, "Politics and Education," *The School Administrator,* American Association of School Administrators (April 1971), pp. 7-10.

11. Charles S. Benson, *The Economics of Public Education,* 2nd ed. (Boston: Houghton Mifflin, 1968), p. vii.

12. Mark Blaug, ed., *Economics of Education,* vol 1 (Baltimore: Penguin Books, 1968), p. 8.

11

Educational Administration and Social Science: An Integrative Approach

Donald J. Willower

In this chapter, an example of the use of social science ideas in a preparation program in educational administration is presented. The illustrations are drawn from two of my graduate seminars on organization theories and educational administration. At the outset, it should be made explicit that what actually happens in the classroom is a good deal more precarious than it sounds when written about. Reality is apt to diverge from plans on the basis of feedback, timing, and those other factors that can make teaching anything but a static enterprise. Moreover, things sometimes go badly, and the purposes I have in mind are not sufficiently attained. Since the account sketched here depicts the seminars more or less ideally, it is somewhat utopian and, occasionally, tinged with fiction.

It will be difficult to place the present essay in relation to others in this book that furnish illustrations of social science emphases in educational administration. As I understand it, they are devoted to cases based on a single discipline or on a multi-discipline emphasis. If a multi-disciplinary emphasis means the use of frameworks like decision making or system theories that cut across traditional disciplines, then this chapter does not display that kind of emphasis. Nor is it particularly devoted to a single discipline emphasis.

Although I would not want to underemphasize the content of theories, the teaching of such content is not my primary aim. After all, content is dated and changes as knowledge grows or is modified. Disciplines are themselves human inventions that represent traditional ways of organizing knowledge, and present alternate, but often overlapping perspectives of the world. I prefer to stress particular methods, concepts, and theories, not disciplines as such. Primary emphasis is placed upon the individual and his efforts to understand the nature of events, in this case, those that occur in a particular institutional setting — educational organizations. Throughout, the focus is on the individual as a critic of theories, as well as a user of theories. As Schwab put it, "A sophisticated and cynical grasp of about a dozen separate ... bodies of theory are [sic] indispensable to good administration."[1]

I have called the approach used, perhaps somewhat pretentiously, an integrative one. However, the term is not used here to refer to an attempted synthesis of theories. Theories are treated as instrumentalities, and the attempted integrations are those of theory and practice, ideas and events, content and application. I would argue that, in the teaching situation, it is important to interrelate theories about educational organizations and their proper modes of utilization by students of educational administration. Student knowledge of theoretical content is a necessary but not a sufficient condition for success in the program described here. First place is given over to the development of a reflective or scientific temper; the search for ideas and explanation conjoined with a probing skepticism.[2] When the tone and manner provided by those qualities is missing, theoretical content may be learned as a matter of form but remain dormant knowledge, forgotten and unused when "reality" is confronted; or, at the other extreme, content may be treated faddishly, as if it furnished panaceas for all of the problems of school administration, without an appreciation of the substantial limitations and potential abuses of the approach.

I turn now to the seminars themselves and consider, first, the background material that introduces them; then, make explicit the criteria used to select the social science content employed; and finally, attempt to show the particular ways to which content is used to pursue the aim of producing students able to critically assess and utilize relevant theories in confronting the problems that characterize educational organizations.

Background

The introductory material is comprised of a brief history of the use of theory in administration in general and in educational administration in particular, a discussion of certain of the terminology of theory building, and a treatment of some of the problems of the theory-practice relationship.

The historical overview of administration is primarily a matter of individual reading by seminar participants, along with some group discussion. In general administration, sources may include Bennis, Etzioni, Gross, and March.[3] In educational administration, Moore, Callahan, and a comparison of recent and early issues of the *Review of Educational Research* on educational organization are helpful.[4] Some students may read Taylor, Fayol, or even Roethlisberger and Dickson as examples of important works in (not on) the history of administration.[5] In addition, some understanding of the commonality of problems educational administration shares with others fields of administration that are also beginning to mature, such as business administration and public administration, can be gleaned from sources in those areas.[6]

The historical overview provides the usual information on names and movements and their relationships to their times and environments, but it also should enable the student to see that the principles of an earlier era may be thought of as proverbs in a later one. Exposure to criticism of such principles, in particular those of classical management theory, can have an additional outcome. At least some of the students, many of whom are practicing school administrators, employ a classical management perspective in their work, although with varying degrees of awareness. For these individuals, the history of administration can have a special, if somewhat disturbing, meaning. It calls into question some of their favorite administrative maxims.

In treating the terminology of theory building, it is neither reasonable nor honest to set forth *the* definition of a term. Hence, the various ways in which a term has been used by various writers are examined. Many of these usages need to be learned but merely learning them is not sufficient in terms of a larger objective, which is to promote an understanding of the instrumental nature of terminology and symbols. It is emphasized that a thing has no "right" name, that there is no necessary connection between symbols and that which is symbolized, and that classification is a matter of interest and utility. To help make this point, Hayakawa's well known story of the animals that come in two sizes, and have round or square heads and curly or straight tails, is useful.[7] Each type of animal is given several names based on functional characteristics that are important to particular namers; the question of what the right names of the animal types are, is quickly seen to be a meaningless one.

The notion of concepts as constructs or inventions is discussed at this point, and some attention is given to the philosophic basis which undergirds it. This discussion is a prelude to a consideration of the arrangement of knowledge in the form of concepts, generalizations, and theories. A number of definitions of theory are presented. These range from the relatively pliant notion of theory, as a body of interrelated, consistent generalizations to the rigorous standard set by Feigl's definition of theory as a set of assumptions from which can be derived a set of empirical laws by logico-mathematical deductions.[8] The former definition is viewed as a modest one, reasonably consistent with the state of the art in the social sciences. The latter (which has been widely cited in the educational administration literature) is seen as most appropriate to the natural sciences, especially physics. The question of whether it is realistic for the social sciences to seek to build theories of this type is discussed. Clearly, they do not come close in any meaningful sense at present.

While it would be too lengthy a task to specify all of the other terms considered, some of them will be mentioned to illustrate their diversity. The term "operational definition" is one that is assigned a like meaning by most writers, but the term "model" is used in numerous ways. Some writers use that term very loosely, as in theoretical model or graphic model, while others give it a more technical meaning, as in mathematical model or in the usage that is concerned with analogy and isomorphism. Some terms are closely bound up with basic questions in the philosophy of science. Evidence, confirmation, fact, and induction are examples. Some terms, like "normative proposition" and "descriptive proposition," set forth important distinctions; others, such as "tautology," point to potential false moves on the part of the theory builder. A number of terms are employed in the literature with subtle emphases to which valuations are attached. Thus, empiricism can be considered as a necessary antidote to an intuitive approach to knowing, or it can be called naked empiricism, that is, atheoretical. Taxonomies have been applauded as crucial to the development of a science, and they have been disparaged as "mere" taxonomies. Some terms have unfortunate every day meanings that can mislead the unwary student; "ideal type" is an example.

These are the kinds of things that are made explicit when terminology is considered, and it is made clear that the same types of limitations and problems found in connection with the vocabulary of theory construction apply as well to the concepts that contribute to the content of theories.

Discussion of the theory-practice problem, which also continues from time to time throughout the seminars, begins with a homely example.[9] It concerns a young man who lacked experience with women and who sought advice from two male acquaintances with reputations as experts on the subject. The first expert counseled the novice to "treat them gently"; the second advised him to "treat them rough." Each claimed that his method had stood the tests of time and been proven in the crucible of experience. Given the conflicting recipes of experts, the young man was faced with a problem that might not have arisen for him had he spoken with only one consultant or had both made the same pronouncements.

An alternative is to approach the problem scientifically. I suppose we could begin by recognizing the variability of women. Study of this variability should lead to a classification scheme, in effect, a typology of women. A second element could be labelled the treatment variable, conceptualized by the experts as either gentle or rough. Whether we choose to examine the effects of these or other variables, we will want to seek greater precision. If the problem of devising a suitable operational measure could be solved, perhaps a continuum ranging from gentle treatment as one extreme to rough treatment at the other would be in order. Finally, it is necessary to be concerned with outcome variables. A multitude of possibilities suggest themselves, but, for simplicity's sake, let us call them success or failure and assume that a satisfactory measure or measures can be constructed. We would now be in a position to mount a research program that, hopefully, would furnish a list of results of the following kind: For type A women, gentleness of treatment is associated with a successful outcome at a specific probability level. If careful theory building preceded our empirical tests and was supported by them, a credible explanatory framework would be available.

Given this information, the practitioner, in this case the young man, is in a position better to understand what he is about. But he ought to be fully aware of the limitations of science. Its results are probabilities, not certainties. They have been obtained under controlled conditions and are implicitly qualified by the phrase, other things equal. Yet, in the world of practice, other things are arrantly unequal. Furthermore, one theoretical perspective has been brought to bear on a very small and artificially segregated segment of the phenomenal world. Other perspectives that might not compete with this one but just differ from it may be equally useful to the practitioner. In any case, he should be prepared to work with new frameworks as science, in its self-correcting wisdom, tells him that what was once pertinent must now be disregarded.

Life has suddenly become more complex for the young man of our illustration. He now has a conceptual framework to guide practice, but the pathways are still hazardous. He must first classify particular women in terms of the theory's typology, a task that is neither easy nor assured of success. He can hope that his application of the treatment variable approximates closely enough that of the scientist, and although he has been alerted to the possibility of confounding variables, he cannot be sure that he has been sufficiently aware of them nor does he always know how to correct for them. A successful outcome still hangs in the balance. Note, too, that the example deals with a problem that is relatively simple compared with one like that of implementing a major organizational change.

Theories can furnish sensitizing concepts and perspectives or "cognitive maps," to use a term some prefer; they do not provide the security that certain individuals find in simple maxims.[10] Nevertheless, with all its limitations, the scientific approach is the best that we have. These are major points that emerge from the general discussions generated by the illustration, a teaching device I have recounted here, because it has appeared to be effective.

CRITERIA

I turn now to the reasons for the selection of the theoretical frameworks that are examined and worked with in the seminars. This is largely a matter of making explicit the purposes of the experience and the criteria for the selection of content generated by them. The problem is in great part a teaching problem. It is not simply one of choosing the organization theories that are best in scientific terms. If it were, we would primarily be concerned with the usual criteria of theoretical adequacy variously described in the literature as predictive power, coherence, explanative power, scope or comprehensiveness, fruitfulness, heuristic value, testability, and parsimony. Of course, these criteria cannot be ignored. We do want to deal with at least some reasonably good theories. In any case, it should be kept in mind that, given the present state of theory construction in the social sciences, the application of these criteria is basically a matter of judgment; it is not a task that can be precisely accomplished.

What then are our major purposes, and what criteria for selection do they imply? One purpose is to learn to work creatively with theory, as contrasted with merely learning about theory. Activities that can reasonably contribute to the attainment of this end are the development of original hypotheses from theory, the application to schools of theoretical propositions that have not been elaborated in terms of the school setting, and the analysis of everyday events in schools in theoretical terms.

Another purpose is to learn a critical stance toward theory; to seek and demand clarity and logic in theoretical formulations; to recognize jargon as opposed to legitimate concepts whether in sociology, education, or any other field; and to examine ideas on their own merits, regardless of source. Activities that can reasonably contribute to the attainment of this end are the critical analysis of hypotheses and other theoretical propositions, the dissection of theory in terms of criteria of adequacy, and the comparative analysis of several theories.

These two main purposes and the activities posited as likely to contribute to their achievement generate the criteria utilized to select particular theories for study. A criterion accompanies each activity; the theory utilized should facilitate the particular activity. All of the criteria are not applied to each theory; each theory has its special uses.

In order to develop hypotheses from theory, at least one theory is required from which hypotheses can be derived without great difficulty. Getzels' version of role theory appears to meet this criterion reasonably well.[11] Two frameworks that have not been elaborated in terms of school organizations but which lend themselves to such elaboration are those of Parsons[12] and Gouldner.[13] To analyze everyday events in the life of the school, the general framework of socio-cultural analysis is employed.

To furnish material for critical analysis, the hypotheses that are derived from Getzels' theory are the first source. In addition, a theoretical approach that lends itself to critical dissection is required. Griffiths' approach to decision-making theory provides our cadaver.[14] Finally, several of these theories can be used for comparative analysis.

Some of the theories used are important in the literature of educational administration. They happen to fit a particular criterion or several criteria; at the same time, our interest is essentially in educational organizations, not in the traditional social science disciplines as such.

Now, the specific uses of these theories in the classroom will be sketched.

Uses

The first theory considered is Getzels'. After it has been studied, along with hypotheses generated from it that have guided research,[15] each seminar member presents an original hypothesis derived from the theory.

Each hypothesis is critically analyzed in terms of the following questions. What are the main concepts and what do they mean? What is the relationship posited between or among them? What is the justification of the proposed relationship; that is, what is the rationale for the hypothesis? How well does it fit, in terms of past research, in terms of our experience in schools? Can a good argument be made for a conflicting explanation? How tight is the derivation of the hypothesis? Does it really follow logically from Getzels? Can ways be presented feasibly to operationalize the concepts? Is the content of the hypothesis interesting? Is it significant? Is it researchable?

Some of the hypotheses presented are excellent; others are hopeless. Sometimes when a hypothesis is improved via the critical analysis, it loses its relationship to Getzels' framework. If the idea is a good one, this is not cause for regret, as long as it is explicitly recognized that a test of such a hypothesis does not furnish evidence on Getzels' theory. A few of the hypotheses turn out to be tautologies. It is not always easy to walk the line between logical identity or tautology, and the logical connection between variables that provides a rationale for their relationship. Some of the hypotheses have a rather limited scope. Often, this stems from a tendency to compare nomothetic and idiographic types, as in the hypothesis: school administrators who employ an idiographic style of leadership will be more accurate in their perceptions of subordinates' need-dispositions than will school administrators who employ a nomothetic style of leadership. Such hypotheses are often interesting in spite of their limitations.

From a teaching standpoint, perhaps the foremost problem is to maintain a delicate balance between the openness and freedom that fosters the development of original ideas and the threat generated by the critical analysis. Thus, it is stressed that hypothesis construction frequently involves false starts; that what seems to be the beginning of an important idea sometimes never crosses the threshold of explicit formulation; that ideas that appear to be full of promise often are found wanting after they have been clearly formulated; that hypothesis building is one of the most demanding and difficult aspects of inquiry.

In any case, whether this experience in critical analysis has been personally gratifying or discomforting to them, seminar participants are fully inclined to raise critical questions about propositions and theories they subsequently encounter in the literature.

The framework next considered is that of Griffiths on decision making. Students first attempt to isolate its major concepts and propositions. Among the questions eventually raised is one on steps in the decision process. Since the steps, which usually begin with the recognition of a problem and end with the selection and implementation of a solution, represent rational decision making, what is their place in a descriptive theory of decision making? Griffiths deals with this problem by interposing concepts like perception, authority, power, and formal and informal organization. Often, it is asked whether these additional concepts buy increased scope for the theory at some cost to its logical coherence or, at least, to the interrelatedness of its parts. The point is that, in keeping with the critical stance toward theories fostered earlier, numerous questions are raised about the adequacy of the framework. Yet, the obvious utility of some of its ideas is recognized and sometimes even extended. For example, one group developed a number of hypotheses that related certain organizational characteristics to the incidence and location of the types of decisions discussed by Griffiths. Examination of Griffiths' and Getzels' theories, in comparative terms, closes this phase of the work.

In considering Parsons' treatment of functionally differentiated levels in formal organizations, the aim is not critical analysis so much as it is to gain experience in the elaboration of possible applications of a general theory to the school setting. It will be recalled that Parsons discussed three organizational levels that reflect qualitative breaks in line structure in organizations and, hence, may be conceptualized as systems having their own special responsibilities and functions. These are the technical system, the managerial system, and the community or institutional system.

Perhaps an example will suffice to show the kind of exploration that occurs at this point in the seminar. Parsons' analysis calls attention to the problems of articulation among the three systems, which in schools are represented by teachers, the administration, and the Board of Education. The example to be presented is a speculation on a particular mechanism of articulation between the technical and the managerial systems in schools, the supervisory role. This position, which is inappropriately named, ordinarily is not a line position. It is devoted to the improvement of instruction by assisting but not rating, teachers. In fact, the maintenance of this latter distinction is almost an article of faith in the literature on school supervision. It is significant that this distinction facilitates the articulation functions of the supervisory position, already something of a boundary role in terms of its location, with assured entry into, but not full participation in, the technical and the managerial systems.

The following make sense in terms of this perspective. The supervisor can work with teachers perceived by the principal to be marginal (perhaps more effectively than the principal could), and he may confirm and thus legitimate the principal's evaluation of such teachers. The supervisor can also report information to the principal that might not otherwise be secured, since teachers may be guarded in their relationships with their immediate line superior. At the same time, the supervisor can act as a mediator of conflict between the principal and teachers, communicating the views of each to the other in softened and more acceptable terms. He can also present the teachers' case to the principal free of the constraints teachers might feel in so doing, and, if he chooses to do so, he is in a favorable position to communicate directly with the central administration, by-passing the principal entirely. While this analysis is plainly conjectural, the kinds of behavior described generally fit the experience of seminar members.

The theoretical framework used by Gouldner in his case study of a gypsum plant is utilized in the same manner. Briefly, two kinds of applications are assayed. One involves the search for structures in schools like those found in the gypsum plant. For example, is there in schools, a functional equivalent to the indulgency pattern, and, if so, does it have similar consequences? This kind of application is essentially horizontal, in the sense that the level of abstraction of the concepts that describe indulgency patterns in each kind of organization, is similar. The second application, like that of Parsons' above, is basically vertical. In this case, Gouldner's notion of bureaucratic patterns—mock, representative and punishment centered—is used to examine various aspects of school organization.

Our final theoretical approach has a strong empirical orientation. It is essentially an attempt to blend the conceptual and the empirical by examining commonplace elements of school life essentially in social system terms, with special attention given to the teacher subculture.[16]

A major purpose is to encourage students to look at the familiar in unfamiliar ways. In this, the posture adopted is much like that of the cultured anthropologist observing in a primitive society. It requires openness to data, but at the same time, the investigator carries theoretical baggage. It consists of concepts such as norms, rules, role expectations, adaptive structures, latent and manifest functions, and others like them that facilitate social system analysis.

Some illustrations of ways in which familiar aspects of school life can be comprehended in terms of this framework follow. Conformity to norms for behavior is demanded in public places, that is, in places of high visibility; thus, teachers exhort their classes to exhibit their best behavior in assemblies. Conflict between teacher and student subcultures fosters norms for custodial and socially distant teacher behavior toward pupils; thus, teachers are advised by their colleagues not to become too friendly with students. Curriculum committees have the latent function of legitimating program changes desired by the school administration or the Board of Education; thus, such committees go through the motions rather ritualistically, rarely veto a proposed change, and confine themselves to minor decisions, such as which text to recommend.

The public school is a vulnerable organization. A number of features of school life can be viewed as adaptive structures that reduce vulnerability and protect the school in its relationships with its publics. PTAs function as legitimating bodies, and public relations programs furnish opportunities for impression management. Public inspection of schools is highly controlled. Parents are encouraged to visit the school when they are expected and a program has been prepared for them; at other times, visitors are directed to report to the office on entering the building. Report cards are constructed to evaluate the student, not the school. The proliferation of specializations in the school and the use of the conference involving several specialists in addition to the teacher and parent functions to reduce the threat of effective parental intervention.

Seminar participants have ordinarily not thought about schools in such terms. They have, then, opportunities to "reconstruct experience" in new ways. At the same time, the tentative and rather fragile bases of these account is emphasized.

CONCLUDING COMMENTS

These, then, are the conceptual frameworks that are considered in the seminars. The question of their relevance to educational administration is essentially a question of their ability to explain coherently what goes on in schools. All of them appear to set forth at least some useful and enlightening content. However, I do not believe that it makes much sense to consider the teaching of content in isolation from the teaching of the creative and critical stances that offer hope that content will be used wisely and well. Because these twin stances seem to me to be desirable in both the practitioner and scholar of educational administration, I do not differentiate the two as sharply as some do, although I recognize that a degree of differentiation is necessary.

Students of educational administration need not be awed by the social sciences. They should recognize the limitations of these fields, as well as their strengths. Only then can they fully appreciate their demanding nature, their utility, and even their elegance.

FOOTNOTES

1. Joseph J. Schwab, "The Professorship in Educational Administration: Theory-Art-Practice," in *The Professorship in Educational Administration,* eds. D. J. Willower and J. A. Culbertson (Columbus, Ohio and University Park, Pennsylvania: University Council for Educational Administration and The Pennsylvania State University, 1964), pp. 59-60.

2. A general statement consistent with the present view can be found in my "The Professorship in Educational Administration: A Rationale" in *The Professorship in Educational Administration,* pp. 87-105.

3. Warren G. Bennis, "A New Role for the Behavioral Sciences: Effecting Organizational Change," *Administrative Science Quarterly* 8, 2 (September 1963): 125-65; Amitai Etzioni, *Modern Organizations* (Englewood Cliffs, New Jersey: Prentice-Hall, Inc., 1964); Bertram M. Gross, "The Scientific Approach to Administration," in *Behavioral Science and Educational Administration,* ed. Daniel E. Griffiths (Chicago: The Sixty-third Yearbook of the National Society for the Study of Education, 1964), pp. 33-72; James G. March, "Introduction," in *Handbook of Organizations,* ed. James G. March (Chicago: Rand McNally and Co., 1965), pp. ix-xvi.

4. Hollis A. Moore, Jr., "The Ferment in School Administration," in *Behavioral Science and Educational Administration,* pp. 11-32; Raymond E. Callahan, *Education and the Cult of Efficiency* (Chicago: The University of Chicago Press, 1962).

5. Frederick W. Taylor, *Scientific Management* (New York: Harper and Bros., 1947); Henri Fayol, *General and Industrial Management,* trans. C. Storrs (London: Sir Issac Pitman and Sons, 1949); Fritz J. Roethlisberger and William J. Dickson, *Management and the Worker* (Cambridge, Massachusetts: Harvard University Press, 1939).

6. See, for example, Robert A. Dahl, Mason Haire, and Paul F. Lazarsfeld, eds., *Social Science Research on Business* (New York: Columbia University Press, 1959).

7. S. I. Hayakawa, *Language in Action* (New York: Harcourt, Brace and Co., Inc., 1941).

8. Herbert Feigl, "Operationism and Scientific Method" in *Readings in Philosophical Analysis*, eds. Herbert Feigl and Wilfrid Sellars (New York: Appleton-Century-Crofts, Inc., 1949), p. 505.

9. This example is taken from something I heard or read some years ago, but I cannot recall the source. Perhaps the attribution would be less than eagerly welcomed anyway.

10. In this connection, see the description of younger school administrators "getting the word" in the form of definite answers to a host of administrative problems in Neal Gross, "The Use and Abuse of Sociological Inquiry in Training Programs for Educational Administrators," in *The Social Sciences and Educational Administration*, eds. Lawrence W. Downey and Frederick Enns (Edmonton, Alberta: University of Alberta and University Council for Educational Administration, 1963), p. 23.

11. J. W. Getzels and E. G. Guba, "Social Behavior and the Administrative Process," *School Review* 65, 4 (Winter 1957): 423-441; and J. W. Getzels and H. A. Thelen, "The Classroom as a Unique Social System" in *The Dynamics of Instructional Groups*, ed. N. B. Henry (Chicago: The Fifty-ninth Yearbook of the National Society for the Study of Education, 1960), pp. 53-82.

12. Our focus is primarily on his treatment of functionally differentiated levels in organizations. See Talcott Parsons, "Some Ingredients of a General Theory of Formal Organizations," in *Administration Theory in Education*, ed. Andrew W. Halpin (Chicago: Midwest Administration Center, University of Chicago, 1958), pp. 40-72.

13. A. W. Gouldner, *Patterns of Industrial Bureaucracy* (Glencoe, Illinois: The Free Press, 1954); the companion piece is *Wildcat Strike* (Yellow Springs, Ohio: The Antioch Press, 1954).

14. Daniel E. Griffiths, "Administration as Decision-making," in *Administrative Theory in Education*, pp. 119-149; and *Administrative Theory* (New York: Appleton-Century-Crofts, Inc., 1959).

15. Egon G. Guba and Charles E. Bidwell, *Administrative Relationships* (Chicago: Midwest Administration Center, University of Chicago, 1957) contains a number of hypotheses tightly derived from the theory. D. J. Willower, "Leadership Styles and Leaders' Perceptions of Subordinates," *Journal of Educational Sociology* 34, 2 (October 1960): 58-64, is an example of a looser derivation.

16. Relevant sources are Howard S. Becker, "The Teacher in the Authority System of the Public School," *Journal of Educational Sociology* 27, no. 3, (November 1953), 128-41; Charles E. Bidwell, "The School as a Formal Organization," in *Handbook of Organizations*, ed. James G. March (Chicago: Rand McNally and Co., 1965), p. 972-1022; Matthew B. Miles, "Some Properties of Schools as Social Systems," in *Change in School Systems*, ed. Goodwin Watson (Washington: National Training Laboratories, cooperative Project for Educational Development, 1967), pp. 1-29; Willard Waller, *The Sociology of Teaching* (New York: John Wiley and Sons, Inc., 1932); D. J. Willower, "The Teacher Subculture and Curriculum Change," *Samplings* 1, 3 (April 1968): 45-60; and D. J. Willower, T. L. Eidell, and W. K. Hoy, *The School and Pupil Control Ideology* (University Park, Pennsylvania: Penn State Studies Monograph No. 24, 1967).

12

Content Selection in Organizational Theory and Behavior in Education

James M. Lipham

In making the plea for the use of theory in educational administration over a decade ago, one of my esteemed professors took great delight in taunting past, present, and prospective practitioners with the petard, "School administrators can tell you what they do and even how they do it, but just ask one why he does what he does and he is apt to choke on his own saliva." Now, I must admit, being faced with the prospect of having to justify why one teaches what he teaches gives me the same choking sensation. No doubt this is due to my commitment to the theory based orientation to administration which traditionally has eschewed the ad hominem approach to knowledge.

The issue of what knowledge is of most worth has perplexed people from the time of Plato to the present. As has been shown in previous chapters, our misery is shared by colleagues in the social sciences; there also is evidence that on occasion, the issue plagues perceptive professors in the humanities and even in the biological and physical sciences. In this regard, I am reminded of my superb graduate chemistry professor who, when faced with a clutch of curious students enrolled in a course in quantitative and qualitative instrumental analysis in a laboratory bulging with apparatus and equipment, remarked somewhat as follows: "Now you don't know what you really need to know, and I don't know what you really need to know, but one thing is damn sure. You're going to learn the damn art of this damn science." Damned if we didn't.

In this chapter, the assumption is made that a converse, and perhaps equally obfuscating, injunction is presently appropriate in the field of educational administration. We need to learn the science of the art. Already, beginnings have been made toward the development of administrative science through adopting, adapting, and applying (sometimes in reverse order) some general or specific theories, models, constructs, taxonomies, concepts, and findings (often in random order) from the social or behavioral sciences. It is assumed that the prospective practitioner or professor of educational administration should, at least, be aware of such developments; at most, his future behavior thereby should be modified. It is also assumed that a major portion of the responsibility for incorporating such knowledge rests with Departments of Educational Administration. Hence, the necessity for conscious, albeit self-conscious, attention to the criteria that one might utilize in fulfilling this responsibility should be obvious.

It does seem appropriate at this juncture, however, to sound the note that one should be careful when he engages publicly in self-conscious analysis of his profession. Judging from the rash of publications which have given us "new" perspectives on preparation programs, the professorship, philosophy, knowledge production, change, research, and the social sciences in educational administration, it might be supposed that the profession's capacity for assimilating such heavy doses of introspection and flagellation has been surfeited.[1] Even so, another attempt can be justified by appeals to the infancy of the field.

At the most general level, the issue of which criteria govern the selection of content, techniques, and materials for graduate courses and seminars in organizational theory and behavior in education is no different from any other curricular development problem. In even a post hoc attack on the issue, therefore, we can turn to existing curricular principles, such as those outlined in Tyler's taxonomy, which called attention to both the sources of curricular objectives and the screens through which the curricular objectives may be filtered.[2] At a more specific level, decisions then must be made concerning the selection of organizing concepts and organizing centers for instruction which will elicit precise and probable (if not predictable) changes in student behavior. The sources and screens for the objectives will be discussed after a précis of the course offerings in organizational theory and behavior in the Department of Educational Administration at the University of Wisconsin is presented.

Offerings in organizational theory and behavior at Wisconsin consist basically of a course, Organizational Theory and Behavior in Education and a seminar in Organizational Theory and Behavior in Education. These offerings may be augmented with research and independent reading. The basic catalog description is as follows: Theoretical concepts and research relating to administrator behavior in organizations with special reference to educational organizations. The course typically is elected after at least one introductory, graduate level course in educational administration; it is a prerequisite for the seminar. Both the course and the seminar are prerequisites for doctoral level research or independent reading in the specialization.

Over the past decade, enrollments in the course have varied from 15 to 70, but courses usually have been sectioned, partially sectioned, or team taught when enrollments exceeded 30. Enrollments in the seminar have varied from 5 to 30, but seminars have been sectioned when enrollments exceeded 15. Enrollments in research and independent reading have averaged, respectively, 5.8 and 2.8 students per professor per semester. The course is offered each semester both on-campus and off-campus at approved locations having adequate meeting, library, audio-visual, and computer terminal facilities. The seminar, research, and independent reading are provided on campus only.

As the basic titles imply, there is a bifurcated emphasis, organizational theory and organizational behavior. Emphasis on theory is achieved through lectures and readings; emphasis on behavior is achieved through student participation in simulation experiences in the course and in research development activities in seminar, research, or independent reading experiences. Role playing, case study analysis, computer interacting, and other behavioral sampling and evaluating techniques are utilized to establish bridges between theory and behavior or between content and practice. In addition to the typical expectations held for students to read, to listen, to talk, and to write, an additional expectation is held for them to provide actual behavioral samples as a basis for analysis by self, others, and a computer.

Concerning the offerings in organizational theory and behavior, there are certain relevant sources from which the educational objectives are derived.

SOURCES OF EDUCATIONAL OBJECTIVES

The sources of educational objectives include the nature of the students enrolled in educational administration, the nature of life in contemporary organizations, and the nature of administrative science as a discipline.

The Student of Organizational Theory and Behavior

Since education is a process of changing the behavioral patterns of people, attention must be given to the nature of the students enrolled, if only to identify some major gaps between actual status and some standards of philosophic value held by the institution, the instructor, and the student regarding what should be.[3] Such gaps, typically termed "needs" or "interests," often defy quantitative assessment but, at least, call for an accurate and systematic data base on the students as a starting point. At the University of Wisconsin, such a relevant, computer-based data file on each student and on each course has been developed and is maintained.

Analysis of the data file has shown that the anachronistic term, "bounded heterogeneity," best describes the students of organizational theory and behavior. "Bounded" is used in the sense that the students are graduate candidates or post-doctoral fellows who are interested in the behavior of administrators in organizations. Although a detailed description of "heterogeneity" would be superfluous here, observations concerning some of the major variables appear to be in order. Regarding age, the range is from 22 to 64 years, bimodally distributed around age 27 and age 34. The younger students typically represent research trainees, computer specialists, and principalship aspirants, while the older students typically represent practicing superintendents, supervisors, and professorship aspirants. Regarding race, 96 per cent are white; 4 per cent, other. Eighty-four per cent are male; 16 per cent, female. Approximately 78 per cent of the students completed undergraduate programs for teacher certification in a variety of subject fields; the remainder completed programs in such fields as liberal arts, business, and nursing. The median number of full-time positions held, exclusive of military, prior to enrollment is 3.8; the range, from 0 to 14. Approximately 12 per cent of the students are majoring at the graduate level in fields other than educational administration.

While the foregoing data are valuable as indicators of diversity of student "needs," objectives can never be identified automatically by collecting information from students. The process becomes some-what more powerful by collecting information from students. As a first order of business in the course in organizational theory and be-havior, therefore, the student is requested to update and augment existing data by providing written input concerning himself (utiliz-ing a personal data card), his expectations for the course (utilizing an objectives and activities form), and his level of current knowl-edge (utilizing a potpourri pretest). The planning process is moni-tored largely informally throughout the course; it is monitored more formally at the end of the course (utilizing student evaluations of course and instructor, after grades are in).

Analysis of the student as a source of objectives reveals that the content of student input may be broadly grouped according to concerns related to administrative problems, administrative skills, or administrative attitudes. Student concern with administrative problems is roughly analogous to acquiring cognitive knowledge of the administrative functions and is expressed by students as a need for help with such tasks as selecting, assigning, evaluating, and negotiating with employees; understanding organizational sub-publics; improving basic work processes; and working with subordi-nates in organizations. Concern with administrative skills is roughly analogous to the application of knowledge of the administrative process and is expressed by students as a need for help with plan-ning, decision making, communicating, coordinating, or evaluating types of activities. Attitudinal concerns are roughly analogous to affective involvement in administration and relate to attitudes to-ward status, authority, leadership, change, innovation, and partici-pation in organizations.

Although one can only conjecture regarding what criteria stu-dents utilize in making inputs, one might assume that they stress the criterion of "relevance for me as perceived by me-in-situation." Even though such inputs may suffer the weaknesses of being narrow, inappropriate, or inadequate, there is little doubt that the content, approaches, techniques, and activities of the course are continually altered in the give-and-take of students and instructor working and learning together. While this is not to suggest the syndrome of "instructor-as-pawn," it is to indicate that of the many times that the course and seminar have beeen offered they never have been identical. The nature of the student, therefore, becomes critical in such operational matters as deciding which focal roles in contem-porary educational organizations (school superintendency, secon-dary principalship, or elementary principalship) will be selected for the simulation activities.

Life in Contemporary Organizations

Two major criticisms exist concerning the analysis of contemporary organizational life as a source of course objectives. One is that the study of contemporary behavior does not indicate whether or not such behavior is "desirable." This criticism can be overcome only if the derivation of objectives does not depend solely upon the study of contemporary life.[4] The other is that because life is continually changing, preparing students for today will build in an incapacity for dealing with tomorrow. Except for the anthropological-historical approach, which includes yesterday, there seem to be few viable alternatives.

It is somewhat anachronistic that while so much time and energy are spent in coping with life in contemporary organizations, so little is spent in trying to understand it. In essence, this anti-analytic stance is comparable to an anti-theoretical bias. It is not uncommon, therefore, to encounter an individual who feels that he already knows all about organizations because he has lived in one — as in the case of the demagogue who poses as a pedagogue because he once went to school. Except for some probably archaic notions about line and staff, some rudimentary knowledge of the legal structure for education, and some passing acquaintance with job descriptions, the typical student of administration in the field of education is illiterate in organizational theory.

Analysis of the nature of contemporary organizational life constitutes a line of endeavor all its own, particularly with regard to dividing the study of organizations into manageable areas for investigation. From excellent existing works,[5] however, the following exemplary topics emerge as possible organizing concepts for instruction: organizational boundaries and goals; organizational size, growth, or change; organizational responsiveness to the larger environment; organizational health; organizational technologies; organizational technologies; organizational structure; organizational dynamics; and organizational-individual articulation.

Two limitations regarding the preceding topics should be noted. The first is that presently there is no systematic treatment of educational organizations that is anywhere nearly so complete as that of others, such as business organizations. Heavy reliance must be placed upon transfer of learning — to the dismay of some who express fear that inappropriate transfer will be made. The second limitation is that the topics stress treatment of the organization as an entity. This cuts across the grain of many students in education who have been conditioned to focus upon the individual as an entity. Thus, the student from education may feel that his world is cast askew and that he is struggling to cope with an alien discipline.

Administrative Science as a Discipline

The nature of a discipline, with its traditional lines of inquiry ensconced in textbooks, undoubtedly serves as the major source for objectives in most of what passes for education in schools and colleges today. Unfortunately, or fortunately as the case may be, the boundaries of both the total discipline of administrative science and of its subspecializations are by no means clear. It may be defensible to describe administrative science as that particular aspect of organizational science that focuses primarily upon administrative, managerial, or supervisory roles and relationships. As all applied disciplines should do without apology, both organizational science and administrative science draw heavily upon theories, taxonomies, terminology, and techniques from numerous basic disciplines, including sociology, psychology, political science, economics, history, anthropology, philosophy, and humanities — perhaps in that order.

A substantial body of literature in administrative science has been developing, at differing levels of generality, which provides us with such organizing concepts as: power, influence, and authority; leadership and change; decision making, policy making, and planning; compliance; communication; role relationships; and motivation and productivity, among others.[6] Even in this primitive stage, the problem of content selection is enormous.

While it is beyond the scope of this paper to combat fully the current criticism that the nature of administrative science does not constitute a legitimate source of objectives, two interrelated viewpoints should be countered. One ostrich-type view holds that administrative science should be ignored because it doesn't account for everything; there is neither extant, nor on the horizon, any grand, unifying theory of administration. There probably never will be. Another view decries the cafeteria-style nature of the discipline. Cafeterias do, of course, serve meat.

Derived from whatever source—the nature of the students, the nature of contemporary organizational life, or the nature of the discipline—the disparate objectives must be screened or processed to render them operational in administrator preparation programs.

SCREENS FOR EDUCATIONAL OBJECTIVES

The screens for processing educational objectives in organizational theory and behavior include the nature of the preparing institution, the nature of the individual instructor, and the nature of adult learning.

The Preparing Institution

The institutional milieu within which the educational process is attemped serves as a powerful screen for educational objectives either formally or informally, either consciously or unconsciously, either conscientiously or unconscientiously. The capacity of a university to attract quality students in the first place, to develop imaginative programs of instruction, and to implement programs to change the behavior of its students depends upon the quality, vision, and value commitments of the staff; the quantity and accessibility of the resources necessary for the task; the organizational structures and relationships that may facilitate program change and implementation; and the extent to which these factors are sustained through time. Since my friend and colleague the late Professor Virgil E. Herrick delineated in detail the major parameters within which the research function at the University of Wisconsin is fulfilled,[7] only some of the formal and informal mechanisms within which the teaching function is fulfilled should be mentioned.

Regarding the formal mechanisms, several factors condition selection and screening of educational objectives to insure that they are relevant to target populations of students at the University of Wisconsin. The first grows out of the fact that individualized student programming in multidisciplinary and interdisciplinary options is typical procedure; consequently, required and prerequisite courses are held to a minimum. Under these conditions "bad" courses usually die. The second is that course and seminar review and approval procedures are seriously monitored at both departmental and social science divisional levels. Overlapping "junk" usually does not get through. The third is that large classes and seminars are sanctioned. There is adequate opportunity to teach and to learn. The fourth is that necessary assistance, supplies, and facilities are provided. There are few "lame excuses." The fifth is that student involvement in course evaluation is sought. Effort is made to reward excellent teaching. Finally, each professor is alloted a percentage of his load (a minimum of 20 percent in Educational Administration) for research. Hopefully, teaching is thereby rejuvenated.

Regarding the informal mechanisms, which are probably even more powerful than the formal ones, course objectives are influenced and screened through student and professor interaction and involvement in issues ranging from general concerns of the universe to specific concerns of the individual. In our systematic follow-up of graduates, it is predictable, therefore, that they would cite "being in Madison, U.S.A.," "brown bag lunches," "cram sessions for exams," and "Lorenzo's" and "Mr. Giblin's" pubs as some of the more powerful determinants of their understandings, skills, attitudes, and behaviors.

The Individual Instructor

That the background, training, experience, need-dispositions, perceptivity, values, and philosophy of the instructor serve as a potent screen for objectives is obvious. In this regard, I am reminded of a former colleague who used to rant as follows when new courses were being reviewed: "Most professors have one good course in them; an outstanding one perhaps has two. So why don't we stop this program nonsense and offer Greggology 700, Wakefieldology 700, Liphamology 700, and so on, and let the student take only one course from each professor until he has had all that he can stand!" This perceptive view can be reduced to the operating maxim so widely followed throughout the academic world, "Pick the professor."

In staffing the program in educational administration at the University of Wisconsin, careful attention has been given to matching the man and the specialty. The day of the generalist professor who can teach anything and everything in the administration of education has passed. Of the five professors who have taught organizational theory and behavior at Wisconsin during the past decade, all have had substantial study at least equivalent to joint majors or doctoral minors in related social science disciplines, have had sustained interest in and involvement with developments in organizational and administrative sciences, have had substantial study or experience in education, have had specialized preparation in the use of simulation training techniques, and have conducted or supervised research related to the specialization. That some institutions, in the rush to become respectably "theoretical," would ignore such minimal prerequisites for the professor of organizational theory and behavior is a crime.

Qualifications of the instructor, however, constitute only a point of departure. Considerable time and effort must be spent with students in mutually planning and evaluating course objectives and with colleagues in discussing and sharing approaches, techniques, and materials deemed relevant to the learner.

The Nature of Adult Learning

Occasionally, one despairs as to whether or not it is actually possible to teach an adult anything that really matters. It is certainly naive in the extreme to presume that a 16 to 18 week, two to three hour course or seminar will alter significantly the basic adult personality from which most behavior derives, hence, the need for greater attention to recruitment and selection of prospective educational leaders. Even so, the nature of the learning process provides at least two general screens for reducing some of the disparity in objectives. Without subscribing to any particular theory of learning, we have found the screens of placement of learning activities and involvement of students to be useful in promoting learning.

Regarding placement of learning activities, the universal concern with scope and sequence is based upon the assumption that in order for a student to acquire and synthesize knowledge it is first necessary for him to have had meaningful, concrete experiences to which the new knowledge can be related. Since bounded heterogeneity characterizes the students of organizational theory and behavior, it has been found useful to immerse them early (during the second and third class sessions) in simulation training exercises which provide some common experiential background. For this purpose, the UCEA Madison and URBSIM simulation materials have been used, emphasizing such focal roles as superintendent, secondary principal, or elementary principal, depending upon the student's needs or interests. In addition to providing a common background, the student behaviors sampled are utilized to test and illustrate theory at subsequent junctures throughout the course.

Regarding involvement, it has been amply demonstrated that learning is maximized when the role of the learner is shifted from passive recipient to active participant. While there are degrees of involvement in typical class activities, the course in organizational theory and behavior utilizes small group analysis of "mini-case studies" or in-basket episodes, as well as individual analysis in the form of on-line interaction with a computer. During such interaction the student obtains specific feedback; that is, he receives subsequent problems requiring decision and action which are instantly coded, analyzed, scored, and fed back to him. Except for actual placement on a job, it is difficult to conceive of a more active situation for learning.[9]

Having considered some of the more global sources and screens for objectives, we may now turn to more specific criteria which govern the choice of particular organizing centers for instruction in organizational theory and behavior in education.[10]

CRITERIA FOR SELECTING ORGANIZING CENTERS FOR INSTRUCTION

Since organizational theory and behavior has a Janus-like orientation, one might turn either to administrative theories or to the sampled behaviors of students as organizing centers for instruction. It is possible, therefore, to select a given theory, such as decision theory, as an organizing center or to select specific behaviors, such as student decisions on an in-basket item, as an organizing center. Although behavioral samples having a common base are available, the typical practice at the University of Wisconsin is to utilize theories as organizing centers and then deduce illustrative student behaviors, rather than to utilize student behaviors as organizing centers and then induce illustrative theories. Both are sometimes done. As Culbertson has indicated in Chapter 1, there is inevitable movement between the two approaches. At best, the bridges are tenuous.

Since theories of organizational and administrative science are utilized as organizing centers, characteristics that others have delineated previously as criteria for "good" theory become relevant to the case at hand.[11] Even so, the use of such criteria is difficult because lists which describe "good" theory are similar to those which characterize "good" anything. As criteria become encompassing, they become contradictory. For example, it is held that "good" administrative theory should be general, yet specific; inclusive, yet limited; abstract, yet concrete; verified, yet novel; and phenomenological, yet transcendent. From such bipolar propositions we are able: (1) to conceptualize the criterion problem in terms of characteristic continua, (2) to place such characteristics into putative dimensions and factors; (3) to construct a comparative schema utilizing the dimensions and factors; (4) to rate and profile theories according to such schema; and (5) to draw comparisons among the theories so profiled.

Criteria for assessing theories as organizing centers for instruction in organizational theory and behavior in education might be presumed, a priori, to load on both valuational and descriptive dimensions. The valuational dimension can be conceived as comprised of linear factors and specific characteristics within factors which could be scored, for example, from low to high, bad to good, or 1 to 5.[12] The following factors are viewed as comprising the valuational dimension: (1) clarity, (2) vitality, and (3) utility.

Some characteristics illustrative of each factor and some theories scored on each factor will be cited briefly. The theories cited constitute a majority of the organizing centers for instruction that are currently utilized at the University of Wisconsin.

Concerning the valuational factor of clarity, administrative theories vary on such characteristics as exactness, precision, and operationality. For example, decision theory[13] would score lower on clarity than would the behavioral theory of the firm.[14] To ameloriate the language problem across disciplines and applied fields, exact, precise, operational theories are needed.

The factor of vitality relates to the degree to which a theory can be characterized as heuristic, dynamic, and powerful. Classical theory of bureaucracy[15] would score lower on vitality than would social systems theory.[16] As students have observed; better theories don't "just sit there," they "have wheels" — accounting for such variables as synergy, direction, and change.

The factor of utility includes such characteristics as relationality, causality, and intervention capacity. In this regard, leadership theory[17] would score higher than compliance theory.[18] While some theories may fall within the diagnostic range of "nice to know," if a theory is to be internalized and utilized, it should provide some hints, clues, or guides for action.

The descriptive dimension is comprised of those factors, and specific characteristics within them, on which a theory could be scored not from "bad to good," as in the valuational dimension but from "this to that." Factors that are viewed as comprising the descriptive dimension include: (1) generality, (2) complexity, and (3) currency.

Regarding the descriptive factor of generality, a theory may range from broad to narrow, inclusive to exclusive, or macroscopic to microscopic in the nature and range of organizational and individual situations encompassed. Systems theory,[19] as compared with role theory,[20] is general in nature. Some specific theories have been found to be as high in clarity, vitality, and utility as general ones.

On the factor of complexity, a theory may range from complicated to simple, intricate to evident, or many to few in the number or relationship of variables posited. Hage's axiomatic theory of organizations is based upon a complex, interactive set of dependent and independent variables.[21] Conversely, models of power relationships by Merton, Selznick, or Gouldner are elegant in their simplicity.[22] That which is simple also can be general.

The factor of currency may range from established to emergent, old to new, familiar to novel. In this regard, Weber's theory of bureaucracy[23] can be contrasted with Getzels' theory of administration as a social process.[24] The locus of a theory on this factor will change through time, and such change may be cyclical in nature.

As may be seen in Figure 1, the foregoing dimensions and factors may be utilized for evaluating, comparing, and selecting theoretical content for learning experiences in organizational theory and behavior. According to this schema, the writer would rate Getzels' social process theory as follows: clarity, very high; vitality, high; and utility, very high; generality, macroscopic; complexity, intricate; and currency, established. Hage's axiomatic theory of organization would rate: clarity, high; vitality, very high; and utility, average; generality, very macroscopic; complexity, very intricate; and currency, emergent. Although the profiles differ, both theories rate high on the valuational factors; they merit strong consideration for inclusion as organizing centers for instruction in organizational theory and behavior in education. Such systematic evaluation of many theories by many people is needed both immediately and in the years ahead if commonality of content in the specialization is viewed as desirable.

Factor	*Score* *
Valuational Dimension	
Clarity	Low ————— High
Vitality	Low ————— High
Utility	Low ————— High
Descriptive Dimension	
Generality	Microscopic ————— Macroscopic
Complexity	Simple ————— Intricate
Currency	Established ————— Emergent

x————Getzels' Social Process Theory

o————Hage's Axiomatic Organizational Theory

$\eta = (1; df,0.)$

Figure 1 *Profiles of Two Administrative Theories*

Toward the Future

Although organizational theory and behavior already has become widely incorporated as a substantial component in preparation programs for educational leaders,[25] it is appropriate to speculate at this juncture regarding the directions that study in the specialization may take in the future. In so doing, we may return briefly to the nature of the student, the nature of contemporary life, and the nature of the discipline.

Given that the nature of students in organizational theory and behavior is heterogeneous, some UCEA institutions have seen fit to minimize such heterogeneity by segregating and structuring specialized programs for more homogeneous groups, either by job title or by organizational level. Thus, separate programs and courses are structured for elementary administrators, secondary administrators, general administrators, community college administrators, vocational education administrators, and higher education administrators. More recently, some UCEA institutions appear to be segregating and structuring specialized programs for urban administrators; presumably, specialized programs for suburban and rural administrators are other alternatives. For study in organizational theory and behavior, neither of these approaches, specialization by level or specialization by locus, seems particularly viable. The present stance is that administration in all fields has much in common. If this be true, then surely administration within a field, such as education, has even more in common. Thus, if unique and specialized programs are to be structured, it would appear that this should be done at other than the theoretical level.

Given that the nature of contemporary organizational life is becoming ineffably complex, some have argued cogently for a return to basic philosophy, the humanities, and even the arts in a search for "first principles." This argument appears to avoid the issue. Undoubtedly, there is danger in excessive reliance upon social sciences in the preparation of educational leaders. Thus far, however, few institutions that prepare administrators have found meaningful mechanisms for incorporating the humanities. If knowledge, skills, and attitudes heretofore presumed to fall within the category of general education are to be substituted for knowledge, skills, and attitudes demonstrated to fall within the specialization, then arguments for such substitution must be compelling, indeed. In the extreme, such arguments render the entire effort to prepare administrators as nonsense.

Given that administrative science is a burgeoning field, some UCEA institutions have seen fit to divide the discipline into a proliferation of courses. In some universities, organizational analysis is separated from organizational change. In others, such organizing centers as leadership, decision making, and planning are singled out for separate course treatment. In still others, multi-faceted organizing centers, such as negotiating with community groups, faculty, or students; enhancing self-understanding and acceptance; and resolving conflict appear as course titles. In yet others, administrative theory and administrative behavior never seem to meet. At the University of Wisconsin, we are experimenting with mini-course modules of varying credit and duration focused upon certain of the organizing centers. With completion of construction of our computerized simulation facility which will have the capacity for simultaneously monitored, individualized instruction, we plan to reexamine the entire question of balance between group and individual learning environments. Hopefully, instructional methods, materials, and scheduling practices in colleges and universities will be able to catch up to those already being utilized in some better elementary and secondary schools.

Regardless of specific institutional adaptations, it is hoped that discussion of the issue raised herein concerning the sources of educational objectives, the screens for processing these objectives, and the criteria for selecting organizing centers for instruction will be useful to those who are charged with the responsibility for preparing educational leaders.

FOOTNOTES

1. Jack A. Culbertson and Stephen P. Hencley, eds., *Preparing Administrators: New Perspectives* (Columbus, Ohio: University Council for Educational Administration, 1962).

Donald J. Willower and Jack Culbertson, eds., *The Professorship in Educational Administration* (Columbus, Ohio, and University Park, Pennsylvania: The University Council for Educational Administration and the College of Education, University of Pennsylvania, 1964).

Robert E. Ohm and William G. Monohan, eds., *Educational Administration — Philosophy in Action* (Norman, Oklahoma: College of Education, University of Oklahoma and University Council for Educational Administration, 1965).

Terry L. Eidell and Joanne M. Kitchel, eds., *Knowledge Production and Utilization in Educational Administration* (Columbus, Ohio and Eugene,

Oregon: University Council for Educational Administration and Center for Advanced Study of Educational Administration, University of Oregon, 1968).

Max G. Abbott and John T. Lovell, eds., *Change Perspective in Educational Administration* (Auburn, Alabama: School of Education, Auburn University and University Council for Educational Administration, 1965).

Jack A. Culbertson and Stephen P. Hencley, eds., *Educational Research: New Perspectives* (Danville, Illinois: The Interstate Printers and Publishers, Inc., 1963).

Lawrence W. Downey and Frederick Enns, eds., *The Social Sciences and Educational Administration* (Edmonton, Canada: Division of Educational Administration, University of Alberta and the University Council for Educational Administration, 1963).

Keith Goldhammer, *The Social Sciences and the Preparation of Educational Administrators* (Edmonton, Canada: Division of Educational Administration and the University Council for Educational Administration, 1963).

W. W. Charters, Jr., et al., *Perspectives on Educational Administration and the Behavioral Sciences* (Eugene, Oregon: Center for Advanced Study of Educational Administration, University of Oregon, 1965).

Donald E. Tope, et al., *The Social Sciences View School Administration* (Englewood Cliffs, New Jersey: Prentice-Hall, Inc., 1965).

2. Ralph W. Tyler, *Basic Principles of Curriculum and Instruction* (Chicago: University of Chicago Press, 1950).

3. Despite the fact that these standards of philosophic value are utilized herein as a screen for objectives, it should be recognized that they also may serve as a source of objectives.

4. Tyler, *Principles of Curriculum and Instruction*, p. 13.

5. Cited as examples only are the following: Philip B. Applewhite, *Organizational Behavior* (Englewood Cliffs, New Jersey: Prentice-Hall, 1965).

Chris Argyris, et al., *Social Science Approaches to Business Behavior* (Homewood, Illinois: Richard D. Irwin, Inc., 1962).

Anthony G. Athos and Robert E. Coffey, *Behavior in Organizations: A Multidimensional View* (Englewood Cliffs, New Jersey: Prentice-Hall, 1968).

Gerald D. Bell, ed., *Organizations and Human Behavior* (Englewood Cliffs, New Jersey: Prentice-Hall, 1967).

Peter M. Blau, *Bureaucracy in Modern Society* (New York: Random House, 1956).

Fred D. Carver and Thomas J. Sergiovanni, *Organizations and Human Behavior: Focus on Schools* (New York: McGraw-Hill, 1969).

Rocco Carzo, Jr. and John N. Yanouzas, *Formal Organization: A Systems Approach* (Homewood, Illinois: Richard D. Irwin, Inc., 1967).

L. L. Cummings and W. E. Scott, *Readings in Organizational Behavior and Human Performance* (Homewood, Illinois: Richard D. Irwin, Inc., 1969).

Richard M. Cyert and James G. March, *A Behavioral Theory of the Firm* (Englewood Cliffs, New Jersey: Prentice-Hall, 1963).

Bertram M. Gross, *The Managing of Organizations* (New York: The Free Press of Glencoe, 1964).

Paul R. Lawrence, et al., *Organizational Behavior and Administration* (Homewood, Illinois: Richard D. Irwin, 1965).

Robert Presthus, *The Organizational Society* (New York: Alfred A. Knopf 1962).

William G. Scott, *Organization Theory* (Homewood, Illinois: Richard D. Irwin, Inc., 1967).

James D. Thompson, *Organizations in Action* (New York: McGraw-Hill, 1967).

James G. March, ed., *Handbook of Organizations* (Chicago: Rand McNally and Company, 1965).

6. Regarding each of these possible organizing centers such an impressive body of literature exists, largely in periodicals, that citation of samples herein would be unwieldy.

7. Virgil E. Herrick, "Guidelines for Facilitating Research in Universities," in *Educational Research: New Perspectives*, eds. Culbertson and Hencley, pp. 59-85.

8. For the creative work in this domain we are indebted to Gerald R. Boardman and Donald N. McIsaac, "A Computer Based Feedback Model for Simulation Exercises Involving School Administrators," USOE Project 8-E-167 (Madison, Wisconsin: University of Wisconsin, Department of Educational Administration, 1969).

9. Systematic observation and analysis of learning in such situations will constitute a major line of future research on administrator behavior in the Department of Educational Administration at the University of Wisconsin. Suffice it here to mention simply that gross student affective involvement has been observed to range from that of sweating, telling lies, and then kicking the computer to that of smiling, giggling, and then hugging the terminal.

10. An apology must be made to curriculum theorists for the discontinuity in this approach. Were our particular objective here to illustrate the utility of curriculum theory we would first derive a specific objective, filter it through the multiple screens, express it in behavioral terms, divide it into manageable threads, and then demonstrate the utility of each selected organizing center for achieving each objective and sub-objective. The hope is that what may be lost in depth by the approach herein may be gained in scope.

11. Excellent treatments of this issue in the field of educational administration include: W. W. Charters, Jr., "Anthropology and the Study of Administration: Response," in *Social Sciences and Administration*, eds. Downey and Enns, pp. 91-93 and Robert E. Sweitzer, "An Assessment of Two Theoretical Frameworks," in *Educational Research: New Perspectives*, eds. Culbertson and Hencley, pp. 201-203.

12. Through future empirical research or seminars on theory, minimal cutting scores on the valuational factors could be established and theories scoring lower than such minima might be ignored.

13. Irwin D. J. Bross, *Design for Decision* (New York: The Macmillan Company, 1953).

14. Richard M. Cyert and James G. March, *A Behavioral Theory of the Firm.*

15. Max Weber, *The Theory of Social and Economic Organization*, trans. Talcott Parsons (New York: The Free Press, 1947).

16. Talcott Parsons, *The Social System* (New York: The Free Press, 1951).

17. Andrew W. Halpin, "How Leaders Behave" in *Theory and Research in Administration*, ed. Halpin (New York: The Macmillan Company, 1966).

18. Amitai Etzioni, *A Comparative Analysis of Complex Organizations* (New York: The Free Press, 1961).

19. R. A. Johnson, F. E. Kast, and J. E. Rosenzweig, *The Theory and Management of Systems* (New York: McGraw-Hill, 1967).

20. Theodore R. Sarbin and Vernon L. Allen, "Role Theory," in *Handbook of Social Psychology*, ed. Gardner Lindzey (Reading, Massachusetts: Addison-Wesley Publishing Company, 1968), pp. 488-567.

21. Jerald Hage, "An Axiomatic Theory of Organizations" in *Organizations and Human Behavior,* eds. Carver and Sergiovanni, pp. 91-110.

22. James G. March and Herbert A. Simon, *Organizations* (New York: John Wiley and Sons, Inc., 1958).

23. Max Weber, *Theory of Organization.*

24. Jacob W. Getzels, James M. Lipham, and Roald F. Campbell, *Educational Administration as a Social Process* (New York: Harper and Row, 1968).

25. Judson Shaplin, "The Professorship in Educational Administration: Attracting Talented Personnel," in *The Professorship in Educational Administration,* eds. Willower and Culbertson, pp. 1-14.

Part Four

Criteria for Selecting Social Science Content

Authors preparing chapters for this part, in contrast to those preparing chapters for Part Three, were not constrained by practice. Their task was to project ideal guidelines of use to those interested in selecting social science content in preparatory programs.

Each of the four chapters is written from a different perspective of relevance. Chapter Thirteen deals with the career-based concept of relevance. Guidelines for those interested in a problem-based perspective of relevance are presented in Chapter Fourteen. Chapter Fifteen offers criteria for those selecting content from a discipline-based perspective, while the final chapter in this part projects criteria from a theory-based perspective.

In each chapter, the sources from which the criteria are derived are identified. For example, the sources of criteria for career-based perspectives are inherent in functions performed by differing specialists in educational administration, while the sources of criteria for the theory-based perspective are inherent in the nature of theory. The various chapters also seek to shed light on the relationships between criteria and relevant social science content.

13

Specialized Career Patterns and Content Selection

Jack Culbertson

INTRODUCTION

A widely recognized criterion of any profession is a knowledge base sufficient to undergird and affect its practice. Past experience shows that a profession cannot obtain an adequate knowledge base unless and until it attains well defined and effective specializations, including specialized career patterns for its members. Specialization, in advanced professions, generally has two expressions which are suggested by the following questions: What bodies of knowledge should be mastered by specialists in the field. What specialized uses should be made of the bodies of knowledge? In educational administration, the politics of education and organizational behavior are illustrative bodies of knowledge or content specializations. Research, development, synthesis, and administration are illustrative of processes which require specialized uses of bodies of knowledge. The processes of research, development, and synthesis function in every mature professional field regardless of the content specializations which define it.

Typically, the development of specializations in any field is a long and laborious process. For example, John Morgan, the first professor of medicine in the United States, argued strongly in 1765 that such established sciences as anatomy, physiology, botany, and chemistry should be viewed as branches of medicine; further, that these branches should be used to develop knowledge to combat the myths of practice in the medical field.[1] However, it was not until this century, and largely during the period 1940–70, that medicine experienced a quantum jump in research and development.[2]

Educational administration, which only began the search for a knowledge base and for defined specializations in this century, is obviously in an earlier state of development than medicine. In part because educational administration is a relatively young field, neither its content specializations nor its specialized ways of using knowledge are as yet defined in ways that are clear, precise, and widely accepted. This presents a problem to those who would design preparatory programs for specialists in the field. This chapter seeks to shed some light upon specialized uses of knowledge in educational administration and to develop some of the implications for preparing differing specialists in the field. The discussion will be limited to four specializations: research, synthesis, development, and administration.[3] Clearly, all of these require increasingly skilled and specialized uses of social science content by those in the field of education generally and in educational administration specifically.

Three fundamental assumptions underlying this paper are as follows: first, researchers, synthesizers, developers, and administrators in educational administration perform different functions in different settings to achieve dissimilar objectives; second, differing competencies and motivations are needed by researchers, synthesizers, developers, and administrators to pursue different objectives and to perform different functions in diverse contexts; third, preparatory programs for researchers, synthesizers, developers, and administrators should be differentiated in ways that recognize their needs for acquiring differing professional competencies.

If preparatory programs are to be differentiated in specific ways, then the first step is that of clarifying how research, synthesis, development, and administration differ. Such clarification can proceed through an examination of the aspirations, outputs, processes, work concepts, and other elements associated with all four specializations. Through such an examination, differences in each specialization can hopefully be identified and the implications for program differentiation can be made more explicit. From the results obtained, guidelines can be derived for designing programs which will meet the special needs of those pursuing differing career objectives.

SPECIALIZED CAREER PATTERNS

While the discussion to follow will highlight differences in career specializations, it should be emphasized from the beginning that there are common bonds between and among research, synthesis, development, and administration. The results produced by these specialists all serve, if in somewhat different ways, educational institutions. Thus, as specialization develops, the need for effective interdependence between and among research, synthesis, development, and administration becomes increasingly evident. This point should be kept in mind as the differences in specializations are highlighted below.

Table 1

Knowledge-Related Specializations: Some Subclassifications

Research	Synthesis	Development	Administration
1. Conclusion Oriented or Basic Research (a) Relationships between leadership and power structures (b) Relationships between selected early childhood experiences and later academic achievement	1. Concept Oriented Synthesis (a) Economics of education (b) Organizational behavior	1. Idea Oriented Development (a) The educational park (b) The voucher system	1. General Administration (a) Superintendency (b) Principalship
2. Decision Oriented or Applied Research (a) Impact of state financing on its programs for education. (b) Decision implications of a school district achievement scores for reading and arithmetic in its elementary schools.	2. Practice Oriented Synthesis (a) Collective negotiations in education (b) Business-education relationships	2. Product Oriented Development (a) Computer programs (b) Instructional materials for preparing administrators	2. Special Administration (a) Personnel (b) Business

In the systematic examination of specializations in educational administration, problems of definition are inevitably encountered. The problems are complicated by the fact that there are somewhat differing classes and concepts of research, synthesis, development, and administration. Table 1 illustrates some of these differences.

An examination of the content in Table 1 will indicate that the categories are not discrete. There is, in other words, an interaction between and among the categories of research, synthesis, development, and administration, as well as the subclassifications in these categories. These interrelationships should be kept in mind because *selected* subclassifications are treated in greater detail below. The subclassifications selected for illustrative treatment are conclusion oriented or basic research, concept-oriented synthesis, product-oriented development, and general administration.

Specialized Careers in Basic or Conclusion-oriented Research

Basic researchers in educational administration, and in other fields for that matter, aspire to advance the frontiers of knowledge. A strong curiosity motivates them to inquire into unknown relationships and to ask questions in ways not previously formulated. Since they are typically not concerned about immediate problems of practice, they are content to see others translate their own findings and generalizations into development or decision results. They work to acquire data and to develop generalizations which describe and explain dimensions of administration in new and more valid ways. They strive to shed light upon significant relationships between and among variables inherent in or impinging upon educational administration. Economists in the 1960s, for example, illuminated the relationships between investments in education and the economic returns to society in more specific and objective ways. During the same period, psychologists shed new light on the relationships of early childhood learnings to later educational achievements.

The major and more immediate knowledge-related tools of the basic-oriented researcher are theories, modes of inquiry, and specific procedures of investigation. The essential process is one of basic inquiry, and this process proceeds selectively. Instead of dealing with countless variables, as does the administrator, the basic researcher concentrates his inquiry upon a limited number of clearly defined variables. Even a few variables, such as leadership or power structure, can guide a lifetime of search for knowledge. The main tangible and immediate artifacts of his work are research reports, articles, and monographs.

Since the basic researcher tends to be interested in applying the knowledge he gains to produce additional knowledge instead of to field decision problems, he tends to communicate principally with fellow researchers. His own peers serve as the chief sources of quality control insofar as his inquiry is concerned. While he may be interested in the work of synthesizers and he may communicate with developers to gain insights into areas of needed new knowledge and with administrators to obtain data necessary for his research, these latter specialists are not his primary reference groups.

The university is the typical work place of the basic researcher, although he may reside in the growing number of relatively independent research centers, institutes, and non-profit corporations. In the work setting of the basic researcher, individual effort is highlighted, as a rule. Individuals pursue knowledge under conditions of academic freedom. This means that their work is characterized by a high degree of autonomy and, therefore, minimum supervision. It also means that time constraints which affect administrators constantly, synthesizers to some degree, and developers to a substantial degree are much less binding on basic researchers. Attaining general consensus on goals, an action requirement for the administrator, is not essential for basic researchers. Thus, he and his colleagues can and often do pursue inquiry from quite different perspectives and from diverse conceptualizations. Since the basic researcher is not required to take actions which affect society immediately nor to gain public legitimation for the specific objectives he decides to pursue, he usually is not nearly as much concerned about the politics of public legitimation as is the administrator who must frequently be sensitive to a variety of publics.

Basic researchers need time to acquire concepts, skills, and attitudes necessary for inquiry. However, it also seems clear that the most important research findings in the general scientific community generally have been developed by persons in their twenties and thirties.[4] Thus, the capacity to raise fundamental questions and to pursue them in highly fruitful ways seems in some ways to be dependent upon the relatively fresh and flexible perspectives of younger researchers. This means that seasoning achieved through a range of experience in school districts, usually presumed to be an important foundation for effective general administration, is not necessary for the basic researcher. There is some evidence that extended administrative experience may even be antithetical to an effective career oriented toward basic research.

Specialized Careers in Concept-Oriented Synthesis

Concept-oriented synthesizers aspire to achieve broadened meanings of educational administration through the comprehensive ordering of concepts and research findings. The outcomes desired by synthesizers are organized bodies of knowledge which illuminate selected aspects of educational administration. The motivation of the concept-oriented synthesizer is not, as is the case typically with the basic researcher, to develop valid generalizations concerning a limited number of variables but rather to achieve sets of generalizations about a range of variables affecting educational administration.

First steps in synthesis are the identification and mastery of scholarly works bearing upon defined aspects of educational administration. Defined aspects could encompass such subjects as the economics of education, the politics of education, organizational behavior, or group dynamics in administration. Having mastered pertinent references, there is the challenge of discovering how research findings and conceptualizations shed light on aspects of administration selected for study. Further, there is the task of discovering and elaborating those organizing principles which can provide bases for a comprehensive and integrated ordering of the knowledge mastered and examined. Thus, the essential process is synthesis. Synthesis involves the effective integration of well understood and somewhat fragmented bodies of knowledge into a larger whole.

Important knowledge-related tools of the concept-oriented synthesizer are the pertinent theories and findings produced by researchers. In addition, he makes use of modes of inquiry associated with definition, classification, and scholarly generalization. While synthesis requires an integration among parts, the process often involves an ordering of knowledge in smaller parts within a larger organizational framework. Thus, typical by-products of the synthesizer are textbooks and articles on aspects of educational administration selected for study. Before a textbook is completed, for example, synthesis of parts of it (e.g., chapters), is typically effected. Since the content of such chapters is often communicated initially in the form of classroom lectures, the synthesis of knowledge in educational administration is often associated with the teaching function. Put differently, synthesized knowledge is an important tool of the teacher and a servant of the learner.

A typical work setting of the concept-oriented synthesizer is the university. However, other agencies, including non-profit agencies, can provide a home for those performing the synthesis function. In contrast to the basic researcher who is concerned with a limited number of variables, the synthesizer typically concentrates upon a substantial number of variables. Synthesis tends to proceed largely through individual effort. However, several individuals may be involved in a given synthesis effort when an effective division of labor can be achieved. Synthesizers experience a high degree of autonomy and, as is the case with basic researchers, public legitimation of specific objectives is not usually necessary. Since they must often master and order the results of many studies, they typically require long periods of work, especially in the creation of larger synthesis. While sometimes constrained by publication dates and contracts, they, in contrast to administrators, are not sharply pressed by time limits.

The concept-oriented synthesizer does not immediately or primarily concentrate upon problems of practice. However, since he is concerned with the larger meanings of educational administration, he is more likely to be interested in informing and instructing educational administrators than is the basic researcher. Those versed in the conduct of scholarship are likely to be the principal quality control agents of the synthesizer, however, other consumers of his work, including practicing administrators, express and pass judgment on his performance.

Specialized Careers in Product-Oriented Development

Product-oriented development in education generally, and in educational administration specifically, is much more inchoate and of more recent origin than is research, synthesis, or administration. The process, it is generally agreed, involves the systematic use of knowledge in the design of useful materials, processes, systems, technologies, and related products.[5] Instructional materials designed for the in-service training of educational administrators or computer programs created to process data necessary for decision making are specific examples of product-oriented development.

The aspiration of the developer in educational administration is that of achieving products which will be generally useful in educational organizations and in administration. Such products could be instructional materials of use in the in-service education of principals or information systems to support the decision making of administrators. Development products are designed to be useful not just to one school system but to many.

The essential process basic to development is invention. This process requires both effective problem defining and problem solving. Problem defining must be based upon real situations and have applicability to a range of similar problem situations in different school settings. The process initially is guided largely by analysis. The problem-solving dimension of development must be based upon concepts and information which go beyond the immediate contexts of problems. The attainment of new relationships between ideas and practice is important in effective problem solving since inventions require new arrangements and structures. Put differently, effective product-oriented development requires the bringing together of concepts and applied problem definitions in new ways. Ideally, product-oriented development is a bridge of theory-practice gaps par excellence. The essential knowledge-related tools involved are information and data concerning organizational and administrative problems and concepts and ideas derived from theories, research findings, and inventive thinking. The immediate and tangible artifacts of development work are specifications for design or prototypes.

The settings of product-oriented developmental work in educational administration are more diffused than is the case with research. The regional laboratory is one important work place. Industry and non-profit organizations also provide settings for developers.

While research and synthesis are expressed largely through the creative work of individuals, product-oriented development tends to proceed principally through team efforts. A range of competencies is required by development teams, and these can only be defined within the context of specified problems. In general terms, however, some team members must be able to bring to bear data-gathering and analytic skills during the process of problem defining while others must be able to draw upon a range of theoretical inquiry and concepts during the problem-solving phase of development.

Product-oriented development is more constrained by specific time limits than is basic-oriented research and, to a lesser degree, concept-oriented synthesis. Significant generalizations by researchers or synthesizers cannot be easily forced by arbitrary time limits. However, development is less constrained by time than is the work of the administrator who is continually pressed for immediate decisions. By the same token, the developer, since he generally selects one or a few problem areas on which to work at a given time, has many fewer variables with which to contend than does the administrator who, even in short time periods, participates in many decisions involving countless variables. On the other hand, the developer must deal with a wide range of variables even for one development task. Thus, he is not as free as the basic researcher to limit the number of variables with which he must deal. The autonomy of the developer is likely to vary depending in part on the stage of developmental work in which he is involved and in part on whether or not he works in a profit or non-profit organization. Greater autonomy is likely to prevail in earlier than in latter stages of development, and there is some evidence that autonomy is more likely to abound in non-profit than in profit agencies. In any case, it seems reasonable to believe that the developer has more autonomy than the administrator in the conduct of his work but less than that of the researcher and synthesizer.

Quality control for product-oriented developers is achieved largely through informed judgments made by potential or actual users of the products created. The process can be initiated at the point where design specifications are formulated; at the stage when a prototype is completed; or even after wide diffusion and use of products. In all cases, feedback can lead to adaptations in later design and production efforts. Developmental efforts, in other words, at this stage in educational history, is more responsive to user needs and user experience than to valid and reliable evaluative data. The latter have generally been difficult to achieve. Thus, product developers tend to be more immediately concerned with external publics than researchers and synthesizers although they are not generally as much concerned with the processes of political legitimation as have administrators.

Specialized Careers in Educational Administration

Educational administration, in this chapter, as already implied, refers to the official actions of those who head schools or school districts. It is assumed that such persons can and should express both administrative and leadership behaviors. Put differently, they must at times be involved in the execution of existing policies and, at other times, should be involved in the creation of new purposes, policies, programs, or structures.

The central aspiration of the effective educational administrator is not that of creating useful development products, advancing scientific understanding, or ordering bodies of knowledge. Rather, his central aspiration is that of achieving organizational effectiveness and educational improvement. Ideally, he measures much of his work in terms of the degree to which the goals and programs of the institution he administers are effectively attained. While he uses knowledge, information, and developmental products generated largely by others to achieve institutional goals, he must be concerned with effective action, both his own and that of others.

The essential process guiding his actions and the actions of those with whom he works is decision making. Major knowledge-related tools of immediate use to him in decision making are data about conditions and decision situations in the organization where he works, and pertinent research findings, concepts, bodies of knowledge, and developmental results created by synthesizers, researchers, and developers external to his setting. Even though there are increasing amounts of internal data, external research, and development resources available to him, he continually makes decisions under conditions of uncertainty, in part because of the innumerable variables affecting his decision situations.[6] Not only do knowledge-related tools shape the decision processes in which he participates, but also critical values held by him and others with whom he interacts. Immediate and tangible artifacts of official administrative decisions reside in minutes and recorded actions. More intangible residues are found in the memories and actions of those making up the informal networks, past and present, of the organization he heads.

A typical work setting for the administrator is a school district which in turn is linked to a larger community. Within this larger context, the educational administrator, in contrast to the researcher, synthesizer, and even the developer, is subjected to many pressures and has limited freedom and autonomy. He is severely constrained by time in decision-making situations and is continually pressed to take actions. Since he is much more closely linked to the political and community environment than are researchers, synthesizers, and developers, his decision-making arena is much more extended and complex. Since organizational decision making has been defined as groups of people interacting upon one another toward some conclusion, the individual emphasis in research and synthesis and the single team expression in development do not typify decision situations in administration.

Since schools are intimately related to society, the administrator, much more than the researcher, synthesizer, and developer, must be concerned about politics and economics. He must also be more concerned about the public interest of given communities, broadly defined, and about how the organization in which he works should be linked to the immediate and broader community served. While his peers in other educational institutions evaluate to some degree his behavior, the quality of his performance, much more than for the researcher, synthesizer, and developer; he is evaluated ultimately by the public, or by its designated representatives. This is particularly true for the school superintendent.

SUMMARY OF KEY DIFFERENCES IN SPECIALIZED CAREER PATTERNS

Idealized descriptions of researchers, synthesizers, developers, and administrators help highlight differences in specialized career patterns in education generally and in educational administration specifically. The uses of knowledge and the conditions of knowledge application differ for these patterns. Table 2 summarizes some of the key differences reflected in the specialized activities of *selected* types of research, synthesis, development, and administration.

GUIDELINES FOR SELECTING CONTENT

A variety of implications for preparatory programs can be deduced from patterns as they are described in Table 2. Since this chapter deals specifically with career-based relevance, the guidelines to follow will be concerned principally with the questions of why and how social science content in preparatory programs should differ for researchers, synthesizers, developers, and administrators. However, some attention will also be given to the attainment of needed linkages between and among the specializations during preparation. Generalizations will be limited to the following types of specialists: basic researchers, the concept-oriented synthesizer, the product-oriented developer, and the general administrator. Therefore, the generalizations are illustrative and not comprehensive. More specifically, they do not include specialists in decision-oriented research, practice-oriented synthesis, idea-oriented development and central office administration.

Fundamental Criteria

The fundamental criteria for selecting program content from the social sciences for use in preparing researchers, synthesizers, developers, and administrators should be the differing career goals of these specialists. A major thesis advanced above was that the goals pursued by administrators, synthesizers, researchers, and developers differ substantially. To briefly summarize: conclusion-oriented researchers aim to achieve valid findings and generalizations that will advance the frontiers of knowledge in educational administration; concept-oriented synthesizers strive to achieve newly ordered bodies of knowledge; product developers seek to produce new materials, processes, systems, technologies, and related products; and general administrators strive to make decisions which will lead to improved organizational effectiveness and to optimal learning op-

Table 2

Selected Specialized Career Patterns in Educational Administration:
Some Significant Differences

DESCRIPTIVE CATEGORIES	Specialists			
	Conclusion-oriented Researchers	Synthesizers	Developers	Educational Administrators
General Aspirations	Scientific understanding	Larger and more comprehensive meanings of educational administration	Useful products	Improvements in educational policies, programs, and organizational effectiveness
Desired Outcomes	Valid findings and generalizations	Organized bodies of knowledge	New materials, programs, organizations, processes, or technologies	Effective decisions and actions
Knowledge-Related Resources Typically Used	Selected theories and modes of inquiry	Modes of inquiry required for mastering and ordering a wide range of concepts and research findings	Analytic studies of "field" problems and knowledge relevant to them	School system data and externally developed research findings and concepts
Essential Processes	Basic inquiry	Synthesis	Product invention	Organizational decision making
Illustrative Work Places	Universities	Universities	Regional laboratories	School districts

Some Characteristics of Work Setting and Processes	1. Not so constrained by time 2. High degree of autonomy 3. Individual effort highlighted 4. Public legitimation of specific research objectives not usually necessary 5. Uninvolved in solving immediate problems of practice 6. Relatively small number of carefully defined variables involved	1. Considerably constrained by time 2. Substantial degree of autonomy 3. Individual effort required 4. Public legitimation not usually necessary 5. Uninvolved in immediate administrative practice 6. Large number of variables usually involved	1. Substantially constrained by time 2. Considerable degree of autonomy 3. Team effort critical 4. Public legitimation helpful 5. Definitely involved with selected problems of practice 6. Substantial number of variables involved	1. Highly constrained by time 2. Limited degree of autonomy 3. Many groups and individuals interacting 4. Public legitimation frequently essential 5. Continually involved with a wide range of problems of practice 6. Countless variables involved
Illustrative Artifacts of Practice	Research monographs	Textbooks	Design specifications	Officially recorded decisions in minutes of meetings
Significant Quality Control Agents	Fellow research specialists	Reviewers of textbook manuscripts	Product users	Boards and designated professional personnel

portunities in educational institutions. What more fundamental criteria can there be for selecting program content from the social sciences than these career goals? They should be central not only to professional activity but also to professional preparation.

Definite Criteria

More definite criteria for selecting social science content can be achieved through an analysis and breakdown of the general career goals of researchers, synthesizers, developers, and administrators into more specific objectives. Generally stated, career goals to be useful in content selection need to be analyzed and broken down into specific objectives. An illustrative, initial breakdown of general goals is found in Table 3.

The first-step analysis of career goals in Table 3 has implications for those selecting social science content to prepare research, synthesis, development, and administrative specialists. However, the analysis is only a beginning. For more definitive criteria, each subgoal needs further analysis. For example, the administrator subgoal, "Help create organizational arrangements to ensure continuous program improvement," can be broken down further as follows:[7] establishing adaptation as an important normative standard for educational institutions; helping develop a greater organizational capability for fostering and using education research and development; helping develop more systematic programs for the continuing education of school personnel; helping establish new forms of organization to facilitate such functions as educational planning and evaluation; facilitating the design of more functional information systems and more systematic ways of accounting to the public; and experimenting with temporary structures, external cooperative systems, project teams, and other organizational arrangements designed to facilitate program change. Clearly, a more specific breakdown of sub-goals for each of the specialized careers results in more specific guides for selecting social science content in preparatory programs.

Perspective of Discipline-Based Relevance

The perspective of discipline-based relevance can be especially useful to those selecting social science content to prepare basic researchers. The researcher, as already noted, concentrates upon a relatively few variables within some limited aspect of the larger reality with which educational administrators must deal. The social science disciplines themselves function, even if somewhat imper-

Table 3

Goals of Researchers, Developers, Synthesizers, and Administrators:
An Initial Analysis

Conclusion-oriented Researchers	Concept-oriented Synthesizers	Product-oriented Developers	General Administrators
1. Identify and describe research problems	1. Identify and master a range of concepts and research findings	1. Analyze and define significant dimensions of development problems	1. Help schools and communities formulate desired educational purposes and policies
2. Conceptualize pertinent research strategies and designs	2. Classify and order the knowledge mastered	2. Identify concepts and research findings pertinent to dimensions defined	2. Help generate programs designed to achieve defined purposes and policies
3. Operationalize needed methods and instruments for data gathering	3. Discover relationships and organizing principles in the range of knowledge mastered	3. Relate concepts and findings to dimensions of development problems in new ways	3. Manage financial and human resources to implement programs
4. Gather and analyze data and project their larger meanings	4. Synthesize concepts and findings into larger bodies of knowledge	4. Invent and bring into being products specifically designed to help resolve problems of administrative practice	4. Help create organizational arrangements designed to ensure continuous programs improvement and effectiveness

fectly, to bound different dimensions of reality as reflected by the fact, for example, that economics encompasses different variables than does sociology. Consequently, given social science disciplines can provide researchers limiting frameworks for inquiry and, in turn, guides for selecting content basic to preparation.

Since the basic researcher concentrates on a limited number of variables, he needs greater in-depth understandings of selected theories, concepts, and modes of inquiry than do synthesizers, developers, and administrators who deal with more numerous variables. The researcher needs, for example, more specialized insights into modes of inquiry, including their statistical and mathematical bases than does the synthesizer, developer, or the administrator. This is true, in part, because the latter specialists tend to use concepts and findings generated by researchers, rather than to use modes of inquiry to generate basic knowledge for themselves. Thus, discipline-based relevance has special significance for the researcher since it offers an opportunity to study intensively one relatively defined body of knowledge and to acquire the specialized concepts and skills needed to produce knowledge.

Those in colleges of education have traditionally viewed psychology as *the* relevant discipline in the study of education and especially in the investigation of teaching and learning. However, educational administration, because of its encompassing nature, clearly needs to have a broader concept of relevance including not only knowledge of psychology but also of sociology, political science, social psychology, economics, and anthropology. Researchers with depth training in the various dimensions of one discipline can effectively contribute to the broad base of knowledge needed for informed administrative decision making, effective synthesis, and creative developmental work in educational administration.

Specified Dimensions

Specified dimensions of educational administration should be used to select social science content in programs to prepare concept-oriented synthesizers. Concepts in educational administration tend to be ordered either within the context of substructures of disciplines (e.g., politics of education) or within the context of bodies of knowledge which transcend disciplines (e.g., leadership). Both these contexts provide useful bases for selecting social science content for those preparing to become concept-oriented synthesizers.

Bodies of knowledge pertinent to general administration include those which illuminate such processes as leadership, communication, decision making, morale, change, systems analysis, and planning. Concepts relevant to these processes and substantive areas can be found in a variety of disciplines. In addition, concepts pertinent to these processes have been generated through research in various applied fields including business, government, hospital, and educational administration. For example, concepts pertinent to communication are found in various fields of administration and in such disciplines as social psychology, sociology, and anthropology. As a consequence, personnel preparing to specialize in the synthesis of social science knowledge bearing upon aspects of administration need intensive experiences in identifying, mastering, and ordering scattered and wide ranging units of knowledge.

Those synthesizing content within the context of disciplines face less encompassing tasks than those concerned with knowledge transcending disciplines. This is especially true in such discipline substructures as the economics of education and the politics of education where concerted research began only in recent decades. However, synthesizers working within the substructures of social science disciplines with the aim of ordering knowledge need an understanding of the larger discipline involved. Therefore, content designed to enable prospective synthesizers to understand thoroughly the basic structure and modes of inquiry in a chosen discipline is important for their future career work.

Specified Problems

Specified problem areas affecting educational administration are especially useful in the selection of social science content relevant to the preparation of product-oriented developers. Since problems or, more accurately, problem areas are the beginning points for development, carefully defined dimensions of them constitute important bases for selecting content to prepare developers. It should be emphasized that development problems are different from administrative problems. Administrative problems arise as open expressions of everyday operations in educational organizations while development problems are not always as obvious. For example, problems involved in evaluating a teacher under *existing* policy and procedures in a given school are different from those encountered in developing new teacher evaluation *systems* designed for use in a variety of school districts. For one thing, development problems are generally more complex, and their resolution demands more time and energy. In part, because these problems are typically complex, programs for preparing developers should require more intensive experience with a much more limited number of problem areas than programs for preparing administrators. The attainment of basic skills and processes required generally for development work will be important since only a relatively small number of development problems can be experienced during preparation and these inevitably change with time.

There are, as already implied, different kinds of problems bearing upon product development: systems (e.g., manage information); processes (e.g., communication); materials (e.g., training manuals); and technologies (e.g., cassettes). Content from the social sciences, as a rule, is relevant to most all types of problems of product development in educational administration, although technological and especially "hardware" problems, for example, may require content from math, chemistry, physics, and so forth.

During preparation, developers need opportunities to analyze significant problem areas, to identify major components of problems, and to establish developmental tasks to be achieved. As these processes are experienced, prospective developers need to move back and forth between concepts and conditions of administrative practice. Let us take the problem area of principal accountability systems, for example. In arriving at the dimensions of the problems and the specific development tasks to be undertaken, careful studies would have to be made first within a number of field situations where the problem resides. Even during the process of field work, social science concepts might be selected for use in analyzing and delineating existing expressions of accountability and in defining the development needs to be met. When dimensions of the problem were defined, developmental tasks oriented toward clearly defined accountability systems could be set forth. These tasks in turn could serve as guides for identifying and studying relevant concepts, theories, and findings in the social sciences and in other areas. In most, if not all development efforts, the search for concepts would likely not end in one but in a number of disciplines including the science of administration. Preparation should encourage students of development to move back and forth intermittently between study and practice contexts not only during initial problem analysis but throughout the various stages of the development process. Thus, criteria of relevance should change and become more refined in a given development effort as the search for inventive solutions progresses.

Perspective of Problems-Based Relevance

In the selection of social science content to prepare general educational administrators a perspective of problems-based relevance is especially appropriate. As already noted, the number of problems and the number of variables with which administrators deal are countless. Even the ways of classifying problems are numerous. The general administrator, in contrast to the product-oriented developer, is generally concerned with problems within the single context in which he works. Thus, the test of proposed alternatives and decisions in his case is not that of general applicability, as is the case with developers, but the decision requirements of his own situation and the impact of decision results on that situation.

Since administrators experience a large number and wide range of decision problems and since these can be viewed from varied conceptual perspectives, administrators need a greater breadth of social science content during their preparation programs than do researchers, developers, and even synthesizers. While prospective researchers in preparatory programs are acquiring depth knowledge in one discipline, developers are studying varied content relevant to selected development areas. Synthesizers, on the other hand, explore a wide range of social science knowledge on specified dimensions of educational administration, while administrators will be acquiring social science content pertinent to administration and policy problems from a number of social science disciplines.

As in the case of the developer, however, it is unreasonable to assume that administrators can be prepared to deal with all of the specific problems they will encounter in practice. There are simply too many specific problems and even a total catalogue of problems developed at any one time is highly susceptible to change; further, such a strategy would encounter the danger of trained obsolescence. As a practical matter then, only certain classes of problems can be used as criteria for selecting social science content; therefore, the development of certain social science knowledge utilization skills which apply generally to problem solving and decision making must be important targets of preparatory programs.

First, there are perennial problems which are central to the life of most organizations related to purpose setting, community dynamics, organizational change, human relationships, the acquisition and management of resources, planning, communication, and decision making. A second class of problems are those which are very visible at given periods but change as events change. They pose important issues of policy. Currently, problems associated with race and education, with student militancy, and with teacher militancy are illustrative of these types of problems. Finally, prospective educational administrators need opportunities to practice using social science content during preparation relevant to specific decision making situations. The latter can be represented in cases and simulated situations or in internship situations.

There is so much social science content relevant to problems of administration that no one person can master it within the limited time span involved in preparation. The specific content used should vary to some degree for each person depending upon his background, interests, and capabilities. In addition, as team decision making in educational institutions evolve, varied social science content and leadership skills will be needed by individuals on administrative teams.

Need for Flexibility

There is a greater need for flexibility in organizing and presenting social science content in programs for general administrators than in programs for concept-oriented synthesizers, product-oriented developers, and basic-oriented researchers. Those responsible for preparing researchers, synthesizers, developers, and administrators should strive for flexibility in programs for *all* these personnel. At the same time, the thesis that more marked flexibility is needed in programs for administrators than in programs for synthesizers, researchers, and developers can be supported. Content to prepare basic researchers, given a discipline-based orientation to relevance, is already organized to serve the functions of research. This is true in large part because past efforts of many scholars have resulted in relatively well ordered bodies of knowledge called social science disciplines which are organized to support basic inquiry to a greater degree than decision making, invention, and synthesis. In addition, emergent social science content tends to be presented in scholarly journals which serve research more than administrative, development, or even synthesis needs. For researchers, then, there is less need for departing from traditional ways of organizing and presenting social science content than for administrators, synthesizers, and developers. This minimizes the need for flexible and varied ways of selecting and organizing content for researchers.

Social science content to prepare administrators, as already noted, can be drawn from many disciplines and theories because of the countless variables and problems affecting decision making in educational institutions. If this thesis is accepted, another argument for flexibility in content selection and organization in preparatory programs is evident because of the numerous options for selecting social science content and the untold number of combinations for organizing the content. This flexibility can take a variety of forms: the administrative or leadership problem areas used for selecting content: the disciplines or theories selected as most immediately relevant to problems chosen for use; the arrangements used for presenting content (e.g., independent study, seminars, courses, workshops, or field studies); and so forth.

Content to be used in synthesis, as previously stated, can come from a variety of theories and social science disciplines. Even in synthesizing knowledge about selected dimensions of administration pertinent social science content is dispersed in a variety of journals and publications. It is not as ordered as discipline-based knowledge. Consequently, the content cannot be as focused as in programs for preparing basic-oriented researchers. This means that in programs for synthesizers, there is a need for greater flexibility in the search for and selection of social science content.

Programs for preparing product-oriented developers should involve the study of many variables and a range of social science content selected from different disciplines. Theories designed to illuminate specific variables bearing upon problems and to provide clues about needed solutions to these problems are especially pertinent. Since there can be substantial variations in problems chosen for development study and in the content judged to be relevant to chosen areas of study, greater flexibility is needed in content selection and use in programs for preparing developers than in programs for preparing basic researchers. On the other hand, the number of variables and the range of content would not be as great for developers as for administrators because of the limited number of problem areas dealt with in differentiated programs for developers. It follows, then, that the need for flexibility in these programs would not be as great as in programs for administrators.

Social Sciences in Field Settings

The application of social science content in field settings during preparation should vary for prospective administrators, researchers, synthesizers, and developers. One aspect of variance in the different specializations has to do with the nature and scope of the field settings within which social science content is applied during preparation. For reasons already expressed, the scope of field settings for administrators is greater than for other specialists in educational administration. Not only can applications be made to a great number and variety of decisions within school districts during administrator preparation, but increasingly, field experience and internships for administrators are involving work in state and federal education agencies, community agencies external to schools, and government agencies.

The dimensions of the settings in which social science findings can be applied by prospective basic researchers are more limited in scope than are the settings for administrators. This is true because field work for researchers will tend to be circumscribed by the variables selected for use. Using the concept, "power structure," within political science to guide research, for example, limits the field of application. Field experiences for researchers would tend to be associated with research projects carried out by research centers, bureaus, research agencies, or independent researchers.

Applied work for developers is likely to be defined by intensive work in a few problem areas. Content from varied social science disciplines, for example, may be applied in field settings to such problem areas as those having to do with management information systems, training systems, or evaluation systems. Thus, field settings for a prospective developer is likely to be defined by a few problem areas. Thus, the scope of social science content used in field settings will likely be more proscribed for prospective developers than it will be for prospective administrators. Developers may achieve field experience in research and development centers, regional laboratories, Title III Centers, and profit and non-profit corporations.

A major field setting for the concept-oriented synthesizer is the library. He uses findings and concepts of many researchers and theorists whose ideas are found in the written word. While many of these researchers and theorists will themselves have acquired data from settings in which administrators work, the concept-oriented synthesizer does not need to repeat their work. He is one type of specialist in educational administration who does not need much immediate contact with administrative practice to pursue his career objectives.

Social Science Content Used Differs for Each Career

In programs for preparing administrators, developers, synthesizers, and researchers, the social science content selected and the uses to which it is put in culminating activities should be substantially different for different specialists. Traditionally, the doctoral dissertation has been *the* culminating activity in advanced programs to prepare personnel in educational administration. This activity was borrowed in the early part of this century from the larger university community where it has long helped scholars to become more effective researchers. In theory, the dissertation, as originally conceived, was designed to promote "original" research on the part of those completing doctoral programs. The doctoral dissertation, then, is especially relevant as a culminating activity for prospective basic researchers in educational administration. Within the context of the current discussion, this culminating activity for researchers not only needs to be continued but to be improved. One way of improving basic research in educational administration is to ensure that those pursuing doctoral dissertations have an intensive grounding in social science concepts and modes of inquiry in a specific discipline *before* undertaking the dissertation. The test of a dissertation for researchers should be (1) whether or not new knowledge and/or bases for new knowledge are attained, and (2) whether or not persons carrying through dissertations achieve needed research skills, understandings, and attitudes which can continue to be used in the study of educational administration.

The dissertation can also serve in the preparation of concepts-oriented synthesizers. However, its purpose for synthesizers should be that of helping them to acquire skills associated with identifying, mastering, and synthesizing existing knowledge in contrast to creating new knowledge. It should produce larger meanings from varied specialized and fragmented research efforts. These meanings could be generated from research and concepts within a specific social science discipline or from research and concepts which transcend any given discipline. Sources of data would be limited to recorded reports of research and conceptualization.

The doctoral dissertation, as traditionally conceived, does not provide the most appropriate culminating activity for either the administrator or the developer, because it is designed to advance research, rather than administration and development. Consequently, different culminating activities in preparatory programs are needed which are designed to advance effective decision making in administration and invention in development. In such culminating activities, written reports might be involved but the form, purposes, and criteria for evaluating the activities should be different from those associated with dissertations, as traditionally defined.

More specifically, the culminating activities for developers should facilitate the use of social science and other content to define and invent solutions to significant problems in educational administration. Thus, the focus should be on affording opportunities to learn development rather than knowledge advancement skills. The scope and specific purpose of a culminating activity should vary depending upon the nature and difficulty of the development problems addressed. In a problem area such as administrator evaluation, a central purpose might simply be that of identifying and describing precisely some targets where developmental work might fruitfully be undertaken. In a more limited area, such as that of developing training materials to prepare principals in selected aspects of planning, candidates might conceptualize a training system and develop prototype materials basic to the system. In both cases or in others that could be suggested, the test would be whether or not prospective developers actually achieved or learned better how to achieve more fruitful definitions of development problems and/or solutions to them. Written reports undoubtedly could be useful in illuminating the process of development, but the quality of the products themselves (e.g., prototype training materials) would constitute the test for evaluating the success of culminating activities.

The doctoral dissertation, as it is used in knowledge advancement, seems particularly inappropriate as a culminating activity in programs designed to prepare administrators. Rather, activities are needed which respect both the action orientation of administration and the need for strengthening action through informed decision making. One type of culminating activity, for example, might be that of having prospective administrators work for a year in a specific school district where the design of an action program and its legitimation for implementation would be the major activity. Criteria for evaluating such an action program might include the potential of an action program for actually being implemented, its capacity for improving education, administration, or leadership in the district in question, and the degree to which it has been shaped by social science and other relevant knowledge.

Another type of culminating activity could be more broadly based than a specific action plan. A broadly based activity, for example, could be achieved within the context of an internship experience involving a range of administrative decisions over time, and accompanied by seminars and guided readings of social science and other references. A major purpose of the seminar could be that of diagnosing and evaluating selected administrative decisions in which interns participated. Social science and other content could be introduced into the discussions in order to extend understandings of the processes and consequences of decisions. Seminars could be supplemented by guided reading designed to shed light upon the decision process generally; upon specific substantive issues involved in decision making; and upon specific dimensions of administrative and organizational behavior. The tests of such a broadly based activity would be found in the extent to which decision making on the part of interns was changed and the quality of insights achieved through diagnosis and study was improved.

Programs Must Insure Understanding

Programs, while concentrating upon providing differentiated learning experiences for administrators, developers, synthesizers, and researchers, should also help ensure that specialists obtain needed common understandings of social science and other content during preparation. While developers, administrators, synthesizers, and researchers perform differing functions designed to achieve dissimilar purposes in diverse settings, they are all part of the larger complex of educational administration. Since these various specialists are part of a larger professional field, they will need to communicate with and to understand one another throughout their careers. Therefore, preparatory programs should be concerned with cementing effective professional relationships and with establishing needed bonds between and among administrators, synthesizers, researchers, and developers.

One way of developing bonds among those pursuing differing specialized careers in educational administration is to ensure that they have common opportunities for exploring the purposes of education, including the relationships between educational purposes and societal needs. Through such study, which might take place in the earlier phases of preparation programs, specialists can be helped to see the larger ends of education and how their own unique outputs can contribute to and be related to these ends. Social science content can illuminate societal needs and provide bases for exploring relationships between these needs and the purposes of educational institutions.

Another approach to the attainment of common bonds is represented in learning situations in which researchers, developers, synthesizers, and administrators seek to understand and appreciate one another's respective roles, how these roles can complement and support one another, and how they can mutually contribute to the advancement of education. Such understandings can be developed in a variety of ways: the sharing of experience and the mutual analysis of social science concepts; the joint addressing of phenomena in simulated and real administration situations from the perspective of differing roles and social science perspectives; interaction between and among those pursuing different roles on specific problems of inquiry, synthesis, invention, or decision making; and examining and jointly discussing formal descriptions of research, development, synthesis, and administration roles and how these roles can be affected by insights gained from the social sciences.

SUMMARY

This chapter has set forth guidelines for those interested in selecting social science content in differentiated programs to prepare the following specialists in educational administration: basic researchers, concept-oriented synthesizers, product-oriented developers, and general administrators. Other specialists in educational administration have been identified and briefly described, including practice-oriented researchers, practice-oriented synthesizers, idea-oriented developers, and special administrators; however, since the purpose of the chapter was to be illustrative, rather than comprehensive, guidelines for selecting social science content in differentiated programs to prepare these latter specialists have not been presented.

The guidelines presented were derived from several basic assumptions. A fundamental assumption is that basic researchers, concept-oriented synthesizers, product-oriented developers, and general administrators perform different functions to achieve dissimilar purposes in diverse settings. A second major assumption is that different competencies are required to perform differing specialized functions in differing settings. Finally, it is maintained that programs for different specialists in administration need to be designed in ways which will enable them to achieve competencies unique to their respective specializations. The guidelines are derived from conceptualizations of ideal types in which differences between and among the various specialists are treated. While it is assumed that specialists should have common learning experiences during the first year of their preparation, it is argued that there should be substantial differences in the social science content selected and used in later stages of their preparation. Guidelines are developed for selecting social science content in differentiated programs to prepare diverse specialists. These guidelines relate to differing instructional purposes, concepts of relevance, field experience including internships, culminating activities, and other aspects of preparation.

The substance of the chapter may be summarized in still another way by illustrating content emphases in programs to prepare differing specialists. The illustrations to follow assume that there should be a three-year period of preparation for specialists in educational administration and that the last two years should be substantially differentiated.

Assuming an individual wanted to prepare for a career as a basic-oriented researcher in the economics of education, what kinds of social science content might be incorporated into his program during the last two years of preparation? First, his program would have a strong base in the discipline of economics. In addition to introductory courses, he might study micro-economic theory, macro-economic theory, statistical theory, urban economic growth, the economics of poverty, the financing of urban government, economics of education, school finance, school plant planning, and business management, for example. Discipline-based relevance, in other words, would have a strong influence on decisions about content.

Since the prospective basic researcher would concentrate upon the study of the economics of education, his internship desirably would be with a leading researcher in the economics of education. His culminating activity should be a dissertation designed to advance knowledge in a chosen problem area directly related to the economics of education. The study should be a rigorous one informed by depth knowledge of the concepts and modes of inquiry in economics.

If a person wanted to prepare to specialize in concept-oriented synthesis, what social science content might be incorporated into his program? First, it seems clear that theory based concept of relevance would strongly influence decisions about content in his program. After determining an area of study in which he wanted to concentrate, he would undoubtedly draw from a number of social science disciplines for content. Let us assume, for example, that he was interested in synthesis related to communication processes and structures in organizations. There would be various disciplines from which he could draw. He might, for example, study references in social psychology, sociology, and political science, as well as varied studies in educational administration. As a prospective synthesizer, he would be seeking to understand a range of concepts and to develop skills in the integration of them. He might well work under the tutelage of persons who had demonstrated skills in synthesis. His culminating activity would likely be a dissertation in which he worked in some defined area of administration to achieve new meanings and newly organized bodies of knowledge.

What about social science content for those preparing to become product-oriented developers? Let us assume, for example, a person was interested in the design of more effective management information systems. His objectives would be to master pertinent literature and to understand information problems for which better systems were needed. The literature would go beyond social science disciplines to encompass such subjects as management science, games and decision strategy, accounting for decision making and control, management information systems, computer organization, computer-based information systems, systems programming, data structures, administrative management and systems analysis, and computer programming languages. At the same time, he might study the sociology of organization, the social psychology of groups, and other concepts from the social sciences. The area development would be a major criterion for content selection.

His field or internship experiences would be oriented to the actual study of management information problems and needs in a number of districts. He should have experience during his preparations with those who have demonstrated effective developmental work, and his culminating activity might very well be that of designing a prototype information system or subsystem.

What social science content should be incorporated into programs for a general administrator? The concept of problem-based relevance would strongly shape decisions about content in programs for the general administrator. If one of the problems chosen for study, for example, was the general area of education and race, social science concepts illuminating racial attitudes in America, the psychology of human relations, intergroup conflict and prejudice would be relevant. If the problem to be studied had to do with institutional change, then social science content on bureaucracy, diffusion theory, and attitude information would be pertinent. Clearly, a range of problems could be used for selecting content. In addition, special syntheses achieved by both concept-oriented and practice-oriented synthesizers could be incorporated into programs.

The field experience should involve problems and conditions experienced by general administrators in educational institutions and by related leaders in communities. The culminating activity might well be an internship over an extended period of time supplemented by careful independent study designed to enable the prospective administrator to understand effective organizational performance. He should have experience with outstanding administrators and practice-oriented synthesizers during his culminating work.

FOOTNOTES

1. John Morgan. *A Discourse Upon the Institutions of the Medical Schools in America* (Baltimore: The Johns Hopkins Press, 1937).

2. For a discussion of the growth of research and development in medicine and its impact, see George Miller, "The Professorship in Medicine" in *The Professorship in Educational Administration,* eds. Donald Willower and Jack Culbertson (Columbus, Ohio: The University Council for Educational Administration and The College of Education, the Pennsylvania State University, 1964).

3. Other specializations could be treated as, for example, clinical applications of knowledge and the dissemination of knowledge.

4. Harvey C. Lehman, *Age and Achievement* (Princeton: Princeton University Press, 1953), p. 117.

5. For an insightful discussion of educational development, see Richard Schutz, "The Nature of Educational Development," *Journal of Research and Development in Education* 3, 2 (Winter 1971) : 39-62.

6. Joseph Schwab has estimated that there are 50,000 kinds of problems facing educational administrators, and he maintains that most of them interact with one another. See Joseph Schwab, "The Professorship in Educational Administration, Theory-Art Practice" in *Professorship in Administration,* eds. Willower and Culbertson, p. 54.

7. For a recent analysis of goals associated with administration, see Jack Culbertson et al., *Preparing Educational Leaders for the Seventies* (Final Report, Project No. 8-0230, Grant No. OEG-0-8-080230-2695 [010] Columbus, Ohio: The University Council for Educational Administration, 1969).

14

Using Social Scientific Concepts in the Preparation of Educational Administrators

Keith Goldhammer

THE SOCIAL SCIENCES AND EDUCATIONAL ADMINISTRATION

Education has long been plagued with the idea that knowledge is an end in itself and has no other necessary purpose for being. This concept was readily seized by the medieval scientists who thought they had a sound basis for escaping persecution for what might be their heretical discoveries. It has been perpetuated by savants throughout all ages to protect them against the prejudices arising from conservative, fundamentalist, and anti-intellectual thought. It has served scholars well and has probably enabled scientific advances in knowledge which an inelastic society would have proscribed.

Unfortunately, this concept has also been used within the modern university as a means of avoiding accountability and escaping the necessity for building relevance into the curriculum. When professors of educational administration began to discover the pertinence of the social and behavioral sciences for the preparation of educational administrators, they had two alternatives from which to select their instructional strategy. Either they could send their students to the social scientists for instruction in the basic content of the social sciences, or they could develop some competence in the social sciences on their own and relate their knowledge of the content to the basic problems of educational administration. Both tracks have been followed, but with growing awareness that it is increasingly difficult to get educational and administrative relevance from the social scientists, and that professors of educational administration are easily seduced into the academic reward system of the university, which places high prestige upon indifferent, highly theoretical, fundamental research while it is supercilious to that research and conceptualization which is professionally practical and relevant to field problems.

Industry discovered that academic science departments could not be held accountable for the practical application of their research, so they encouraged and frequently supported schools of engineering which would develop the findings of fundamental research into action strategies or systems which would be relevant to industrial needs. The chemical engineer is no less a chemist than his academic department counterpart. But to survive, he has to be pragmatic in his applications of knowledge. A similar concern appears to be only slowly developing in the field of educational administration. Professors of educational administration have become increasingly concerned about the study of administration, which is certainly essential. However, the study of administration is a social scientific endeavor, while the application of the knowledge gained to the realistic problems confronted by school administrators is an essential professional activity sorely needed if educational administrators are to become increasingly competent to deal with the complex problems of schools in contemporary society.

The social sciences have become increasingly research oriented, and courses in the various fields have come to emphasize a research approach to the more effective handling of conceptual and theoretical problems. They are designed primarily to train students as social scientists. Many students as administrators-in-training have discovered that this training is to a large degree dysfunctional for preparation as administrators — a fact which may account for the large number of graduate students in administration who disdain returning to the field of practice after the completion of their graduate training. One reason for this is that the scientist avoids ambiguity and seeks to deal with precise information so he can draw his conclusions with as much statistical precision as possible.

The administrator, on the other hand, constantly deals with ambiguous and problematical situations, in which it is impossible statistically to determine the probabilities for securing the consequences he desires. The scientist views the world as ordered, structured, reducible to laws which define the immutable motion of phenomena. The administrator, too, hopefully deals with a structured universe, but he recognizes that human situations are not reducible to laws which specifically define the probabilities for securing desired consequences. The raw data with which the school administrator deals are data about people as individuals and in groups. The behavior of an individual is idiosyncratic even if one can predict the consequences of a group action with a fair degree of reliability. The administrator does not have at his command the precision tools with which he can accurately and reliably predict the consequences of the decisions which he makes relative to the solution of specific problems. Not only does he have to formulate his decisions without these precise tools, but the data which may be required to make adequate predictions may not always be available. Consequently, practically all decisions on critical problems made by administrators are high-risk decisions based upon strategies which have unknown probabilities for success.

The essential point of concern here is that the administrator operates in an entirely different kind of intellectual realm than does the scientist. The scientist needs a terminology and a conceptual base that is heuristic. Each step that he takes in seeking to understand the variables pertinent to a problem is also a step toward the identification of new problems and new theoretical interpretations. The scientist never solves a problem; he opens up new means for being able to ask more sophisticated questions or to provide a more complete theoretical understanding of them. As a scientist, he is not seeking to gain control over problems of his field; he is seeking to gain more complete understanding as a means of filling in the missing pieces in the theoretical puzzle.

The administrator, on the other hand, is constantly attempting to find closure on his problems. His goal is not so much to understand the nature of the interrelationships of phenomena as it is to maintain a social stability that will enable the work of his organization to proceed without disruption. In effect, the administrator uses the content of the social sciences in a manner never intended by the social scientists and in some ways which might be conceived as a contamination of the scientists' efforts. This may be one reason why the scientist and the administrator are so frequently in conflict.

The purposes for including social scientific content in the curriculum of administrators-in-training are two-fold. First, to provide the administrator with a language and a set of concepts through which he can identify the critical factors with which he must deal in any situation. An unsophisticated administrator may hold to the position that birds of a feather stick together. Knowing this, he does not necessarily have a means for identifying potential sources of conflict with respect to given school issues either inside of the school system or in the community of which it is a part. However, if he has studied social psychology and is acquainted with reference group theory, he will know the bases upon which individuals find anchorings in specific reference groups and ideologies, and he will have a means for identifying the cohesiveness of various groups and the degree of identification of individuals with various groups which might be facilitators or barriers to the development of adequate school policies.

But mere knowledge of a concept and the ability to distinguish the pertinent elements associated with any kinds of organizational or social phenomena does not necessarily give the administrator-in-training the power to deal effectively with the problems when they occur in his own school. The administrator must be able to deal *diagnostically* with the school organization and the community relations which involve the schools. He must not only know the concepts of the social sciences which are pertinent in the analysis of given situations, but he must also know how he can use these concepts to identify both the healthy and the pathological functioning of the organization or the community. Hence, to increase his power to assess what needs to be done to relieve pathological conditions, remove constraints to the healthy functioning of his organization, or, in other ways, to improve the health of his organization; he must have an excellent grasp on social science concepts.

In other words, the social scientific content of the administrative preparation program should provide a basis for clinical diagnosis and treatment of organizational pathologies. Lawrence J. Henderson once attempted to analyze how the physician applied scientific knowledge about the human organism to the identification and treatment of human disease. He said that the physician must have three things as a skilled clinician: first, *an intimate, habitual, intuitive familiarity with the subject matter* which is pertinent to his area of operations; second, *systematic knowledge about his field of endeavor*; and, third, *an effective way of thinking about the subject matter of his field.* He said that the intuitive familiarity was not sufficient in itself, but it had to embrace systematic knowledge, as a conceptual means for dealing with both his knowledge and the professional problems to which that knowledge is to be applied.

From this point of view, the clinical approach to the study of administrative problems will involve several steps:

1. The administrator must be able to identify that data which he believes are necessary and pertinent for his understanding the situation and developing both an adequate diagnosis of it and a

strategy which will lead to the solution of the problem. In identifying the data which he needs, the administrator makes a preliminary or hypothetical diagnosis of the situation based upon his conceptualization of what he thinks is involved.

2. The administrator must secure the data which he needs, while at the same time he searches for additional information which will enable him to determine the validity of his hypotheses relative to the situation or to discard his preliminary hypotheses for those which are more consistently related to the data as they emerge.

3. The administrator then arranges or organizes the data in accordance with a conceptual model which gives him the power to interpret their significance with respect to the problem.

4. At this stage, it is then possible to bring to bear basic concepts, laws, understandings, theories which appear to be pertinent in the analysis and interpretation of the data at hand. In other words, the administrator must call up any knowledge which he has about these data and their interrelationships within his conceptual scheme which will help him to interpret their significance and arrive at conclusions which will enable him to deal effectively with the situation.

5. At this point, it is possible to develop at least a tentative diagnosis of the situation. The administrator, in effect, asks to what extent he sees malfunctioning of the organization or of relationships that have produced the problem and how these malfunctions are related to the continuing, healthy functioning of the organization. Now the administrator relies heavily upon his systematic knowledge of school organizations, of social phenomena, and of the conceptual means through which this knowledge can be effectively related to the problems which he must solve.

6. On the basis of this knowledge and careful diagnosis of the situation, the administrator then attempts to synthesize his analysis based upon his knowledge and experience, or, as Henderson stated it, his intimate, intuitive familiarity to develop a strategy or prescription of how he can deal effectively with the problem. He should be aware that at this stage of the clinical analysis he goes beyond the state of knowledge and actually makes his judgment to act on the basis of both that knowledge and his intuitive familiarity.

7. The pragmatic administrator will be concerned about taking the slightest risks possible in the action gambles in which he is engaged. He, therefore, will attempt to assess the potential consequences of his decision, weighing against this decision other possible

remedies and their potential consequences. In the final analysis, he will select that strategy which appears to have the most desirable consequences for the school organization, as well as that strategy which can produce the desired consequences most expeditiously, effectively, and economically.

The intuitive familiarity of the administrator for dealing with the problems of the school organization will be developed through experience and association with other administrators who share their experiences with him. For many situations, the administrator will be fairly secure in dealing with his problems on the basis of his experiences. For the most critical situations, however, an individual's experiences alone will be a very unsatisfactory guide. The knowledge of organizational and societal dynamics which the administrator will need both to test his experience and to help him develop an adequate conceptual base beyond what he has actually personally viewed can be achieved only through a careful study of selected social scientific content. The fields of the social sciences are too broad for the administrator to study all of them with the degree of depth and sophistication he needs. Consequently, very careful selection of content is essential to give him the basis for having some fundamental knowledge which can be used effectively in his clinical diagnoses and for having enough sophistication in the use of social scientific literature that, when confronted with specific issues, he can explore the social scientific literature further to provide for his needs.

SOCIAL SCIENCES IN THE PREPARATION OF EDUCATIONAL ADMINISTRATORS

The basic proposition upon which the foregoing discussion is based is that the administrator needs a sound basis upon which he can do two related things. First, he must be able to have the knowledge and skills necessary to determine the basis upon which organizational processes are either functional or dysfunctional for the accomplishment of the organizational objectives. Second, he must have the knowledge and skills for being able to predict with a high degree of accuracy the consequences of prescriptions (strategies) that he might apply to relieve organizational dysfunctions and return the institution to a state of healthy or normal functioning, maximizing to the extent possible the effectiveness of the utilization of the scarce resources allocated to it. An administrator's ability to manage an organization successfully will depend upon the degree to which he selects appropriate strategies of action which accomplish their major purposes. An essential aspect of strategy development is the selection of strategies that are appropriate to the particular problem at hand and which secure the desired consequences.

The social sciences have four basic contributions to make to the administrator for the achievement of these ends. *First,* the social sciences will provide terms and concepts which enable the administrator to identify phenomena with which he must deal. As in all learning, terms and concepts are essential for being able to identify elements, to specify the exact characteristics of elements so as to distinguish them from other elements, and to provide a shorthand or formulary basis for dealing with complicated situations which are characterized by complex interrelationships of various factors. Many old-time administrators could go into lengthy discussions about the people within their school districts who could block or facilitate the achieving of specific objectives. The concept of power structure enables administrators to deal more economically with the complexity of factors associated with gaining public support for essential school programs.

Second, the administrator needs to have knowledge of the patterns involved in human and group response to various types of situations, as well as to administrative strategies and policies. Although the regularities in social events are not as discretely identified as regularities in natural or physical events, nevertheless social scientists have been able to detect a number of characteristic patterns in which individuals and groups react. Although one cannot assume the finite generalizability of these patterns to a precise situation, they are a far better basis of prediction than the less exact and more erratic intuitive familiarity of the administrator. The research and theory on organizational change, for example, provides a fairly sound basis upon which the administrator can make his decisions and does not leave him completely helpless in predicting the potential for success of the change strategies that he may wish to employ.

Third, the administrator needs to have, at hand, knowledge of the dynamics of various types of organizational, societal, and group situations and processes that are related to organizational dynamics. As the physiologists have been able to identify the structure and function of various organs within the living body, so too, the organizational scholars have been able to identify the ways various types of organizational structures, societal structures, and group processes function when particular types of dilemmas occur. Knowledge of the related literature will give the administrator a better basis for making his judgments, predicting consequences, and selecting strategies than relying on his instincts and prejudgments of the situation.

Fourth, social sciences can help the administrator identify significant factors which are involved in various types of organizational situations, thereby calling his attention to those particular elements within structures and processes of the organization with which he has to be concerned in order to deal effectively with specific kinds of problems. In identifying elements pertinent to various social processes, the social scientist has provided a strong basis for developing typologies of functional and pathological conditions in various organizational processes. Knowledge of these elements is fundamental to the administrator.

Concepts of the Social Sciences Particularly Relevant to Administrators

The list of concepts particularly relevant to school administrators is almost endless. They can be derived from all of the fields of the social and behavioral sciences, and it would be impossible to state which ones are more important to a school administrator than others. Obviously, to the administrator faced with a community upheaval involving various organized dissident groups, the knowledge of community structures and processes is of utmost importance. It is unlikely that any administrator will complete his career without having to deal with some type of community problems. In the large urban centers, knowledge of the problems of social class and differentiated social norms and values which give rise to conflictual situations is extremely important. In many rural communities, however, there is still a social homogenization which does not necessitate that the administrator spend a great deal of his time in the vortex between differentiated social values as related to the public schools. Other factors of community life must be understood. It is also unlikely that an administrator will complete his career without having to concern himself with the problems of conflict and conflict management within the organization. However, there may be, at times, problems within his organization which are far more oppressive and which arise from less significant and overwhelming social scientific constructs. The problem for the administrator is to have access to the type of social scientific knowledge that he needs at the particular time that a critical concern confronts his organization. Some careful prediction of what administrators need must be made. However, the initial or pre-service training program cannot possibly include everything which may confront the administrator in the course of his immediate or future career.

After two decades of concern about the social sciences in relationship to educational administration, it seems as though some of the ingredients of the initial thrust are still pertinent. The administrator-in-training should certainly be exposed to the basic conceptual structures involved in each of the social and behavioral sciences. He should have the familiarity with the language employed by the various disciplines and the sources through which the literature of the social and behavioral sciences can be explored, so that he can find the information or the concepts that are most relevant to him. For the scholar, the organizing of these materials around the various traditional disciplinary segments of the behavioral and social sciences seems most advisable, but for the administrator who must use these concepts to develop diagnoses of malfunctioning and appropriate strategies of action, social scientific concepts can more realistically be organized about an analysis of organizational structures, characteristics, and processes. It is the organization that provides the central focus for the administrator, and social scientific content becomes pertinent to the extent that it relates to these characteristics of healthy functioning of the organization. For the administrator, economics is not an end in itself but rather provides a conceptual basis through which the administrator gains power both to assess organizational functioning and to predict the consequences of his strategies. The traditional social scientific courses are not as adequate for the administrator as are experiences through which an administrator comes to use the concepts of the disciplines for furthering his diagnostic insights. The theoretical knowledge of the social sciences for the administrator is an aid toward organizational analysis, and a system must be devised for his being able to use such knowledge as a tool toward clinical diagnosis, rather than as a means toward obtaining further, more sophisticated, and more refined knowledge about the phenomenon under consideration. In educational psychology, we learn that transfer of training takes place when it is specifically sought in the teaching situation. The ability to apply social scientific knowledge will be achieved, accordingly, to the extent that the preparatory program is specifically oriented toward this end.

The issue immediately arises as to how the administrator learns to use social scientific research and concepts in his clinical diagnosis of organization problems. We would not think of eliminating clinical experiences in the preparation of physicians, dentists, teachers, or guidance workers. It is no less important that we provide clinical experiences for individuals who will become administrators, both to secure the critical insights (or intuitive familiarity) which administrators need and to establish the patterns through which they can apply their knowledge about organizational dynamics to the concrete types of problems which they will confront as administrators.

Clinical experiences in educational administration, it seems to me, can be secured in three ways. The first is to build a significant amount of the work in the pre-service program around actual problems in educational administration. Case studies have proven to be very vital means of building both the critical insights and experience in the application of knowledge to various fields including educational administration. The case problems approach should be valuable in helping the administrator deal realistically with a wide variety of problems in the various components of the field of educational administration, providing that the structure of analysis of the cases is systematically developed to insure that pertinent data will be identified and appropriate concepts will be applied to the case as the administrator is helped to develop realistic strategies for dealing with the problems involved. The didactic instruction in the fundamentals of administration should be accompanied with the use of case materials which help the administrator-in-training perceive the relevance of the principles involved.

A second method for providing clinical experiences in the preparation program is to employ simulated situations which require the administrator-in-training to react and to make diagnoses which lead to his devising appropriate strategies. Simulated situations provide a means for placing the student in a relatively non-stressful but challenging position where he has pertinent knowledge about an organization and its operations, which necessitates that he make a diagnosis of dysfunctional or pathological conditions, apply his knowledge for the development of appropriate strategies, and, at least theoretically, determine the consequences of his interventions. Desirably, through computerized simulation, it may become possible to produce the consequences of his decisions so that the whole chain of administrative events arising from administrative action may be secured within the relative security and aseptic conditions of the laboratory.

The third method for developing the clinical experiences is to place the candidates in situations where they have an opportunity under expert guidance to make actual clinical diagnoses of live problems and to suggest the strategies that can be most appropriately employed to relieve dysfunctionality or achieve a higher level of organizational health. This means that the more advanced students must be involved for more extended periods of time in actual field situations where they must collect the data, develop hypotheses, make the necessary diagnostic analyses, and be accountable for the consequences which they secure.

There are particularly five elements that must be viewed by the diagnostician as he reviews case data and attempts to secure closure upon critical educational problems. These five elements suggest the broad areas around which social scientific content can be organized.

First, he must focus his attention upon people. The attitudes, feelings, aspirations, and motivations which people bring to an organizational problem comprise the basic data relevant to the problems or the conflictual situations in organizations. In focusing upon people, the administrator must be able to determine the unique or idiosyncratic characteristics of human beings as they perform their various functions. He must be able to determine whether or not behaviors are expected, eccentric, or anomalistic when confronted with the precise situations which are involved. The psychology of human interaction, the social psychology of individuals within groups, value system, and codes of behavior both personal and social are all relevant factors that must be explored in being able to diagnose and understand the human components of organizational problems.

Second, the diagnostician must focus attention upon ideological systems which have a bearing upon the problem. Although in his study of people who are involved the analyst will be concerned with their values and attitudes, he must also formulate his analysis with reference to how these values and attitudes relate to larger ideological movements. The individual today is the target of many diverse communications and many groups for a variety of reasons are attempting to capture the minds of the populace. Structures of relationships and events can be completely understood only when the broader involvements of people in social and ideological movements are understood.

Third, the diagnostician must focus upon the structure, both formal and informal, of relationships in which the problem occurred.

Human and social events do not take place in a vacuum. They take place under the structural arrangements which define the zones of tolerance for various kinds of behaviors or responses and include the structure of authority and control relationships, as well as the definitions for expectations for role performance of individuals. In effect, one cannot define idosyncratic or anomalous behavior unless he has viewed the structure adequately to determine that which is legitimated, both formally and informally, within the organization.

Fourth, the diagnostician must focus upon the actual ecological and social situations in which the case exists. As human beings differ, no two social situations are ever exactly alike. Before one can actually diagnose concretely for the immediate situation, he must be able to identify the actual ecological conditions in which it arises, its unique components, and how it may be similar to or unlike characteristics of other situations with which the individual may be familiar or in which some of the basic, pertinent knowledge has been secured. Each definition of the situation will present the particularized constraints, imperatives, or potentials within the given field of operations with which the diagnostician must be familiar.

Fifth, the diagnostician must concentrate attention upon particular events as they emerge from the patterns of human interactions within the structure and the specific situation in which this structure of relationships has taken place. The events constitute the manifestation of both the healthy and dysfunctional operations of the school organization. They may be characterized as anticipated or as unanticipated events. They will be anticipated to the extent that the analysis of the data which we collect about people, structure, and situations leads us to the conclusion that we could expect this event from the interrelationships involved. They will be unanticipated or anomalous to the extent that we could not predict them on the basis of the data available. When events are characterized as anticipated but a conflictual situation arises, the sources of the conflict should be readily identifiable and remediation strategies may also be clearly indicated. When, however, the events are unanticipated on the basis of the data at hand, it is clearly evident that either additional data must be obtained or the administrator must gamble on what he expects to be the sources for the unanticipated consequences. When critical problems arise, it is probably more likely that the administrator will be dealing with these unanticipated problems to a much greater extent than those that are anticipated, but it is also in dealing with these unanticipated problems that the particular skill of the administrator will be reflected.

These five elements — *people, ideological systems, structure, situation,* and *events* — provide a strong conceptual framework both for the organization of social scientific concepts relevant to administrative problems and for providing a basis for the administrator's systematic ordering of knowledge and data in a fashion usable in the diagnosis of administrative problems. It is around these ingredients that a systematic curriculum for developing the knowledge and skills which administrators need can be established.

CONCLUSION

The main point which I have attempted to stress is that the content of the social sciences particularly relevant to the school administrator-in-training is that which helps him to develop the clinical insights that he needs for adequately diagnosing specific types of educational problems and devising appropriate strategies for dealing with them. The administrator in modern society can no longer realistically be viewed as the paternalistic boss who gives the orders and expects his servants to carry them out. The administrator today must be viewed more as the facilitator of the processes through which the organization achieves its goals and the evaluator of the degree of effectiveness through which the various components of the organization operate. To this extent, his diagnostic or evaluative skill, his skill as a strategist, and his skill in applying knowledge of human and group processes to the particular situation in which he is involved is a key factor in his professional success.

SELECTED REFERENCES

Bennis, Warren G. et al., eds. *The Planning of Change.* New York: Holt, Rinehart & Winston, 1969.

Cabot, Hugh and Joseph A. Kahl. *Human Relations: Concepts and Cases in Concrete Social Science.* Cambridge: Harvard University Press, 1953.

Charters, W.W. et al. *Perspectives on Educational Administration and the Behavioral Sciences.* Eugene, Oregon: Center for the Advanced Study of Educational Administration, University of Oregon, 1965.

Culbertson, Jack A. et al. *Administrative Relationships: A Casebook.* Englewood Cliffs, N.J.: Prentice-Hall, 1960.

Downey, Lawrence W. and Frederick Enns. *The Social Sciences and Educational Administration.* Edmonton, Oregon: University of Alberta, and The University Council for Educational Administration, 1963.

Eidell, Terry L. and Joanne M. Kitchell, eds. *Knowledge Production and Utilization in Educational Administration.* Eugene, Oregon: University of Oregon, 1968.

Goldhammer, Keith et al. *The Social Sciences and the Preparation of Educational Administrators.* Columbus, Ohio: University Council for Educational Administration, 1963.

Goldhammer, Keith et al. *Issues and Problems in Contemporary Educational Administration.* Eugene, Oregon: Center for the Advanced Study of Educational Administration, University of Oregon, 1967.

Gouldner, Alvin W. and S.M. Miller. *Explorations in Applied Social Science.* New York: The Free Press, 1965.

Lazarsfeld, Paul F. et al. *The Uses of Sociology.* New York: Basic Books, 1967.

Lee, Alfred McClung. "The Clinical Study of Society." *American Sociological Review* 20 (December 1955):648–753.

Sargent, Cyril G. and Eugene Belisle. *Educational Administration: Cases and Concepts.* Boston: Houghton Mifflin, 1955.

Tope, Donald E. *A Forward Look — The Preparation of School Administrators.* Eugene, Oregon: Bureau of Educational Research, University of Oregon, 1960.

Tope, Donald E. *The Social Sciences View School Administration.* Englewood Cliffs, N.J.: Prentice-Hall, 1965.

15

Social Science Disciplines and Content Selection

William A. Harrison, Jr.

This chapter is concerned with whether the social science disciplines themselves can provide criteria for determining which knowledge is important for the preparation of educational administrators.

Although social scientists and educational administrators have drawn upon each other's fields for many years, relations between the two types of practitioners have not always been harmonious. To social scientists, much of the writing on educational administration has seemed unduly polemical, prescriptive, and lacking in theory. To educational administrators, many findings of social science have seemed vague, trivial, and of little practical value. To each field, the other has seemed overly jargonistic.

These divergent viewpoints no doubt reflect the different role expectations of the two fields, as reinforced by training, socialization, and experience. The social scientist seeks primarily to gain knowledge of aspects of the social environment; the administrator seeks primarily to act on and in that environment. The social scientist frequently resorts to higher levels of abstraction and technical language in search of explanatory power; the educational administrator needs to use low-level abstraction and everyday language in order to communicate with a variety of persons. For the social scientist, the prime constraints are the demands of scientific rigor. For the practicing administrator, they are the legal and political responsibility to act — frequently without authority commensurate with their responsibilities and almost always with less than complete information upon which to base their judgments.

Most scientific research in the administration of education falls into what political scientists call "policy" research, of which we can discover two types. One is done with the objective of deriving strategies for social intervention, that is, directing administrators and other political actors to do certain things in order to achieve certain results. The other informs us about the way some part of the world works but does not inform us about how to modify relations we discover. Administrators and politicians usually seek the former. If we provide them anything through scientific endeavors, it almost always fits into the latter category.

Small wonder, then, that many school administrators chafe at social science propositions and findings that are too abstract, untimely, and trivial to help them. Small wonder, too, that many social scientists chafe at school administrators who fail to fathom the nature of the scientists' work and fail to appreciate the seriousness of their purpose.

Probably the different perspectives and purposes of social science and educational administration make some degree of confusion among the practitioners inescapable. But if we are to bring more resources to bear upon the tasks of organizing, managing, and governing the public schools — and knowledge is one of the most crucial resources for this purpose — then further means will have to be found to improve these relationships. An important contribution to this end is the recognition, as Culbertson and Shibles point out in Chapter One, that the field of educational administration includes activities of research, synthesis of research findings, program development, and application of administrative knowledge. It is hoped that the relationships discussed in this chapter will also contribute to that end.

In this chapter, I will propose not so much a set of substantive criteria, as a *process* for selecting knowledge deemed appropriate by the social science disciplines. First, I will review some characteristics of the social science enterprise and the academic social science disciplines. Then, I will outline a matrix of relationships between social science and educational administration to illustrate several kinds of relevance beween the two fields and to suggest criteria for selecting social science knowledge for use in training school administrators.

WHAT IS SOCIAL SCIENCE?

The social sciences deal primarily with the behavior of man in his relation to his fellow men and the environment they share.[1] Basically, the method is to observe patterns in social life and then to identify the principles which determine these patterns. That is, social scientists seek to discover regularities in the human experience of "social life," in the mutual modification of human behavior. And then they seek to explain these regularities — to "explain all cases" — by finding a set of laws that, taken together, describe all cases of the phenomena observed.

There is some disagreement on the scope of the term, "social science."[2] Many people feel that, when applied to the non-social concerns of psychology, the term is something of a misnomer. For that reason, the term "behavioral science" has come into recent popularity. Behavioral science does have some advantages for this use, but it also has some distinct disadvantages as a generic term to replace social science. Insofar as it suggests that social scientists are interested in nothing but behavior, it is too narrow to be descriptive. To the extent that it suggests that the behavior of physical and organic entities is of prime interest to social scientists, it is too broad. There does not seem to be a fully satisfactory general term for the field. Therefore, for our discussion we shall stick to social science as the generic term but with the understanding that we are extending this designation to psychology.

Social science means both *process* and *product*.[3] It is similar in this respect to such terms as "swim," "education," and "educational administration," All refer to a certain activity or process and also to an outcome, eventuation, or end product of that process. As we shall see, both meanings of social science have relevance for both meanings of educational administration.

Social science as a process rests upon three major assumptions: First, that there exists a world beyond the senses; second, that this world is knowable by humanity through some process which allows communication of this knowledge; and third, that the results of interacting with that world (and thereby accumulating knowledge of it) is valuable.[4]

It is also understood that two norms underlie all social scientific procedures.[5] One is the norm of publicity; all operations must be open to review by other social scientists. The other is the norm of constant reversibility of decisions. No specific issue is ever closed once and for all.

Usually, the problems that social scientists inquire into grow out of change and resulting conflict. Scott Greer has identified three broad classes of such problematic situations: "Policy problems" are the problems of everyday life in the society, problems of practical urgency, whose resolutions "must be in empirically testable terms."

They grow out of value conflict, out of the disparity between what is and what is desired. The goal of the researcher or problem solver is to move actuality toward the ideal state of things. The salience of this class is clear, says Greer, ". . . in the general concern with social and clinical problems and the industries (social welfare, psychiatry) that have emerged to deal with them. Much of the public acceptance of the social sciences today comes from the average citizen's concern with poverty, race relations, mental illness, and crime."[6]

A second source of problems is social philosophy. Here the problem is to fit new experiences into the given context of the culture, to reconcile the conflict between an ideology and new experiences. The aim of the researcher or problem solver is to re-create an intellectual order, an integrated world view.

A third source of problems is generic to the scientific community or "discipline." These problems emerge from conflicts between existing theories, between theories and findings, and from gaps in empirical proof for accepted propositions. Here the researcher or problem solver seeks to "extend the theoretical structure in the light of new data which he has created through observation, and he tries to extend the meaning of the empirical known by the new theory he has created to accommodate the facts."[7]

The method of social science (as distinguished from its techniques of discovery) is essentially the same as that for any other science. The social scientist begins with a problem. The problem is conceptualized in such a way as to suggest a trial solution. (A "model" is constructed in the mind, one that places the problem in a larger frame of reference.) The trial solution is tested logically and empirically. The test results are then evaluated against what was expected. The test procedures are also evaluated to determine if they were a fair test of the hypothesis. Finally, the test results are used to extend or edit the theory. The revised frame of reference, in turn, gives birth to new problems for further investigation.[8]

Social science as a product is also similar to other sciences. The structural characteristics of a social science theory are the same as those of any other scientific theory: "a theory is a systematically related set of statements—including some lawlike generalizations—that is empirically testable."[9] To the extent that a theory has been fully articulated in some formulation, it will achieve an explicit deductive development and interrelationship of the statements it encompasses. Theories that are formulated as completely articulated deductive systems are sometimes referred to as "fully formulated."

If fully formulated theories abounded in social science, it would be a relatively simple matter to establish criteria for selection. We could simply begin with the fully formulated theories, since virtually all of social life can be considered within the possible purview of education and therefore of educational administration. Unfortunately, fully formulated theories are rare in science generally and, thus far, nonexistent in social science.

What is a Social Science Discipline?

Although the disciplines which form the basis for organizing much knowledge are labeled social sciences, they are not concerned exclusively with social science.[10] Typically, social scientific fields or disciplines begin with the identification and delineation of patterns or regularities among some concrete phenomena of interest to a scientist. Usually they are of practical interest to a good many others in the society as well. This initial identification and delineation of patterns is usually done in the everyday terminology of the larger society. Consequently, many of the early concepts in a discipline are apt to be essentially unanalyzed abstractions.

Once some patterns in social life have been discovered, the questions and explanations developed by social scientists can proceed in any direction. They may try to account for the *origins* of the patterned phenomena, for what *maintains* the patterns, or the *effects* of the regularities. They may draw upon concepts and knowledge at hand, or they may borrow formulations — concepts, models, modes of inquiry — from other fields. The result is likely to be an empirical science or field or discipline closely tied to everyday concerns and not delineated neatly by boundaries.

When a scientific field is theoretically delimited, the emphasis is upon its explanatory laws. In this book, knowledge organized in this fashion has been called theory-based.[11]

Disciplines, of course, are not organized solely according to theories. Although theoretically organized knowledge occasionally can be found within the confines of a single discipline, the disciplines resemble communities more than logical sets. They are groups of people identified by interests in some roughly common subject matter and some loosely common methods of study. The groups may be mutually exclusive, but their subject matters are not. If one were interested in the production and authoritative allocation of values for a society, for example, he might profitably look into university departments of economics, political science, sociology, and anthropology — all of which profess to hold these problems as more or less central concerns. So the boundary lines between the disciplines of social science are more than a little arbitrary, are frequently indistinct, and usually are more the products of historical accident and evolution than of any theoretically related set of categories.

Social science disciplines also differ from theory-based knowledge because their concerns go beyond empirical theory. Historically, the modern social sciences have evolved out of the classical discipline of social philosophy, which always encompassed questions of "what ought to be," as well as "what is." The social science disciplines retain something of this normative concern. This is most easily seen in an explicitly labeled subdiscipline, such as political philosophy or historical sociology. But vestiges remain in the self-conscious or unself-conscious choice of questions to investigate and in other activities. Social scientists are by no means agreed upon how to handle these normative concerns or in some cases whether they even exist. Typically, some of the greatest controversies in the disciplines turn precisely on questions of whose values and priorities are built into the analytic constructs and whether or not conscious advocacy of social values is proper behavior for members of the disciplines.

THE RELEVANCE OF SOCIAL SCIENCE KNOWLEDGE TO EDUCATIONAL ADMINISTRATION

The relationships between social science disciplines and educational administration are something more than simply the relationships of theory to practice or pure research to applied research. The question of relevance is complicated by multidimensional nature of the social science disciplines and the several types of activity included under the rubric of educational administration.

Nevertheless, if we view educational administration as a field which includes a range of activities — including research, synthesis of research findings, program development, and application of administrative knowledge — then we can recognize at least four ways in which social science disciplines have impact upon educational administration. Three of the ways were introduced by Culbertson and Shibles in the first chapter of this volume.

To review briefly, they suggested that concepts and modes of inquiry from given social science disciplines could be used to study "actual problems, conditions, and variables in school systems and their environment" in order to develop substructures of knowledge within the social science disciplines (i.e., "politics of education," and "economics of education"). "These substructures would have immediate relevance since they would be based upon actual research in educational systems or their environments." (See page 13.) The advantage of such substructures, it is argued, is that sets of concepts or theories developed in educational settings would better highlight significant causal relationships among decision variables facing educational administrators, helping them to see variables differently and to achieve better control over administrative and educational events.

A second view of discipline-based relevance involves establishing logical connections between social science content and specific dimenions of educational administration. The purpose is to sensitize administrators to environmental factors and relationships that will help them view more realistically and incisively the complex set of forces at work in their social environments.

The third view of discipline-based relevance centers on having administrators obtain a liberalizing education. This view includes two somewhat different concepts of relevance: (1) "exploring content from disciplines in relation to major societal problems," and (2) "intensive study of one discipline to develop a 'disciplined' way of thinking which can be applied generally by educational administrators in posts of leadership."

A fourth conception of relevance, I submit, inheres in the *interactive* relationship between the social science disciplines and educational administration. Since this characteristic has not been discussed earlier, it bears some exploration here.

Social science and educational administration are mutually interactive. The fields influence each other. Insight into this relationship can be gained from the important and persuasive treatise in the sociology of knowledge of Peter Berger and Thomas Luckmann.[12] Their treatise asserts that *all* knowledge, including our individual notions of self, are the products of social interaction. Our very notions of reality are influenced by our habituated ways of seeing and thinking about things, which in turn are approved or disapproved (all of our lives) by those with whom we come into contact. By the same process, we help shape the realities perceived by others. Thus, we gain and enforce expectations about the behavior of others and ourselves through social interaction. All knowledge—including scientific knowledge—is subject to continuing affirmation or negation as people interact with each other in the dialectic between nature and the socially constructed worlds of our experience.

In practice, the social science disciplines affect educational administration in a very fundamental way by altering the very conceptualization of the field. This has happened, for example, when economists introduced the concept of "education as investment," when sociologists portrayed schools as social systems and school systems as bureaucratic organizations, and when political scientists introduced the notion that policy formation and policy administration are not dichotomous but merely inseparable aspects of the same policy-making continuum.

For its part, educational administration affects the disciplines by feeding back reactions on the utility of their conceptualizations and by bringing new problems to the attention of social scientists. The controversy in recent years over decentralizing big-city school systems, for example, was generated out of the very urgent, practical desire to make complex systems more responsive to new needs and demands—albeit in this case primarily from the *clients* of educational administration, rather than from the administrators themselves.[13] Although social science concepts ("accountability," "community," and "responsiveness") were quickly conscripted by parties to the controversy—not necessarily in a very well-defined or accurate manner—the controversy itself did not stem from any new social science formulations.

As American society continues to change, social change itself being more and more a product of interaction among increasingly interdependent people, the relationship between social science and educational administration will continue to be dialectical, through the interactions of the two fields and their respective realities.

Finding New Criteria of Relevance

The discussion thus far has revealed that social science disciplines have several dimensions. They have substantive (or product) dimensions, procedural (or process) dimensions, and normative dimensions. Each of these have potential for knowledge useful in the preparation of school administrators.

The discussion has also revealed that the social science disciplines have impact upon educational administration in at least four ways: (1) in creating subdisciplines concerned with education, (2) in developing liberally educated persons for the profession, (3) in studying educational administration within applied settings, and (4) by entering into reciprocal processes of defining and confirming or denying alternative views of reality.

Therefore, the question of whether the social science disciplines can provide criteria for determining which knowledge is relevant

Table 1

Matrix of Possible Contributions of Social Science Disciplines to Educational Administrator Preparation Programs

| | Social Science/Educational Administration Relationships ("Ways of Conceiving Relevance") | | | |
	Liberalizing Education	Exchange	Establishing Logical Connections (with practical problems)	Developing a Substructure of Knowledge Within the Discipline
Substantive Dimension I: Theories	Heuristic guiding metaphors (institutionalization, authority, communication bureaucracy, leadership, socialization, attitudinal and belief-system change)	Heuristic guiding metaphors	Formulations that purport new conceptualizations of education or educational administration	Heuristic guiding metaphors
Substantive Dimension II: Findings	Findings bearing upon theoretical formulations Findings uncovering "problems" (social and attitudinal change)	Findings bearing upon theoretical formulations Findings uncovering "problems" (social and attitudinal change)	Findings bearing upon theoretical formulations Findings uncovering "problems" (social and attitudinal change)	Findings bearing upon theoretical formulations Findings uncovering "problems" (social and attitudinal change)

	Firm predictions of alternative futures	Firm Predictions of alternative futures	Firm predictions of alternative futures	Firm predictions of alternative futures
Procedural Dimensions:	Problem-solving ability (conceptualizing)	Scientific method	Scientific method (educational administration as a social science)	Levels of analysis Scientific method and research techniques
Normative Dimensions:	Purposes of educational administration	Purposes of educational administration	Normative implications of administrator practices	Changes in what administrators perceive as "right;" changes in what publics want and perceive as "right."

turns out to have a number of sides to it, primarily because of the different aspects of social science disciplines and the different purposes to which the knowledge may be put in training educational administrators.

All disciplines have some basic organizing questions and some methods or approaches for inquiring into these questions. Our problem is to find useful bases (not too broad and not too narrow) suggested by the disciplines themselves for choosing among these. For this purpose, it is useful to have a systematic framework to keep us clear about the various relationships and ensure that we examine as many aspects of relevance as possible. We can then explore each of the dimensions of social science activity—substantive, procedural, and normative—for contributions in each of the areas in which the social sciences have impact upon educational administration.

In Table 1, these elements are set into a matrix. At the top of the matrix are the four relationships or ways of conceiving relevance between the two fields. At the left are the dimensions of social science disciplines, with the substantive dimension split for clarity into a category emphasizing theoretical formulations and a category emphasizing research findings or empirical generalizations. The cells in the matrix represent *contributions* that each dimension of social science disciplines can make in each of the areas of relevance. For reasons to be discussed shortly, some additions of content could be made in many of the cells. Some specific nominations of relevant knowledge for inclusion in administrator preparatory programs are proposed, illustrating the procedure by which the matrix might be used by other students to derive further criteria.

Substantive Criteria I: Theoretical Formulations

In principle, the logical starting point for selecting social science content is to seek the best theories we have. We should seek the theories we are most confident of, well-confirmed bodies of statements from well-explicated regions of inquiry. Unfortunately, as we noted earlier, we do not yet have any fully formulated, satisfactorily interpreted theories in the social sciences. And strictly speaking, there are no social science models (developed theories that are isomorphic to undeveloped ones).[14] So there can be no absolute theoretical criteria for selecting social science content.

The theoretical formulations which the social sciences do have to offer are at best "guiding metaphors." These are constructs created by analogizing, by applying forms useful in other contexts to a problem at hand. The concepts of the "game," the "machine," and the "organism" as applied to social life are familiar guiding metaphors. The chief utility of the guiding metaphor is heuristic, rather than explanatory, and this importance should not be overlooked. But this characteristic does not make the task of finding orderly criteria of selection any easier. Which metaphors to choose, if one can be aware of the choice at all, depends upon the problems one is interested in. The problems, as reviewed earlier, may come from policy needs, from needs of social philosophy, or from other theoretical work in the disciplines. Frequently, the preception and definition of problems is altered by new empirical knowledge from the social sciences themselves. Ultimately, the choice of metaphors, like the choice of problems, is intuitive.

If we seek knowledge in the areas of greatest social scientific activity, where the most work has been done and where social scientists are most confident of their knowledge, then two problems result. One, there still is too much knowledge to draw upon, and so we need to find further criteria to narrow the selection of knowledge. Two, the older concepts may not necessarily be the most heuristically promising ones. Newer concepts and methods of inquiry may prove to be of much greater heuristic value which is, after all, our goal. Of course, there is no way to know for sure in advance which ones will prove fruitful.

Speaking intuitively and granting that there is much room for overlapping among categories, some guiding metaphors may be more appropriate to some of our four ways of conceiving relevance than to others. For example, for the purpose of liberalizing education, especially useful metaphors might include those regarding institutionalization, authority, communication, bureaucracy, leadership, socialization, social cost, social benefit, and attitudinal and belief-system change.

If one's approach is to establish logical connections between social science and various aspects of school administration, then social science formulations which purport new conceptions of education or educational administration (i.e., new ways to look at them) would be high priority items. For example, David Easton's concepts of "demands" and "supports" as the principal inputs into political systems can be employed as well to visualize the inputs into administrative systems.[15] In this way, school administrators come to be viewed as key actors within systems of educational governance, which is to say political systems. Another example is Howard Becker's characterization of societies along a sacred-secular continuum. Iannaccone and Lutz have applied the sacred-secular distinction in analyzing school districts and have argued that the two types of communities imply quite different role expectations for school superintendents and other administrators.[16]

Another concept which would appear to be timely for purposes of establishing logical connections could be called "political bonding." All social institutions and systems require support from their constituents to maintain themselves and their functions. Sometimes it is hard to realize how much this is so until we witness how quickly some loss of support can disrupt them.

Practicing school administrators usually develop ideas from experience and intuition about what will work in one community or another. Practically speaking, they have to solve this problem of developing adequate support or lose their jobs. Social scientists appear to have little knowledge of the processes by which such support is cemented. We know little about the social or political bonding through which the corporation necessary for social and institutional life is welded or about the procedures through which new bonds of social cooperation are established, new institutional patterns created, and new content put into old institutional shells.

In many areas of public life, we seem to be currently witnessing legitimate authority in public institutions becoming eroded. Many traditional routines which have been evolved to handle problems in an institution or community no longer seem to have their anticipated effect. These situations may remain unstable until a new leader or leaders can pose courses of action compatible with the values of the community and attract sufficient cooperation for a new and viable institutional life. If leaders can successfully forge new political bonds, a new basis for legitimate authority and institutional viability will be formed.

This is the notion of political bonding in the abstract. If it is to be useful to practicing administrators, the concept needs to be operationalized, and the attitudes and behaviors which produce it identified and developed in administrator preparation programs.

If one's approach is to develop substructures of knowledge within the discipline (for example, to develop further the "politics" or "economics" or "sociology" of education), then all of the preceding metaphors would seem to be potentially useful. Developing subdisciplines is essentially no different from the basic procedures of social science described earlier. It probably matters little except as a matter of personal style, whether a researcher starts with a problem and proceeds to develop theoretical formulations or starts with a theoretical formulation and then tries to test it in the world of educational administration. Which is *best* for generating useful knowledge? Since we have such limited experience with the successful development of social theory to draw upon, who can say?

The study of education and educational administration have many things to offer to the social sciences. Because of its ostensibly important role in socializing the young, the educational system is an important phenomenon for *all* of the social sciences. Similarly, educational systems have provided important source events and behaviors for those interested in bureaucracy, economic return on investment of resources, and the inculcation of political norms and attitudes.

Some other aspects of educational systems have not been mined so extensively. Persons interested in change in complex systems could find additional fruitful materials here and in settings more accessible and of more manageable size than, say, entire societies or the national and international realm. The same is true of persons interested in the development and erosion of legitimate authority, leadership, communication, and crisis in institutions. From a political science point of view, educational systems offer a particularly intimate kind of policy making, since the policy bears rather directly upon values in a basic unit of society, the family. Furthermore, it requires an extraordinary degree of cooperation and mutual dedication from the top of the policy-making hierarchy to the teacher in the classroom to bring about successful implementation of policy decisions.

From the viewpoint of preparation programs for school administrators, this is a curious category because it is probably more relevant to social scientists working in the disciplines than it is to school administrators. The most relevant knowledge from the subdisciplines would seem to be that which uncovers new connections between what administrators do and the outcomes of the school system in the society.

The relationship which I have described as interactive between social science disciplines and educational administration may not be a source of many guiding metaphors. Recognition of the relationship is important, however, because of the tendency for social scientists to reify the abstractions they create and, perhaps more importantly, because of the strong tendency in many practicing administrators to feel that their knowledge from experience is unique and the only genuine knowledge. Persons from either group can be "right," but the only way to establish this is through genuine confrontation and interaction about the experience of the "real" world.

There can be no scientific basis for choosing among alternative guiding metaphors. Their utility is measured primarily by the imaginative connections between things and events in social life which they inspire.

Substantive Criteria II: Findings

In principle, certain findings from social science are musts for inclusion in administrator preparation programs. In practice, it is not always easy to identify them. We can recognize three types, and all three can contribute to each of the four types of relevance that we have identified.

One type consists of findings which bear upon the theoretical formulations selected for administrator preparation programs. By and large, these formulations would be our basic definitions and conceptualizations of educational administration. An example would be Norman Kerr's finding that school boards can function chiefly as agencies of legitimation.[17]

A second type consists of findings which uncover "problems" — either empirical problems (schools administered in a certain way do not do what we thought they did) or normative problems (schools administered in a certain way produce undesirable outcomes). These can include change in the objective conditions of social life or in attitudes and values through which social conditions are viewed and evaluated. This type should not be confused with what has been called in this book problem-based relevance. That refers to the case of an administrator who realizes that he has a problem and goes to the social scientists for help. In the case I have in mind, a school administrator (or school administrators in general) may be unaware of a problem or potential problem until a social scientist discovers or predicts it. For example, speaking from hindsight, it would seem that most of the metropolitan problems and urban disorders of the 1960s were entirely predictable with the knowledge and techniques we had beforehand, if only it had occurred to more scientists to look and to other persons to listen to their analyses. Similarly, the current teacher surplus in this country seems to have arrived unnecessarily and unexpectedly.

A third type of mandatory finding are those which produce "firm predictions" of alternative futures. There are no very precise boundaries to distinguish predictions based upon relatively "complete" theoretical constructs from mere projections extended from findings or empirical generalizations. By "firm" predictions, I have in mind projections made with some substantial degree of detail, intellectual rigor, and conceptual sophistication, and referring to extensive areas of social life (large social classes or characteristics of entire societies, for example). They are relevant because education takes place in the social milieu and because knowledge of the future is always useful to any practitioner but, especially, those charged with designing and operating institutional structures and processes for particular social milieu. These products of social science are potential inputs for each of the ways of identifying relevance.

Procedural Criteria

Much of school administration has been and continues to be traditional in nature. Administrators learn what to do mainly from their experience in schools or in a particular school system and then continue largely to run schools as they always have been run. In this circumstance, there is little need for knowledge of the procedures of social science.

As school administration becomes increasingly innovative, as it becomes bombarded with new knowledge from research and confronted with conditions of social change, the need to do research and to be able to evaluate the quality of research becomes indispensable for those charged with the responsibility of leading the schools to become viable institutions.

Two kinds of content are needed for administrator preparation programs: knowledge of social science procedures (including philosophy and techniques of social science research) and skills in performing them. These are obviously needed for the research part of educational administration which is in effect, though not in name, a social science.

They are also needed for purposes of providing liberalized education for would-be administrators. In this regard, probably the most important contribution that the social science disciplines can make is through modes of inquiry which exemplify and develop problem-solving ability. By this, I mean not merely that administrators should learn a set of research techniques which are appropriate for a predefined type of research problem. Rather, administrators need to have the cognitive flexibility and confidence to look at things in new ways. Student administrators should have practice in trying to conceptualize problems from real life in new ways that suggest paths to solution or resolution. This experience is important because in times of rapid social change the ability to define new problems from ambiguous situations of social life in ways that suggest paths to solution seems to be the one indispensable skill of an educational leader and, indeed, of an educated person generally. It is probably the skill which separates the innovative administrator or leader from the administrator who can merely maintain the pre-existing routines and procedures whether they still perform their intended function or not. Social science experiences and modes of inquiry which exemplify and develop these capabilities in individuals seem high-priority items.

When so many other persons take their cues for interpreting complex situations from the administrator in legal authority, it is manifestly important that the administrator have appropriate conceptual "boxes" or categories in mind in which to classify the behavior he witnesses. Behaviors which disrupt the status-quo — students or parents who demonstrate against school practices, for example — may or may not be "good" or "justified." But the administrator who fails to comprehend the social forces, the motives, and the functions of the behaviors within his own system and within its environment, who classifies the behaviors into inappropriate conceptual "boxes," cannot hope to be an effective leader toward solutions. He may simply exacerbate the problems and encourage others to exacerbate them, to the detriment of the basic mission of the schools.

It is useful for all four types of relevance to be able to judge the quality of a given theory, orientational view, or concept. For this purpose, the seven criteria elaborated by Charters are appropriate. To recapitulate, Charters suggests that formulations may be judged for their potential contribution to administrative training according to how well they (1) articulate the theory or concept set, (2) incorporate dynamic referents into the theory or concept set, (3) incorporate person-environment interaction referents, (4) permit operationality, (5) account for reasonably substantial amounts of variance in phenomena with which the practitioner must deal, (6) propose intervention capacity, and (7) contribute a gain in power from a theory or concept set.[18]

I would add one other criteria in this category. Knowledge which extends the levels of analysis of educational administration problems is desirable. Most social phenomena of interest to social scientists and educational administrators can be understood to be affected (determined) by both *structural* variables within the particular social institution, system, or situation in question and by *contextual* variables from its environment. In trying to account for the performance behavior of a particular school, for example, one might fruitfully look at structural variables, such as groups, individuals, roles, and intra-psychic behavior. He might also fruitfully look at such contextual variables as community attitudes, the legal and fiscal support system at local, state, and national levels, the administrative style of the school superintendent, and the physical constraints of the school facility itself. In extending the levels of analysis, we may or may not raise the level of abstraction of our concepts. But we will have tried to improve our understanding through understanding as many relevant variables as possible.

Normative Criteria

Various normative criteria exist for evaluating administrative behavior. Indeed, one of the hallmarks of a leader (or the "executive" in Chester Barnard's classic discourse)[19] is the ability in a situation involving conflicting values to suggest which path leads to or manifests the higher morality and to have this course accepted by the followers or the organization. Nevertheless, two general kinds of criteria come to us from the tradition of moral philosophy through the social science disciplines and are widely used for answering moral questions of governmental or public policy.[20] One kind is traditionally called "deontological." It commands that "one ought to do that which is inherently fair or just or right, as determined either by direct consideration of the act and its situation of itself, or by reference to some general formal principle (often one whose denial is self-contradictory)."[21] The other criterion is called "teleological," and it commands that "one ought to do that which will have the best consequences, do the most good, maximize utility."[22] The utility may be maximized for society or mankind as a whole (utilitarian) or only for the individual agent (egoistic). In seeking knowledge from social science disciplines, knowledge of these criteria and their involvement in administrative practices (some of which are being uncovered or are yet to be uncovered through empirical means) is important in several ways.

There has been much polemical prescription in the literature of educational administration and educational reform. Undoubtedly much of it has resulted from the deficient state of empirical research in the field, especially on many recent and difficult problems associated with supplying educational services to an increasingly urban, technological, and geographically mobile society. Social scientists, as well as educational administrators, have served as the polemicists. By both positive and negative example, this writing shows that the liberalizing education conception of relevance needs new content on the purposes of educational administration. This does not mean simply learning a static professional code for use throughout the rest of one's career. Rather, it means developing the capability to apply normative criteria in evolving new purposes of education and educational administration as social conditions and social demands change. It means acquiring the skill to develop adaptive codes of professional behavior. The same need applies to the conception of relevance of interaction between social scientists and administrators.

The normative dimension of the social sciences can also contribute to the task of establishing logical connections between the fields. Here the application is in discovering the normative implications of administrative practices: "Whose ox gets gored in the public schools?" The answers, of course, change with changing conditions and changing social values. Educational administrators frequently profess the goal of developing the schools to serve the needs of the individual learner. They much less often announce explicitly who defines the needs. Nor do they seem to raise to the explicit level (unless forced by community reaction to do so) the question of whether or not the hidden curriculum rooted in the organizing processes of schools—especially in their impact upon the affective attributes of independence, self-discipline, social skills, and occasionally, love—go against family or community values. Nor do they make clear how these program decisions, many of which result unintentionally, can be morally justified.

In the task of developing a substructure of knowledge within the social science disciplines, the normative dimension has application in suggesting empirical research on changes in what administrators perceive as "right," changes in what various publics *want*, and changes in what the public(s) perceive as "right" in public schools.

In the foregoing matrix of social science dimensions and conceptions of relevance between the social sciences and educational administration, we have not tried to generate an exhaustive set of new criteria for inclusion of knowledge in administrator preparation programs. We have, instead, tried to propose a systematic basis for considering new criteria and have sought to fill in some of the cells with what seem to be useful contributions that the various social science dimensions can presently make. Some of the cells are woefully empty, due no doubt to the lack of imagination and insight by the author, rather than to any inherent limitations of the social sciences. Hopefully, this outline of relationships will provide clarity enough to enable other students with more inspiration to add different and better contributions to the cells in correspondence to their own insights into what is important in the field.

One final word on the value and limitations of criteria from the social science disciplines. There is no inherent superiority of discipline-based knowledge over theory-based or problem-based knowledge. Discipline-based knowledge is designated such for rather arbitrary and conventional reasons. One slight advantage, perhaps, is the somewhat more explicit orientation in some disciplines toward normative concerns, along with those of developing empirical theory. In the end, however, criteria for the inclusion of knowledge in training programs must be based on intuition. There can be no *formula* of relevance. There is no scientific predictor of science. It must be intuition that guides our borrowing of knowledge. Hopefully, it will be intuition guided with moral concerns for alternative futures reliably discovered and predicted by educational administrators and social scientists.

FOOTNOTES

1. Special Commission on the Social Sciences, *Knowledge into Action: Improving the Nation's Use of the Social Sciences* (Washington, D.C.: National Science Foundation, 1969), p. 7.

2. Richard S. Rudner, *Philosophy of Social Science* (Englewood Cliffs, New Jersey: Prentice-Hall, Inc., 1966), pp. 3–4.

3. Ibid., pp. 7–8.

4. Scott Greer, *The Logic of Social Inquiry* (Chicago: Aldine Publishing Company, 1969), p. 21.

5. Ibid., pp. 6–7.

6. Ibid., p. 9.

7. Ibid., p. 13.

8. Ibid., p. 4.

9. Rudner, *Philosophy of Social Science*, p. 10.

10. This section is based largely on Scott Greer's discussion in Chapters 1 and 13 of *The Logic of Social Inquiry*.

11. See Chapter 1, Table 1.

12. Peter L. Berger and Thomas Luckmann, *The Social Construction of Reality* (Garden City, New York: Doubleday and Company, Inc., Anchor Books, 1967).

13. A chronology of events in the most significant case, New York City, can be found in Melvin Urofsky, ed., *Why Teachers Strike* (Garden City, New York: Doubleday and Company, Inc., Anchor Books, 1970).

14. Rudner, *Philosophy of Social Science,* Chapter 2.

15. David Easton, *A Systems Analysis of Political Life* (New York: John Wiley and Sons, 1965).

16. Laurence Iannaccone and Frank W. Lutz, *Politics, Power and Policy: The Governing of Local School Districts* (Columbus, Ohio: Charles E. Merrill Publishing Company, 1970), Chapter 2.

17. Norman Kerr [pseud.], "The School Board as an Agency of Legitimation," *Sociology of Education* 38 (Fall 1964): 34–59.

18. See Chapter 1 of this volume. Charters' criteria are taken from W. W. Charters, Jr., "Anthropology and the Study of Administration Response," in *The Social Sciences in Educational Administration,* eds. Lawrence W. Downey and Frederick Enns (Edmonton, Canada: Division of Educational Administration, The University of Alberta and The University Council for Educational Administration, 1962), pp. 91–93.

19. Chester I. Barnard, *The Functions of the Executive* (Cambridge, Massachusetts: Harvard University Press, 1938).

20. See Alan Gewirth, *Political Philosophy* (London: The Macmillan Company, 1965), pp. 5–9.

21. Ibid., p. 5.

22. Ibid.

16

The Theory-Based Perspective: Selection and Organization of Content

A. R. Crane and W. G. Walker

It is the task of this chapter to ask how one responsible for an administrator preparation program decides what is relevant and to ask just what parts of the relevant material should be included in such a program. In a sense, the chapter asks the question that Spencer put so succinctly a century ago: What knowledge is of the most worth?[1]

Employing Theory in Administration Preparation

What knowledge is of the most worth for the educational administrator? Though this question will be discussed at length in this chapter, for a beginning it may not be too trite an observation to point out that the practitioner is concerned above all else with human beings in a variety of settings both as individuals and as groups. He is concerned with the individual as a personality, a member of the organization, a member of one or more formal and informal units and, of course, a member of society at large.

In the "lonely crowd"[2] society of the present, and, one must assume, of the foreseeable future, the practising administrator needs resources which will help him to understand not only the individual in the contexts referred to above but also the social context in which he himself works, especially as it relates to the buzzing confusion of the administrative day. Clearly, the resources will need to provide guides for action, to suggest to him what and when to change, as well as what and when not to change; when to innovate and when to maintain the status quo; and when, indeed, to *lead* the organization for which he is responsible. He needs, moreover, to ask not merely the questions, "What is?" "What happens if . . . ?" and "Why?" but also, "What is happening to me?" "How do I maintain *myself* while maintaining and leading the organization for which I am responsible?"

The planner of curricula for the preparation of educational administrators who is conscious of the personal needs of the practitioner, with his value system and his concept of the nature of man, might turn in part to philosophy, to the humanities or to religious studies for his raw material. But insights into the "oughts" of administrative behavior are no longer enough. It is to the "is's" that we increasingly turn for answers to the age-old question, "What do I do now?" The source of the "is's" lies predominantly in the social sciences where, as Culbertson and Shibles point out, the emphasis is increasingly upon objectivity, reliability, validity, and replication.[3]

It is a truism that the word theory is no longer used in scholarly writing to mean impractical, but there is no harm in emphasizing at this stage that the authors of this chapter see theory as practical, as operational, as possessing within itself the power to generate hypotheses, to explain and to predict. In fine, theory is seen as providing rich sources of guides to action.

We do not — cannot — deny that normative guides to action are derived from philosophy, religion, and the humanities, from theories in those fields which attempt to explain and account for the behavior of man as an individual, as a member of a group, of an organization, and of society at large. Yet, the fact must be stressed that the practice of educational administration, like that of any profession, depends upon more insights than the domain of the normative alone can provide. Professional practice is both an art and a science, and the practitioner as an artist may turn to philosophy, religion, and the humanities, but as a scientist, he must turn to the social or behavioral sciences as the source of disciplined general propositions that vouchsafe insight into the dynamics of organizational life and the impact of the organization on his own behavior. Such social science disciplines may, of course, be categorized in a number of ways. For the purpose of this chapter, they are categorized as historical/political, economic, sociological/anthropological, social psychological, and psychological.

The intellectual core of administrator training and thus the concern of this chapter, then, lies primarily in the social or behavioral sciences. As we have seen in earlier chapters, educational administration, like the other professions, relies heavily for the foundations of its practice upon the insights provided by certain basic disciplines. It is not, of course, merely a matter of mastering one or more of those basic disciplines. The question of the relevance of the discipline to the administrator's task is crucial. Within any discipline, there is the question of the greater relevance of some parts than others.

It is true that theory based on one of the basic disciplines, such as social psychology or politics is illuminating and useful for administrators, especially when each separate discipline is treated as a source of relevant concepts and modes of enquiry. However, as Snyder has pointed out, "an inter-disciplinary program which envisages the swallowing of five or more core disciplines is a prescription for frustration or indigestion or both."[4]

The multidisciplinary approach being advocated in this chapter seems to be an effective way of avoiding Snyder's indigestion. This is so because the approach does not regard each discipline as a discrete source. It takes as its focus an administrative task or an organizational problem and then searches the disciplines for relevant material which is then integrated in such a way as to give a coherent theoretical account of the administrative or organizational phenomenon being studied.

Whilst the scientist-researcher's desire for tight control of variables leads him to work within the bounds of a single discipline, the administrator's needs almost inevitably lead him to a multidisciplinary study of the state of affairs by which he is surrounded and within the matrix of which he must make his decisions. Breadth of insight is crucial to his very existence. What is the point of achieving the organization's goals if, in the long run, the organization itself is destroyed? Few administrators wish to lead their organizations to such Pyrrhic victories. What is the point of adopting an economic solution of an educational problem if it wrecks faculty morale? Indeed, only the most insensitive and inflexible administrator would operate consistently on the basis of theory derived from a single discipline. Callahan's study, *The Cult of Efficiency*, gives a salutary warning by showing what happened when educational administrators were captured and constrained by a partial view of their task.[5] Even if an administrator has selected significant concepts from what he considers to be a key discipline, he is wise to look at what other disciplines have to say before he commits himself to action.

DETERMINING THE RELEVANCE OF THEORIES

From the theory-based perspective there is a rich reservoir of multidisciplinary resources which have with educational administration the "traceable, significant and logical connection" for which Culbertson and Shibles plead as the criterion for their inclusion in a preparation program.[6] It might well be that these connections are not always at first glance obvious to practising administrators, but they are nevertheless there and recognisable as such by the perceptive scholar and curriculum planner. Part of the aim of a course of study planned in this way is to reveal and clarify these connections.

It is probably platitudinous to state that all administrators, irrespective of the organization in which they are working, share common roles and functions; all are concerned in one way or another with the process of administration. Yet, if we accept Parson's tripartite division of an organization into institutional, managerial, and technical levels,[7] it becomes clear that administrators working at different points in the organization will need different repertoires of knowledge, insight, and skill if they are to perform their functions completely. It is significant here to notice that any administrator's task will span two of Parson's levels. He works on the boundary between levels and, indeed, one of his most important tasks is the translation of communication generated at one level into the language of the next. The administrator whose task spans the institutional/managerial levels will need, at least in part, a different training program from the administrator who spans the managerial/technical levels.

If we keep in mind the conception of the administrator as an "organizational level spanner" as we survey the social sciences to locate those areas most relevant for inclusion in an administrator training program, it is possible to detect also levels of theories. There are those which deal with the universal, sweeping developments that affect all mankind. Much of the work of such writers as Toynbee, Marx, Rousseau and Marcuse, for example, may be included here. Then there are theories concerned with man in more limited social settings, such as nations, communities, and large organizations. The works of Hunter, Barnard and Presthus are but a few examples. Thirdly, there is a group of theories concerned with man as a member of a workgroup within an organization. Here names such as Taylor, Argyris and Halpin come to mind. (See Selected References for a list of the authors' works.)

In the best of all worlds, every administrator in training would be brought face to face with many theories at all three levels. Of course, he could not be expected to study more than a small number in any depth, yet it is reasonable to expect that he be familiar with at least two or three at each level and in some depth, irrespective of where in the organization his administrative task is located. However, the extent to which he is confronted with further theories will depend largely on which organizational levels he will find himself spanning on the completion of his course.

There are good reasons why the administrator working in the institutional/managerial sector should be brought face to face with the great systems of values which have changed and are changing the world. One wonders, for example, how senior educational policy makers in today's interdependent world can hope to lead a school system without at least a nodding acquaintance with the great political forces which are the warp and woof of modern civilization. They should be familiar with the great movements in history: Christianity; democracy as seen by a Jefferson or a Rousseau; Fascism by a Mosca or a Pareto; Communism by a Marx or a Lenin or a Mao; even the world of chaos as seen by a Marcuse or a Fanon or an Eldridge Cleaver. (See Selected References for list of authors' works.)

It seems axiomatic that the director of a national or state department of education, for example, needs to be sensitive to political theorizing at a rather different level from that of the superintendent of a small city school system. For the former, Pareto's *The Mind and Society* may have considerable relevance,[8] but for the latter, Hunter's *Community Power Structure* may be far more pertinent.[9] The principal of a school, on the other hand, is likely to be much more concerned with theories relevant to the internal problems of the school and instructional leadership. For him, the work of Halpin[10] and of Guba[11] and Getzels[12] for example, are of focal significance.

It has already been said that to a significant degree the curriculum for preparation programs will be shaped by the kinds of decisions that administrators will need to make and the tasks they will carry out on the completion of their preparation. But we would hope that no administrator training is so narrow as to be blinkered by this sole criterion. Our aim is to widen horizons, not to restrict them.

Perhaps what we need to decide what knowledge is of the most worth is a nice balance between a liberal education, a generalist administrative preparation, and a specialist administrative preparation. Certainly this balance is not likely to be achieved by means of the frequently inward-looking, rather pathetic little "how-to-do-it" courses still often found in university departments of educational administration.

At this stage, it would be convenient to summarize the ground rules which we have so far discussed and which are pertinent to providing an answer to the question of what knowledge is of most worth to the administrator.

1. Theory provides a reservoir of insight on which action can be based.

2. Theory based in a single discipline is less likely to provide a broad perspective of the factors involved in administrative behavior at its various levels than theory derived from a number of disciplines.

3. Theories overlap considerably and cover a vast spectrum of human behavior. However, for our purposes, they can be conveniently labelled political/historical, economic, sociological/anthropological, social psychological, and psychological.

4. No one administrator can hope to master all of the theoretical constructs which might prove valuable to him in selecting amongst alternatives for action, in providing bases for his decision making, and in explaining and predicting human behavior. While the tyro administrator might and should be introduced to a large number of theories, the education of administrators must perforce limit the number of such theories that can be studied in depth.

5. Over and above this selected corpus of material designed to enrich the insight of all administrators, there will be a further selection based upon the organizational level at which the student will be working on completion of his period of preparation.

The model illustrated by Table 1 is based on the concept of organizational levels and provides guidelines for the selection of theoretical constructs relevant to the understanding of each level of organizational life. The crosshatched area on the model represents the theoretical areas of greatest relevance in terms of worth to the student. Thus, at the institutional level the emphasis is on historical/political, economic, and sociological/anthropological theory; whereas, at the managerial level, the emphasis shifts to sociological/anthropological and social psychological theory. At the

Table 1

Showing Relevance of Theory to Administrators Preparing for Responsibility at Various Levels

THEORY RELEVANCE

	Historical/Political	Economic	Sociological/ Anthropological	Social Psychological	Psychological
INSTITUTIONAL LEVEL					
Boundary spanning administrator					
MANAGERIAL LEVEL					
Boundary-spanning administrator					
TECHNICAL LEVEL					

Direction of Occupational Mobility

N.B. Cross-hatched area is area of special relevance for preparing administrators for levels shown.

397

technical level, the shift is toward both social and individual psychology.

In general, the model argues as follows: At the institutional level of large systems (federal, state, big city, or city-state) the most pregnant theories are those which explain how influence is wielded in the corridors of power; how economic developments and planning affect the operation of school systems; how societies change in response to social, political, or economic movements; and how race, color, and public mores affect or are affected by the allocation of resources. The top level policy maker is also concerned, though less so, with theories describing the behavior of groups in organizations or with the individual in the organization; yet he must be aware of the likely impact on the organization of the decisions being made. That is why he has earlier in the chapter been designated a "level spanner."

At the managerial level, concern is less with the suprasystem and more with the system itself, with the politics and sociology of the surrounding community, rather than the society in toto. Responsibility for the control of individual schools in the system calls less for concern with major economic principles, more with theories of financial control; less with the great forces changing mankind, more with the individual and his problems in adapting to the organization and to groups within it.

At the technical level, there is a clear and immediate concern with teachers, both as individuals and as members of groups, and of course, with children.

Naturally, these divisions are artificial. It has indeed already been emphasized that each administrator has a hand in at least two of the divisions. This could suggest that all administrators should be familiar with all theories, but reality makes it only too clear that this is a hopeless proposition and that, therefore, the curriculum builder must exercise a ruthless and discriminating selection. Yet, it still remains true that every educational administrator needs some knowledge of great worldwide social movements, some knowledge of the political context of the school system, and some knowledge of the behavior of individuals within educational organizations, but the emphases on each of these areas will vary according to the position he will hold within the organization. It is assumed, further, that as he proceeds up the organizational ladder, he will read and probe the literature and select from such theories as set out in Table 1. As suggested above, this table indicates the focus of theory around which the curriculum for preparing administrators

Table 2
Multidisciplinary Theory Grid

Discipline \ Level	Institutional	Managerial	Technical
HISTORICAL/ POLITICAL	MILL, TOYNBEE	KEYNES, HUNTER	STRAYER AND MUNRO
ECONOMIC	MOSCA, PARETO, MACHIAVELLI, SOROKIN, MARX, MARCUSE, FANON, WEBER	BENSON, VAIZEY	TAYLOR, FAYOL
SOCIOLOGICAL/ ANTHROPOLOGICAL	OSBURN, MERTON	PARSONS	CARLSON, GOULDNER
SOCIAL PSYCHOLOGICAL	GETZELS, ETZIONI	BARNARD, SIMON, HALPIN, GROSS, PRESTHUS, ARGYRIS, FOLLETT	MAYO
PSYCHOLOGICAL	GUBA		HOMANS, MASLOW

at the various levels will be concentrated. It does not mean that the theories shown outside the crosshatched portion should be excluded. It merely suggests that they are not of *central* concern to the levels indicated.

In Table 2, an attempt has been made to spell out in greater detail the use that can be made of the grid in highlighting those theories which should be scrutinized by program builders. From such a table as this, it is easy to see the kind of material which is available to those constructing courses for administrators at one or another organizational level.

This section of the chapter has done no more than illustrate a rough criterion for adjudging the relevance of certain families of theories for certain levels of administration. In the following section, we shall be searching for criteria to assist in deciding what is best of what is relevant. There are, however, one or two caveats which should be noted before proceeding.

The first of these is the assumption that the possession of ideas about something necessarily leads to intelligent action. Even relevant, high quality theory does not necessarily influence behavior. Much depends on the quality of the interaction between professor and student. A well-constructed curriculum does not ipso facto produce wise decision making, but it is the basis upon which wise decisions might be founded. Let us remember and be warned by the excesses of Taylorism and of the theory of democratic decision making when they were applied to school administration.

The second caveat relates to the assumption that the key to understanding the administrative process will be found only in the social sciences. If this leads to a rejection of literature, history, or philosophy as sources of relevant insight, it will be a great mistake. It is possible, especially in these closing years of the twentieth century, to become obsessed with empiricism. Halpin gives a salutory reminder when he pungently quotes from E. E. Cummings.

> While you and I have lips and voices which
> are for kissing and to sing with
> who cares if some one-eyed son of a bitch
> invents an instrument to measure spring with?[13]

ASSESSING THE VALUE OF RELEVANT THEORIES

Up to this point, an attempt has been made to indicate where a curriculum builder might look for material to include in a program for educational administrators. This section sharpens the focus of inquiry and suggests some guiding principles about what to look for amongst the plethora and the complexities of the areas of enquiry that have been indicated in Table 1 and spelt out in Table 2. It is proposed, therefore, to explore in more detail the criteria which could guide the selection of the building bricks of a coherent course of study.

It is not claimed, nor is it suggested, that the criteria to be discussed here are mutually independent. This is certainly not so. They are merely systematic ways of approaching the mass of knowledge presented for our scrutiny. In other words, they are mental sets that develop a state of readiness to recognize those sections that should be seriously considered for inclusion in a curriculum.

Dependability

Here are some of the questions which this criterion suggests that we ask of a theory. Does it appear to explain phenomena with which the administrator is concerned? Can it be depended upon to provide insight into states of affairs? Can it indicate to the practising administrator possible sources of trouble? Can it help in the diagnosis and remedy of troubles that have already occurred?

The idea behind dependability is probably akin to that of relevance which has already been discussed, but here the focus is sharpened onto a point of time when a decision has to be made. The work of Toynbee, for example, is relevant but is not, in this sense, dependable;[14] whereas parts of Weber[15] and even of Machiavelli[16] could be both relevant and dependable. This is because of these two theories the administrator can gain a glimpse of the realistic parameters of possible action and the probable consequences of any particular action.

Range

In considering just what theories to select, one decisive factor will be the area of the administrative process that is illuminated by the theory. One theory, for example, might throw light on a single level of administration or even a single administrative process; whereas, another could have significance over a much wider area. The works of Barnard[17] and Mary Parker Follett[18] have wide range in this sense, whereas, that of Carlson[19] is narrower.

Such a criterion as this could be used to differentiate between the material that could be common to all administrator preparation programs and the material that could be specifically directed toward administrators at a particular organizational level.

Fertility

The center of concern here is the potential of the theory to widen the horizons of the administrator and to indicate to him new sources for the understanding of the process in which he is engaged. Examples of theories of high fertility are found, for example, in the work of Etzioni, Gouldner, Presthus and Halpin. (See Selected References for list of authors' works.)

Dynamism

The educational administrator is working in a continually changing arena, and any preparation program must recognise and embrace this fact. It is, therefore, fair to ask whether the theory under scrutiny includes change and innovation within its orbit. Is it a dynamic as against a static theory? The work of Weber could, for example, be considered as rating low on dynamism whereas that of Argyris, Guba and Getzels would rank rather higher. (See Selected References for list of authors' works.)

Adventurousness

It must be admitted that this criterion in itself is rather adventurous. It differs from the others in an interesting way. They attempt to give guidance to the questing curriculum builder as he surveys material already adjudged as relevant to his task. This one would lead us to suggest that there could be bodies of ideas or theories which, on the surface, appear irrelevant or even eccentric but which might in fact turn out to be sources of creative and unexpected insight.

For generations in England, it was assumed that the best training for the future administrator, whether of a large and distant colony or a single school in England itself, was attendance at one of a small number of Public Schools followed preferably by reading the Greats at Oxford. This might sound today an eccentric idea, but it is one which still deserves serious discussion. A further example, this time from the other side of the Atlantic, is Maslow's conception of Eupsychean management.[20]

One day an apple might fall on the head of an administrative Newton, and the world will never be the same again. Eccentricity and illumination have often proved to be closely related.

Empiricism

So much discussion about all aspects of education, including its administration, is based on what can fairly be described as myth, tradition, value judgment, shibboleth, or circular statement. This criterion suggests the questions: To what extent is the theory under discussion built on hard data? Has it been empirically tested? If not, does it lend itself to such testing?

In the present state of both organizational and administrative studies, it could be said that a theory can be dependable without its having been rigorously tested in educational organizations. Some theories that have been tested in industry, in civil service, hospitals, and prisons have produced results that are highly suggestive of wider application. Outstanding examples are the work of Argyris,[21] Presthus,[22] Blau,[23] and Jones.[24]

Fortunately, the amount of relevant and dependable theory empirically based on educational organization is growing apace. Outstanding examples may be found in the work of Gross,[25] Carlson[26] and Halpin.[27]

Appropriateness

This criterion again differs from all those that have gone before. Here the major concern is the background of knowledge and expertise possessed by the student. For example, the course of reading suggested for, and the theories brought to, the attention of a student with a background in political science could well differ from those considered desirable and appropriate for one with a background in mathematics or psychology. It is important to emphasize that no course of reading can be equally appropriate for all students. Another possible term to describe this criterion would be "readiness." The question here is directed to the needs of a particular student and not to the curriculum itself.

We have here suggested some guidelines to help the curriculum builder in his search for appropriate material, but it is clear that not all program designers could use these guidelines in the same way or would be looking for the same things. What they will be looking for will, to a significant degree, depend on the aims of the courses under construction and the contexts, both social and organizational, for which the administrator is being trained to work. For example, if he is working in a situation of increasing centralization, then the work of Weber could be pregnant with significance.[28] On the other hand, in a situation of increasing devolution of authority, the work of Etzioni[29] and Bennis[30] could be of special relevance. Again, the course being prepared for administrators likely to work in a multiracial American megalopolis would have a different content and emphasis from the course designed for an

Australian or New Zealand headmaster of a rural elementary school.

It is for the program builder to decide which of the suggested criteria should be given priority and emphasis in any particular course pattern. In Table 3, an attempt has been made to assign High, Medium, or Low values to a number of theories on the basis of the criteria previously discussed. The values shown in the table are relevant only to a program, such as the one conducted at the University of New England where the majority of the students will be straddling the managerial/operational levels in centralized systems struggling towards greater collegiality and devolution of authority.

Table 3

Showing Criteria and Level of Value of Selected Theories

Theory	Depend-ability	Range	Fer-tility	Dy-namism	Adventur-ousness	Empiricism
Weber	H	H	L	L	L	L
Etzioni	H	H		H	L	L
Presthus	H	H	H	L	M	M
Parsons	H	H	H	M	M	L
Argyris	H	H	H	H	M	M
Maslow	L	L	H	H	H	L
Getzels-Guba	H		H	H		M
Marcuse	L	H	H	H		L
Jones	H	H	M	L	M	H
Griffiths	H	H	M	M	L	L
Mayo	H	H	H	H	H	H
Halpin	H	H	H	M	M	H

N.B.   H = High
       M = Medium
       L = Low

It is the task of each program builder to clarify in his own mind the specific purposes of his course and then sit down and work out some such table for himself. In the case of the New England course, for example, emphasis is first on the Dependability and Range of theories which are of value in the understanding of the present organizational context of the administrator's task. Its second, but not secondary, focus is on Dynamism and Adventurousness with the deliberate aim of opening the minds of the students to other than bureaucratic solutions to organizational and administrative problems.

CONCLUSION

We began this chapter by asking, from the point of view of the curriculum planner in educational administration, the critical question which Spencer asked a century ago: What knowledge is of the most worth? We have attempted to indicate some of the directions in which the inquirer might seek answers to this question. To suggest that there are not other answers, other directions, and other criteria for choice among answers would be contrary to the eclectic and exploratory spirit of this book. However, as Hilda Taba has reminded us, the curriculum planner must rely on some criteria,[31] and clearly the choice of criteria becomes a matter of crucial concern when those exposed to the courses developed from them are destined to be the leaders of those described so eloquently by Sir Percy Num as "Ambassadors of Society to the Kingdom of the Child."[32]

SELECTED REFERENCES

Argyris, Chris. *Personality and Organization: The Conflict Between the System and the Individual.* New York: Harper, 1957.

Barnard, Chester I. *The Functions of the Executive.* Cambridge, Mass.: Harvard University Press, 1938.

Benson, Charles S. *The Economics of Public Education.* Boston: Houghton Mifflin, 1961.

Cleaver, Eldridge. *Soul on Ice.* New York: Dell, 1968.

Etzioni, Amitai. *A Comparative Analysis of Complex Organizations.* Glencoe, Ill.: Free Press, 1961.

Fanon, Frantz. *The Wretched of the Earth.* Marmondsworth, Mddx.: Penquin, 1967.

Fayol, Henri. *General and Industrial Management.* London: Pittman, 1956.

Getzels, Jacob W. "Theory and Practice in Educational Administration: An Old Question Revisited" in *Administrative Theory as a Guide to Action*, eds. Roald F. Campbell and James M. Lipham. Chicago: Midwest Administration Center, 1960.

Gouldner, Alvin. *Patterns of Industrial Bureaucracy*. Glencoe, Ill.: Free Press, 1954.

Guba, Egon G. "Research in Internal Administration: What Do We Know?" in *Administrative Theory as a Guide to Action*, eds. Roald F. Campbell and James M. Lipham. Chicago: Midwest Administration Center, 1960.

Halpin, Andrew W. *Theory and Research in Administration*. New York: Macmillan, 1966.

Homans, George C. *The Human Group*. New York: Harcourt, Brace, 1950.

Hunter, Floyd, *Community Power Structure: A Study of Decision Making*. Chapel Hill, N.C.: University of North Carolina Press, 1953.

Keynes, J. Maynard. *General Theory of Employment, Interest and Money*. London, Macmillan, 1936.

Lenin, V.I. *The Teachings of Karl Marx*. New York: International, 1933.

Mao Tse-Tung. *Quotations from Chairman Mao*. Peking: Foreign Language Press, 1967.

Marcuse, Herbert. *One-Dimensional Man*. London: Routledge and Kegan Paul, 1964.

Marx, Karl. *Capital*. New York: Modern Library, 1932.

Mayo, Elton. *The Human Problems of an Industrial Civilization*. New York: Viking Press, 1960.

Merton, Robert K. *Social Theory and Social Structure*. Glencoe, Ill.: Free Press, 1957.

Mill, John Stuart. *Utilitarianism, Liberty and Representative Government*, ed. A. D. Lindsay. New York: Dutton, 1910.

Mosca, Gaetano. *The Ruling Class*. New York: McGraw-Hill, 1939.

Ogburn, William F. *Social Change*. New York: Huebach, 1922.

Padover, Saul K. *Jefferson: A Great American's Life and Ideas*. New York: Mentor, 1952.

Parteo, Wilfredo. *The Mind and Society*. New York: Brace, 1935.

Presthus, Robert. *The Organizational Society*. New York: Knopf, 1962.

Rousseau, Jean Jacques. *The Social Contract*. New York: Hafner, 1954.

Simon, Herbert A. *Administrative Behavior*. New York: Macmillan, 1951.

Sorokin, Pitirim. *The Crisis of Our Age*. New York: Dutton, 1946.

Taylor, F. W. *The Principles of Scientific Management*. New York: Harper, 1911.

Toynbee, Arnold J. *A Study of History*. Oxford: Oxford University Press, 1946.

Vaizey, John. *The Economics of Education*. London: Faber, 1962.

FOOTNOTES

1. Herbert Spencer, *Education: Intellectual, Moral and Physical* (London: Watts, 1911).

2. David Reisman, *The Lonely Crowd* (New Haven, Conn.: Yale University Press, 1950).

3. Jack A. Culbertson and Mark Shibles, "The Social Sciences and the Issue of Relevance" (Chapter 1, this volume).

4. Richard C. Snyder, "The Preparation of Educational Administrators: Some Problems Reconsidered in the Context of the Establishment of a New Graduate School of Administration" in *Educational Administration: International Perspectives*, eds. George Baron, Dan H. Cooper, and William G. Walker (Chicago: Rand McNally, 1969).

5. Raymond E. Callahan, *The Cult of Efficiency* (Chicago: University of Chicago Press, 1962).

6. Jack A. Culbertson and Mark Shibles, Chapter 1.

7. Talcott Parsons, "Some Ingredients of a General Theory of Formal Organization" in *Administrative Theory in Education*, ed. Andrew W. Halpin (Chicago: Midwest Administration Center, 1958).

8. Wilfredo Pareto, *The Mind and Society*.

9. Floyd Hunter, *Community Power Structure*.

10. Andrew W. Halpin, *Theory and Research*.

11. Egon G. Guba, "Research in Internal Administration: What Do We Know?" in *Administrative Theory as a Guide to Action*, eds. Roald F. Campbell and James M. Lipham (Chicago: Midwest Administration Center, 1960).

12. Jacob W. Getzels, "Theory and Practice in Educational Administration: An Old Question Revisited," Ibid.

13. E. E. Cummings, "IS 5: Poem 157," *Collected Poems* (New York: Harcourt, Brace, 1938) quoted by Andrew W. Halpin in "Training for Research in Educational Administration: A Rationale" Chapter 19 in *Educational Research: New Perspectives*, eds. Jack A. Culbertson and Stephen P. Hencley (Danville, Ill.: Interstate, 1963), p. 324.

14. Arnold Toynbee, *A Study of History*.

15. Max Weber, *The Theory of Social and Economic Organization*, trans. A. M. Henderson and Talcott Parsons, ed. Talcott Parsons (Glencoe, Ill.: Free Press, 1947).

16. Niccolo Machiavelli, *The Prince* (Marmondsworth, Mddx.: Penquin, 1961).

17. Chester I. Barnard, *Functions of the Executive*.

18. H. C. Metcalf and L. Urwick, *Dynamic Administration: The Collected Papers of Mary Parker Follett* (London: Pitman, 1957).

19. Richard O. Carlson, "Environmental Constraints and Organizational Consequences: The Public School and its Clients" in *Behavioral Science and Educational Administration*, 63rd Yearbook, N.S.S.E., ed. Daniel E. Griffiths (Chicago: University of Chicago Press, 1964).

20. A. H. Maslow, *Eupsychean Management* (Homewood, Ill.: Irwin, 1965).

21. Chris Argyris, *Personality and Organization.*

22. Robert Presthus, *The Organizational Society.*

23. Peter M. Blau, *Bureaucracy in Modern Society* (New York: Random House, 1956).

24. Edward E. Jones, *Ingratiation: A Social Psychological Analysis* (New York: Appleton-Century-Crofts, 1964).

25. Neil Gross and R. E. Herriott, *Staff Leadership in Public Schools: A Sociological Inquiry* (New York: Wiley, 1965).

26. Richard O. Carlson, *Executive Succession and Organizational Change* (Chicago: Midwest Administration Center, 1962).

27. Andrew W. Halpin, *Theory and Research.*

28. Max Weber, *Social and Economic Organization.*

29. Amitai Etzioni, *Analysis of Complex Organizations.*

30. W. G. Bennis, *Changing Organizations* (New York: McGraw-Hill, 1966).

31. Hilda Taba, *Curriculum Development—Theory and Practice* (New York: Harcourt Brace, 1962).

32. Percy Nunn, *Education: Its Data and First Principles* (London: Arnold, 1920).

Part Five

Summary and Projection

The first chapter in this part summarizes the major findings and generalizations in the book which bear upon the selection and use of social science content in preparatory programs. Pertinent data from studies not reported in the book are also included in the summary. Again, the four perspectives on relevance provide a framework for summarizing many of the findings and conclusions.

The final chapter projects general directions for future program design and change. Basic premises concerning likely developments in the field of administrator preparation and the social sciences are set forth as a framework for projections. Generalizations concerning needed specializations in the field of educational administration are elaborated, and their implications for the use of the social sciences in preparatory programs are delineated. An increase in differentiated preparation within a context of career-based relevance is projected. Several courses of action, which will likely result from increased differentiation, are presented. These are related to the four perspectives for viewing relevance.

17

The Social Sciences in Preparing Educational Leaders: An Interpretive Summary

Robin H. Farquhar

> It is one thing to recognize broadly that the social sciences have a significant contribution to make to the study of educational administration. It is quite another to design administrator training programs which will utilize social science materials in a significant way.[1]

Implicit in the above statement, written almost a decade ago, is a challenge that constitutes the primary motivation for this book. Since that time, developments within school administration and the social sciences have rendered the challenge increasingly formidable. On the one hand, the need for enlightened educational leadership, and for improved programs to prepare those who must assume responsibility for it, has been exacerbated dramatically by numerous technological advances, critical sociocultural changes, and increased client demands (and frequently conflicting expectations) for better schools. Those preparing educational leaders require all the help they can get from the cognate disciplines. On the other hand, substantial growth has occurred within the social sciences, not only in the level of sophistication achieved but also in the sheer amount of knowledge produced. Blough presents data indicating that the membership in five selected social science associations (American Anthropological Association, American Economic Association, American Historical Association, American Political Science Association, and American Sociological Association) nearly quadrupled between 1947 and 1967. As he states:

> It may be reasonably assumed that an increase in the number of scholars engaged in teaching and research in the social sci-

411

ences will be accompanied by an increase in the production of
social science knowledge. The implication of this growth for
those allied fields, like educational administration, which wish
to make selected use of social science knowledge is clear: the
task of identifying and selecting social science knowledge of potential relevance to the allied field is compounded in difficulty.[2]

The present volume is intended to help meet this difficulty.

Two primary tasks are attempted in this book. One (in Part Two)
is to present a synthesis of the major concepts and modes of inquiry
comprising each of the five social science disciplines generally con-
ceded to be most relevant to the study of educational administration (anthropology, economics, political science, social psychology,
and sociology). These chapters were written by social science
scholars. The other (in Parts Three and Four) is to explicate and
illustrate, on the basis of both actual experience and ideal conception, the identification and application of criteria for selecting
relevant social science content to incorporate into educational
administration preparatory programs. These chapters, written by
professors involved in administrative preparation, are intended to
illuminate four somewhat distinct ways of viewing relevance (the
discipline-based, theory-based, problems-based, and career-based
perspectives).

The purpose of the present chapter is to summarize those that
precede it. A descriptive chapter-by-chapter summary, however, is
not attempted. The "social sciences" chapters are already in summary form; it is difficult enough to synthesize the nature of a discipline in twenty-odd pages and virtually impossible to do it in a
paragraph or two. The "relevance perspectives" chapters, because
they contain descriptions of experiences and projections of ideas,
are both complex and comprehensive; they cannot be succinctly
summarized (beyond what Culbertson and Shibles have already
achieved in Chapter 1) without omitting crucial elements, simpli-
fying significant complexities, and obscuring important comparisons. Thus, a descriptive summary would be more of a hindrance
than a help to the reader seeking to determine what this book
"says." Greater assistance can be provided, in the author's opinion,
by an interpretation of the major "messages" that the volume seems
to communicate. This chapter, then, is an interpretive summary.
As such, it seeks to identify and illuminate those points in the
preceding chapters that bear most directly upon the major purposes
of the book.

Accordingly, the chapter has three main sections. In the first, some generalizations about the social sciences are offered with respect to their basic characteristics, relationships among them, and directions in which they appear to be moving. In the second, some generalizations about the relevance perspectives are offered with respect to the contribution they make, relationships among them, and their operationalization. In the third, an assessment of where we are now is presented with respect to the employment of social science content in educational administration preparatory programs, the resolution of the ubiquitous relevance problem, and the limitations of this volume as an attempt to advance the preparation of educational leaders. It is suggested in the chapter that, while the relevance perspectives offer some new and fruitful guidelines for selecting social science content, they do not, as reflected in this book, generate criteria for content selection that are sufficiently specific to be operational. The summary is selective and reflects the perceptual biases of the author; but this is true of any effort at synthesizing, and particularly of an interpretive summary.

THE SOCIAL SCIENCES

What is the general status of the social sciences as they are presently understood? In response to this question, Bennis has painted the following, rather disconcerting picture:

> The pivotal characteristics are these: unevenness in development and in status of theories and methodologies; necessary coupling of theory and instrumentation; fuzzy boundaries between certain of the disciplines; probably the widest spectrum of methodologies available, from rigorous experimentation to naturalistic observation; tension between the "two cultures" of science [subjective and objective study of phenomena]; as yet, no unified theory (such as "general systems" theorists have striven for) — not even, within the disciplines (aside from economics) is there an accepted general theory.[3]

If one accepts Bennis' depiction—and considerable support may be found for it among the chapters within this book—then he surely must approach with timidity the task of understanding the social sciences sufficiently to select intelligently from them content relevant to educational administration. The social sciences do not comprise a neatly integrated group of discrete, static, easily comparable disciplines within which scholars have achieved consensus as to the purpose, substance, and method of what they are about. On the contrary, the social sciences are overlapping, changing, variegated, and conflict-ridden bodies of knowledge. There is considerable disagreement, in fact, on what disciplines comprise the social sciences, and even on whether some typically included bodies of knowledge are really disciplines at all.

It is in characteristics such as these, however, that the vitality of the social sciences lies, and it is in their vitality (along with their common focus upon man and his relationships to his environment) that their potential relevance to school administration lies. To exploit this relevance requires that those preparing educational leaders become familiar not only with the basic concepts and modes of inquiry within selected disciplines but also with such general characteristics of the social sciences as those noted above. Progress toward meeting the former requirement can be facilitated by reading the chapters in Part Two of this volume, which synthesize the basic content of anthropology, economics, political science, social psychology, and sociology.

Drawing largely upon Chapters 3 through 7, some generalizations are presented below in an effort to capture the "flavor" of these disciplines at their current state of development. Among the traits that help define some contemporary characteristics of the social sciences and directions in which they are moving are their variability, indiscreteness, change, conflict, social utility, and interdisciplinarianism. These traits are derived from previous chapters and have been selected for attention here.

Variability

Because of their different primary targets of inquiry and their different stages of historical development, the social science disciplines vary in a number of ways. Several dimensions of variability have been identified by Fosmire and Littman. For example, on the dimension of individualism, they contrast psychology with other social sciences, noting that "psychology provides an understanding of the processes and outcomes of the individual as he interacts with others while the other disciplines provide an understanding of the collective results of the interaction of individuals."[4] On the dimension of impersonality, they distinguish between the attention to personal attributes which characterizes anthropology, psychology, and sociology and the focus on relations between individuals (but not the individuals themselves) that typifies economics and political science.[5] Distinctions among the former three disciplines are drawn on the dimension of molarity, with psychology (emphasizing individual behavior) being the most molecular, sociology (emphasizing group phenomena) being more molar, and anthropology (emphasizing culture and race) being the most molar. They view economics and political science as being at a molar level similar to sociology but with a different focus (as indicated above).[6]

There are numerous other dimensions along which the social science disciplines differ. They vary, for example, in the degrees to which they have achieved conceptual precision, intellectual rigor, theoretical power, and social utility. They also vary in their quantitative orientation and methodological objectivity, and the relative emphases they place on deductive and inductive approaches.

Several of these differences are evident in the chapters of Part Two. Daniere, in particular, contrasts economics with the other disciplines, pointing out such distinctions as the following: a heavier quantitative and numerical component (although Walberg notes that some social psychological theories also can be expressed mathematically, and Daniere observes that economists do considerable work with qualitative models as well); a longer history of scientific inquiry (although controlled experimentation is more characteristic of the other disciplines); a superior predictive capability; a greater tendency to "spin off" independent mathematical and statistical methodologies (like econometrics), some of which have been adopted or adapted for use in other disciplines; and a greater capacity to discover optimizing social interventions. Distinguishing characteristics such as these, he states, derive from the facts that the economic domain is as much in the physical as in the human or social world, and that the economist manipulates only a small fraction of the social and behavioral variables that are of concern to the sociologist and social psychologist.

Other authors in Part Two also comment on variations among the social sciences. There is, for example, the significant contrast between Gallaher's mention of the "holistic" tradition in American anthropology, wherein the discipline is viewed as a "holding company" for several sub-fields of study all tied together by the basic concept of culture, and Walberg's reference to social psychology as "pluralistic," with no core of integrated, universally accepted concepts and paradigms. Gallaher also points out that the anthropologist places greater stress upon patterned (as opposed to unpatterned) phenomena and qualitative (rather than quantitative) aspects of data in his work than do other social scientists. Walberg notes that the social psychologist more frequently employs experimental research designs and is more concerned with causality (in contrast to correlation) than other social scientists. Minar discusses the relatively undeveloped theories and research techniques of political science (although they are becoming more sophisticated) and suggests that it is difficult to approach the study of politics objectively, which is not as true of investigations in the other disciplines.

The above references illustrate the variability that exists among the social sciences. This is not to say, however, that the disciplines are unrelated. On the contrary, there are many instances in which the variance within them exceeds that between them, and there are certainly many points at which they overlap—which relates to the second characteristic to be discussed here.

Indiscreteness

Many definitions of the social sciences recognize, implicitly or explicitly, the difficulty of discerning definite boundaries between them. Haller, for example, expresses the belief that, while these disciplines "represent clusters of related perspectives on social phenomena in which, as it were, the between-group variance is greater than that within groups," the distinctions among them are not always clear;[7] Fosmire and Littman observe that "from each of the different sciences one can assemble a number of theories that are mutually supporting and which resemble one another more than they resemble some other theories developed within their own disciplines."[8] In the present volume, Harrison illuminates this issue by distinguishing between the content and the people involved in the social sciences, defining disciplines as "groups of people identified by interests in some roughly common subject matter and some loosely common methods of study." He goes on to say that "the groups may be mutually exclusive, but their subjects are not.... So the boundary lines between the 'disciplines' of social science are more than a little arbitrary, are frequently indistinct from almost any point of view except pure convention, and are more the products of historical accident and evolution than of any theoretical related sets of categories."

Numerous other writers have commented on the overlapping nature of the social sciences. Bennis refers to the "fuzzy" distinctions between disciplines.[9] Handy, in examining what social scientists had to say about the scope and nature of their work, found that "quite often the official definition given for one discipline was practically the same as that given for other disciplines."[10] Fosmire and Littman note that the differences they identified (reported earlier in this section) between economics and political science, on the one hand, and anthropology, psychology, and sociology, on the other hand, are diminishing and that "identical situations are being studied by investigators from each of the various behavior sciences."[11] And a recent survey published jointly by the National Academy of Sciences and the Social Science Research Council indicates that "the behavioral and social sciences have enlarged and diversified so much in recent years that there are many misconceptions about the 'division of labor' among the various disciplines and about the range of topics within any of these."[12]

More specifically, illustrations of overlapping substance and common methodologies among the social sciences abound throughout the chapters of Part Two in this book. The second table in Walberg's chapter clearly identifies some of the overlaps in content between social psychology and other disciplines, especially sociology. Walberg also mentions the growing psychological emphasis that has developed during the past half-century in economics, political science, social anthropology, and sociology. An examination of Corwin's chapter suggests that sociology may be the least discrete of the social sciences. In addition to its convergence with social psychology, it overlaps with anthropology both in substance (concepts such as role, rank, function, status, prestige, conflict, and class are common to both) and method (case studies and other field techniques are employed in each). It also overlaps with political science, particularly with respect to a shared concern with power (although they typically employ different approaches in power studies). As is clear from Minar's chapter, political scientists have interests in common with anthropologists and/or sociologists in several other constructs, such as institution, system, authority, conflict, change, culture, and social structure, and with economists in a shared concern with the allocation of resources. Minar also observes that data sources, research techniques, and theories in political science are often borrowed from, or shared with, other social sciences.

There is, then, substantial overlap among the social sciences with respect to both concepts and modes of inquiry. It thus should surprise no one that many social scientists have at least as much interest in common with scholars in other disciplines as they do with colleagues in their own. Differing perspectives within disciplines are, in fact, quite typical; accordingly, they constitute the next characteristic to be discussed here.

Conflict

The chapters in Part Two of this volume provide ample evidence of intra-disciplinary conflict in the social sciences. Daniere refers to the "noisy controversies between various schools of thought" in

economics. Minar discusses the current disagreement among political scientists about what the subject matter of their discipline is
and examines the main questions now at issue, pointing out that
political science is in a relative state of disarray compared with
other disciplines. Walberg characterizes social psychology at present as "irrelevant, fragmented, and gloomy," suggesting that it (like
other social sciences) reflects the "fragmentation, doubt, and existential anxiety" that typify the ideology and tone of society today.
Corwin identifies the varying "aims" of sociology espoused by different scholars (explanation, description, understanding, and evaluation) and highlights some major disputes currently rampant
within the discipline, including disagreements over the relative
merits of sophisticated models and field methodologies in research
and of neutrality and advocacy in orientation.

With respect to the latter issue, Corwin observes that some sociologists undertake studies to "grind their own private axes," which
highlights an important cause of the intra-disciplinary conflict
within the social sciences—the unavoidable subjectivity and personal bias of scholars. Harrison explains this well in his chapter,
where he says: "Typically, some of the greatest controversies in the
disciplines turn precisely on questions of whose values and priorities
are built into the analytic constructs and whether or not conscious
advocacy of social values is 'proper' for members of the disciplines."
The typicalness of investigator bias within the social sciences is
clear from the fact that it is specifically mentioned not only by
Corwin but by Gallaher, Minar, and Walberg as well.

Just as the personal biases of scholars can lead to conflict within
the disciplines, so can conflict result in change. This is the next
characteristic of the social sciences to be discussed here.

Change

As suggested previously, the social sciences are not static. Their
substance is constantly revised by experience, and their primary
purposes differ over time. Through research, theories are tested
against actuality, and the former get changed accordingly. As Haller notes, "social science theories have not been immutable; few
have survived the empirical crucible exactly as originally formulated."[13] According to Harrison in this book, no fully formulated
theories have been developed yet in the social sciences, although
this is an important product objective. Thus, the quest will continue and so will its concomitant substantive change.

Historically, changes in the disciplines tend to occur in certain
directions more than others with the result that trends become

evident and different "schools" achieve dominance at particular times. Thus, Walberg traces the ancient bifurcation of social psychology from Plato's analytic distinction between individual and society to the early twentieth century disciplinary discreteness of psychology and sociology; and he identifies three important trends that have emerged since the 1930s reflected in the study of group dynamics, the effort to structure and integrate substantive content, and the application of knowledge in social policy and action. He also mentions the following three basic assumptions that social psychologists have held about the nature of man and that have dominated the work of scholars at different times: rationality, as reflected in Gestalt and cognitive theory; egoism, as reflected in behaviorism and stimulus-response theory; and hedonism, as reflected in psychoanalysis and dynamic theory. In economics, Daniere traces the development from the early classicists who tended to be political economists, through the analysts of industrial capitalism and competitive models in the late nineteenth and early twentieth centuries, to the central concern with distribution and stabilization around mid-century, and finally to the preoccupation in the 1960s with sophisticated theoretical advances and elegant mathematical model-building, optimization and cost-benefit analysis, and prediction and rational policy formation. Similarly, Minar considers the historical trend in political science, away from the classical concern with determinism, speculation, and intuition, and toward the contemporary emphasis upon empiricism and sensory evidence. Gallaher discusses the general trends in anthropology away from the study of simple, primitive societies toward the study of more complex, differentiated societies, and toward greater specialization within the discipline.

As illustrated above, then, each of the disciplines changes continually, and over time the changes tend to accumulate in the form of general trends or historical movements. Some trends are characteristic of the social sciences collectively, and it is the more emergent of these that are probably of greatest interest to many readers of this volume. Thus, two of the most apparent tendencies of this type have been selected for attention in the remainder of this section.

Social Utility

Implicit in much of the preceding discussion is the persistent issue of whether the social scientist should strive for value neutrality or should employ his knowledge to seek societal change that he deems desirable. Some time ago, Goldhammer classified the latter endeavor as "social philosophy" and the former as "social science," which he said is "valueless."[14] Dahlke, on the other hand, has stated that the social sciences, and sociology in particular, cannot be value-neutral: "Insofar as they are practical disciplines, they must perforce involve themselves in value judgments."[15] Among social scientists today there is, as Bennis states, "a basic tension, a role dilemma, between commitment and detachment."[16] But it is his opinion that there is currently "a growing disenchantment with the moral neutrality of the scientist, a belief that it has led to a decline in vision and has been used as a hedge against responsibility," and that "we are moving closer to a shift in outlook from the contemplative mode to the manipulative mode."[17] This view receives some support from a recent study which found that about three-fourths of this century's major advances in social science were stimulated by practical social demands.[18]

A tendency toward greater emphasis upon the social utility of the social sciences is justified in the survey report by the National Academy of Sciences and the Social Science Research Council,[19] and is evident in the chapters of Part Two in the present book. Thus, Daniere suggests that economists, more than other social scientists, are willing to use their models toward practical ends, such as policy advocacy toward social welfare, although he recognizes that there are tendencies in this direction among the other disciplines as well. Minar predicts that political science study in the future will be directed more than previously toward reform, toward influencing decisions in the service of freedom, dignity, and equality. Walberg similarly states that social psychologists must respond increasingly to the pressing individual and social problems of today. Corwin perceives a current movement in sociology away from a value-free, neutral, and objective science toward a more liberal "new sociology" committed to social improvement.

No major societal problem, however, falls neatly within the aegis of a particular social science discipline. Such problems are complex and wide-ranging in both their sources and their expressions. Adequate "handles" on them cannot be gained from a unidisciplinary perspective. It is essential that they be approached with a multidisciplinary orientation. A tendency in this direction is beginning to emerge, as indicated below.

Interdisciplinarianism

If the chapters in Part Two are any indication, it seems clear that social scientists today are very aware of the overlaps among their disciplines. Increasingly, as Daniere and Minar recognize explicitly, the potential of these overlaps for fruitful interdisciplinary efforts is beginning, and will continue, to be realized. As Walberg notes, this tendency has been facilitated by the growing recognition on the part of those in professional schools, including schools of education, that the social sciences have relevance to their fields and the consequent encouragement of social scientists from several disciplines to cooperate in the instruction of students and the conduct of research in applied areas. The tendency has also been encouraged by the development within universities of special (often temporary) centers at which scholars from several disciplines collaborate in the multidisciplinary study of selected problem areas or professional fields.[20] In an effort to further movement in this direction, the National Academy of Sciences and the Social Science Research Council have recommended that "universities consider the establishment of broadly based training and research programs in the form of a Graduate School of Applied Behavioral Science (or some local equivalent) under administrative arrangements that lie outside the established disciplines."[21]

The success of efforts to promote interdisciplinarianism among social scientists, however, depends at least as much on psychological variables as on structural arrangements. Mutual respect, shared interests, joint commitment, and serendipity are significant factors. Bennis makes a telling point when he says:

> I have found ... that inter-disciplinary collaboration is practically impossible to plan, that it depends as much on conviviality and propinquity as it does on anything else, and that when it does occur, it happens quite spontaneously between two or more scientists from different fields, who share a common methodology, captivation with a common problem, and a nearby bar.[22]

Perhaps future designers of facilities for departments of educational administration should include a prominently placed cocktail lounge in their blueprints.

THE RELEVANCE PERSPECTIVES

Recognition of characteristics such as the above, which seek to capture the "flavor" of the current state of development in the social sciences, is essential to those seeking to identify and select content from the disciplines that is relevant to educational administration. But this is only a first step. Once one has become familiar with the nature of the source pool, he faces the more difficult task of determining which content he should select from that pool to best achieve his purposes. He must confront the vexatious issue of relevance.

At a general level, the main dilemma underlying this issue has been posed by Cunningham, Downey, and Goldhammer as follows: "whether to begin with the substances of the various social sciences and attempt to extract from these such materials as appear to be of most use to the administrator, *or* to begin with a specification of the substance of administration and attempt to identify the areas in which this overlaps with the substance of the various social sciences."[23] Tope has stated it in similar terms.[24] While posing this dilemma helps define the issue of relevance, it is not sufficiently specific to be of much assistance in developing criteria that can contribute effectively to resolving this issue. The four relevance perspectives that provide a framework for much of the present book represent an attempt to conceptualize the issue of relevance at a level specific enough to generate criteria for selecting social science content.

The relevance perspectives were identified inductively from literature reviews and first-hand observation and are defined by Culbertson and Shibles in Chapter 1. They are (1) the discipline-based perspective, which starts with and assesses relevance by reference to concepts, research findings, generalizations, and modes of inquiry in social science disciplines; (2) the theory-based perspective, which starts with and assesses relevance by reference to theories of administration and organization associated with the "science" of administration; (3) the problems-based perspective, which starts with and assesses relevance by reference to problems confronting or likely to confront educational administrators or leaders; and (4) the career-based perspective, which starts with and assesses relevance by reference to career objectives and functions of personnel preparing to use knowledge in educational administration within different settings and for different purposes. Culbertson and Shibles examine the distinguishing historical events from which these perspectives developed, and they identify some of the general instructional goals through which each is expressed. They note that the perspectives are interrelated, interactive, over-simplified, and typically employed in some combination; nevertheless, they have considerable conceptual distinctiveness and, thus, have heuristic value in addressing the issue of relevance.

As Culbertson and Shibles observe, the discipline-based and theory-based perspectives fall largely within the first approach identified by Cunningham, Downey, and Goldhammer, while the problems-based and career-based perspectives more closely resemble their second approach. Yet, distinguishing characteristics are claimed for each of the perspectives. For example, the discipline-based and theory-based perspectives differ as the latter draws upon more than one discipline, aspires more toward value neutrality, and is typically implemented through professional schools, rather than social science departments; whereas, the opposite is true of the former. The problems-based and career-based perspectives differ since the former focuses upon the substantive targets of administrative behavior; whereas, the latter emphasizes the leadership functions performed.

Whether or not these relevance perspectives are functional in identifying and applying criteria for selecting social science content can be determined to some extent by examining the chapters in Parts Three and Four of this book. Although it must be remembered that these chapters were written explicitly to demonstrate the functionality of the perspectives, the experiences reported in Part Three preceded and informed the conceptualization of the perspectives. The present section focuses upon the following three topics that are central to assessing the usefulness of the perspectives: the contribution they make to resolving the relevance issue, the nature of relationships among them, and the factors affecting their operationalization.

Contribution

Are the perspectives discussed in this book any more helpful than previous efforts to grapple with the issue of relevance? Numerous writers have expressed in general terms a belief that the social sciences are pertinent to educational administration. Many of them leave it at this point, and one senses in their motivation a rather desperate attempt to locate a legitimate source of substance for their field of study or to discover a means by which it might be rendered more academically respectable. Others have sought to indicate why these disciplines are relevant. Their efforts, however, have typically lacked precision. Usually, they have consisted of lists of administrative skills, processes, tasks, or functions, followed or preceded by a vague statement about how obvious it is that the social sciences can contribute to preparing administrators for these skills, processes, tasks, or functions. Little or nothing is said about how one can determine what social science content can contribute most or best (although some examples, apparently selected almost at random, are often given). Still others have started with the disciplines and derived lists of concepts, theories, and methodologies for which they claim relevance to educational administration. But seldom do they specify what in administration they are relevant to, why they are relevant, or (with the exception of Charters' singular establishment of provisional criteria[25]) how the quality of their relevance can be determined.

There is no intent here to denigrate the efforts of those who, in the sixties, applied thrust to the social science movement in educational administration. Their arguments in support of relevance were persuasive; but they did not generate criteria by which others could determine and assess relevance. The result has been that while some (represented by several of the authors in this book) have been capable of developing and applying satisfactory relevance criteria on their own, others have recklessly jumped on the social science band wagon without really knowing (or having any control over) where they were going. If the relevance perspectives in this book have a primary contribution to make, it is probably by helping the latter through reporting and analyzing the experiences of the former.

The selection of social science content for administrative preparation is an exercise in curriculum development and should be conducted in accordance with the best theory and practice in that field, as Lipham demonstrates well in his chapter. The four relevance perspectives are designed to facilitate this, for they are derived from the differing instructional objectives of professors. They recognize that the aims and philosophy with which a professor approaches his task strongly affect his definition of relevance and, hence, are central to the kinds of criteria he should employ in selecting social science content. By classifying various definitions of relevance into four somewhat distinct categories differentiated primarily in terms of instructional objectives, the perspectives not only permit a professor to select a definition of relevance that is congruent with his own aims and philosophy, but they also generate relatively specific guidelines by which he can identify and apply criteria for selecting social science content that will help him achieve his instructional objectives.

It is in these respects, then, that the primary contribution of the perspectives to resolving the relevance issue lies. To a greater extent than previous approaches, they provide the professor conceptual frameworks which enable him to examine and clarify his instructional objectives, and they have potential for generating explicit criteria according to which he can determine the relevance of social science content to his instructional objectives. As noted later, however, this potential is not fully realized in the present volume. Some possible reasons for this are discussed below.

Relationship

Despite the disclaimer by Culbertson and Shibles to the effect that the relevance perspectives are not wholly discrete, the rationale for positing them rests rather firmly on the assumption that the instructional objectives from which they derive and the selection criteria that they should generate are essentially distinct. This does not necessarily mean that different social science content will be selected depending on the relevance perspective involved; but it does mean that the content will be selected for different reasons. Whether or not this can occur as a result of viewing relevance in terms of the four perspectives is a good test of their value. Because distinctiveness among them is postulated as a conceptual more than an operational level, it seems more appropriate to explore this question with reference to the ideal conceptions presented in Part Four of the book than with reference to the actual experiences reported in Part Three. (In operationalizing the perspectives, numerous extrinsic variables serve to confuse the issue of conceptual distinctiveness, as noted later in this section.)

While virtually all of the authors in Part Four agree with Culbertson and Shibles that preparation programs should involve frequent movement back and forth between social science knowledge and administrative practice, the perspectives are differentiated in terms of where the movement starts and on which side the greatest emphasis is placed in determining relevance. In this regard, it seems that the problems-based perspective is potentially the most distinct. In operationalizing it, one analyzes the component dimensions of a problem and then selects whatever social science content is available (concepts or theories, undisciplinary or multidisciplinary) to help illuminate and resolve these dimensions. It must be admitted, however, that this is not clearly indicated in Goldhammer's treatment of the problems-based perspective; rather than emphasizing the dimensions of problems as criteria generators, he focuses more upon the functions and procedures involved in recognizing, diagnosing, prescribing for, and implementing cures for problems. Nevertheless, his chapter does demonstrate the relative distinctiveness of approaching the issue of relevance from a primary orientation to organizational pathologies.

The discipline-based and theory-based perspectives are less distinctive. It is apparent from both Harrison's chapter and the one by Crane and Walker that these two perspectives cannot be very easily differentiated. There are, after all, theories indigenous to particular disciplines, although these generally differ from the interdisciplinary theories of organization and administration involved in the theory-based perspective. Further, elements of the problembased perspective enter Harrison's discussion of the discipline-based perspective (but from a proactive rather than a reactive viewpoint) as do elements of the career-based perspective (particularly with regard to differing social science related research abilities required by those pursuing differing careers). Nevertheless, Harrison does demonstrate how the primary guidelines for selecting content can be found in the nature of a discipline itself, which is the essence of the discipline-based perspective.

It appears from the Crane and Walker chapter that the theory-based perspective cannot be easily isolated from the other three. Their primary justification for the theory-based perspective contains strong elements of the problems-based rationale. Their initial classification of theories in accordance with Parsons' organizational levels and in terms of the relative particularism of various social sciences contains strong elements of the career-based and discipline-based perspectives, respectively. In the latter part of the chapter, they adopt more directly the theory-based perspective in their classification of theories according to indigenous criteria. These are qualitative criteria, however, and one wonders whether they could serve effectively as selection criteria without explicit reference to the problems-based, career-based, and discipline-based considerations presented earlier in the chapter.

Finally, the career-based perspective seems the least distinctive of all, at least as a generator of criteria for selecting social science content. While it does stem from a unique purpose in preparation and provides an heuristic conceptual framework to guide the development of differentiated preparatory programs, it appears to become incorporated with the other three perspectives when it is applied to the identification and application of selection criteria. As Culbertson demonstrates, the career-based perspective facilitates a determination of the differing nature, goals, and functions of different careers in educational administration and these, in turn, help to generate guidelines for selecting content. However, when one faces the task of identifying and applying criteria for the actual selection of social science content, he finds himself (as Culbertson observes) operationalizing other perspectives. Thus, in selecting content to prepare conclusion-oriented researchers, the discipline-based perspective is employed; content to prepare concept-oriented synthesizers is selected from a combination of the discipline-based and theory-based perspectives; and content to prepare product-oriented developers and general administrators is selected largely from the problems-based perspective, although the nature of developmental and administrative problems differs. The career-based perspective, then, is less a distinct relevance perspective than a rationale or "screen" for determining which of the other perspectives to employ in selecting content.

That the four perspectives appear less conceptually distinct than might have been hoped by no means negates the value of the chapters in Part Four or of the perspectives themselves. They have potential for generating selection criteria related to instructional objectives, as these chapters demonstrate and, thus, they represent a more systematic, comprehensive, and useful approach to the problem of selecting relevant social science content than any previously published attempts in educational administration. What happens when they are operationalized in actual preparatory programs is the next topic for discussion.

Operationalization

Numerous factors impinging upon administrative preparation programs affect not only the operationalization of the four relevance perspectives but also the very choice of perspectives to be employed. The central significance of instructional objectives has already been mentioned. Other variables also have a major impact, as the chapters in Part Three indicate; these variables may be classified generally as personal, institutional, societal, and substantive in nature.

Two kinds of personal variables are dominant in the selection of social science content. One involves the professors' values, interests, and competencies. The impact of these variables is well illustrated by comparing the chapters by Lipham and Willower. While both demonstrate the operationalization of the theory-based perspective, the selection guidelines they follow are quite different. This is true in part because of the high importance Willower personally assigns to approaching theory with a "probing skepticism." The importance of the professor as a variable is also exemplified in Horvat's statement that his first criterion for selecting social science concepts was that the instructor be acquainted with them, and in the view expressed by both Hartley and Lipham, the professor who selects and teaches the content should have a firm grounding in the social sciences at the graduate level. A second kind of personal variable involves the students' needs, aspirations, and interests. Horvat points out that an important determinant of the content he employed in his negotiations workshop was the realization that his students were relatively unsophisticated practicing administrators interested in learning as quickly as possible the processes and techniques for face-to-face bargaining. Similarly, among the assumptions from which Hartley works in selecting content for his Economics of Education course is that his students have not previously studied economics. Lipham identifies students' needs and interests as a primary source of objectives for his teaching of theory, and it is from his objectives that his selection criteria are derived.

Lipham also indicates the importance of societal variables, in his recognition of the nature of life in contemporary organizations as another important source for his instructional objectives. Horvat implies that the negotiations workshop he discusses might not have been offered at all had it not been for the fact that a recent state law had forced his clients to confront the bargaining problem. Institutional variables also have an impact on the selection of social science content. As Cronin and Iannaccone point out, the career-based differentiations between the Chicago and Harvard programs emerged in large part because of such factors as the inclusion of Chicago's program as an integral component of the university's Division of Social Sciences, the strength of Harvard's Center for Field Studies, and the differing orientations of key individuals on the faculties of the two universities during the programs' formative years. Further, Lipham notes the significance to content selection of a university's mechanisms for program change and of the facilities and materials available. In the latter regard, it is likely that Horvat's approach to content selection would have been quite different had the "bargaining game" (which he developed) not been available for his use. Finally, there is the variable of substance, which is recognized explicitly by Lipham as a major source for his instructional objectives. The selection of social science content is surely influenced by what content is available and particularly by that which has emerged recently.

Thus, numerous contextual variables serve to constrain (or enhance) the operationalization of the relevance perspectives. These variables influence the establishment of instructional objectives, as Lipham clearly demonstrates. Because selection criteria are (or should be) generated by instructional objectives, the relevance perspectives cannot be operationalized independently of the contextual variables. It is not clear which (the perspectives or the variables) take precedence in a professor's determination of selection criteria; this probably varies from one individual, institution, or time to another. It is apparent, however, that the end result, the determination and following of guidelines for selecting social science content, may be classified as reflecting one perspective toward relevance more than another, and that four such perspectives are represented by the chapters in Part Three of this book. And so we have come full circle; for it was on the basis of this kind of induction that the relevance perspectives were postulated in the first place.

WHERE ARE WE?

It has been suggested that the social sciences are in a state of flux which in some instances approaches chaos, and that the four relevance perspectives postulated in this book are neither conceptually distinct nor operationally pure. This does not mean, however, that the social sciences do not represent a rich source of content pertinent to educational administration or that the relevance perspectives do not constitute an important new aid in the identification and application of criteria for selecting content. On this uncertain note, it would seem worthwhile to reflect briefly on where we are at present in educational administration with respect to the employment of social science content in preparatory programs, the resolution of the continuing problem of relevance, and the limitations of this volume as a contributor to improved administrative preparation.

Employment of the Social Sciences

There is no question that there has been a "social science movement" in educational administration within the past fifteen years. The literature bulges with expressions of support for this trend, and the vast majority of North American universities employ some means to incorporate social science content into their administrative preparation programs. However, the success of these efforts is debatable. A few years ago, Goldhammer found in his survey of school superintendents evidence of "a scarcity of consistent programs with well-developed rationales for the use of the behavioral sciences in preparing administrators for the achievement of specified goals.[26] Miklos observed that "when we consider critically the total impact of the behavioral science-administration relationship upon the field, when we consider the many areas in which there appears to have been little or no impact, when we compare what is with what might be or should be in view of the length of the association, our observations tend to be disquieting."[27] Both Hills and Shaplin reported data suggesting that those preparing educational administrators may talk a better game than they play in regard to employing the social sciences.[28] More recently, though, the UCEA survey of programs preparing school superintendents indicated that the incorporation of subject matter from the social sciences was one of the four most frequently cited strengths in program content, that the most common recent change in content was the incorporation of additional social science material, and that the most frequent change in staffing during the previous five years was the addition of professors with competencies or backgrounds in the social sciences.[29] The same survey, however, yielded evidence of a strongly perceived need for more and better use of the social sciences in administrative preparation. As Haller and Hickcox remark in Chapter 2 of the present book, many prospective professors of educational administration still take no social science courses during their graduate study, and most take less than 15 per cent of their course work in the social sciences. Haller and Hickcox also indicate that some apparently relevant disciplines receive far less attention than others in preparatory programs.

The same authors identify the following three common strategies for incorporating social science content into administrative preparation: the requirement strategy, whereby students must take course work in the disciplines; the minor member strategy, whereby doctoral students must include non-educationists on their advisory committees; and the in-house strategy, whereby professors of educational administration introduce social science content into their own courses. Haller and Hickcox find that the in-house strategy is the most commonly employed of the three, which conflicts with the UCEA survey finding that the most typical approach to incorporating content from the disciplines is to send educational administration students across campus.[30] Either strategy has problems, however. Haller and Hickcox observe that the requirement or across campus approach often results in a dysfunctional cafeteria technique and leaves to the student the difficult task of integrating the social science disciplines with educational administration, a task which the practitioners participating in Goldhammer's study found problematical.[31] The in-house strategy suffers from the fact that, as Taylor has observed along with Haller and Hickcox, most professors of educational administration are unqualified or ill-qualified to teach social science content.[32]

Thus, while the employment of the social sciences in administrative preparation is increasing, it continues to be generally inadequate, uneven, and problem-ridden. Some of the problems, as observed in Harrison's chapter, stem from the vast differences in perspectives, purposes, and methods between the social scientist and the educational administrator. Others have undoubtedly resulted, as Miklos suggests, from the tendency of those designing administrative preparation programs to underestimate the magnitude and complexity of the task, overemphasize the necessity of bringing prospective administrators into direct contact with social scientists, underemphasize the significance of the professor of educational administration, fail to learn how to work with social scientists, and be overly cautious in approach and too loose in program structure.[33] Probably the most significant source of problems in employing the social sciences, however, is the relevance issue.

Resolution of the Relevance Problem

As stated earlier, the four perspectives postulated in this book contribute productively to the resolution of the relevance problem since they have potential for the more systematic generation of criteria for selecting social science content in accordance with instructional objectives. For a variety of reasons mentioned previously, this potential has not been fully realized, at least in the present volume. A brief review of the major contributions of chapters in Parts Three and Four illustrates this point.

Crane and Walker select a substantial number of social science theorists, classify their works along a kind of "individualism continuum" ranging from political/historical theories to individual psychological theories, and relate this classification to the three organizational levels posited by Parsons, thereby suggesting the kinds of social science theories that appear most relevant in preparing educational administrators to perform as boundary spanners between different levels in Parsons' framework. In addition, they develop seven criteria which can help guide the professor in making qualitative judgments about social science theories, and they rate a dozen well-known theorists according to whether (in the authors' judgment) their work is high or low on several of these criteria. But, as the authors suggest, criteria for selecting from among "good" theories must depend in large part on the relative merits the selector assigns to the various qualitative characteristics, and they offer little specific guidance in this regard.

Cronin and Iannaccone analyze in considerable detail the historical development and productiveness of the Chicago and Harvard programs, which have traditionally employed the social sciences in different ways. They examine the differing purposes, institutional arrangements, key personnel, and instructional approaches that evolved in these two universities; the impact of these developments upon attitudes toward and the employment of the social sciences in administrative preparation; and the resultant differentiation between general career lines typically followed by graduates of the two programs. However, (aside from mentioning the very general depth-versus-breadth contrast) they do not indicate how or whether differentiated criteria for selecting social science content have been employed at these universities.

Also on the differentiation theme, Culbertson develops the idea that programs for preparing those pursuing different specialized career patterns in educational administration should be differentiated in several ways, including their employment of social science content. He selects four specialized career patterns; explicates how they differ in goals, functions, competencies, aspirations, and a number of other characteristics; and presents some of the implications of these distinctions for differentiated preparation in the form of ten guidelines for determining instructional content and experiences. He concludes with some examples that illustrate the operationalization of these guidelines. But his criteria for selecting content remain implicit within the guidelines.

Goldhammer conceptualizes problem solving in educational administration as a clinical process and discusses the major elements in this process. He explores and illustrates the ways in which social science content can help prepare administrators to identify, diagnose, and treat organizational pathologies, and discusses some of the clinical experiences that are useful in such preparation. In addition, he identifies five elements of problems that must be examined by the administrator-as-diagnostician, each of which contains implicit guidelines for selecting social science content from the problems-based relevance perspective. However, he does not explicate specific criteria by which one can identify and select pertinent content related to these elements.

Harrison provides helpful definitions of "social sciences" and "disciplines," and considers in some depth the substantive, procedural, and normative dimensions of the social sciences. He then relates these dimensions to four ways of conceiving relevance according to the discipline-based perspective and demonstrates how each dimension can contribute content pertinent to each of the ways of conceiving relevance. However, operational criteria by which one can select content into the cells of his grid are not presented.

Hartley also deals with the discipline-based approach, presenting a systematic analysis of its implementation in a course on Economics of Education. He identifies the major purpose of the course, indicates its basic assumptions, and specifies twenty criteria (organized within five priority-ordered categories) which he employs in selecting social science content. He illustrates how the PPBS concept meets his criteria and presents a course outline to indicate the other kinds of economic content selected. In addition, he discusses the procedure of content selection and some of the problems encountered in pursuing it. His chapter probably comes closer to generating operational selection criteria than any other in the book.

Horvat deals with the problems-based perspective, presenting an analysis of a workshop on collective bargaining. He describes the setting and activities of the workshop, discusses the major instructional problems inherent within it, and presents a conceptualization of the dimensions (organized according to four bargaining subprocesses) comprising negotiation as an administrative problem. He then provides a number of examples of social science concepts relevant to each of the problem dimensions, but the criteria he says were employed in selecting these concepts are at such a general level as to be of little assistance to a professor attempting to use them for his own purposes.

Lipham illustrates the application of curriculum theory to the selection of social science content in accordance with the theory-based relevance perspective. He begins with the establishment of instructional objectives, identifying three sources for objectives and three screens through which objectives are selected. Then, to facilitate the use of social science theories as organizing centers for instruction to achieve his objectives, he explicates six criteria for selecting theories, half of them valuational in nature and the other half descriptive. He indicates how, in his judgment, a number of social science theories rate on each of these criteria and develops schematic profiles on them for two selected theories. While his valuational criteria are useful in the same way that those of Crane and Walker (and Charters) are, his descriptive criteria are actually qualitative continua that can help generate selection criteria but are not criteria themselves.

Willower also illustrates the operationalization of the theory-based perspective. He emphasizes his purpose of teaching students to work creatively with and develop a critical stance toward theory, rather than merely to learn about theory. He reports the kinds of instructional activities through which these purposes are achieved, provides examples of theories selected to facilitate these activities, and illustrates how some theories are employed to involve students directly in theory-analyzing, theory-testing, and theory-building experiences. However, he does not specify criteria by which theories can be selected to achieve the purposes he identifies.

On the basis of the above review, it seems fair to state that in most instances, while these chapters provide numerous guidelines (with illustrations) that can help direct one's search for relevant content, the step from guidelines to criteria still remains to be taken. It may be, as Harrison suggests, that there can be "no *formula* of relevance for determining selection criteria — only intuition." Tope may be correct in his opinion that "it will probably never be satisfactorily determined which material gleaned from social science study and research is most relevant to a field like school administration."[34] Yet, it seems too soon for those in educational administration to relinquish the quest for some resolution of the relevance problem. A significant advance has been made in this book. Suggestions for further advances are implicit in its contents. Certainly, efforts should be made to refine, validate, and test the many guidelines and qualitative characteristics presented by the chapter authors and to determine their capability for generating reliable and applicable selection criteria, much in the way that Blough has examined Charters' work.[35]

Limitations of This Book

Preparatory programs are complex and comprehensive entities. Content is only one of numerous program elements. (Others include structure, recruitment and selection, instructional approaches, field-related experiences, staffing patterns, evaluation methods, etc. — most of which have been mentioned only in passing, if at all, in this volume.) The selection of relevant content is only one of several content-related tasks in programs. (Its organization, presentation, and evaluation are others.) This book is limited to the consideration of only four, inductively determined perspectives for viewing relevance. (Other perspectives are undoubtedly operationalized by professors, and still others could probably be developed by deduction.) The social sciences constitute only one source of content relevant to educational administration. (Certainly, the humanities, the emerging management sciences, mathematics, and various applied fields of study have provided important content for many preparatory programs.) Finally, the five disciplines emphasized in this book do not exhaust the sources of relevant content within the social sciences. (Psychology and, by some definitions, history are among the other social science disciplines that have some pertinence to educational administration.)

No book can do it all, and only a very small portion can be done well in any single volume.

CONCLUSION

This book was written primarily to help program designers and students who are interested in the relevance of social science content to educational administration. One of its major contributions to this end is the synthesis of central concepts and modes of inquiry presented for each of the five social science disciplines most commonly viewed as relevant to educational administration. These summaries serve to delineate the source pool from which pertinent substance can be selected. The volume's other main contribution is the identification, explication, and demonstration of four perspectives on relevance that can enhance the selection of social science content in accordance with one's instructional objectives. The perspectives differ just as instructional objectives do and when they are clearly conceptualized and operationalized, they tend to generate differing guidelines for selecting content.

But too much must not be claimed for the perspectives. As presented, they have provided a useful conceptual framework within which to organize and analyze the varying approaches to content selection that have been reported; however, they have not resulted in the specification of criteria that can be directly applied by those seeking to solve the problem of selecting relevant content. This burden still rests with the judgment of individual program designers and students, but the load has been lightened by the guidelines generated through the perspectives discussed herein.

Although the transition from guidelines to criteria has not been fully achieved in this book, it is not necessarily an unattainable goal. The way to further advances in this direction has been opened, and some issues have been identified for further investigation. It may be, for example, that clear criteria are not typically applied in the actual process of selecting social science content; the level of general guidelines may be as specific as anyone ever gets, can get, or needs to get. Alternatively, criteria may be applied but at such a subjective and personalistic level that it is impossible to be explicit about them. Or criteria may be applied, and it may be possible to explicate them but not within the framework provided by the four relevance perspectives treated in this book; some other conceptualizations of relevance may be necessary to foster the identification of operational selection criteria. These, and other, possibilities emerge from the contents of this volume and should be explored systematically.

Thus, important challenges still confront those who would improve the employment of social science content in preparing educational leaders. Some suggestions concerning how they may be approached in the future are offered by Fogarty in the final chapter.

FOOTNOTES

1. Lawrence W. Downey and Frederick Enns, "Introduction to Part V" in *The Social Sciences and Educational Administration,* eds. Lawrence W. Downey and Frederick Enns (Edmonton: The University of Alberta, 1963), p. 95.

2. John A. Blough, "Knowledge for Action: An Analysis of the Relevance of Selected Social Science Concepts to the Preparation of Educational Administrators" (Unpublished research proposal for doctoral dissertation, The Ohio State University, 1971).

3. Warren G. Bennis, "Future of the Social Sciences," *The Antioch Review* 27, 2 (Summer 1968): 232–233.

4. Fred Fosmire and Richard L. Littman, "The Behavior Sciences — An Overview" in *The Social Sciences View School Administration,* eds. Donald E. Tope, et al. (Englewood Cliffs, N.J.: Prentice-Hall, Inc., 1965), p. 54.

5. Ibid., p. 55.

6. Ibid., pp. 37–8.

7. Emil J. Haller. "The Interdisciplinary Ideology in Educational Administration: Some Preliminary Notes on the Sociology of Knowledge," *Educational Administration Quarterly* 4, 2 (Spring 1968): 66.

8. Fosmire and Littman, "The Behavior Sciences," p. 55.

9. Bennis, "Future of Social Sciences," p. 229.

10. Rollo Handy, "Some Philosophical Issues in Metropolitanism" (Paper delivered at the Ninteenth UCEA Career Development Seminar, Buffalo, 1969), p. 1.

11. Fosmire and Littman, "The Behavior Sciences," p. 38.

12. National Academy of Sciences and Social Science Research Council, *The Behavioral and Social Sciences: Outlook and Needs* (Englewood Cliffs, N.J.: Prentice-Hall, Inc., 1969), p. 27.

13. Haller, "Interdisciplinary Ideology in Administration," p. 74.

14. Keith Goldhammer, *The Social Sciences and the Preparation of Administrators* (Edmonton: Division of Educational Administration, University of Alberta; and Columbus, Ohio: The University Council for Educational Administration, 1963), pp. 6–7.

15. H. Otto Dahlke, "The Study of Value Systems," *Alberta Journal of Educational Research* 15, 3 (June 1969): 93.

16. Bennis, "Future of Social Sciences," p. 252.

17. Ibid., pp. 242–243.

18. Robert Reinhold, "Social Science Gains Tied to Big Teams of Scholars," *The New York Times* (March 16, 1971), p. 26C.

19. National Academy of Sciences and Social Science Research Council, *Behavioral and Social Sciences*, p. 93.

20. An example pertinent to the subject of this book is the Center for the Advanced Study of Educational Administration at the University of Oregon.

21. National Academy of Sciences and Social Science Research Council, *Behavioral and Social Sciences*, p. 12.

22. Bennis, "Future of Social Sciences," p. 249.

23. Luvern L. Cunningham, Lawrence W. Downey, and Keith Goldhammer, "Implications for Administrator Training Programs" in *The Social Sciences and Educational Administration*, p. 97.

24. Donald E. Tope, "Equipping the School Administrator for His Task" in *The Social Sciences View School Administration*, p. 30.

25. W. W. Charters, Jr., "Anthropology and the Study of Administration— Response" in *The Social Sciences and Educational Administration,* pp. 91–93.

26. Keith Goldhammer, et. al., *Issues and Problems in Contemporary Educational Administration* (Eugene: Center for the Advanced Study of Educational Administration, University of Oregon, 1967), p. 114.

27. Erwin Miklos, "The Behavioral Sciences and Educational Administration: Some Reconsiderations" in *Educational Administration: International Perspectives*, eds. George Baron, Dan H. Cooper, and William G. Walker (Chicago: Rand McNally & Company, 1969), p. 169.

28. Jean Hills, "Educational Administration: A Field in Transition," *Educational Administration Quarterly* 1, 1 (Winter 1965): 58–66.
Judson T. Shaplin, "The Professorship in Educational Administration: Attracting Talented Personnel" in *The Professorship in Educational Administration*, eds. Donald J. Willower and Jack Culbertson (Columbus: The University Council for Educational Administration; and University Park: The College of Education, The Pennsylvania State University, 1964), pp. 1–14.

29. Jack Culbertson, et al., *Preparing Educational Leaders for the Seventies* (Final Report, U. S. Office of Education Project No. 8–0230, 1969), pp. 339, 401, and 423–424.

30. Ibid., p. 431.

31. Goldhammer, et al., *Issues and Problems,* pp. 154–155.

32. William Taylor, "Issues and Problems in the Training of the School Administrator" in *Educational Administration and the Social Sciences* eds. George Baron and William Taylor (London: Athlone, 1969), p. 109.

33. Miklos, "Behavioral Sciences," pp. 178–181.

34. Tope, "Equipping the School Administrator," p. 27.

35. John A. Blough, "Knowledge for Action: An Analysis of the Relevance of Selected Social Science Concepts to the Preparation of Educational Administrators" (Unpublished Ph.D. dissertation, The Ohio State University, 1971).

18

The Social Sciences and Educational Administration: A Projection

Bryce M. Fogarty

We are not found wanting for efforts to project what society as a whole, the educational enterprise in particular, or the specific professional area of educational administration will be like in ten or fifteen years or, even, at the advent of the elusively exciting "Year 2000." Amateur futurists abound, and the clinical practice of futurism is rapidly developing a coterie of proponents and an increasingly specialized body of knowledge. In spite of occasional charges of escapism, many are finding that forecasting the future has several innate attractions. It doesn't involve precise manipulation of hard data; it cannot incorporate elaborate verificational tests. If projections do not come to pass, it will be of little consequence to the prognosticator who, by the time reality descends, presumably will be directing his attention toward a newly defined future and operating from a different body of knowledge and set of premises. Most important, it is an absolutely essential activity if significant evolutions are to be identified and, perhaps, directed and if major problems and issues are to be anticipated and, perhaps, avoided.

With all the forecasts available and with the limitations on scholarship which forecasting entails, why contribute to the deluge? There are basically two reasons: 1) the structure of this book logically flows from past to present to future. Uses of social science knowledge in preparatory programs in educational administration during the past have been described; criteria used currently to select social science content have been analyzed and illustrated. Therefore, some attention must be given to what the future may

entail if the assessment of the past and present has implications for
program development; and 2) despite the spate of future-oriented
literature currently available, little attention is devoted to the specific subject of content and criteria for selecting this content which
will be basic to preparatory programs in the years ahead. Much
more of what has been written is directed toward new administrative structures, instructional mechanisms, and societal relationships, subjects that will be explored only tangentially here.

Projections are only as rational as the premises from which they
evolve. Obviously, any projection regarding content selection for
preparatory programs in educational administration is ludicrous if
one is operating on the assumption that there will be no such thing
as an educational administrator by, say, 1980. There are eight major
assumptions which form the framework for much of the future-
oriented thinking which will be presented in this paper. Each of
these premises is subject to question, and particular biases could
lead to totally different starting points for discussions related to the
identical subject. Nevertheless, it is essential that they be stated
here explicitly so that assessment of projections can be analyzed
from a particular frame of reference, albeit an arbitrary one.

Premise 1: Education will continue to take place within social
organizations designed and established to guide learning. Such organizations may well be diverse in structure, particularistic in goal orientation, and temporary
in character.

Premise 2: Although hierarchical relationships within these social organizations charged with the task of educating
may well be different from those found today in
schools, there will be still the need for administrators
of the educational organization and of the learning
process.

Premise 3: Those individuals aspiring to achieve administrative
positions in educational organizations may come from
widely divergent educational, societal, philosophical,
motivational, and experiential backgrounds.

Premise 4: Academic preparation for prospective administrators
will continue to be provided in the educational environment of the university. Structures within universities for identifying and transmitting the academic
knowledge base will be as divergent and particular-

istic as the organizations in which individuals will be required to serve.

Premise 5: The academic knowledge base for prospective practicing administrators will be expanded in meaningful ways through the development of various types of field experiences which will facilitate role orientation, problem analysis, knowledge application, and institutional socialization. Specific individuals in the preparatory institutions will be identified and charged with developing strong relationships between academic knowledge and field experience.

Premise 6: Significant evolving issues in educational administration will have their roots in societal problems and conditions, and understanding of these various issues will be gained through expanded study of the social sciences, either through existing means or through processes yet to be identified.

Premise 7: While increasing recognition will be given to the importance of social science knowledge in understanding the many dimensions of the significant issues in educational administration, a parallel development in the social sciences will result in a substantial movement of social scientists away from a tight interpretation of their disciplines and their roles as scholars in favor of greater activism in the study of societal issues and institutions.

Premise 8: The convergence of the recognition that significant issues in educational administration have their genesis in broader societal conditions which can best be explored from a base of social science knowledge and of the interest of social scientists in the application of their disciplines to the analysis and possible solution of societal problems will provide a condition for cooperation, experimentation, and learning hitherto unknown in preparatory programs in educational administration.

Within the bounds prescribed by these premises, certain generalizations about future preparatory programs in educational administration can be explicated. It is, for example, clear that social science content will constitute the bulk of the academic knowledge base used in preparing educational administration professionals — both practitioners and professors. The selection of social science content will follow diverse patterns determined by the relevance of content to particular levels of preparation and by the expectations identified as pertinent to specific roles which individuals are being prepared to assume. As the ultimate, one can envision a two stage program consisting of a common social science base for all students of administration and a specialization stage in which social science content is identified and selected according to its adjudged relevance to such divergent professional roles as those of the practicing administrator, the synthesizing professor, the field synthesizing professor, the discipline-based professor, and the disciplined-based researcher. It is suggested, therefore, that no single set of criteria can be applied universally to the task of selecting social science content which may be relevant to all levels of preparation or to all of the roles likely to emerge in educational administration. Rather, criteria for selecting social science content will be sharply defined and highly differentiated.

The common base for all students of educational administration, regardless of their future professional orientation, is regarded as essential to the development of professional interrelationships and communication channels among practitioners, professors, and researchers. The lack of a common knowledge base has created serious barriers for the development of a profession. Theory — practice gaps, practitioner — professor antagonisms, and field-university schisms, most notably in the area of research, can all be traced either directly or indirectly to the absence of knowledge common to all. Such knowledge may provide the foundation or core for future professional preparatory programs. This core however, will be unlike many traditional foundation programs common in universities today. It will be different in organization, as well as in content selection.

The "common" program is seen as being organized on the basis of critical centralizing themes in society and in education. Some movement in this direction can be seen today with the establishment and spread of introductory courses in organization theory which draw heavily upon social science content from several disciplines. But such courses are still limited to a very small number of themes, and the multidisciplinary approach in many programs is still overwhelmed by moves early in the preparatory program toward specific role oriented courses and courses focused upon a single function of administration. Broadly based knowledge directed toward the analysis and understanding of significant issues in administration is often far overshadowed by the unseemly haste toward specialization, either according to role or to functional performance.

Centralizing themes which might appropriately provide foci for marshaling social science content can be readily identified. Some which seem pertinent today and will presumably maintain their character of timeliness in future eras are as follows: urbanization and metropolitanism, complex organizations, political processes, power relationships, participatory decision making, change dynamics, school-community organization analyses, emerging roles and expectations, group processes, permanent and temporary systems, and the positive and negative aspects of conflict. Such centralizing themes, it is suggested, may well provide a base for courses and seminars developed and organized to contribute to the foundation or core program which will be pursued by all students of educational administration.

The common characteristic of the centralizing theme approach is the fact that all of the themes can be studied from a variety of disciplined approaches provided by the social sciences. None of the themes is founded in a single social science, and none can be analyzed thoroughly from a single perspective. Thus, the criterion for the selection of social science content in the core phase of preparatory programs will be the relevance of content found in the disciplines to the analysis and understanding of identified centralizing themes. Because of the nature of the themes, relevant content will usually be multidisciplinary in character with certain themes requiring more knowledge from more disciplines if they are to be completely understood.

In the second phase of preparation, greater emphasis will be given to role and performance specialization, and, consequently, criteria for the selection of content for inclusion in programs for future administrators will be differentiated from those used in the selection of content for use in preparing professors. Further, delineation of divergent professorial roles will be determined, and particular criteria for content selection relevant to each of these roles will be identified.

For prospective administrators, the common base of social science knowledge will be expanded through extensive field experiences and through courses related to the functions of administration. Through this process the essential practicality of administration will be noted, and the value of direct participation by future administrators in the identification and solution of problems will be accepted. Field experiences of various types will be correlated with seminars in which knowledge of functional administration, as well as content from the social sciences, will be brought to the analysis and possible solution of significant issues to which the student is being exposed in the field. The essential criterion for the selection of social science content for inclusion in the advanced preparation of administrators will be its relevance to the understanding of roles and issues found under field conditions. The identification of criteria to be applied in selecting social science content for use in the preparation of university-based personnel is not as simple. It is complicated by the conjecture that not only will future programs differentiate between the preparation provided for administrators and professors but also that sharp functional differentiation will be noted in the preparation of particular types of personnel to be found in various roles which will emerge in university departments of educational administration. As suggested earlier, four specific roles can be identified: 1) the synthesizer, 2) the field synthesizer, 3) the discipline-based professor, and 4) the discipline-based researcher. Such differentiated staffing will require, of necessity, the application of differentiated criteria for selecting social science content for incorporation into preparatory programs.

A definition of these diverse university based roles and suggested content selection criteria would encompass:

1. The synthesizer will be the individual who will bring multidisciplinary based social science content to the organization, analysis, and teaching of centralizing theme foundation or core courses and seminars. While the temptation to classify such individuals as generalists is great, it is avoided. The connotation of the generalist as one with broad but shallow knowledge does not suit the concept of synthesizer. Rather, the synthesizer is seen as one who has studied several of the social sciences in depth and has the ability to focus content from these several disciplines on significant centralizing themes. Criteria utilized in selecting social science content for study by the future synthesizer will be its relevance to the development of a multidisciplined approach and its relevance to the expanded understanding of identified and emergent critical themes.

2. The field synthesizer will be the individual who will bring multidisciplinary based social science content to the analysis and understanding of field problems. Such an individual will also be responsible for developing field experiences for students and for conducting seminars in which field expe-

riences are analyzed in light of diverse social science knowledge. The central criterion for selecting social science content for incorporation into the preparation of the field synthesizer will be the relevance of the content to the definition, analysis, and solution of field problems.

3. The discipline-based professor will be the individual who can bring an in-depth knowledge of a single social science discipline to the analysis and understanding of essentially unidimensional areas in the preparatory program. Examples of such areas would be the Sociology of Organizations or the Economics of Education, wherein the ramifications of such courses may be broad but essential tools for understanding are firmly rooted in a single discipline. The criterion for selecting social science content to be included in the preparation of the discipline-based professor will be the significance of the content to the development of an extensive knowledge of a discipline and a disciplined approach to the study and application of a particular area of academic endeavor.

4. The discipline-based researcher will be the individual who can bring an in-depth knowledge of a single social science discipline to the identification and study of significant areas of research. His preparatory program will include, in addition to social science knowledge, extensive study of research methodology and statistics. The criterion for selecting social science content for incorporation into the preparatory program of the discipline-based researcher will be the relevance of the content to the development of an understanding of the discipline and of significant modes of inquiry basic to the discipline.

Thus, for the four specific roles likely to emerge in departments of educational administration in the future, differentiated criteria for selecting appropriate social science content for inclusion in role preparatory programs are identified. While some similarity in criteria is seen for content selection for the synthesizer and field synthesizer, as well as for the discipline-based professor and researcher, the functions expected of incumbents in these roles are sharply different. This suggests that content selection and application will follow divergent patterns for each of the roles defined.

If differentiated criteria for the selection of content from the social sciences are to be viable characteristics of future preparatory programs, how is such an approach similar to, yet different from, the various methods identified earlier in this book as presently being utilized? The following four principal approaches have been described and illustrated as encompassing procedures currently in use: 1) the differentiated program approach, 2) the problem approach, 3) the single discipline approach, and 4) the multidisciplinary approach. Obviously, the proposed differentiated criteria approach has elements of all the present designs, yet it has characteristics uniquely different from any approach totally implemented in existing preparatory programs.

Differentiation in program approaches have largely been devoted to the development of separate curricula and experience opportunities for prospective administrators and for prospective professors. In the process, however, program differentiation has resulted in virtual states of isolation in which administrators know and use few of the social science concepts relative to significant field issues, and professors have a limited understanding of field problems. In a differentiated criteria approach, there is the recognition that there is room for the pure practitioner and the pure professor, but that in between there is also a need for a common frame of knowledge based primarily upon synthesized content and secondarily upon in-depth knowledge available in the social sciences. Exploring further, the differentiated criteria approach suggests that quite different social science content should be incorporated into preparatory programs related to specific roles as defined in the field or in university settings and that social science content relevant to the roles of administrator, synthesizer, field synthesizer, discipline-based professor, and discipline-based researcher may be, in each case, strikingly different. Most significant, however, differentiation according to role is seen as something which may be desirable only after a common social science base has been learned by all potential professionals in educational administration.

The problem focus approach, now widely used, is recognized as a legitimate basis for selecting and organizing social science knowledge as part of the specialized preparation for practitioners and field synthesizers. It does not appear to be particularly germane to content selection as related to discipline-based professors or discipline-based researchers. While obviously related to the preparation of synthesizers, the problem focus is seen as narrow and possibly restrictive for selecting social science content to be incorporated into the foundation or core programs. The broader concept of centralizing themes is proposed as a substitute for the problem orientation.

The single discipline approach is recognized as legitimate and necessary in the selection and ordering of social science content for prospective discipline-based researchers and for those prospective discipline-based professors who require a structure and a mode of inquiry for the study of evolving issues and for the teaching of specialized bodies of knowledge. The single discipline approach is seen as being inappropriate for selecting social science content to be incorporated into the preparation of potential practicing administrators and of those potential professors who see the necessity for knowledge synthesis, both in practice and in instruction.

Present approaches to social science content selection which can be classified as multidisciplinary are recognized as being basic to the incorporation of such content into the projected foundation or core program focused upon centralizing themes. In addition, this approach will be essential in selecting and including social science content in the specialized programs which will have to be developed for prospective professors desiring to synthesize knowledge either for classroom or field purposes. The multidisciplinary approach, however, is seen as being particularly inappropriate for the selection and incorporation of social science content into the specialized programs developed for prospective discipline-based professors and discipline-based researchers who require in-depth knowledge of a social science discipline and its related mode of inquiry for the conceptualization and conduct of research and for the teaching of specific single discipline based content.

Based on the preceding, it would appear that all of the various approaches which have been used in the past, as well as currently, will continue to be pertinent to the task of social science content selection and use in the future. It seems clear that the multidisciplinary approach will be given increased emphasis in the development of core or foundation phases of future preparatory programs. As one moves into later phases of preparation, however, greater recognition will be given to the idea that the efficacy of a particular approach is closely related to the differentiated roles for which individuals will be prepared.

Differentiation in role description and in consequent content selection will not, of course, leap full-blown upon the preparatory scene. Instead, expanding degrees of differentiation will be observable over a period of several years. The earliest stage, in which many universities are already functioning, will involve differentiation in content selection based upon roles to be assumed by students in the future. Essentially, current differentiation practices are limited to programs for the preparation of practitioners and somewhat different programs for the preparation of professors. The serious gap which this form of differentiation creates, however, is increasingly being recognized, and various forms of linkages between the field and the university environments are being proposed.

Synthesizer and field-synthesizer roles are described here as specific links between the practicing administrator and the university instructional unit. As such, these roles are indispensible, and their early definition and implementation will contribute much to overcoming the existing theory-practice barrier. A second weakness of present staffing procedures in university departments of educational administration is less widely recognized and accepted. This weakness is due to the failure to see the difference in essential knowledge and skills required of the effective teacher of administration and the productive researcher in the area of educational administration. The result of this weakness is clearly observable in the paucity of significant quality research in educational administration. The profession is suffering from a lack of hard data necessary to the development and direction of curricula which are both relevant and conceptually sound. Only when preparatory programs reach the point where the role of researcher is distinguished from the role of teacher will there likely be an upsurge in research output, as well as in teaching effectiveness.

There are a number of significant problems which must be overcome if the degree of differentiation projected is ever to be achieved. One of the serious barriers to such differentiation will be the implications it has for staffing. It is conjectured that the true synthesizer, both professor and field, will be the most difficult to identify and recruit. The synthesizing professor who will work, essentially, in the centralizing theme core program will have to have the knowledge of several social science disciplines and the ability to focus this multidisciplinary knowledge on identified themes. His total educational background will have to be reviewed, and it is probable that he be found among individuals who have an undergraduate major in one social science discipline and minors in others. Further, his graduate work will include a master's degree also in the social sciences and a doctorate in educational administration in which a strong minor field area of concentration is incorporated.

The field synthesizer must have all the characteristics of a synthesizing professor plus extensive experience in field settings. The role will involve not only the relating of relevant social science content to practical problems, but also the expansion of opportunities for the application of social science concepts to extant issues through such devices as case studies, role playing, simulation analyses, field studies, internships, and community participation.

The combination of qualities necessary for effective performance in this role is rare, and special programs for the preparation of individuals to function as synthesizers may well be necessary.

Discipline-based professors and researchers, although currently not found in great numbers in departments of educational administration, are not as difficult to identify as the synthesizers. They will be individuals with extremely strong backgrounds in one of the social sciences and a doctorate either in one of the social sciences or in educational administration. The key criterion will be the degree to which they possess an in-depth knowledge of a discipline and its indigenous modes of inquiry. While easily described, such individuals may be difficult to recruit. Educational administration and the potential which the field offers for teaching and study will have to be presented as both an exciting profession and as a field in which career opportunities are both challenging and rewarding.

As the significant import of social science content to the development of viable knowledge bases for preparatory programs becomes increasingly accepted and as differentiated criteria for selecting social science content become progressively more sophisticated, related phenomena will emerge and be observable in the preparing institutions. First among these will be the establishment of ad hoc relationships among social scientists and professors and practitioners of educational administration for the purpose of exploring avenues for furthering the already extensive efforts to identify relevant social science content, to incorporate such content into preparatory programs in educational administration, and to put social science theory to greater use in research directed toward understanding of the dimensions of educational organizations and administrative practices.

A second phenomenon will be directed toward expanding the formal relationships between the social sciences and educational administration. One of the ways in which this can be accomplished will involve extensive use of joint appointment procedures, whereby qualified individuals will hold dual positions as professors in one or more of the social sciences and as professors of educational administration. The discipline-based professor and researcher as envisioned would likely possess the necessary qualifications and credentials for multiple appointments to university departments.

Another expected consequence of the movement toward differentiated criteria for content selection will be the continuation of experiments in the joint instruction by social scientists and professors of educational administration of courses and seminars in which social science content is applied to issues in educational administration. In this form of team teaching, the role of the social scientist is that of a resource scholar in his particular field of expertise, while the role of the professor of educational administration is that of translator of theories and concepts of the social sciences to the empirical world of administration. As the projected differentiated staffing of departments of educational administration progresses, teaching teams in these types of courses and seminars will likely evolve into instructional combinations among the discipline-based professor and either the synthesizer or the field synthesizer.

Still a fourth situation will emerge as the social sciences and educational administration further converge. This will involve the virtual elimination of institutional barriers to the movement of students between departments of educational administration and the social science areas either for in-depth or breadth study. The stagnant isolationism of too many departments of educational administration will no longer be acceptable. All of the resources of the university must be utilized if the complex issues of administration are to be better understood and resolved.

A fifth development which will likely take more time to be widely observed will encompass broad acceptance of an administration *qua* administration philosophy. As social science content is increasingly incorporated into preparatory programs in educational administration, a similar situation will occur in such other applied fields as public administration, business administration, and hospital administration. The social science content identified for incorporation into preparatory programs in all these areas will be similar; and as its similarity becomes ever more recognized, there will be a healthy movement of these separate professional preparatory programs toward reliance on a knowledge base of overwhelming commonality. This observation may in time provide the impetus necessary for widespread development of graduate programs in administration, with no delimiting adjective necessary.

Without taking much of a risk, it may be conjectured that if any single word can describe society in the decades ahead, the word is "change." Societal institutions and social conditions will be in constant flux as new directions are identified and as new means for achieving desired goals are explicated. If institutions charged with preparing individuals to function as leaders of significant organizations in society are unwilling or unable to anticipate and respond to expectations and demands with creativity and immediacy, then society will turn to other means for identifying and educating its leaders. The challenge to those responsible for formulating and directing university preparatory programs in educational administration is great; a significant part of a successful response to the challenge will be found in the knowledge provided by the social sciences.

INDEX

Adler, Mortimer, 77
Administration as a Social Process: Theory, Research and Process (Getzels, Lipham and Campbell), 237
Administrative Behavior in Education (Campbell and Gregg), 5-6, 15
Administrative Relationship (Guba and Bidwell), 236
Administrative Science Quarterly, 15, 54, 69
Administrative Theory in Education (Halpin), 228, 232
Administrative Theory as a Guide to Action (Campbell and Lipham), 228
administrators:
  goals of, 340, 341
  urban school, 235
Administrator's Notebook, 223, 232, 236
Allport, Gordon W., 64-65, 68, 78, 79, 82, 213
American Anthropological Association, 411
American Association of School Administrators, 3, 205
American Economic Association, 275, 411
American Educational Research Association, 218
American Educational Research Journal, 69
American Historical Association, 411
American Political Science Association, 411
American Psychological Association, 76
American Sociological Association, 411
Anderson, Homer, 201

Andrews, John, 27
anthropology, 117-136, 415
  core concepts of, 121-136
  modes of inquiry in, 119-121
Argyris, Chris, 394, 403
Aristotle, 64
Aronson, Elliot, 68-71

Bailey, Steven, 214
Bane, Frank, 222
Banfield, Edward C., 22, 210
Barnard, Chester I., 213, 387, 394, 401
Barnard, Henry, 15, 199
Bay City schools study, 197, 203, 218
Becker, Howard, 210, 381-382
Belisle, Eugene, 19, 203, 211-213, 218
Benedict, Ruth, 127
Bennis, Warren G., 295, 403, 413, 416, 420, 421
Benson, Charles S., 196, 208-209, 214, 218, 234, 240, 284
Bentham, Jeremy, 78
Berger, Peter, 376
Bidwell, Charles, 227, 232, 235, 236
Binswanger, Robert, 213
Blake, Robert R., 263
Blau, Peter M., 209, 403
Blaug, Mark, 290-291
Blough, John A., 411-412
Boston (Mass.), 202, 203
Boston University, collective negotiations workshop at, 245-265 *passim*
Boulding, Elise, 250
Boulding, Kenneth E., 250
Bowles, Sam, 210
Bowman, Mary Jane, 235, 278-279
Boyan, Norman, 197
Briner, Conrad, 233, 237
Brockton (Mass.), 215
Brotz., Howard M., 99-100
Burkhead, Jesse, 214
Burton, William, 201

458 *Index*